D1596558

Empire of Friends

EMPIRE OF FRIENDS

Soviet Power and Socialist Internationalism in Cold War Czechoslovakia

RACHEL APPLEBAUM

CORNELL UNIVERSITY PRESS
ITHACA AND LONDON

Cornell University Press gratefully acknowledges receipt of a grant from
the Office of the Dean of Arts and Sciences, Tufts University, which
aided in the publication of this book. Publication was also made possible
in part by a grant from the First Book Subvention Program of the
Association for Slavic, East European, and Eurasian Studies.

First published 2019 by Cornell University Press

Library of Congress Cataloging-in-Publication Data
Names: Applebaum, Rachel, 1980– author.
Title: Empire of friends : Soviet power and socialist internationalism in
    Cold War Czechoslovakia / Rachel Applebaum.
Description: Ithaca : Cornell University Press, 2019. | Includes bibliographical
    references and index.
Identifiers: LCCN 2018029905 (print) | LCCN 2018030904 (ebook) |
    ISBN 9781501735585 (pdf) | ISBN 9781501735592 (epub/mobi) |
    ISBN 9781501735578 (cloth)
Subjects: LCSH: Czechoslovakia—Relations—Soviet Union. | Soviet
    Union—Relations—Czechoslovakia. | Socialism and culture—
        Czechoslovakia. | Czechoslovakia—Civilization—Soviet influences.
Classification: LCC DB2078.S65 (ebook) | LCC DB2078.S65 A67 2019
    (print) | DDC 943.704—dc23
LC record available at https://lccn.loc.gov/2018029905

For Joshua

Contents

Abbreviations

ČSM	Československý svaz mládeže
	Czechoslovak Union of Youth (1949–1968)
ČSR	Československá republika
	Czechoslovak Republic (1945–1960)
ČSSR	Československá socialistická republika
	Czechoslovak Socialist Republic (1960–1990)
KPSS	Kommunisticheskaia partiia Sovetskogo Soiuza
	Communist Party of the Soviet Union
KSČ	Komunistická strana Československa
	Communist Party of Czechoslovakia
LKR	Lidové kursy ruštiny
	People's Russian Courses
MGU	Moskovskii gosudarstvennyi universitet
	Moscow State University
MPEA	Motion Picture Export Association

OSChD   Obshchestvo sovetsko-chekhoslovatskoi druzhby
        Society for Soviet-Czechoslovak Friendship
ROH   Revoluční odborové hnutí
        Revolutionary Trade Union Movement
RSFSR   Rossiiskaia Sovetskaia Federativnaia Sotsialisticheskaia
           Respublika
        Russian Soviet Federative Socialist Republic (1922–1991)
SČSP   Svaz československo-sovětského přátelství
        Union of Czechoslovak-Soviet Friendship
SSOD   Soiuz sovetskikh obshchestv druzhby i kul'turnoi
        sviazi s zarubezhnymi stranami
        Union of Soviet Friendship Societies
TsK   Tsentral'nyi komitet
        Central Committee [of the Communist Party of the Soviet
           Union]
ÚV   Ústřední výbor
        Central Committee [of the Czechoslovak Communist Party]
VKP/b   Vsesoiuznaia kommunisticheskaia partiia (bol'shevikov)
        All-Union Communist Party (Bolsheviks) (1925–1952)
VOKS   Vsesoiuznoe obshchestvo kul'turnoi sviazi s zagranitsei
        All-Union Society for Foreign Cultural Ties

Note on Translation and Transliteration

Unless otherwise noted, all translations from Czech and Russian are my own. I have used the Library of Congress guidelines for transliterating Russian words, with the exception of well-known names (for example, I use Maxim Gorky instead of Maksim Gor'kii, and Maya Plisetskaya instead of Maia Plisetskaia).

EMPIRE OF FRIENDS

INTRODUCTION

A Tank in Prague

On July 29, 1945, Czechoslovak and Soviet dignitaries gathered on Štefánik Square in central Prague to celebrate the unveiling of a monument to the Red Army. The monument was a Soviet tank—allegedly the first to have entered Prague during the Soviet Army's liberation of the city from German occupation two and a half months earlier. The tank stood on top of a massive granite pedestal. A bronze plaque proclaimed "eternal glory" to its deceased drivers, "eight Red Army soldiers, who sacrificed their lives for Prague's freedom."[1]

Berlin in 1953, Budapest in 1956, Prague in 1968: a tank on the streets of a Central European city is the paradigmatic symbol of Soviet oppression in the Eastern bloc during the Cold War. A Soviet tank in Prague on a summer's day remains an especially indelible image of the USSR's violent efforts to maintain control over its socialist empire in Europe. In this familiar narrative of the superpower's use of force against its satellite states, the 1945 Monument to the Soviet Tank Crews in Prague would appear to be the foundation of Soviet hegemony in Czechoslovakia and the rest of the Eastern bloc. Yet long

Figure 1. Prime minister of Czechoslovakia Zdeněk Fierlinger speaks at the unveiling of the Monument to the Soviet Tank Crews on Štefánik Square in Prague, July 29, 1945.
Credit: Česká tisková kancelář.

before the monument became a quintessential symbol of Soviet hard power, it was part of an audacious but far less well-known experiment in power of a different kind: the attempt to use transnational friendship to create a cohesive socialist world. This experiment, which involved cultural diplomacy, interpersonal contacts, and the trade of consumer goods across national borders behind the Iron Curtain, linked citizens of the superpower and its satellites in an empire of friends that lasted until the fall of the Berlin Wall.

The Red Army's liberation of Central and Eastern Europe at the end of World War II marked the beginning of this wide-ranging friendship project, which would transform the lives of people from Berlin to Vladivostok.

Figure 2. Portraits of Klement Gottwald, leader of the KSČ, and Joseph Stalin
at the unveiling of the Monument to the Soviet Tank Crews on Štefánik Square in Prague,
July 29, 1945. The banner says, "With the Red Army for Eternity."
Credit: Národní archiv, Fotodokumentace 1897–1981, inv. č. 1229.

The goal of this project was to unify the diverse countries in the region into a transnational, socialist community led by the Soviet Union. The Soviets and their Eastern bloc allies commonly referred to this project as "socialist internationalism" or "proletarian internationalism." These terms originated in the mid-nineteenth century in Karl Marx's call for "working men of all countries" to "unite" across national borders to overthrow international capitalism.[2] After the October Revolution in 1917, the concept of socialist internationalism became synonymous with "world revolution"—the Bolshevik conviction that the new Soviet state's success was dependent on a wave of revolutions breaking out across Europe and in its colonies.[3] Following World War II and the creation of Soviet satellite states in Eastern Europe, socialist internationalism changed from an aspirational concept to a pragmatic challenge: stabilizing the new transnational socialist system in the realm of everyday life. The development of socialist internationalism in the Eastern bloc also drew on the rhetoric and practices of the Soviet campaign of "friendship of the peoples" from the 1930s, which attempted to create an overarching multicultural identity in the USSR by highlighting the achievements of individual Soviet nationalities and the love and affection among them.[4]

Empire of Friends tells the story of the rise and fall of this friendship project between the Soviet Union and Czechoslovakia—a story that provides the boldest illustration of the project's paradoxes. At the end of World War II, out of all the countries of the future Eastern bloc, Czechoslovakia offered the best chance for a successful friendship with the USSR. The Czech lands had a history of peaceful relations with their Slavic neighbor to the east; unlike Poland, which was partially annexed by the Russian Empire in the eighteenth century and fought a war with the Soviet Union in 1920; and unlike Hungary, Romania, and Bulgaria, which were German allies for periods of World War II.[5] In 1945, after six years of German occupation, Czechoslovak politicians from across the political spectrum, and a majority of the public, supported a close alliance with the USSR.[6] Despite these favorable indicators, the Soviet Union and Czechoslovakia made strange friends: the USSR touted itself as a model for Czechoslovakia's development, yet the soon-to-be satellite state was in fact wealthier and more industrialized than the nascent superpower. In addition, Czechoslovakia had a history of close ties with the West.[7] This book examines the evolution of the unlikely friendship between the Soviet Union and Czechoslovakia during the Cold War, in tandem with the dramatic shifts in their alliance: from Stalinism to de-Stalinization and from the Prague Spring to Soviet occupation.

The Soviet-Czechoslovak friendship project was multifaceted, encompassing everything from the coproduction of films, to collaboration between factories, to scientific exchanges. *Empire of Friends* focuses on the project's influence on everyday life: the export and reception of Soviet films, music, and fine art in Czechoslovakia; the postwar construction of the mythology of the Soviet liberation of Czechoslovakia; interpersonal contacts between the two countries' citizens, including student exchanges, tourism, friendship societies, pen-pal correspondences, and veterans' relations; and the exchange of consumer goods. These transnational connections reveal that the friendship project was central to the construction, the maintenance—and ultimately—the collapse of the European socialist world.

A Friendship Forged in War

From the fall of 1944, when the Red Army liberated Romania, to the spring of 1945, when the Red Army engaged in the Berlin and Prague offensives, rank-and-file Soviet troops, accompanied by secret police and propaganda units, helped lay the foundation for an eventual takeover by local Communist parties in the region.[8] The liberation provided the Soviets with the logistical and moral basis for the construction of a new empire in the region—the empire of friends.

The context of the Red Army's liberation of Czechoslovakia underscored the country's singular position within this new empire. In much of the rest of Central and Eastern Europe, the Soviet liberation in fact meant occupation. Soviet wartime propaganda portrayed German civilians as enemies.[9] When Soviet troops entered German territory in the winter of 1945, Red Army posters proclaimed the country "The Lair of the Fascist Beast."[10] Soviet commanders openly instructed their troops in both Germany and its erstwhile ally, Hungary, to avenge the terrible violence that Hitler's forces had committed on Soviet soil. Red Army soldiers responded by committing war crimes of their own, including, most notoriously, the rape of hundreds of thousands of German and Hungarian women.[11]

By contrast, the six years the Czechs spent annexed to the Reich made them, from the Soviet perspective, unequivocal victims of German aggression. The situation in Slovakia was more ambiguous. For three and a half years Slovakia functioned as a German puppet state under the leadership of the Catholic priest Jozef Tiso. In August 1944, Slovak partisans initiated an uprising against Tiso that was brutally crushed by the German government. As a result, Slovakia, too, fell under German occupation. Following this geopolitical reversal of fortune, the Soviet government portrayed Slovaks as their natural allies.[12] This background elucidates the instructions the Soviet command issued to the soldiers of the First and Fourth Ukrainian Front as they began the liberation of Slovakia in the fall of 1944: "Explain to all the soldiers that Czechoslovakia is our ally, that the forces of the Red Army must behave in a friendly manner toward the inhabitants." The soldiers were also warned not to confiscate property from locals and were threatened with punishment if they violated this order.[13]

The Soviet liberation of Czechoslovakia was the most important factor in shaping the postwar friendship project. It was a singular event for people in both countries. For the Red Army, the liberation of Czechoslovakia was distinguished by the high number of casualties sustained—an estimated 140,000 soldiers were killed—and because it was the final theater of battle after four exhausting years of war.[14] But the friendliness of the Czechoslovak population—in stark contrast to the hostile and fearful reactions from Germans and Hungarians—also made a strong impression. "The people were throwing flowers into the vehicles, shouting '*Ura!*' ["Hooray" in Russian] and '*Na zdar!*' ["Hello" in Czech] and offering us food and other refreshments," a Soviet veteran recalled of his regiment's arrival in the Czech lands via a pass in the Sudeten mountains. He continued, "In one town . . . the column became stuck amidst a dense crowd. Shliakhov, who was standing on the hood of a Dodge truck, tried to reason with the people in Russian to bring them back to their senses so they would part and make way for our column. However, the crowd mistook his exclamations and gestures as a salutatory speech and replied with yells of '*Na zdar!*' and '*Zet zhie!* [Hello! Long live!]."[15] Another Soviet veteran remembered, "In no other country that we came to be in during the war, were we, Soviet soldiers, greeted so warmly as in Czechoslovakia. The entire population, but especially the elderly, women, children, [and] young ladies threw themselves at us in tears and kissed us, as if we were their closest relatives. Such an encounter can never be forgotten."[16]

Many Czechs, too, portrayed their encounters with the Soviet soldiers as extraordinary, almost magical experiences. A few days after the liberation of Prague, a Czech journalist depicted a drive he took with a Soviet officer through the capital as if it were a love scene in a Hollywood film. As cheering crowds lined the streets offering food, water, and bouquets of lilacs to the Soviet troops, the Soviet officer whispered, "'Magnificent people . . . you Czechs are a magnificent people.'" The journalist added, "He clasped my hand. I was so moved that only my heart echoed his words."[17] Czech photographs from the liberation highlight this theme of genuine friendship. They show Red Army soldiers playing the accordion and guitar to entertain Czech women, sitting down to drinks at the home of a Czech family, and tenderly holding a succession of Czech babies and young children.[18] In the postwar period, the memory of these spontaneous expressions of friendship would lay the groundwork for the official, more scripted friendship project between the two countries.

These heartfelt testimonies and images of warm encounters between the Red Army and Czech and Slovak civilians help account for the friendship project's relative success over the four and a half decades following May 1945. Yet the liberation also had a darker side, which foreshadowed the interplay between friendship and violence that would equally characterize Soviet-

Czechoslovak relations for the duration of the Cold War. "The Russians received an enthusiastic welcome when they entered Czechoslovakia, but this brotherly Slavic love and friendship did not last," alleged a fall 1945 report by the U.S. Army, which had liberated parts of Western Bohemia.[19] Even though Red Army troops in Czechoslovakia were instructed by their commanders to "behave in a friendly manner," civilians filed numerous reports complaining of criminal behavior. They accused Soviet soldiers of plundering their homes, stealing food and livestock as well as personal possessions, including jewelry, linens, and clothes.[20] Even more damaging to the nascent friendship between the two countries was a rash of violent crimes perpetrated by Soviet soldiers, including rapes and murders.[21] These crimes confounded the Communist Party of Czechoslovakia (KSČ), which emerged from the war in a position of unprecedented popularity and political strength. In September 1945, a provincial branch of the party's friendship society with the Soviet Union, the Union of Friends of the USSR, protested that the Soviet soldiers' actions were undermining their campaign to enroll new members, "Complaints about their behavior are coming in from many sides. We have tried to make excuses for this behavior at [our] meetings. But how can we explain the foul play that occurred on the night of September 22, 1945, in the village of Gerštorf to the Čech family, when three of its members were fatally wounded? . . . How do we explain to the inhabitants that a Russian lieutenant shot Josef Roubíček, the chairman of the National Committee in Donín, on September 20, 1945?"[22] In the Brno region, the district secretary of the KSČ reported, "Every day and night incidents occur from the side of Russian soldiers, who steal, pillage, rape Czech women (not to even mention German women)." He highlighted one horrific crime: in the village of Popice, four Soviet soldiers had broken into the postmaster's house and held him at gunpoint while they raped his wife. These kinds of incidents, the district secretary complained, were tarnishing not only the Soviet Union's reputation, but also that of its staunchest ally in Czechoslovakia, the KSČ. "Many of our comrades are being poisoned by these kinds of things and have deviated from work for the party, or else they go about it lacking in spirit and sufficient taste."[23] Even Joseph Stalin was forced to concede to Czechoslovak leaders that his soldiers were "no angels."[24] Ultimately this tense situation was only resolved by the departure of the Soviet troops, who returned home at the end of November 1945, at the same time as their counterparts from the U.S. Army. By the end of 1945, Czechoslovakia was the only future Soviet satellite state that was not occupied by the Red Army.

The Evolution of Friendship

Throughout the Cold War, Soviet and Eastern bloc officials used the term "friendship" to describe the relationships among their countries. Friendship was supposed to emphasize the singularity of international relations in the socialist world: to connote alliances based on shared ideology and goodwill, rather than on hard power or realpolitik. In this book, I use the term "friendship project" to describe the strategies Soviet and Eastern bloc officials developed to extend this concept of friendship from the sphere of high politics to the realm of everyday life. These strategies included cultural diplomacy, a variety of transnational, interpersonal contacts, and the trade of consumer goods. In the case of the Soviet-Czechoslovak alliance, the nature of friendship between the two countries as well as the terms of the friendship project evolved significantly over the course of the Cold War. This evolution was shaped by important shifts in the countries' domestic politics and by broader political, social, and cultural changes on both sides of the Iron Curtain.

During the short-lived Third Republic in Czechoslovakia (1945–1948), officials from the Soviet Union and the KSČ began to develop the friendship project. The first phase of this project centered on Soviet cultural exports to Czechoslovakia. The Czechoslovak government was a National Front, consisting of four Czech and two Slovak political parties. The KSČ wielded the greatest power in this coalition: its members headed the Ministries of the Interior, Defense, Information, Education, and Agriculture.[25] In June 1945, the Ministry of Information signed a landmark agreement with the Soviet All-Union State Office for Film Export and Import (Soiuzintorgkino), giving Soviet films the right to occupy 60 percent of screen time in Czechoslovakia's movie theaters.[26] That fall, the Ministry of Education mandated the teaching of Russian as a foreign language in Czechoslovak schools.[27] Soviet exports of music, art, and literature further introduced Czechoslovak citizens to their new "friend."

The Soviet government and the KSČ hoped that these cultural imports would convince the Czechoslovak public of the need to build socialism. As the Cold War began, the Soviet government and the KSČ also looked to Soviet cultural imports to combat Western influence in Czechoslovakia, particularly from Hollywood films. Instead of promoting socialist internationalism, however, Soviet culture inadvertently bolstered Czechoslovak nationalism. Czechoslovak cultural critics, ordinary moviegoers, and exhibition viewers—even, in private, some leaders of the KSČ—employed Soviet films and paintings, in particular, as foils to define their country as more Western and culturally sophisticated than the USSR. Czechoslovaks thus concluded that their country needed to pursue its own, unique, path to Communism. During the Third Republic, the majority of Czechoslovaks considered the need for friendship with the USSR axiomatic, but they unexpectedly attempted to use Soviet culture as a proxy to set the terms of this friendship to their own advantage.

Over the course of the Third Republic, the KSČ, supported by Moscow, maneuvered for greater control over the National Front. In May 1946, the party won a plurality in free parliamentary elections, with 38 percent of the vote. The KSČ hoped to win a majority in the next set of elections, which were scheduled for the spring of 1948. When it became clear that this was not likely to happen, the party employed extralegal means to augment its control, including stacking the security services with its supporters, and intimidating members of the other parties. In February 1948, the KSČ took power in a coup.[28] The stakes of the friendship project immediately intensified. Soviet and Czechoslovak officials now relied on Soviet culture to cement the country's new position as a member of the socialist world.

In the spring of 1948, a split between Stalin and the Yugoslav leader Josip Broz Tito threatened to undermine Soviet hegemony in the nascent Eastern bloc. In response, the KSČ worked in tandem with Moscow to Sovietize most aspects of Czechoslovakia's political and cultural life, with the slogan, "The Soviet Union Is Our Model." During the Stalinist period in Czechoslovakia, which lasted until the mid-1950s, the party oversaw a veritable cult of the USSR: rhetoric of "friendship" now largely served as a cover for Soviet domination. Public debates over relations with the Soviet Union were prohibited. Western cultural imports were effectively banned; Czechoslovakia's movie theaters, libraries, concert halls, and galleries were inundated with Soviet socialist realist art, or Eastern bloc imitations. Even cultural exchanges between the two countries were supposed to highlight Soviet supremacy. When the Czechoslovak Army's musical ensemble toured the Soviet Union in 1952, Soviet cultural officials criticized it for not performing enough Soviet songs.[29]

The friendship project was further undermined during the late 1940s and early 1950s by campaigns in the USSR to cleanse the country of foreign influences. As a result, few Soviets and Czechoslovaks, aside from participants in high-level political and cultural delegations, had the opportunity to meet in person, and few Czechoslovaks were allowed to visit the Soviet Union. The one exception was several hundred Czechoslovak students, drawn from the Communist elite, who went to study at Soviet universities and institutes. Soviet xenophobia prevented these young people from fully integrating into life in the USSR; for example, the Soviet government's ban forbidding its citizens to marry foreigners thwarted transnational romances. Yet the students' sojourn in the USSR nonetheless taught them important Stalinist political tactics that proved essential for forging—and surviving—the new socialist world.

After Stalin's death in 1953, de-Stalinization in the USSR caused three significant changes to the friendship project in the Eastern bloc. First, cultural contacts among the socialist countries became more reciprocal, based on bilateral exchange agreements. Second, they became more populist, encompassing the broad participation of ordinary citizens in the USSR and its satellites. Third, they became more modern, in convergence with new practices of leisure and consumption developing across the Eastern bloc. In the broader Cold War, the structure of international relations on both sides of the Iron Curtain became yet another form of competition between the superpowers. Soviet officials seized on the allegedly benevolent international relations among the socialist countries to provide a contrast to what they viewed as Western, imperialist practices.[30]

During Stalinism, the friendship project had been largely aimed at Czechoslovaks, who were supposed to emulate Soviet culture and politics. After 1953, Soviet citizens began to participate in the project more actively. In Czechoslovakia, two friendship societies with the Soviet Union had been founded in the interwar period, and soon after the 1948 coup they were amalgamated into the Union of Czechoslovak-Soviet Friendship (SČSP), which became the second largest mass organization in the country, after the trade unions. In 1958, the Society for Soviet-Czechoslovak Friendship was founded in Moscow. In the 1950s and 1960s, Soviets and Czechoslovaks began to visit each other's countries as tourists, to correspond as pen pals, and to subscribe to glossy magazines detailing the lives of their foreign "friends." Friendship propaganda encouraged Soviets to buy Czechoslovak-made underwear, perfume, and shoes, and urged Czechoslovaks to purchase Soviet-made cameras, television sets, and cars. Soviet veterans of the liberation of Czechoslovakia in World War II began to renew contacts with the civilians who had sheltered and cared for them in 1944–1945. Their gratitude to these Czechoslovaks undermined the Stalinist dichotomy of Soviet superiority and Czechoslovak supplication.

These new bilateral contacts established more intimate connections between individual Soviets and Czechoslovaks, yet they also revealed political and cultural differences that undermined the larger goal of creating political cohesion in the Communist bloc. In the mid-1960s, Czechoslovakia embarked on a series of political and cultural reforms that challenged Soviet authority—and by extension, the friendship project. Soviet tourists who traveled to Czechoslovakia were shocked to encounter abstract art, pornography, and hippies, not to mention outspoken guides who praised the United States and Western Europe and denounced the Soviet Union. Back in the USSR, readers of the Czechoslovak-produced, Russian-language magazine *Sotsialisticheskaia Chekhoslovakiia* (Socialist Czechoslovakia) were exposed to a far more sophisticated consumer culture than was available in the Soviet Union, and to reviews of films and excerpts from Czechoslovak novels that were considered too unorthodox for release in the Soviet Union.

The expansion of interpersonal contacts between Soviet and Czechoslovak citizens also revealed new tensions between friendship as a form of state politics, and friendship as a mode of intimate relations between individuals. In their propaganda, the Soviet and Czechoslovak governments claimed that personal friendships between their citizens would help bolster their countries' alliance. "Friendship between nations is also based on personal friendships between people," declared Oldřich Pavlovský, Czechoslovakia's ambassador to the Soviet Union.[31] Yet when it came to managing tourism, pen-pal correspondences, and veterans' relations, Soviet and Czechoslovak officials betrayed fears that such friendships might threaten the stability of the transnational socialist system.

Tensions between the Soviet Union and its satellite state came to a head during the 1968 Prague Spring experiment in reform Communism. As the KSČ took the dramatic steps of rehabilitating Stalinist political prisoners, opening the country's borders, and lifting censorship, Czechoslovakia became the darling of leftists around the world. In response, the Soviet Union ordered a massive invasion. On the night of August 20–21, Soviet troops entered Czechoslovakia for the second time in twenty-three years.

The invasion might logically appear to have crushed the friendship project, along with the Prague Spring. Yet even as Soviet troops occupied Czechoslovakia for the next two decades, the friendship project endured. This happened for two reasons. First, Czechoslovak citizens drew on the rhetoric and practices of the friendship project to protest the invasion, and in the process, inadvertently helped the project to survive. Second, Soviet leaders and the government of Gustáv Husák (the first secretary of the KSČ) actively worked to restore the friendship project in order to "normalize" relations between their countries. The two governments' efforts further blurred the distinction between violence and amity; and hard and soft power that had defined the friendship project since 1945. The Soviet government sent tourists to Czechoslovakia to renew friendly ties, while the SČSP instructed its members to treat the Soviet troops occupying their country as tourists. The Czechoslovak government rewarded supporters of normalization by sending them on "friendship trains" to the USSR. The Soviet government even instructed its troops in Czechoslovakia to participate in the friendship project by playing chess matches and soccer games with local youth.

The friendship project became a key component of normalization in Czechoslovakia, and remained an integral part of everyday life up until the Velvet Revolution in 1989. "Czechoslovak-Soviet friendship was a routine thing for me because I grew up with it. It seemed completely normal to me," a middle-aged Czech recalled of the 1970s and 1980s in a 2009 television documentary.[32]

Empire of Friends

The friendship project presents a new way to understand Soviet-Czechoslovak relations, which have remained almost entirely unexplored beyond the realm of high politics.[33] It also offers a new way to conceptualize the Eastern bloc as a whole. During the early Cold War, Western scholars understood Soviet relations with Eastern Europe as Sovietization, which they defined as the USSR's attempt to transform politics and state institutions throughout the region in its own image. With this framework of totalizing Soviet control, they dismissed the role of "internationalism" as a cover for "nationalism on behalf of the Soviet Union."[34] Following the events of 1956 in Hungary and Poland, which demonstrated the limits of Soviet power in the region, Zbigniew Brzezinski argued for a new approach. He cited "new and more complex interrelationships between the [Eastern bloc] states," such as the Council for Mutual Economic Assistance and the Warsaw Treaty Organization, as evidence that a supranational system of power had developed in the region.[35]

Since the collapse of Communism, scholarship on Soviet relations with the Eastern bloc has begun to extend beyond high politics, and in the process has further challenged the utility of the Sovietization approach. John Connelly's comparative study of higher education in the Stalinist period in East Germany, Czechoslovakia, and Poland has revealed a degree of Soviet indifference toward their new satellite states. He has shown, for example, how Soviet officials often chose to outsource the restructuring of education in the satellite states to local Communists.[36] V. Pechatnov and A. S. Stykalin have further undermined the image of the USSR's hegemonic power abroad by revealing how Soviet propaganda efforts in early postwar Eastern Europe and the West were stymied by organizational problems, a lack of resources, and state-led xenophobic campaigns.[37] Norman Naimark and Peter Kenez have explored Soviet efforts to use culture, including literature, education, and film as a means of augmenting authority in the Soviet occupation zone of Germany and in Hungary, respectively.[38] Jan Behrends and Alan Nothnagle have, respectively, examined Polish and East German Communists' attempts to use propaganda promoting friendship with the USSR to consolidate their power in the late 1940s and early 1950s.[39] Patryk Babiracki has argued that Soviet and Polish midlevel officials sought to use soft power, in the form of cultural relations between their countries, "as a means to gain influence and establish unity."[40]

This scholarship reveals that the USSR's relations with its satellites in Eastern Europe were more complex than Cold War arguments about "captive nations" suggest. At the same time, the vast majority of the scholarship concludes that Soviet efforts to use art, education, and friendship to unify the socialist bloc were a failure. For example, in his work on the League for Polish-Soviet Friendship during the late 1940s and early 1950s, Behrends argues that in the Eastern bloc after Stalin's death in 1953, Soviet power entered into "prolonged decline," as the Eastern European Communist parties began to substitute nationalist rhetoric and policies for Sovietization, in an attempt to foster political legitimacy at home.[41] Similarly, Zbigniew Wojnowski contends that in the post-Stalinist period, cultural contacts between Soviet Ukraine and Czechoslovakia, Hungary, and Poland backfired, undermining socialist internationalism and augmenting Soviet patriotism.[42]

Empire of Friends challenges this story of failure in three ways. First, I highlight the friendship project's longevity and geographic breadth. Most of the literature on Soviet cultural relations with Eastern Europe focuses on the Stalinist period, or, in the case of Wojnowski's work, concerns the decades after Nikita Khrushchev's Thaw in the mid-1950s. By detailing the evolution of Soviet relations with Czechoslovakia over the longue durée of the socialist experiment, I show that the friendship project proved surprisingly durable and flexible—able to survive the dramatic shifts from Stalinism to de-Stalinization and from the Prague Spring to normalization. The project's success can also be measured geographically: from 1949 to the 1970s, Soviet officials used it as a blueprint to expand the empire of friends to China, Vietnam, and Cuba, and to try to attract the newly independent countries in Africa and Asia to the socialist camp.[43]

Second, I argue that while the Soviet friendship project with Czechoslovakia and the other Eastern bloc countries failed to achieve a stable, transnational socialist community led by the USSR in high politics, it succeeded in creating a cohesive socialist world in the sphere of everyday life. This seemingly paradoxical contention builds on recent scholarship that examines the history of the transnational socialist system in relation to its influence on material culture, social practices, and collective memory.[44] As Elidor Mëhilli argues, socialism "engendered a shared material and mental culture across national borders without ensuring political unity."[45] In *Empire of Friends*, I reveal how the friendship project influenced the most intimate aspects of the everyday lives of Soviet and Eastern European citizens, including what they wore, where they traveled—even who they married. As ordinary citizens participated in cultural, interpersonal, and commercial exchanges, they helped shape the friendship project—and with it—the socialist world.

Third, I contend that the friendship project succeeded *through* its political failure. In the case of Soviet-Czechoslovak relations, the very cultural, interpersonal, and commercial contacts that were supposed to augment the countries' alliance were so successful that they actually undermined it. During the Prague Spring, for instance, Soviet citizens were able to learn about the reform movement in Czechoslovakia by travel on official tour groups to the country. The friendship project thus provides a new approach to understanding the eventual failure of the socialist world. This was a world that collapsed not only because the Soviet Union and its socialist allies abroad took increasingly divergent political paths after Stalin's death but also because their cultural and interpersonal spheres became so intertwined.

By examining Soviet power in Eastern Europe through the lens of everyday life, *Empire of Friends* contributes to a rich literature about the symbiotic relationship in socialist regimes between state politics and the quotidian sphere (particularly in the post-Stalinist period). Studies examining sexuality, familial relations, housing, and consumption during socialism show how party leaders tried to satisfy their citizens' social welfare needs and consumerist desires, and how in return, ordinary people supported the state with a range of behaviors, including participating in propaganda, serving in social organizations, and acting as secret police informers.[46] This complex relationship between authoritarian regimes and their citizens challenges the binaries traditionally used to characterize life in Communist countries, such as the state versus society and collaboration versus resistance.

In her history of East Germany, Mary Fulbrook argues that it is often difficult to distinguish between "the East German state" and "East German society" because the two were so entwined. She thus dubs East Germany, "a participatory dictatorship."[47] *Empire of Friends* reveals a similar paradox in the relationship between the Soviet Union and its satellite states in Eastern Europe. This relationship was of course explicitly hierarchical, and it relied extensively on hard power, as Soviet military interventions in 1953, 1956, and 1968 so clearly demonstrate. At the same time, however, Soviet power in the Eastern bloc did not rely exclusively on force and coercion. Soviet and Eastern European citizens helped construct the Eastern bloc by participating in such everyday activities as going to the movies, studying, and shopping.

The story of the friendship project between the Soviet Union and Czechoslovakia also contributes to recent work on the relationship between hard and soft power in international relations, and on illiberal forms of internationalism. In the late 1990s, Akira Iriye argued for a new approach to the history of international relations that would privilege what he called "cultural internationalism": cross-border contacts between citizens for peaceful purposes, such as student exchanges and tourism. In Iriye's view, cultural internationalism stands in opposition to "power"—that is, warfare and high-level diplomacy among states.[48] A few years later, Joseph Nye popularized the concept of "soft power," which he defined through a similar binary—a country's ability to rely on "attraction rather than coercion or payments" to realize its geopolitical goals abroad.[49]

Iriye's and Nye's contention that cross-border contacts helped spread liberalism and democracy has become a common argument in studies of twentieth-century internationalism, and the cultural Cold War.[50] Yet the argument ignores how illiberal regimes employed similar types of transnational contacts to promote authoritarianism. As Ana Antic, Johanna Conterio, and Dora Vargha have recently argued, examining the efforts of fascist and socialist governments to use transnational contacts "shows that internationalist endeavours often could sit uncomfortably well with imperialist, violent and chauvinistic political or cultural projects."[51]

In this book, I argue that the relationship between the Soviet Union and its Eastern European satellites constituted an empire of friends. I use this term to highlight the paradoxes in the relationship: between high politics and the realm of everyday life; amity and violence; cultural exchange and authoritarianism; and hard and soft power. On its own, "empire" is an imperfect term to describe Soviet power in the region. Even during Stalinism, the Eastern bloc countries ostensibly maintained their sovereignty. Traditional imperial hierarchies were reversed in the European socialist world: the periphery—that is, the satellite states—was wealthier (and more westernized) than the imperial center—the Soviet Union. Yet in the late 1940s and early 1950s, the Soviets employed many of the tools of empire in their relations with Eastern Europe, including economic exploitation, the subjugation of ruling elites, and mass repression.[52] At the same time, the USSR developed a new type of imperial control over its satellite states, in which Soviet and Eastern European citizens were bound together not only by military force but also by transnational cultural contacts and personal encounters.

In the case of Soviet relations with Czechoslovakia, the 1945 Monument to the Soviet Tank Crews in Prague best illustrates the paradox of this framing of Soviet power in Eastern Europe as an empire of friends. The monument employed a tank—a symbol of military force—to connote Soviet liberation and friendship. At the time, the tank would likely already have held a dual meaning for many Czechoslovaks as an emblem of salvation from German occupation and as a reminder of the crimes perpetrated by the Red Army. Over the course of the following four and a half decades, the tank monument became the most iconic symbol of friendship between the Soviet Union and Czechoslovakia.

Following the Soviet army's invasion in 1968, many Czechoslovaks came to see this symbol of Soviet soft power as a reminder of Soviet hard power. In the spring of 1991, in the aftermath of the Velvet Revolution and not long before the collapse of the Soviet Union, a young Czech artist named David Černý engaged in a famous act of political protest art when he painted the tank pink. Not long afterward, the Czechoslovak government moved the offending monument to a military museum, where it remains today.

The Structure of Friendship

Chapter 1 examines the export of Soviet culture to Czechoslovakia during the Third Republic (1945–1948) and in the Stalinist period (1948–1953). Chapter 2 follows the experiences of Czechoslovak exchange students in the Soviet Union during late Stalinism. Chapter 3 charts the friendship project's transition from Stalinism to de-Stalinization by examining the evolution of the legacy of the Red Army's liberation of Czechoslovakia from the early postwar period until the 1960s. Chapter 4 continues the story of the de-Stalinization of the friendship project, describing how, in the late 1950s and 1960s, the project became more reciprocal, populist, and entwined with the new emphasis on popular culture and consumption across the Eastern bloc. Chapter 5 uses mass tourism as a lens to examine the upheaval in the friendship project during the Prague Spring and the Soviet invasion. Finally, chapter 6 examines the attempts by the Soviet government, led by Leonid Brezhnev, and the Husák government in Prague to reinstate the friendship project in the decade after the invasion, against the backdrop of the Soviet occupation of Czechoslovakia. In the conclusion, I return to the Monument to the Soviet

Tank Crews in Prague. I discuss how, in the spring of 1991, following the collapse of Communism in Czechoslovakia, the monument became a focal point with which Czechoslovak and Soviet citizens could debate the legacy of the friendship project. The monument's removal, in June 1991, represents the collapse of the empire of friends.

Chapter 1

CULTURE WARS

A revolution in people's thinking does not happen as
quickly as the nationalization of industry.

—VÁCLAV DAVID, 1950

A "visual extract of the Soviet world" appeared in Prague in April 1947, in the form of a major exhibition of socialist realist paintings from the USSR.[1] The Communist Party of Czechoslovakia (KSČ) hailed the exhibition as a means to cement Czechoslovakia's friendship with the Soviet Union. A headline in the party's newspaper, *Rudé právo* (Red Right) boasted, "The Exhibition of Soviet Art: The Further Rapprochement of Soviet Culture and Ours."[2] Yet rather than bring the countries together, the exhibition inspired an extraordinary debate in Czechoslovakia about the merits of Soviet culture and the stakes of the nascent friendship project. This debate developed among critics in the Czechoslovak press and among ordinary viewers in the exhibition's comment books. "No exhibition has aroused so much interest and polemics," the newspaper *Svět práce* (World of Labor) reported.[3]

The socialist realist art exhibition—along with the export of other types of Soviet culture to Czechoslovakia, including film, music, and literature—marked the beginning of the postwar friendship project between the two countries. Following the Red Army's liberation of Eastern Europe, the Soviet

Union embarked on the creation of a "cultural sphere" in the region to augment its military power and to combat Western influence.[4] Soviet cultural imports in Czechoslovakia and the other future Eastern bloc countries had "ceremonial and didactic functions." They were supposed to showcase the USSR's new status as a world power and promote socialist ideology and socialist realist aesthetics to local citizens.[5] From the point of view of Soviet officials, the primary purpose of sending films, novels, and paintings to Czechoslovakia and the other countries in Eastern Europe was thus to provide political enlightenment, not entertainment. As the Soviet Ministry of Cinematography explained in an internal document, "Soviet films in these countries play the role of a transmitter [*provodnik*] of socialist ideals among the broad masses."[6]

When representatives of the six political parties that formed Czechoslovakia's postwar National Front government met for the first time in Košice in April 1945, they agreed that friendship with the USSR was central to the reconstruction of the Czechoslovak state. "As an expression of the Czech and Slovak people's undying gratitude toward the Soviet Union, the government will make the closest alliance with the victorious Slavic power in the East the unassailable leading line of Czechoslovakia's foreign policy."[7] The politicians thus framed friendship with the USSR as an expression of fealty, but they also understood it as a means of national preservation. They believed close relations with the USSR were necessary to protect Czechoslovakia's sovereignty in the event of an attack by a revanchist Germany.[8] Their political calculation thus revealed a central paradox of the nascent friendship project: Czechoslovaks viewed Soviet internationalism as a safeguard for their own nationalist project. The KSČ even developed a slogan that encapsulated this paradox, "Without November 7, There Would Be No October 28, 1918!"[9] The slogan thus claimed that the Bolshevik Revolution was responsible for the establishment of Czechoslovakia's independence from the Habsburg Empire at the end of World War I.

At the beginning of the friendship project, the Soviet government tried to use its paintings, films, and symphonies to achieve very specific goals in Czechoslovakia: to augment the USSR's prestige and to spread Soviet-style socialism. At the time, the Soviet government allowed few foreigners to visit, and thus Soviet cultural imports were the main way the Czechoslovak public came to know the country that had become their most important ally. Yet during the Third Republic, Czechoslovak politicians, cultural critics, and the broader public used these Soviet imports not to assimilate Soviet politics but to debate and define their nationalist project and friendship with the USSR.

In the first months after the Soviet liberation, Czechoslovaks across the political spectrum welcomed Soviet culture as a means to combat German influence and to cultivate pan-Slavism. By the fall of 1945, however, the reception of Soviet cultural imports in Czechoslovakia had become caught up in new fault lines that developed in domestic politics. For the KSČ, the promotion of Soviet culture was a way of buttressing the party's long-standing alliance with the USSR and of rejecting Western influence as the cultural Cold War began. In public, the party lavished praise on Soviet cultural imports as symbols of the USSR's political achievements and as models for the development of Czechoslovakia's own cultural sphere. In private, however, some of the party's leaders expressed concern that Soviet films and paintings were too ideologically heavy-handed and simplistic to attract what they saw as their compatriots' more sophisticated tastes. They thus used Soviet culture as a foil as they attempted to create a unique path to socialism, predicated on Czechoslovakia's more advanced economy and history of close political and cultural ties with the West.

Czechoslovak non-Communists, by contrast, employed Soviet culture to publicly critique Soviet politics. Non-Communists included members of the Social Democratic Party (a leftist party closely allied with the KSČ); the Czechoslovak National Socialist Party (a centrist, nationalist party that acted as the KSČ's main opposition); and the People's Party (a Catholic party that promoted Catholic institutions and had the support of many rural citizens).[10] Although there was no official censorship in Czechoslovakia during the Third Republic, there was a taboo against openly criticizing the Soviet Union.[11] Non-Communists supported a close alliance with the USSR, but they used critiques of Soviet culture to try to influence the broader development of the friendship project. They portrayed Soviet culture as backward and non-Western in order to represent Czechoslovakia as more modern and European. They objected to what they saw as the KSČ's sycophantic attitude toward the USSR: for Czechoslovak-Soviet friendship to be strong, they argued, Czechoslovaks must be open with the Soviets about the cultural differences between their countries.

The beginning of the friendship project in Czechoslovakia was entwined with the onset of the cultural Cold War between the Soviet Union and the United States. The two superpowers, for all their differences, shared the conviction that culture was a powerful instrument of political influence. In the mid-1940s, Czechoslovakia thus became a staging ground for the broader cultural offensive between the Soviets and the Americans. Officials from both countries sent films and art exhibitions to Czechoslovakia, tried to develop alliances with Czechoslovak politicians, and supported friendship societies in Prague in a bid to attract ordinary Czechoslovaks to their respective ideological camps. Yet this opening salvo in the cultural Cold War in Czechoslovakia was ultimately unsuccessful for both the United States and the USSR. By 1948, the United States had effectively ceded its efforts to use culture to influence politics in Czechoslovakia to the Soviet Union, viewing Soviet domination of the country as a fait accompli. The USSR, meanwhile, owing to domestic economic and political constraints, had ended up largely outsourcing the promotion of Soviet culture to the KSČ.

In Czechoslovakia, the wide-ranging public debates about Soviet culture and the friendship project abruptly ended in February 1948, when the KSČ took power in a coup and the USSR integrated the country into its "socialist camp" in Eastern Europe. After Joseph Stalin's split with Yugoslav leader Josip Broz Tito in June, the Soviet leader made it clear to his Eastern European satellites that he would not tolerate "national paths" to Communism. Instead, these countries were to model their political, economic, and cultural life on the Soviet Union. In the cultural sphere, Czechoslovak officials responded in two ways. First, they tried to extinguish competition between Soviet and Western culture by banning cultural imports from the United States and Western Europe. Second, they launched highly detailed Sovietization campaigns that instructed Czechoslovak citizens on how to respond to Soviet films, art, and literature. They thus attempted to secure the hegemony of Soviet culture in Czechoslovakia by ensuring it would no longer serve as a subject of debate.

"The Fresh and Powerful Spring of Russian Art"

In the interwar period, cultural life in Czechoslovakia's cities was cosmopolitan. Art devotees could choose between French and Russian exhibitions. Literature lovers had access to hundreds of new works by foreign writers in Czech translations.[12] In 1938, the most popular film in Czechoslovakia was

Disney's *Snow White and the Seven Dwarfs*.[13] Even in the industrial city of Ostrava, on the border with Poland, "The jazz-age had reached out from that faraway, exotic, bewildering continent that was called America," remembered Joseph Wechsberg, an American soldier of Czech origin, who returned to Czechoslovakia in May 1945. "Everybody sang 'Yes, We Have No Bananas' in Czech or German translation. . . . At the theater they played comedies by Verneuil and Birabeau, with the actresses running in and out of bedrooms, undressed in black-lace lingerie."[14]

The Nazi occupation curtailed this cultural heterogeneity. The German government banned films, plays, literature, and music from the allied countries in the Protectorate, largely replacing them with German and Austrian works. In the final year of the war, Joseph Goebbels, the minister of propaganda, shut down all dramatic theaters in the Reich.[15] In the bleak conditions of occupied Czechoslovakia, German films as well as those made by Czech filmmakers who collaborated with the occupation regime achieved an outsized importance: "Many consumer goods were unattainable, apartments were unheated, the city was dark, the police checked on people in cafés and restaurants, public dancing was not allowed most of the time, and so it was said that in the evening people went either to the movies or straight to bed."[16]

At the end of World War II, the newly reconstituted Czechoslovak state faced severe economic, social, and cultural challenges. When Wechsburg returned to Czechoslovakia in May 1945, he found the country's infrastructure in disrepair and its social order upended. "In the streets of Prague there was the smell of powder and smoke and dead flesh." As he traveled across the country, he discovered that trains were dirty and ran slowly because Soviet troop transports had the right of way. At train stations, groups of Sudeten Germans huddled under armed guard, their shirts marked "N" for *Němec*, the Czech word for "German." Former concentration camp inmates dressed in their guards' uniforms were making their way back home.[17] With this economic and social upheaval, cultural life in Czechoslovakia continued to deteriorate. The new government in Czechoslovakia, headed by Edvard Beneš, banned German films and other works of culture, while Western cultural imports remained largely unavailable. Arriving in Prague in August 1945, the Russian American writer Maurice Hindus concluded, "The intellectual impoverishment of the city matched the collapse of its material welfare."[18]

The Soviet government eagerly exploited this cultural vacuum. In April 1945, even as the Red Army continued to fight German forces in the Czech lands, officials from the Soviet All-Union State Office for Film Export and Import (Soiuzintorgkino) took steps to ensure that Soviet films would be screened throughout newly liberated Slovakia, including in the smallest movie theaters.[19] On June 11, 1945, a month after the Red Army's liberation of Prague, Soiuzintorgkino signed a landmark agreement with the Czechoslovak Ministry of Information, which was headed by Václav Kopecký, one of the KSČ's founding members, to give the USSR the right to export one hundred films annually to Czechoslovakia over the next ten years.[20] According to the agreement, Soviet films were to occupy 60 percent of the total playing time in Czechoslovakia's movie theaters. In Prague, they were to be screened at the Alfa cinema, the city's premier movie theater. In small towns and villages where no theaters existed, they were to be built specifically for showing Soviet films.[21] For Soviet cultural officials, the goal of exporting films to Czechoslovakia was "purely political."[22] Soviet authorities had considered film the best medium for spreading propaganda to the masses since the Civil War, when they had sent trains carrying film projectors into the Russian countryside.[23] Now they set out to use the cinema to bring socialism to the heart of Central Europe.

Czechoslovak film critics and the broader public initially reacted enthusiastically to the twenty-four movies the Soviets sent in 1945 as part of the agreement with the Ministry of Information.[24] Yet their interest was shaped more by nationalist concerns than by support for Soviet-style socialism. The majority of the Soviet films had been made during the war about war-related themes. These movies resonated with Czechoslovak viewers who had just lived through six years of German occupation and were eager to expel the country's large German minority.[25] Three of the top five most popular Soviet movies shown in Czechoslovakia during the first year after the liberation were about the war: *She Defends the Motherland* (Fridrikh Ermler, 1943), a drama about the heroism of a female partisan; *Malakhov Kurgan* (Iosif Kheifits and Aleksandr Zarkhi, 1944), a Georgian-Russian production about the battle for Sevastopol during the war; and *Person No. 217* (Mikhail Romm, 1944), a drama about Soviet slave laborers deported to Nazi Germany.[26] These films had been produced to advance the Soviet war effort by contrasting graphic depictions of German atrocities against civilians with heroic portrayals of Soviet resistance.[27] *She Defends the Motherland*, for instance, tells the story of Pasha, a Soviet peasant everywoman who bravely fights the German occupiers with her bare hands after they murder her husband and toddler son.

The KSČ urged Czechoslovaks to watch these films as an expression of their appreciation toward the Red Army for the liberation of their country. *Tvorba* (Creation), the KSČ's cultural newspaper, wrote approvingly that Soviet war films show "all nations the Soviet Union's enormous spiritual strength, the greatness of the sacrifice that had to be endured by the Soviet people so that Europe could be liberated from the fascist reign of terror."[28] A Prague trade unionist echoed this sentiment in a letter to the Czechoslovak Ministry of Information, "Gratitude toward the Red Army should lead the Czech people to love for the USSR, the Russian language, and Soviet film."[29]

Czechoslovaks' initial enthusiasm for Soviet films and other genres of Russian/Soviet culture was, however, shaped more by nationalist concerns than by allegiance to the USSR. As Chad Bryant has noted, Germanophobia became a key element of Czechoslovak identity in the early postwar period.[30] This anti-German sentiment was directed against the legacy of the Nazi occupation as well as against the country's three million ethnic German citizens, who had lived in the Czech lands for centuries. In accordance with the Manichean logic in the early postwar period, Czechoslovaks welcomed Russian and Soviet culture precisely because they viewed it as the antithesis of German cultural hegemony. Celebrating Soviet cultural imports thus became a way of rejecting German influence, and of constructing a new, homogeneous, Slavic state. "Long live the friendship between Czechoslovak and Soviet pedagogues!" a Czech teacher wrote to VOKS, the Soviet All-Union Society for Foreign Cultural Ties, soon after the liberation. The teacher expressed enthusiasm for the Russian language, which became a mandatory subject in Czechoslovakia's schools in autumn 1945, while complaining that during the Protectorate they had been required to teach "seven hours a week of the hated German language."[31]

Czechoslovak cultural critics, in their reviews of the first concerts of Russian music that were performed in Czechoslovakia after the liberation, praised Russian and Soviet culture as an antidote to German influence. A review of a concert of Russian music in Prague in June 1945 in *Svobodné noviny* (Free News), a newspaper sympathetic to the Social Democratic Party, gushed: "Once again we can drink from the fresh and powerful spring of Russian art, we can look forward to the flower and fruit of Slavic individuality, and we can become acquainted with the new exploits and intellectual currents that flow in the great land of the Soviet Union." The review's praise for Russian music was grounded in sympathy for pan-Slavism, rather than socialism. The pieces performed in the concert were, with the exception of works by the Soviet composer Nikolai Myaskovsky, compositions by the nineteenth-century Russian composers Alexander Borodin, Nikolai Rimsky-Korsakov, and Pyotr Tchaikovsky.[32] Enthusiasm for Russian music as a corrective to German influence cut across the political spectrum in Czechoslovakia. An article in the National Socialists' daily, *Svobodné slovo* (The Free Word), with the not-so-subtle headline "Music after the Babylonian Captivity," argued that Czech musicians, like Czechoslovakia's politicians, should shift their allegiance from the West to the USSR. "Czech music will, by solemn and free effort, orient itself toward the great music states of the Slavic East, and will join together far more intimately than before with the creations and feats of Soviet music."[33]

Czechoslovaks' initial enthusiasm for Soviet films, the Russian language, and music also fed into the movement to punish the country's German minority for the occupation. Even before the war ended, Beneš's government in exile in London began laying the groundwork for the expulsion of Czechoslovakia's Germans. The first phase of this ethnic cleansing, known as the "wild retribution" began immediately after the liberation, when ethnic Czechs launched extralegal, violent attacks against their German neighbors, forcing 660,000 men, women, and children to leave the country.[34] Soviet war films, by graphically exposing German war crimes, provided further justification to Czechoslovak viewers for the expulsions. The Communist poet Vítězslav Nezval, who was in charge of film at the Ministry of Information, made this connection explicit in a speech he gave to a visiting delegation of Soviet filmmakers in July 1945. Referring to three Soviet films about the war that were about to be released in Czechoslovakia, he declared: "These films should be mandatory viewing for our National Committees, for our factory councils, for our border areas. For the problem resolved in them was and is our problem as well. In them . . . it is shown that those who plundered and by the most monstrous means desecrated both the Soviet [Union] and our lands are not people, that they are a damned generation that needs to be absolutely neutralized in their defeat."[35]

Figure 3. An advertisement for the Soviet film *Malakhov Kurgan* and a poster celebrating
the Red Army cover up German posters in Prague, spring 1945.

Credit: Národní archiv, f. 1329 [OČRA-1945], Norbert Bezděk, inv. č. 5/17.

In the first months after the liberation, gratitude toward the Red Army, pan-Slavism, and anti-German sentiment informed Czechoslovaks' support for Soviet culture as much as—if not more than—enthusiasm for Soviet-style socialism. Viewing Soviet films, studying Russian, or attending Russian music concerts thus became a way for Czechs and Slovaks to distance themselves from the German occupation and the German minority, and to construct a new, purely Slavic state. Friendship with the USSR in this period was thus, paradoxically, an expression of nationalism.

The Cultural Cold War

As Soviet culture contributed to the construction of Czechoslovak nationalism, it also inspired debates in Czechoslovakia about internationalism. In the first few months after the liberation, Soviet cultural imports, particularly films, were often the only entertainment available in Czechoslovakia. Beneš's government had barred filmmakers and actors who had collaborated with the Germans from working in the film industry. As a result, in 1945, Czechoslovakia's film industry, which had been highly productive in the interwar years, only produced two feature films, and in 1946, fourteen.[36] When Wechsberg reached his native city of Ostrava in May 1945, a friend complained to him about the effects collaboration and the postwar purges were having on Czechoslovakia's film industry: "'They're playing the old pictures all over again,' Anton said. 'All the new pictures were made under German supervision. Some stars fell for that Goebbels swine. You don't want to pay good money to see a girl who slept with K. H. Frank and his gang?'"[37]

In the summer and early fall of 1945, there were no new Czechoslovak films on offer, and few Western films, since the government had not yet negotiated import agreements with Western countries. Given this lack of competition, Soviet films dominated Czechoslovakia's movie theaters.[38] Once viewers had exhausted these Soviet films, they had little else to see. In a "Film of the Week" column on September 1, 1945, *Obzory* (Horizons), a newspaper allied with the Catholic-oriented People's Party, lamented, "To write about film these days is a difficult and tiresome task, for there is no film of the week, there are no new films and thus it is necessary to theorize and plan for the future." The paper reported that theaters in Prague were screening the few new movies that were in circulation for longer than audiences remained interested in them, while cinema repertoires in the rest of the country were filled with reruns of Czech films made during the war.[39]

In October 1945, the Czechoslovak Ministry of Information reached film-import agreements with England and France.[40] The arrival of Western films undermined the success of Soviet pictures.[41] The decline in popularity of Soviet films thus occurred even before Czechoslovakia began to import American movies. In the late 1930s, American films had been the most popular foreign films shown in Czechoslovakia.[42] In the fall of 1945, *Obzory* argued that while "opinions about Hollywood may vary," the Czechoslovak cultural scene would be bereft without its films. "The reality is that Hollywood is the largest film center in the world, and it is there that the pace of new developments in filmmaking is set."[43]

Obzory's calls for the renewal of American film imports highlights tensions in early postwar Czechoslovakia over what constituted internationalism.[44] In the nineteenth century, František Palacký, the Czech historian and "father of the nation," had envisioned the Czech people as mediators between East and West.[45] In the interwar years, Beneš and other Czechoslovak politicians built on Palacký's idea, imagining that their country would serve as a "bridge" between the Soviet Union and the West, thanks to its geographic location in the "heart of Europe," its Slavic population, and its history of close contacts with the West.[46] In the postwar period, calls in the Czechoslovak press for access to both Soviet and Western culture became another variant on the bridge theme. "We hope that the country of Masaryk may become a . . . unifying force between the land of Dostoyevsky and the land of Shakespeare," an article in *Svobodné noviny* declared.[47] This sentiment amounted to a fantasy of cultural internationalism in a time of intense nationalist politics and in an increasingly bipolar world. For some Czechoslovaks, access to culture from the East and the West presented an opportunity to escape both the cultural isolation of the German occupation and the polarization of postwar politics. *Obzory* argued, for example, that access to world culture was essential if Czechoslovakia was to avoid becoming a provincial backwater. "It is absolutely impossible to imagine the development of our film, and above all, our own cultural development, without it being possible to see everything that is valuable and new that has appeared and is appearing in film production *throughout the whole world*."[48]

While Czechoslovak journalists debated the merits of Soviet versus world culture, the country's pro-Western politicians and the KSČ lobbied the U.S.

and Soviet governments, respectively, to use cultural exports to influence Czechoslovakia's political orientation in the nascent Cold War. Czechoslovakia's pro-Western politicians hoped that the initial onslaught of Soviet cultural exports in 1945 would be quickly countered by a similar cultural offensive from the West, especially the United States. In the summer of 1945, as Soviet films flooded the country's movie theaters, Jan Masaryk, the foreign minister, urged U.S. ambassador Laurence Steinhardt to have the United States "send as soon as possible its best motion pictures, books, and press to Prague."[49] The U.S. embassy took steps to establish a cultural presence in Czechoslovakia: it opened an information bureau in Prague, where Czechs could read literature about life in the United States, and launched an American friendship society with a celebratory concert in the capital.[50] Yet Czechoslovakia's pro-Western politicians judged such steps inadequate to counter Soviet activities. In November 1945, Ján Papánek, head of the Czechoslovak Information Service, complained to American officials that they were still failing to fulfill "the great demand of the Czechoslovakian public for information concerning the United States." Papánek stressed the need for American films in particular.[51]

Ambassador Steinhardt saw Czechoslovakia as on the front lines of the emerging Cold War with the Soviet Union, and he agreed with Masaryk and Papánek that film was an especially important medium to spread American influence. Yet, as Igor Lukes has shown, the U.S. embassy in Prague proved largely ineffective in countering the Soviet presence in Czechoslovakia during the Third Republic. Steinhardt's attention to Czechoslovak affairs was haphazard; he frequently interrupted his ambassadorial duties to attend to personal concerns and business dealings back in the United States. Several other embassy officials were similarly lackadaisical about their political work in Czechoslovakia, devoting much of their time to securing residences in the palaces left behind by Prague's German aristocracy and to enjoying the company of Czech women.[52]

Furthermore, commercial and political interests in the United States proved a significant obstacle to a full-fledged American cultural offensive in Czechoslovakia. For almost a year and a half after the war's end, American film exports to the country were stymied by a conflict that developed between the U.S. Motion Picture Export Association (MPEA) and the State Department. In August 1945, the Czechoslovak government nationalized the country's film industry as part of a broader program to exert greater state control over the cultural sphere.[53] In response, the MPEA refused to negotiate with Czechoslovak officials, referring derisively to the country's film "monopoly." The association feared that signing an agreement with Czechoslovakia would set a bad precedent for its operations throughout Eastern Europe.[54]

The State Department's initial response to the MPEA's intransience was not to interfere. Secretary of State James F. Byrnes agreed with Steinhardt about the political importance of screening U.S. films in Czechoslovakia. But he was also reluctant to inject politics into commerce, arguing that the "question of showing commercial films . . . is one for decision by the industry."[55] By the spring of 1946, Steinhardt grew increasingly frustrated with the MPEA's ongoing refusal to negotiate an agreement on importing American films to Czechoslovakia. The country's first postwar parliamentary elections were scheduled for May. The Communists already had a commanding role in the National Front government; now they hoped to increase their power by winning a majority of seats in parliament. The stakes of U.S. cultural policy in Czechoslovakia had thus become even more urgent than they had been in 1945. In March 1946, Steinhardt emphasized the impending elections in a plea to Byrnes to put pressure on the MPEA to accept the Czechoslovaks' latest offer for importing American films, "The Czechoslovak [Film] Association has completed agreements with the British, French, Swedes, Swiss, and the Russians and . . . Czechoslovak production is steadily increasing. . . . Furthermore, the political advantages to the US growing out of the exhibition throughout Czechoslovakia of the best American pictures between now and the elections in May should not be underestimated."[56] Despite Steinhardt's efforts, however, the MPEA did not enter into a formal agreement on the export of U.S. films to Czechoslovakia until September 1946, and the first U.S. feature films from the agreement were not shown in the country until mid-October 1946.[57]

Meanwhile, the May 1946 parliamentary elections resulted in a major success for the KSČ, which won 41 percent of the vote in the Czech lands, and 38 percent nationwide. The KSČ's achievement was part of a broader pattern of political gains by the Soviet-backed Communist parties throughout Central and Eastern Europe in 1946–1947. In January 1947, the Polish Communist Party employed extralegal methods to sway the results of parliamentary elections. In Poland, Hungary, Romania, and Bulgaria that year, the local Communist parties, backed by the Soviet security forces, arrested members of the political opposition, thus consolidating their power.[58] By 1947, Steinhardt viewed Czechoslovakia as the United States' last opportunity to influence what had rapidly become a Sovietized region. He argued that American cultural diplomacy to Czechoslovakia could serve as a firewall to help stem the further spread of Communism.[59]

By the spring of 1947, American movies were showing in all the cinemas in Czechoslovakia, and Steinhardt bragged to the new secretary of state, George Marshall, "[They] absorb [the] bulk of all playing time. Earnings and remittances in dollars to American producers during [the] past six months far exceed earnings and remittances during any similar period."[60] By contrast, in 1947, Soviet films made up only 23 percent of the screen time in Czechoslovak cinemas—far from the 60 percent mandated in the 1945 film agreement between the two countries.[61] Nonetheless, Steinhardt and American diplomatic personnel across Eastern Europe judged the United States' efforts at cultural diplomacy in the region to be inferior to Western Europe's.[62] Steinhardt looked to Great Britain, in particular, as a model for how the United States could expand cultural relations with Czechoslovakia. The British Council and three British Institutes operated successfully in Czechoslovakia.[63] In 1947, Great Britain also negotiated a cultural exchange agreement with Czechoslovakia. Steinhardt argued that the United States should use the British agreement as a template to negotiate its own cultural exchange treaty with Czechoslovakia.

The State Department, however, strongly objected to this idea, arguing that the American public already regarded Czechoslovakia as having effectively fallen under Soviet domination, and would therefore reject a cultural exchange agreement out of anti-Soviet sentiment. Furthermore, the State Department noted that the academic and scientific exchanges Steinhardt had proposed as part of a cultural exchange agreement with Czechoslovakia would be difficult to implement, given American legal restrictions on allowing Communists into the United States. Finally, the State Department worried that any American institutions established in Czechoslovakia as part of such a bilateral cultural agreement would be co-opted by Czechoslovakia's Communists "for propagation [of] politically tendentious material."[64] Steinhardt reacted in frustration: "As to whether it is desirable to conclude such an agreement w/ a country within Soviet sphere it seems to me far more desirable to spread our culture in areas where strenuous attempt is being made to suppress and eliminate it than in countries which are not within Soviet sphere. For example, would it be more desirable to seek to spread our culture at this time in Canada or in Yugoslavia?"[65]

As Soviet influence over Czechoslovakia increased, the U.S. government reacted by pulling back, rather than engaging more intensely. The KSČ's coup in February 1948 caused the State Department to declare conclusively to the American embassy in Prague that the U.S. government had decided it did not make sense to enter into a cultural exchange agreement with Czechoslovakia.[66] In the fall of that year, in what Frank Ninkovich has described as the "end of the [American] pursuit of cultural internationalism in Eastern Europe," the U.S. government ended its efforts at cultural diplomacy in the region.[67]

Although the U.S. government was reluctant to be drawn into the cultural Cold War in Czechoslovakia, the Soviet government and its ally, the KSČ, saw themselves as engaged in cultural competition with the United States and Great Britain from the very end of World War II. In the fall of 1945, Soviet military representatives in Czechoslovakia sent anxious reports to the Council of Ministers detailing how the American embassy had founded the U.S. Information Bureau in Prague and the Union of Friends of the U.S.A. The military concluded that the Soviet government needed to provide more "propaganda and information" in Czechoslovakia in order to counter the Americans.[68]

The Soviet Union would appear to have had clear advantages over the United States in the nascent cultural Cold War in Czechoslovakia. Soviet cultural production and distribution were entirely controlled by the state, while the U.S. government had to reconcile its political priorities with the commercial interests of private organizations like the MPEA.[69] The Soviet government did not have to contend with the influence of its foreign cultural policy on domestic public opinion, while the U.S. government had to reconcile outreach to the socialist world with the American electorate's widespread anti-Communism. Yet as V. Pechatnov has shown, the Soviet government faced other critical obstacles in its cultural outreach to both Eastern Europe and the West in the early postwar period. The first obstacle was that there were at least a dozen different Soviet organizations responsible for creating and disseminating foreign propaganda, which made coordination among them difficult. The second obstacle was that the dictatorial nature of the Stalinist regime stifled the ability of individual government organizations to improve the quality of their foreign propaganda. The third obstacle was that, beginning in the summer of 1946, when Andrei Zhdanov, Stalin's cultural spokesman, launched a series of anti-Western campaigns, Soviet institutions responsible for foreign propaganda, such as the Soviet Information Bureau and Mezh-dunarodnaia kniga (International Book), which was responsible for sending Soviet books abroad, were rocked by purges.[70] Finally, in the case of Soviet cultural relations with Czechoslovakia, Soviet cultural organizations were also stymied by a lack of resources: for instance, for Czechoslovakia VOKS only had one analyst, who lacked sufficient time to read the Czecho-slovak press carefully and to write detailed reports.[71]

The KSČ was frustrated by these shortcomings in Soviet cultural out-reach. "Propaganda about the Soviet Union in Czechoslovakia does not cor-respond to [our] political requirements. Its volume and composition do not counteract Anglo-American propaganda," Bedřich Geminder, the head of the International Department of the KSČ's Secretariat, complained anxiously to the Soviet authorities on the eve of Czechoslovakia's critical parliamentary elections in the spring of 1946. Geminder reported that the editors of the KSČ's newspapers were desperate for material they could use to propagan-dize the Soviet Union. He also complained that the party lacked visual ma-terial to promote the USSR. The party and its affiliates owned more than fifty bookstores in Prague, with display windows that would be perfect for showcasing Soviet propaganda—if only they had something to show. Meanwhile, American posters and other propaganda materials were visible "in many display windows on the main streets of Prague." In addition, while it took almost two weeks for copies of the major Soviet newspapers to reach Czechoslovakia, British and French newspapers appeared on news-stands the day after their domestic release.

Geminder made several recommendations for improving Soviet cultural influence in Czechoslovakia, including creating an unofficial, "independent" press bureau in Prague to provide information to all of Eastern Europe, sending Czechoslovak students and professors on exchanges to the Soviet Union, and sending more Soviet cultural groups to perform in Czechoslovakia.[72] The response from Valerian Zorin, the Soviet ambassador to Czechoslovakia, was curt. He recommended arranging a small number of Soviet cultural events in Czechoslovakia: a concert by the Red Army's folk dance ensemble, a visit by the Obraztsov puppet theater, and a music festival with performances by leading Soviet musicians Lev Oborin, David Oistrakh, and Yevgeny Mravinsky, adding, "This will be entirely sufficient."[73]

In the mid-1940s, both the United States and the Soviet Union believed that the political fate of Czechoslovakia was of crucial importance in the nascent Cold War. Both also believed that culture offered an important means of influencing the country's politics. Yet their cultural outreach to Czechoslovakia was stymied by domestic factors. In the United States, these factors included the MPEA's commercial concerns, and domestic anti-Communism, while in the USSR they included bureaucratic inefficiency, a lack of financial resources, and fear of foreign contacts—even with a close ally.

Cultural Sovietization by Proxy

In the early postwar years, a pattern emerged across Eastern Europe: even as Soviet political power increased, Soviet cultural policy faced significant obstacles. In Poland, as Patryk Babiracki has shown, Soviet cultural exports faced stiff competition from exports from Great Britain and the United States, and local Communists expressed frustrations similar to those of members of the KSČ about structural weaknesses in the USSR's cultural policy. John Connelly has described a comparable situation in the realm of higher education: Communists in East Germany, Poland, and Czechoslovakia were largely left to their own devices regarding how to "Sovietize" universities. In all three countries, the local Communist parties settled on a similar solution: they indigenized the task of promoting the Soviet Union.[74] In Czechoslovakia, as a result of Soviet inaction, it fell to the KSČ to advance Soviet culture.

During the Third Republic, two societies for friendship with the Soviet Union—both founded in the interwar period—assumed responsibility for pro-Soviet propaganda in Czechoslovakia. The first was the Society for Cultural and Economic Ties with the USSR, which was headed by Zdeněk Nejedlý, a musicologist and Communist fellow traveler who also served as Czechoslovakia's minister of schools and education from 1945 to 1946, and minister of labor and social education from 1946 to 1948. The society's 7,000 members were drawn from Czechoslovakia's cultural and scientific elite. The society was divided into thirteen sections, focused on topics such as the Soviet social sciences, medicine, pedagogy, and sports. Its main method for

promoting the USSR was to hold public lectures on Soviet cultural and technological achievements.[75] The second, larger society promoting the Soviet
Union was the Union of Friends of the USSR. It was sponsored by the KSČ;
Jiří Sládek served as general secretary. In 1946, the union had 292,000 individual members in the Czech lands, and an additional 2,000,000 collective
members (that is, individuals in member institutions such as schools and
factories).[76] The union held mass events to celebrate the life of Vladimir
Lenin and important dates connected with World War II and the Soviet
liberation.[77] It published a magazine promoting the USSR, *Svět sovětů*
(World of the Soviets) and a journal for functionaries, *Přítel SSSR* (Friend of
the USSR). It also devoted considerable energy to propagandizing itself. In
1946, it sponsored 3,000 lectures with the title, "What Is the Union of
Friends of the USSR?"[78]

The two Czechoslovak-Soviet friendship societies faced similar challenges
in propagandizing the USSR during the early postwar period. In particular, they lacked sufficient information about the country they were supposed
to promote. Soviet restrictions on receiving foreign visitors meant that many
of the functionaries who traveled around Czechoslovakia advertising the
superiority of Soviet life had never actually been to the USSR. These functionaries were also frequently forced to use propaganda about the Soviet Union
that was ten to twenty years old because Soviet officials failed to supply them
with up-to-date materials.[79] Soviet representatives in Czechoslovakia complained that the friendship societies lacked sufficient ideological dogmatism.
For example, a VOKS official accused the Union of Friends of the USSR of
"not always having been sufficiently militant [*boevoi*]" in combating the "anti-
Soviet propaganda that has been developed by clear and open enemies of
the Soviet Union."[80] The two friendship societies' combined membership
shows that considerable grassroots interest in the Soviet Union existed in
Czechoslovakia before the February 1948 coup. Yet these organizations were
also forced to substitute for Soviet cultural agencies, which either lacked sufficient resources to conduct their own propaganda work in Czechoslovakia
or were simply afraid of engaging in contacts with a foreign country. The
activities of the two friendship societies during the Third Republic set a
precedent for the future of the Czechoslovak-Soviet friendship project; in
the coming decades, Czechoslovak organizations would continue to play an
outsized role in propagating the USSR.

Culture as a Surrogate for Politics

Soviet cultural imports in Czechoslovakia were supposed to highlight the USSR's political authority as the world's first socialist state, and its moral authority as the liberator of Europe from fascism. Yet during the Third Republic, Czechoslovak cultural critics, members of the broader public, and even (in private) leaders of the KSČ employed critiques of Soviet culture to challenge Soviet supremacy. Debates over Soviet cultural imports thus became a platform for Czechoslovaks to construct their nationalist project: an occasion to express their feelings of cultural superiority vis-à-vis their Soviet liberators, on the grounds that their country was more sophisticated and Westernized.

In public, Czechoslovak Communists hailed Soviet cinema as "a celebration of life, the sum of truth and beauty, the leader of humanity to new goals." The party argued that Soviet films served the lofty goal of reforming individual viewers and society at large, while films made in capitalist countries were only useful "to pass the time and [as] lowbrow amusement."[81] The KSČ's press claimed Soviet films had universal appeal because they focused on the concerns of the common man.[82] By contrast, *Přítel SSSR*, the journal of the Union of Friends of the USSR, accused Western films of trying to distract audiences from "the social injustice of the real world." One journalist wrote, "Our public, alas, is still too much in the thrall of old notions about film, in which phony glitz appears instead of the truth. Unrealistic, literally false life on the screen—that is the film of the capitalist era, which deliberately weakens the consciousness of the masses in order to capitalize on their confusion."[83] Similarly, *Rudé právo* argued that Czechoslovak moviegoers could be divided into "two worlds." One "world" mistakenly supported the "pipe dreams" of "Anglo-American" films, with their "strange modern romanticism, clear escape from reality, eyes closed to [life's] difficulties," while the other "world" correctly aligned itself with Soviet movies, which "try to portray life, to help man find his place in society, and to steer him away from the shallowness in life."[84]

A series of articles in *Svobodné noviny*, the newspaper allied with the Czech Social Democratic Party, declared that the decline in Czechoslovak interest in Soviet films after the arrival of British and French movies in the fall of 1945 stemmed not from misplaced values, but from the basic relation between the state and the arts in the Soviet Union. These articles argued that Soviet films were unattractive to Czechoslovak audiences because the doctrine of socialist realism was too narrow to reflect the complexity of real life. They claimed Czechoslovak viewers were alienated by "the tendentiousness that permeates every meter of Soviet film."[85]

The writer and filmmaker Jiří Brdečka argued in *Svobodné noviny* that Soviet film, far from having the universal qualities celebrated by the KSČ, was too closely linked to Soviet life to appeal to Czechoslovak viewers. Brdečka acknowledged the tradition of pan-Slavism in his country: "For more than a century we have been connected to Russia with a deep and conscious sympathy, bordering on delirium." Yet, he argued, a "difference between the Czech and Russian psyche simply exists." Brdečka concluded that Soviet films were "too exotic" for Czechoslovak viewers. He acknowledged that American movies might also be accused of being too "exotic," but argued that, first, Hollywood films had long been familiar to Czech audiences (since they had been shown in large numbers before the war), and second, they were made for export and were thus designed to appeal to viewers throughout the world.

Brdečka also maintained that Czechoslovak viewers were too Westernized and sophisticated to enjoy Soviet films. He claimed that Soviet films were made exclusively with the needs of Soviet audiences in mind—people "who are, in some regions, still very unrefined and primitive." In particular he singled out the film *The High Reward* (Yevgenii Shneider, 1939) as an example of a Soviet film that should never have been released in Czechoslovakia. The film tells the story of a foreign spy whose attempts to steal information about a fast plane built by a Soviet professor are thwarted by a cunning NKVD agent. Brdečka concluded that Czechoslovak moviegoers were "too refined to consume [such films] with satisfaction. They demand complex narratives of the most ingenious variety, but also plausible plots."[86] By claiming that Czechoslovak viewers were too sophisticated to appreciate Soviet films, Brdečka argued against the notion of Soviet superiority that the KSČ advanced, and instead promoted Czechoslovak nationalism.

Although the KSČ lauded Soviet films in public, in private meetings with Soviet officials, high-ranking party members in fact echoed Brdečka's critiques. In 1947, Kopecký, the hard-line Communist minister of information, complained to a Soviet dramaturge visiting Prague about the quality of the USSR's film imports. According to the dramaturge, Kopecký protested that Soviet films "are not interesting to the Czech viewer, and in his opinion, are, roughly speaking, didactic and simply boring." The dramaturge continued, "The Czech comrades, and the overwhelming majority of Communists whom I had conversations with are united in the opinion that in the conditions of Czechoslovakia, the tendentiousness in our films has too much of a heavy-handed [*lobovoi*] character. For our propaganda to have success in the conditions of the Czechoslovak Republic they need films and plays with the political biases hidden more deeply and with less of a heavy-handed character, and more interesting construction in a dramaturgic sense." The Soviet dramaturge further reported that Kopecký and other Czechoslovak Communists had appealed to the Soviets to release films "of an export character, designed for the European viewer."[87] The language in this statement is striking: by labeling Czechoslovak viewers "Europeans," the KSČ implied that the USSR—its ostensible political model—was a less civilized "other." Behind closed doors, Kopecký and other Communists demonstrated that Czechoslovak feelings of cultural superiority vis-à-vis the USSR cut across ideological lines.

The April 1947 Soviet art exhibition discussed in this chapter's opening provides the clearest example of how debates over Soviet culture in Czechoslovakia served as proxies for the construction of Czechoslovak nationalism and for critiques of Czechoslovakia's broader friendship project with the USSR. The exhibition featured ninety works by four of the USSR's leading socialist realist painters: Aleksandr Gerasimov, Sergei Gerasimov, Aleksandr Deineka, and Arkadii Plastov. The paintings, dating from 1937 to 1946, adhered to Aleksandr Gerasimov's famous definition of socialist realism: "realist in form and socialist in content."[88] They depicted iconic Stalinist themes, including joyful life on abundant collective farms, portraits of Stalin and Soviet military leaders, and patriotic Russian landscapes, in an idealized style.

The exhibition was exceptionally popular. During the month it was open, it attracted approximately 45,000 visitors. By contrast, the U.S.-sponsored exhibit "Advancing American Art," which had been shown in Prague the previous month, and which the U.S. embassy judged "a great success,"[89] had attracted 8,500 viewers.[90] The Soviet art exhibition intensified debates in Czechoslovakia about the merits of Soviet culture and the stakes of Czechoslovak-Soviet friendship: these debates played out among critics in the Czechoslovak press, and among ordinary viewers in the exhibition's comment books. The exhibition also marked the last time there would be a major public debate about relations with the Soviet Union in Czechoslovakia until twenty years later, during the 1968 Prague Spring.

The KSČ boasted that the exhibition would bolster Czechoslovakia's friendship project with the Soviet Union. Yet even the exhibition's setting, at the Mánes Gallery in central Prague, highlighted significant cultural differences between the two countries. The Mánes Gallery was a hallmark of Czech modernist architecture, designed in 1930 by Otakar Novotný. In the interwar period, it had become well-known for promoting a kind of art very different from socialist realism. In January 1935, the gallery hosted the debut exhibition of Czech surrealist artists. The previous year, the leftist avant-garde writers Nezval and Bohuslav Brouk had founded the Czech Group of Surrealists as an explicit alternative to Soviet socialist realism, which they excoriated as "'the vulgar Marxist tendency' of 'the official Communist leadership.'"[91]

In 1947, Czechoslovak Communists commended what they claimed was the universal resonance of the Soviet paintings on display at the Mánes Gallery. They thus echoed the themes they had developed in their praise of Soviet films: universality and populism. "The current exhibition clearly shows us how, without reservation, Soviet art comes from man, from his universal and realistic vision of reality, and how it is again directed [back] toward man," an article in *Rudé právo* declared.[92] Czechoslovak Communists argued that even if Soviet art was "young" and the paintings exhibited bore "many mistakes, namely of a technical nature," it should nonetheless serve as an example to Czechoslovak artists. "What art is so spontaneously and completely positively related to all social phenomena?" a review in *Svět práce* asked rhetorically. "What [art] is so inspired by moral and human values? . . . And what art has [met with] so much enthusiasm from the public?"[93] Czechoslovak Communists portrayed the paintings as an example of the special connection that existed between artists and the Soviet people, a connection they claimed had led to stunning national achievements in the USSR, including "the victorious Stalinist five-year plans" and "the historic victory in the Great Patriotic War."[94]

The exhibition's admirers—both Communists and non-Communists—argued that the Soviet paintings' resonance transcended political and national borders. They used the language of pan-Slavism to praise the artwork. One woman wrote in the exhibition's comment book, "I am not a Communist,

nonetheless this Russian art speaks to me in a comprehensible voice."[95] Another woman wrote, "I am happy that finally something so healthy and Slavic
has come to us," adding that the paintings "grab [one] by the heart."[96] Supporters of the exhibition contrasted the Soviet paintings to works by Western experimental painters and the Czech avant-garde. One viewer wrote, "If
Picasso represents the West, and these artists the East, I give my vote for the
East. Gerasimov, not Picasso!"[97] Another viewer applauded the Soviet painters
for showing "no traces of surrealism, cubism, and that sort of thing," which
he dubbed, "the cancer of contemporary art."[98]

Yet as admirers of the exhibition employed pan-Slavism to praise the
Soviet paintings, they inadvertently bolstered Czechoslovak nationalism.
One man wrote in the comment books that the paintings "convey to viewers
the straightforward, generous, and unrefined soul of the Russian man."[99]
A husband and wife who visited the exhibition together wrote, "We are
enchanted, moved, delighted by the fact that we see here Russia as we imagine it—at once simple and great."[100] By drawing on stereotypes of the unrefined, earthy Russian soul, such comments posited the USSR as a foil for a
more sophisticated, Western, and modern Czechoslovakia. Although these
assessments of Soviet culture were positive, they amounted to a backdoor
form of Czechoslovak chauvinism.

By emphasizing the Soviet paintings' lack of artistic innovation, critics of
the exhibition claimed a cultural chasm existed between Czechoslovakia and
the USSR. "They painted like this here [in the Czech lands] 200 years ago,
and they are painting like this in the Soviet Union today," one viewer wrote.[101]
Another concluded, "It is clear that Soviet art was separated from all Western art, which every cultured person recognizes as superior. Therefore [while]
these pictures are fully composed, they are still lacking from a visual standpoint."[102]

In the Czechoslovak press, the harshest critics of the exhibition were leftist, non-Communist intellectuals. They advanced an elitist, nondemocratic
version of Czechoslovak nationalism. They saw the exhibition's broad appeal
to the general public as grounds for censure. The artist Otakar Mrkvička,
who had been a member of the Czech avant-garde group Devětsil in the
1920s, conceded that "a part of society, and we admit it is a significant part,
were satisfied with what they saw [at the exhibition]," but he added haughtily,
"They were precisely those viewers who otherwise don't go to exhibitions."[103]
In the newspaper *Dnešek* (Today), Brouk, the cofounder of the Czech Group

of Surrealists in the 1930s, made an analogy to engineering and physics: nonspecialists, he argued, would not presume to understand how bridges were built, or how the atomic bomb was constructed, yet they did not hesitate to "presume to perfectly understand art," to claim that it "is something so easy [and] simple that everyone can express themselves seriously about it."[104] Brouk's critique of the exhibition, as well as those by other Czech non-Communist intellectuals, can be seen as a continuation of the vicious debates over Soviet culture that had erupted in leftist circles in Czechoslovakia in the late 1930s.[105]

The Soviet exhibition thus raised the question of who had the authority to critique art. This debate carried out directly in the exhibition's comment books. Beneath the pithy dismissal of the exhibit by a Dr. Waltera, "I came, I saw, I was sick," another viewer wrote, "So an intellectual criticizes." Another comment, signed "Your reverse snob" exclaimed, "Mr. Snobs, tear off that mask of 'connoisseurs of modern art' and confess with complete honesty that you have not found in the Russian brothers' pictures a piece of your own soul, a piece of the same temperament."[106]

Both supporters and critics of the art exhibition understood the controversy as part of a larger debate over the nature of Czechoslovak-Soviet friendship. Czechoslovak Communists interpreted any critique of the exhibition as an attack on the Soviet Union's sacred role in their country's political life. To this end, Kopecký excoriated the exhibition's critics as "reactionaries," "philistines," and "collaborators," who "are, in a provocative manner, attempting to concoct a breach between Soviet fine arts and our own." He warned, "No one will succeed in driving a wedge in the heartfelt brotherhood of Soviet and Czech artists . . . however hard they try to create an artificial 'East-West' contradiction."[107]

By contrast, for non-Communists like Brouk, the exhibition served as proof of the essential differences between the Soviet Union and Czechoslovakia, and of the importance of being honest about these differences for the sake of the countries' broader friendship. Brouk argued, "Soviet painting [is] completely foreign to us," and added that it "belongs on the periphery of artistic creation." He decried what he viewed as the Czechoslovak press's willful silence in the face of this obvious truth. People would not be so polite, he argued, if the exhibition had been British or American. The press's failure to critique not only the exhibition, but the Soviet Union more broadly, was leading, he claimed, to Czechoslovaks becoming disillusioned with the very idea of socialism because they failed to understand how different conditions were in the USSR as opposed to those in their own country. In language that echoed Brdečka's critique of Soviet films a year and a half before, Brouk assailed the KSČ's pan-Slavism, and emphasized the USSR's backwardness compared to Czechoslovakia. "Russian socialism has emerged straight from feudal darkness." He argued that due to Czechoslovakia's more advanced economy, it had a better chance of achieving socialism. The "East-West contradiction" that Kopecký had mentioned was not in fact "artificial," Brouk contended, but stemmed from real historical differences between the two countries: the Czechs were inheritors of Roman traditions, the Soviets of those from Byzantium.[108]

Although the KSČ publicly promoted the art exhibition as a means to achieve cultural "rapprochement" with the Soviet Union, in private, one of its leading members seemed to agree with Brouk that a fundamental cultural divide did in fact exist between the countries. In October 1947, six months after the exhibition, a delegation of Czechoslovak writers, headed by Nezval, traveled to the Soviet Union. Nezval argued with his Soviet hosts that "the current art in Czechoslovakia," which he defined as "painting that is strongly influenced by the contemporary French school . . . is the art that best suits the Czech people." In contrast, he spoke condescendingly about Soviet art, "Your Russian painting has lowered its artistic level. Your art is designed for the broad masses, it is accessible to the understanding of the common man, it has become populist, but our artists and intelligentsia stand above popular tastes, and our art follows a different path."[109] Nezval's critique of Soviet art thus echoed the private concerns Kopecký and other KSČ functionaries had expressed about Soviet films.

For Czechoslovak non-Communists, Soviet films and the 1947 art exhibition provided an opportunity to construct an alternate vision for friendship with the Soviet Union from the KSČ's public, fawning stance. Brouk argued that Czechoslovaks should be forthright about their differences with the Soviet Union precisely because the two countries' relationship was so strong. "Our connection to the USSR is . . . much more than a polite one.[110] He continued, "We will never endear ourselves to our friends with sycophancy, be it hypocritical or spontaneous, especially not in Russia, among such a great people, who can live without our art, not to mention our admiration."[111] This idea—that *real* friendship between Czechoslovakia and the Soviet Union meant the ability to talk frankly, to speak the truth—was a common trope among non-Communist Czech intellectuals during the Third Republic. It provided an antidote to what they saw as the KSČ's self-appointed "duty to passionately praise everything even remotely connected with the USSR, and to bow deeply before it."[112] Above all, calls for honesty by non-Communists posited a vision of Czechoslovak-Soviet relations grounded in reciprocity and respect, where Czechoslovaks could critique Soviet culture and be listened to. "Today we need more candor, openness, and genuine criticism," an article on Soviet film argued. "Soviet filmmakers are our friends, they film in Prague, and they look forward to collaborating with us candidly. If we want our friends to remain here, our criticism must be truly friendly—that is, stringent."[113]

The writer and editor Pavel Tigrid (who became one of the most important Czechoslovak opposition figures in exile after 1948) wrote in *Vývoj* (Progress), the newspaper he edited, "We have always conceived of [our] relationship to the Soviet Union as a real friendship and alliance . . . [in which] we are also one of the partners, albeit the lesser one." What is especially interesting is that Tigrid, like Brouk, depicted the Soviet Union as a potential ally for Czechoslovak non-Communists in their struggle with the KSČ for objectivity and honesty in Czechoslovak-Soviet relations. Tigrid insisted that the Soviets would not want Czechoslovaks to flatter them, or to stifle their criticism of the USSR; he claimed they understood that "Sycophancy is always . . . impossible to reconcile with friendship."[114]

The Soviet response to the debates over the art exhibition in Czechoslovakia exposed the naiveté of the Czechoslovak non-Communists and party members alike. Both groups believed they could influence Soviet cultural policy in Czechoslovakia and the development of the friendship project. A few weeks after the exhibition closed in Prague, however, A. Zamoshkin, the director of the Tretyakov Gallery in Moscow, published an article in the Soviet paper *Moskovskaia pravda* (Moscow Truth) about the exhibition's reception in Czechoslovakia. Here Zamoshkin argued for the validity of the very "'East-West' contradiction" that Kopecký had so vigorously denied. "The exhibition gave people who had previously had a weak conception of our painting the opportunity to compare Soviet painting with that of the West, and to express their sympathy [for it]," he wrote. He also rejected the notion of reciprocity between Soviets and Czechoslovaks that Tigrid and other Czech intellectuals had advanced. Zamoshkin argued that the people of Czechoslovakia must embrace Soviet art not only as passive consumers but also in their own cultural production.[115] Zamoshkin's response thus paved the way for a new stage in Czechoslovak-Soviet relations, in which debates over culture would be silenced, and the Soviet Union would seek to impose socialist realism as the only mode of cultural production in Czechoslovakia.

"New, Healthy Views of the World"

On February 20, 1948, the KSČ took power in a coup. The importance of the friendship project in Czechoslovakia immediately intensified. The USSR was no longer simply the guarantor of Czechoslovak sovereignty; it became the country's explicit political, economic, social, and cultural model. The role of Soviet cultural exports in Czechoslovakia changed significantly. First, the KSČ introduced full censorship in the press, thereby suppressing the public debates over Soviet culture and Czechoslovak-Soviet relations that had been raging for nearly three years. Second, under Soviet pressure, the KSČ worked in tandem with the Soviet government to drastically reduce the flow of Western cultural imports to Czechoslovakia, thus eliminating a key source of competition to Soviet culture.

The split between Stalin and Tito in June 1948 marked the first major rift in the nascent socialist world and led the USSR to redouble efforts to foster uniformity among its satellite states. In response, the KSČ initiated a Sovietization campaign aimed at nearly every aspect of Czechoslovak life. The reams of propaganda the party produced to illustrate its ubiquitous slogan, "The Soviet Union Is Our Model," reduced the USSR to a series of tropes: the defender of peace, the builder of the radiant future, the caretaker of women and children.[116] To get to "know" the Soviet Union was no longer a process of discovery, comparison, and analysis, as it had been during the Third Republic, but of memorization, performance, and ritual.

The frontline organization for the promotion of Soviet culture in Czechoslovakia was the new Union of Czechoslovak-Soviet Friendship (SČSP), which was founded two days after the coup by amalgamating the Society for Cultural and Economic Ties with the USSR and the Society of Friends of the Soviet Union. In May 1949, the SČSP took over the operations of the Slovak friendship society with the USSR; by the end of that year it boasted a membership of 1,632,000 in 6,267 branches across Czechoslovakia.[117]

In order for Czechoslovaks to learn from Soviet culture and develop their own culture in accordance with the Soviet model, the SČSP pledged to facilitate the staging of Russian and Soviet plays, the launching of exhibits of Soviet architecture, and the expansion of press coverage of Soviet cultural achievements. Czechoslovak cultural figures who had been to the Soviet Union were supposed to play an active role in these measures.[118] In 1949, the SČSP initiated a network of "People's Russian Courses" (*Lidové kursy ruštiny*, LKR), which taught Russian language and socialist behavior to adults.[119]

Additionally, the SČSP founded special book clubs (*kroužky*) for reading and discussing Soviet literature. In 1951, the suggested reading list amounted to a veritable canon of Soviet socialist realist hits, including Nikolai Ostrovsky's *How the Steel Was Tempered* (1934), Mikhail Sholokhov's *The Virgin Soil Upturned* (1935), and Alexander Fadeyev's *The Young Guard* (1946, revised edition, 1951). Reading these novels was supposed to teach Czechoslovak citizens about Soviet life and morality.[120]

The SČSP developed new periodicals for its functionaries, designed to help them propagandize Soviet culture, including *Kulturní besedy Československo-sovětského přátelství* (Cultural Discussions on Czechoslovak-Soviet Friendship) and *Sovětským filmem* (With Soviet Film). "Our first societal task is to bring ourselves close together with the Soviet people," the inaugural issue of *Kulturní besedy* declared, "To meet this goal successfully, it is necessary that we become acquainted with Soviet culture, which shows us the problems a socialist society encounters, and how they have been solved in the Soviet Union. The USSR is our model. We will use every opportunity to remind our working people how the Soviet citizen labors and grows. . . . Soviet books and Soviet films are powerful assistants in constructing new, healthy views of the world."[121]

What is especially striking about these publications is the level of detail they provided about how to propagate Soviet culture. Almost no aspect of Soviet culture was left open to individual interpretation. For instance, an issue of *Kulturní besedy* celebrating the Red Army included a series of poems by Soviet and Czechoslovak writers, with instructions about the type of occasion they were best suited for (a small meeting or a classroom exercise), how they should be read aloud ("in a calm voice, full of expression"), and the overall message they were supposed to convey (when reading the poem "The Oath" by Aleksandr Prokof'ev, the audience was supposed to be reminded of Soviet battles in World War II, the Munich Agreement, and "our situation at home").[122] The issue also contained detailed instructions, accompanied by illustrations, for performing a Ukrainian dance, the "Katerina": "The costumes should be Ukrainian national dress. If you do not have the opportunity to acquire it, then girls should wear colorful skirts and white blouses with several strands of colorful coral beads, and should put long ribbons in their hair. If the lads don't have high boots and Ukrainian broad, pleated trousers, long white trousers and white shirts will suffice."[123]

The Sovietization of culture in Czechoslovakia was achieved not only by imitation but also by purging Western cultural imports. In 1949, under Soviet pressure, Czechoslovak cultural officials refused to enter into a new contract with the MPEA.[124] The absence of a significant number of imports from Hollywood shifted the balance of films in circulation to the Soviets' favor. By 1951, films from the socialist countries amounted to 93.6 percent of screen time in Czechoslovakia.[125] That year the share of the market held by Soviet films was 50.7 percent—a peak for the postwar period—compared with 23 percent in 1947, 34 percent in 1948, and 40 percent in 1949.[126]

Although the USSR succeeded in temporarily eliminating most of the competition from American movies in Czechoslovakia, the reception of Soviet films was stymied by shortages. Under the terms of the USSR's 1945 film export agreement with Czechoslovakia, it was obliged to send Prague 100 films the first year, with the number to increase by 5 per year until 1950, and then level off at 125 films per year.[127] Soviet films were also supposed to occupy 60 percent of the screen time in Czechoslovakia—a feat that the statistics cited above show was never remotely accomplished even at the height of the Stalinist period. The problem was that from the early 1930s until Stalin's death in 1953, the USSR did not produce nearly enough movies to meet the agreement's terms.[128] From 1945 to 1953, increasingly stringent censorship, combined with the film industry's decision to focus exclusively on producing "masterpieces," resulted in what scholars have called a "film hunger" in the Soviet Union. During this period, the Soviet Union produced a minimum of 9 films per year (in 1951) and a maximum of 44 (in 1953).[129] As a result, in April 1949, the Soviet Ministry of Cinematography reported to the Central Committee that it had exhausted its entire supply of films suitable for export to the satellite states from the past *20 years*.[130]

The reception of Soviet films in Czechoslovakia also suffered due to an overall lack of enthusiasm from local audiences. Throughout the Eastern bloc, Soviet cultural officials registered complaints about their films.[131] Yet these officials never appear to have seriously considered changing the films produced in the USSR to conform more closely to foreign viewers' tastes. In the Soviets' opinion, the solution was not to change their films, but to change the films' viewers. As the KSČ discovered, however, changing people's ideas about a popular form of entertainment was not easy. "A revolution in people's thinking does not happen as quickly as the nationalization of industry," an article in *Přítel SSSR* conceded in 1950.[132]

Czechoslovak officials experimented with a variety of measures to compensate for the shortage of new Soviet films and to counteract the public's ambivalence. They tried repackaging Soviet films already in circulation into themed festivals.[133] Party functionaries also tried to make a virtue out of a necessity by arguing that films like *Lenin in October* (Mikhail Romm and Dmitrii Vasil'ev, 1937) were so important that they needed to be viewed twice in order to be fully understood.[134] They also argued for the continuing relevance of classic films such as *Chapaev* (Sergei and Georgii Vasil'ev), which had first been released in the Soviet Union in 1934. "The film *Chapaev* . . . is a work that remains vital and appropriate, even though it has been almost eighteen years since it first came out," *Sovětským filmem* argued in 1952.[135]

Czechoslovak officials also gave Soviet films preferential screen time on weekends, and halved the number of all film premieres from 1947 to 1949.[136] The SČSP's regional film organizers used *Sovětským filmem* to share their experiences in trying to increase attendance at Soviet films. In 1952, for instance, a friendship society secretary in Krupka explained how his branch had taken over advertising and ticket sales for Soviet films from the local movie theater. They advertised the films on local radio, designed posters, and arranged for lecturers to make a short presentation in the theater before the films were shown. Even after all these efforts, however, they were usually only able to draw 150 people to a theater that could hold 385.[137]

Soviet party and cultural functionaries ultimately decided that the quantity of their cultural exports throughout Eastern Europe was far more important than their quality. They preferred, for example, to fill Czechoslovak cinema repertoires with filmed versions of Soviet plays rather than let Western movies be shown. In Hungary one Soviet film official even told local Communists point blank that "the worst Russian film is better than an American one."[138] In the realm of creative literature, the Soviets argued that "it should be clear even to a child that it is better to have even our most mediocre book on the international market, rather than to substitute it with a book propagating antithetical ideas that are hostile to us."[139] By the late 1940s, Soviet cultural policy in the Eastern bloc had thus become self-consciously centered on the promotion of mediocrity.

The Politics of Culture

During the Third Republic, Czechoslovakia and the Soviet Union were close allies, but the structure of this alliance was in flux. The KSČ sought to construct a unique version of socialism, suitable to the specific cultural and economic conditions in Czechoslovakia. Non-Communists argued that Czechoslovak friendship with the Soviet Union should be based on reciprocity and mutual respect. The role of Soviet culture in Czechoslovakia during this period was similarly fluid; it served as a means of constructing Czechoslovak nationalism, of competing with Western influence, and even of critiquing friendship with the USSR.

The new methods the KSČ implemented for promoting Soviet culture in Czechoslovakia after February 1948 corresponded to a new direction in Soviet-Czechoslovak friendship. After the coup, both Soviet culture and Soviet politics became nonnegotiable. In the wake of the Stalin-Tito split, when the Eastern bloc's Communist parties began to engage in hunts for "enemies" in their ranks, the KSČ abandoned ideas for a "national path" to Communism. Friendship with the Soviet Union could thus no longer be a platform for constructing Czechoslovak nationalism, as it had been in the 1945–1948 period. Instead, friendship became an expression of fealty to the USSR. In the early 1950s, Soviet culture became one component of a full-fledged cult of the Soviet Union in Czechoslovakia.

Chapter 2

"The Land of Our Destiny"

Everyone who spends even a small amount of time in the Soviet Union
returns to us like a different person. It is as if the strength of the Soviet land
enters their veins and increases our strength [to build Communism].

—Czechoslovak newspaper, 1950

At home our people are learning from Soviet comrades, but we,
on the other hand, have isolated ourselves from the Soviet Union.

—Czech student studying in the USSR, 1952

In the spring of 1952, the community of Czechoslovak exchange students
in the USSR erupted in scandal. Soviet officials accused the students of making anti-Soviet statements, demonstrating bourgeois nationalist behavior,
and deliberately isolating themselves from their Soviet classmates. The
Czechoslovak students responded by employing Soviet methods in an attempt
to expiate their anti-Soviet thoughts and behaviors. They traded accusations,
denounced each other for ideological deviations, and held a series of criticism
and self-criticism sessions that ran late into the night. The Czechoslovak
students had come to the USSR to learn from the Soviet model. That spring,
it appeared as if they had failed spectacularly.

From 1946 to 1953, at the height of Soviet isolationism and postwar xenophobia, thousands of young idealists from the emerging socialist countries
in Europe and Asia traveled to the USSR to study at Soviet universities. These
exchange students were the only large group of foreigners to experience daily
life at the center of international Communism during late Stalinism. Their
story thus provides a unique lens into the tensions between isolationism and

exchange, and imperialism and "friendship" in the European socialist world in this period. As the previous chapter demonstrated, during those years, citizens of the nascent Eastern bloc primarily learned about the Soviet Union secondhand, through Soviet cultural exports. "To visit the Soviet Union, to become acquainted with its life in construction [*budování*] with one's own eyes, this is the ardent desire of every friend of the USSR," *Přítel SSSR* (Friend of the USSR) declared in 1946.[1] Tickets to the socialist paradise, however, were hard to obtain for two reasons. First, Soviet authorities were not eager to let their new "friends" from abroad see the massive devastation from World War II. Second, in the summer of 1946, Joseph Stalin's cultural spokesman, Andrei Zhdanov, launched a series of anti-Western campaigns in the USSR, known as the *Zhdanovshchina*. Soviet authorities came to fear the prospect of their citizens engaging in any interactions with foreigners— even from "friendly" countries. Under these circumstances, few Central and Eastern Europeans were able to visit the USSR. The vast majority of those who did were confined to carefully choreographed, official delegations.[2]

The hundreds of Czechoslovak students who came to the Soviet Union from 1946 to 1953 represented the cream of their country's young Communist elite. They were also the only social group in Czechoslovakia at the time that had the opportunity to live in the Soviet Union for an extended period— most stayed for several years. The extensive documentation that exists in the Russian and Czech archives about the students' experiences, and the memoirs several of them later wrote, provide a unique lens into the intimate side of the friendship project.

When the students came to the USSR, "The Soviet Union Is Our Model" was the leading slogan of Czechoslovak propaganda, and many thus looked to their stay in the Soviet Union as an opportunity not only for professional advancement, but for personal transformation. One even declared, "I am sure . . . that we foreign students will return to our home countries not only as good specialists but as Soviet people."[3] Studies of the Soviet foreign student program and other forms of cultural contact between the Soviet Union and the Eastern bloc countries during late Stalinism have argued that these exchanges failed to establish closer ties between the superpower and its satellites, and instead bred disappointment and disillusionment. The literature on the much larger Soviet program to educate students from the Third World in the 1960s–1980s has likewise focused on themes of disenchantment and failure.[4]

On the surface, this narrative of failure appears to apply perfectly to the Czechoslovak students in the Soviet Union: they were often unable to obtain the technical expertise they sought at Soviet universities or to assimilate into Soviet social life. The fact that some of the students accused by the Soviet authorities of anti-Soviet behavior in 1952 would later go on to play important roles in the Prague Spring and then in the Czechoslovak dissident movement in exile would appear to be further evidence that the student program was a colossal Soviet foreign policy failure. Yet a closer examination of the experiences of the Czechoslovak students in the USSR—including those involved in the 1952 scandal—reveals that the Soviet exchange program actually succeeded in one critical respect. The Soviet and Czechoslovak governments employed this program to promote an authoritarian ideology and political practices. The student exchanges facilitated the circulation of Stalinist political tactics across the borders of the new socialist empire, producing an international cohort of young people with firsthand experience in detecting ideological deviations and using Communist "methods" to correct them. The Soviet foreign student program thus proved to be an essential—and successful—instrument in the creation of the empire of friends.

Educational Exchanges East and West

In the fall of 1946, following a Central Committee resolution in August, the first cohort of postwar foreign exchange students arrived in the USSR. The majority of these 500 young people came from the least economically developed areas of the Soviet Union's new sphere of influence, including Yugoslavia, Bulgaria, and North Korea. Twenty students came from Czechoslovakia, which was not yet, of course, a member of the socialist bloc.[5] By November 1952, the Soviet foreign student program had increased over tenfold to include 8,947 foreign students at 213 institutes of higher education in 23 cities. More than 25 percent of these students came from Romania, and the remainder included 1,540 from Poland, 1,464 from Hungary, and 761 from Czechoslovakia.[6]

The postwar Soviet foreign student program had roots in an earlier era of socialist internationalism: in the 1920s, the USSR had founded several special institutes to educate members of the Comintern and other foreign fellow travelers, including the Communist University of Toilers of the East and the Communist University of National Minorities of the West, both founded in 1921, and the International Lenin School, which opened in 1926. These early experiments in Soviet international education were explicitly designed to train foreign Communist operatives in tactics for fomenting revolution in their home countries.[7] By contrast, the foreign student program that the Central Committee launched in 1946 was intended to stabilize the new Communist world by educating foreign students at regular Soviet institutes of higher education, where they would study and live alongside their Soviet peers. The exchange program was designed to develop cadres versed in Soviet political methods and technical know-how, who would return to their home countries to help "build" socialist societies founded on the Soviet model. At the everyday level, the goal of the program was to augment rapprochement (*sblizhenie*) between the USSR and its new satellite states— to create a transnational, socialist community of friends. The Czechoslovak exchange students were thus required to pledge "to work according to [our] best ability to strengthen friendly ties between the peoples of the Soviet Union and our peoples, to contribute to the ever-deeper knowledge of the life and work of the people of both states."[8]

The Soviet foreign student program also developed within the broader context of the nascent Cold War. Both superpowers saw educational exchanges as tools to expand their influence abroad. In August 1946—the same month that the resolution on foreign exchange students was introduced in the USSR—the United States launched the Fulbright Program, which was supposed to further the "promotion of international good will through the exchange of students in the fields of education, culture, and science" and "increase mutual understanding between the people of the United States and the people of other countries."[9] As Frank Ninkovich has shown, the United States had initially tried to develop educational exchange programs with the Soviet Union in the wake of the countries' alliance during World War II. The Soviets' rejection of these efforts combined with their establishment of the foreign student program for Eastern Europeans were among the factors that led the U.S. government to launch the Fulbright Program and other educational and cultural exchange initiatives.[10] In contrast to the Soviet foreign student program with the socialist countries, where expectations for cross-border influence were unabashedly unidirectional,[11] the Fulbright Program was founded on the premise "that America has much to teach in

the world but also much to learn."[12] But by the late 1940s, as American officials anxiously watched the Soviets consolidate cultural influence over Central and Eastern Europe, they began to reformulate their ideas about cultural
exchange along the lines of the Soviet model. In 1950, Senator J. William
Fulbright, who had originally insisted that the program he had developed
should be apolitical, began arguing that it should instead "'bring about a much
closer association of the people still free from the Iron Curtain.'"[13] By the early
1950s, educational exchanges had become cornerstones of both the Soviet and
American efforts to consolidate their respective spheres of ideological influence
in the Cold War.

Study Abroad, Stalinist Style

In the fall of 1951, a cohort of 300 exchange students from Czechoslovakia
arrived in the Soviet Union. The students had been selected by a special section of the Communist Party of Czechoslovakia's (KSČ's) Secretariat from a
pool of 500 nominees advanced by regional party leaders in the Czech lands
and Slovakia. The majority of the students were nineteen to twenty-one years
old, although a significant number (86 out of 300) were twenty-two to twenty-
four years old. Eighty percent of the students came from worker or peasant
families. All were active members of the KSČ's youth league, and 70 percent
were also party members.[14] Given their class backgrounds and prior political activity, the students selected seemed likely to succeed in their mission as
"interpreters" of Soviet modernization and Stalinist politics.[15]

   The young Czechoslovaks had ideological, personal, and professional reasons for choosing to study in the USSR. One of these young people was
Zdeněk Mlynář, who studied law at Moscow State University (MGU) and
later became famous as a leader of the 1968 Prague Spring. In his memoirs,
Mlynář claims that all his Czechoslovak classmates in the Soviet Union in
the early 1950s "belonged to the elite of the young generation of Communists; they had already worked for several years as functionaries in the CPC
[KSČ], and they were naturally all believing Stalinists."[16] This assertion was
true for Mlynář, who had joined the KSČ at the age of fifteen. But some of
his peers came to the Soviet Union for less overtly political reasons. One
of Mlynář's classmates at MGU, the future historian of the Soviet Union,
Michal Reiman (who would, like Mlynář, become a dissident-in-exile after

the Prague Spring) chose to study in the USSR for familial reasons: his father, Pavel Reiman, was a high-ranking KSČ functionary and his mother was a Soviet citizen. Michal Reiman had spent the war years in the Soviet Union with his parents.[17] By contrast, another young Czechoslovak who studied in Leningrad at the time, Radoslav Selucký, who became a leading reform economist in the mid-1960s, asserted in his memoirs that he came to the USSR in 1949 "more or less by accident." As a young party member and journalist in the Moravian capital Brno, he was recruited to go to the USSR by the local party boss, Otto Šling, who argued that he would benefit from the experience on an ideological level and that studying in the USSR would boost his career prospects. Šling advised the young Selucký, "It was good to see the world a bit, to learn Russian well, to get to know the land that had become our destiny, and to overcome the provincialism of Czech journalists."[18]

The vast majority of the Czechoslovak exchange students were sent to study in Moscow or Leningrad, with Sverdlovsk as a distant third. A few also went to Kazan, Saratov, Odessa, Kiev, and Kharkov. The Czechoslovak and Soviet governments decided where they would live. The Czechoslovak government determined their course of study, based on the needs of the country's new socialist economy. The overwhelming majority of the students were sent to the USSR to specialize in technical and scientific fields, including economic and industrial planning, construction, mining, and chemistry, as well as agriculture and medicine. Despite the political significance of studying in the land of Stalin, only a few students were sent to specialize in explicitly ideological subjects such as the history of the Soviet Communist Party and Marxism-Leninism, or cultural fields like film, theater, literature, and music.[19]

The living conditions the Czechoslovak and other foreign students encountered in the USSR underscored the paradoxes of the Soviet Union's imperial project in postwar Eastern Europe: food, clothing, and housing in the "Soviet model" were dramatically inferior to what they were used to back home. Mikhail Gorbachev, who studied at MGU in the early 1950s (where he became friends with Mlynář) recalled in his memoirs that up to twenty-two students had to share a single room in the dormitory. Nonetheless, the standard of living at MGU was a huge improvement over the village where he had spent his childhood. "We had our own cafeteria where we could buy a cup of tea for a few kopecks, with unlimited amounts of bread on the tables. There was a barber's shop and a laundry. . . . We also had our own

Figure 4. Czechoslovak students at the Wilson station in Prague, bound for the USSR, September 7, 1950. The banner on the train says, "The Soviet Union, Our Liberator."
Credit: Česká tisková kancelář/Alexandr Hampl.

polyclinic."[20] These conditions did not seem as impressive to the Eastern European students, who were in many cases coming from countries that were more economically developed than the USSR. Mlynář's recollections of the dormitories at MGU were decidedly less rosy. "For the several hundred [students] on each floor there was only one collective latrine with a washing area and a single common kitchen."[21]

The Eastern European students had been sent to the Soviet Union to learn the technical skills necessary to construct their countries' economies along the lines of the USSR's industrial model, yet they were often stymied in their academic endeavors. They faced two obstacles in particular. First, many arrived in the Soviet Union with limited knowledge of Russian, an obstacle that the Soviets failed to adequately address. A Council of Ministers' decree in February 1952 mandated that students with weak Russian should take a six-month to yearlong preparatory course before beginning their academic studies. But a year later, a report complained that these students were often still sent straight to academic classes, where they performed poorly.[22] The language issue appears to have been less of a hurdle for the Czechoslovak students because, unlike the Hungarians, Albanians, or Chinese, they had the advantage of being native speakers of a Slavic language, and Russian had become a mandatory language of study in Czechoslovak schools in the fall of 1945.

Second, the Soviet university officials responsible for overseeing the foreigners' education often turned out to be afraid of working with them. The launch of the Soviet foreign student program coincided with a series of interrelated xenophobic campaigns in the USSR. The first of these campaigns was the Zhdanovshchina, which was aimed at rooting out Western "decadence" in the arts. This campaign began in August 1946—the same month that the Central Committee launched the foreign student program—with Zhdanov's attack on two prominent Soviet writers, Mikhail Zoshchenko and Anna Akhmatova. Over the next three years, the attacks expanded to include Soviet filmmakers, musicians, and playwrights. A second campaign was directed against Western influence in the sciences: it included a high-profile attack on Grigorii Roskin and Nina Kliueva, medical researchers who were accused of treachery for having shared their research on cancer with Western scientists. The final xenophobic campaign was aimed at purging Jews from political and cultural institutions. It included the secret trial against the Jewish Anti-Fascist Committee, and the arrest, in early 1953, of several Jewish doctors working at the Kremlin, who were accused of plotting to kill Stalin and other Soviet leaders.[23] Although these campaigns were rhetorically directed at "Western influences," in practice, they were often interpreted as applying to the "friendly" countries of the Eastern bloc. The campaigns created the potential for any Soviet citizen who interacted with a foreigner to be accused of "toadying" to the West.[24] In several instances

Soviet university officials and students developed suspicions about the foreign students. In 1946, for example, the Soviets recommended the expulsion of four Czechoslovak students from the USSR because "they negatively influence the foreigners studying in institutes of higher education in the USSR. . . . They do not want to understand our Soviet reality and our postwar difficulties, they do not see what is most important in our Soviet society, and they try to emphasize and exaggerate our shortcomings and to make an insurmountable problem [out of them]."[25]

The Soviets' suspicions about the foreign exchange students highlight an important paradox of the USSR's relationship with its new satellite states. Michael David-Fox has argued that during the interwar period, a "superiority-inferiority calculus" shaped Soviet relations with the West. Soviet officials sought to convince Western visitors of the superiority of the Soviet system. At the same time, they tried to use Western models of modernization to develop their own new society.[26] A similar "superiority-inferiority calculus" informed Soviet citizens' relations with the Eastern European exchange students. As citizens of the world's first socialist state and as victors in World War II, Soviets hailed their own society as the most advanced. "You could find the official claims that it was a Russian, Popov, who invented the radio. The light bulb was invented by Yabloshkov and the steam engine by the Cherepanov brothers," remembered the future Soviet dissident Ludmilla Alexeyeva, who was a student at MGU at the time.[27] This chauvinism led the Soviet students to claim their superiority over their Eastern European "friends." "Whatever was Soviet was the best, whatever was foreign was the worst," Selucký recalled about his student days in Leningrad. "The people's democracies belonged to this [latter category] as well."[28] But these claims of superiority often masked insecurity. Selucký found "the young Soviet generation's notions about the external world at that time truly shocking." One day, an organizer in the Komsomol (the Soviet youth organization) named Sasha asked him whether there were stone buildings in Czechoslovakia. Selucký responded:

> You know Saša [Sasha] . . . we had this tsar called Karel IV. And this tsar had a stone bridge built in Prague in the fourteenth century, it's called the Charles Bridge, and it stands there to this day. Saša calculated that this was six hundred years [ago], and surprised me with a further question. "And do you have schools of higher education?" "Yes," I told him, "this Karel IV founded a

university in Prague in 1348." Saša was completely shocked, . . . "But then tell me Rádĕk, why have you come to us to study?"[29]

As this anecdote shows, the Eastern European students could appear to their Soviet classmates as provocateurs, who exposed their ignorance about the world and who suggested that less mature socialist societies might be more developed than the USSR. If life in Eastern Europe was actually superior to life in the Soviet Union, then the fact that these Eastern Europeans had come to study in the USSR was itself cause for suspicion.

The result of this climate of fear and suspicion was that in some cases the foreign students were not offered sufficient practical training in their future professions at Soviet technical institutes. A Soviet Central Committee report noted that foreign students were not provided with access to factories with new technology and, as a result, were insufficiently prepared for their specializations.[30] At an institute for bridge building, for instance, the foreign students were only given the opportunity to build houses. Despite a decree by the Council of Ministers in July 1953, stating that aside from "closed specializations," students from the people's democracies should be allowed the same practical training (*praktika*) as their Soviet peers, improvement was sporadic.[31]

Friends but Not Lovers: The 1947 Soviet Marriage Law

Soon after the foreign students began to arrive in the Soviet Union, sexual relations emerged as an unexpected crucible of socialist internationalism. "At Leningrad University there has already been a case of a Czechoslovak student's marriage to a Soviet student," a Soviet report noted in 1946. "This case has attracted great attention from the foreign students. . . . There are several students who are planning to marry, but they are waiting for our administration's reaction to the case."[32] The reaction was draconian. In February 1947, the Supreme Soviet issued a law forbidding Soviet citizens to marry foreigners, regardless of their nationality.[33]

The marriage law was undoubtedly intended to discourage intimate contacts between Soviet citizens and foreigners in the context of the Soviet government's broader xenophobic campaigns. It was also likely an attempt to thwart Soviet citizens from emigrating in light of the massive population losses the USSR had suffered during the war.[34] At the time the law was issued, for example, in interviews with American authorities, several Soviet defectors from the Soviet occupied zone in Germany cited romantic relationships with German and other foreign women as one of their main reasons for fleeing to the West.[35] Perhaps for this reason, Soviet laws were implemented in June 1947 and January 1948 prohibiting fraternization between Soviet troops and women in occupied Germany.[36]

The Soviet marriage law can also be understood as part of a broader effort by European governments to regulate transgressive transnational and interracial sexual relationships, which developed out of the unique geopolitical circumstances of World War II and the early postwar period. These included relationships between Germans and Eastern European slave laborers in the Third Reich; French women and Nazi occupiers in Vichy France; German women and allied soldiers (particularly African Americans) in occupied Germany; and between Germans and Jewish refugees in postwar displaced persons camps.[37] The U.S. Army initially outlawed marriages between American soldiers and Austrian and German women, although these bans were overturned in January and December 1946, respectively.[38] In all these cases, however, these relationships were controversial because they developed between groups considered racially incompatible, or between current or previous political "enemies." By contrast, the Soviet government censured postwar romances between its citizens and Eastern Europeans even though they were members of the same political system, whose great friendship was constantly lauded in official propaganda.

The marriage law exposed significant hypocrisy in the socialist internationalist project—this was how it was understood by many of the Soviet and Eastern European students. According to Selucký, "The law was very irrational and cruel—in Leningrad alone it affected hundreds of young people. Not one of the official functionaries was able to explain why it had really been adopted—it was in such sharp contradiction with the theoretical declaration of internationalism, that [any] attempt to justify its legitimacy with rational arguments was forfeited in advance."[39] Although the law technically only applied to marriage, Soviet and Eastern European officials and students generally interpreted it to mean that all sexual relationships between Soviet citizens and foreigners were undesirable. A Komsomol report from 1952, for example, characterized affairs between Soviet students in Sverdlovsk and their peers from North Korea and the Eastern bloc as "incorrect relations."[40]

In the winter of 1953, El'vira Filipovich, a Soviet student at the Timiriazev Agricultural Institute in Moscow, fell in love with her Czech classmate, Ivo. Soon after they began dating, she was called before a Komsomol committee at the institute and ordered to break off her "illicit relations with a foreigner." "I gave a solemn Komsomol promise, 'not to love!'" she related in her diary. "They lectured me for a long time, 'they took preventative measures' *(delali profilaktiku)*. From this I understood that I was being threatened with expulsion from the Komsomol, from the institute, from Moscow, maybe even exile 'to the ends of the earth.'"[41]

The marriage law exacerbated Soviet students' suspicions and hostility toward their Eastern European peers. The overwhelming majority of the romances involved Soviet women and Eastern European men (in the Czechoslovak case, 75 percent of the exchange students were men, a statistic that concerned KSČ officials).[42] This caused jealousy and resentment among some of the male Soviet students.[43] At a meeting of foreign students in Leningrad in 1953, a Polish student complained that this jealousy had contributed toward an atmosphere of distrust and recrimination with his Soviet peers. "I go to the cinema, and they [Soviet students] follow, watch to see who I go with, when I return. This creates a bad atmosphere." The student went on to complain that the Komsomol criticized the romances at meetings that the Eastern European students were not even allowed to attend. "The girls are yelled at. They get scared. [They are told:] 'Watch out when you finish university. You are a traitor to the motherland, a cosmopolitan.' We find this unpleasant, because if they say that, then how are they looking at us?"[44]

Transnational romances were thus often traumatic for the star-crossed couples involved. But they proved to be teachable moments for aspiring young Stalinists from the Eastern bloc. Lisa Kirschenbaum has shown how foreign leftists who studied in the USSR in the interwar period gradually learned that the Soviets interpreted what they had assumed were personal foibles (such as drunkenness) as serious political violations. She argues that these foreigners thus came to realize that "learning to be Bolshevik" involved not only studying Marxism-Leninism but also perfecting their personal behavior.[45] On postwar Soviet campuses, the marriage law provided the young Eastern European Communists with practice in the kinds of behaviors that the Soviet Communist Party and the Komsomol had long demanded from their members, including self-discipline, mutual surveillance, and denunciation.[46] All the foreign students who came to the Soviet Union in this period were required to sign a pledge to respect the marriage law. When transnational romances did develop, the students thus viewed them as violations of this pledge and reacted by launching investigations into one another's personal lives and suggesting appropriate punishments to the authorities. For example, in 1952 the Czechoslovak student association in Leningrad lodged a complaint against one of its members, a young man named Veselý, for his relationship with a Soviet woman. The association accused Veselý of violating the pledge he had made before coming to the USSR. It also rebuked him for isolating himself from the other Czechoslovak students. "Comrade Veselý has separated himself from both the Soviet and our collective; he practically does not live in the dorm anymore, he has moved to his girlfriend's family's apartment. The comrades in the dorm practically never see him."[47] The association also recommended that the Czechoslovak government launch an investigation into a former Czechoslovak exchange student in the USSR, O. Nahodil, who had since returned to Czechoslovakia, leaving behind his Soviet ex-girlfriend and their child. Not only had Nahodil had the temerity to write to Czechoslovak General Secretary of the KSČ Klement Gottwald begging for permission to bring his girlfriend to Czechoslovakia, he had then proceeded to marry a Czechoslovak woman. In the meantime, his jilted Soviet lover had become "a general nuisance," petitioning the Czechoslovak student association in Leningrad for financial assistance to support her child.[48]

The marriage law was clearly an affront to the principles of socialist internationalism. But the fact that so many transnational romances nevertheless developed between Soviet and Eastern European students during late Stalinism demonstrates the surprising success of international socialist integration in this period on a personal level. Despite their peers' suspicions, the threat of being expelled from the party or the USSR, and the likelihood that the foreign students would have to return home alone once they finished their studies, young Soviets and Eastern Europeans fell in love and even had children who—it might be argued—literally embodied the spirit of socialist internationalism.[49]

The ban on Soviet marriages to foreigners was overturned in November 1953, eight months after Stalin's death. The following May, Filipovich wed her Czech boyfriend Ivo, a year and a half after the Komsomol committee at the Timiriazev Institute had forced her to pledge "not to love" him.[50] In 1955, the couple attended a gathering of Czech students in Moscow at which Filipovich noted that almost all the Czechs had Soviet girlfriends or wives. The Czechs even joked, "Our guys come to study in Moscow so that they can marry Russian girls."[51] Selucký, who had by then returned to Czechoslovakia, heard from friends back in the USSR that male students from Czechoslovakia, Poland, and Hungary—the wealthiest countries of the Eastern bloc—had become sought after by Soviet women, who wanted to emigrate.[52]

National Student Associations

The Stalinist foreign student program was above all a political project designed to teach young people from across the socialist bloc how to build and run the Communist organizations necessary to transform their native countries along the lines of the Soviet model. For the foreign students, idealism and careerism were frequently intertwined: they understood that their professional advancement at home depended on their ability to replicate Soviet institutions and work methods. "We must above all receive a political education here, even to a greater degree than our professional education," Jelínek, the head of the Czechoslovak student association in Leningrad declared in 1953, "we must learn organizational-political work, we must participate in the work of Komsomol meetings, we must see how the Komsomol organization decides various issues, how they lead their meetings, how they lead their election campaigns."[53] At a meeting of foreign students in Leningrad in 1953, another Czech student emphasized the importance of political education even for technical work: "You probably know that an engineer-builder cannot build a bridge well if he doesn't know party issues; if he cannot motivate the workers he will not be able to build the bridge in [the necessary] span of time."[54]

The Komsomol, the trade unions, and other organizations on Soviet campuses were supposed to be responsible for the foreign students' political education. Soviet party committees were supposed to provide the Eastern European students with bimonthly reports about their work, as well as information about the prevailing political "moods" of the party organizations at the regional and city levels. The committees were also supposed to select politically significant articles from the party's newspapers to share with the foreign students.[55] Yet, unsurprisingly, there was a discrepancy between official Soviet policies about the political training foreign students were supposed to receive and how that training was implemented. The very Soviet functionaries responsible for mentoring foreign students turned out to be afraid of the potential repercussions of being in contact with them. As late as 1954, a Soviet Central Committee report noted, "Several of the directors of the *vuzy* [Soviet institutes of higher education], are afraid of 'trouble' [*kak by chego ne vyshlo*] and avoid any kind of work with the foreign students." The report went on to chastise campus party organizations for failing to pay sufficient attention to foreign students, accusing these organizations of meeting rarely (if at all) with them to discuss "daily life and ideological questions." At the Leningrad Engineering-Building University, for instance, party officials had not met with foreign students in six years. Students wanted to attend Komsomol meetings, but were not invited. They were given few opportunities to participate in "social work" (*obshchestvennaia rabota*) on campus. The report concluded that all this had led some foreign students to the "incorrect impression that [Soviet students] relate to them with distrust." The result was that some students had resorted to "immoral behavior" and had developed "suspicious moods."[56]

A few months after the inauguration of the foreign student program, the Soviet Ministry of Higher Education settled on an awkward solution to the problem of how to engage foreign students in political work while at the same time maintaining a safe distance from them. Inspired by a group of Bulgarian students in Leningrad, the ministry instructed all foreign students in the USSR to form national student associations (*zemliachestva*, from the Russian word for "land") that would serve as the focal points for their political work.[57] These associations were supposed to function as intermediaries between the foreign students and the Soviet authorities: "At least once per month, by decree of the *starshii* [head of the student association], [the students] must gather for comradely meetings and discussions concerning . . . their studies, and to explain irregularities of the study process and cultural-living services. These meetings and discussions will be run with the assistance of representatives from the party and Komsomol organizations."[58]

The national associations became the most important political organizations the foreign students belonged to in the Soviet Union during the late Stalinist period. From the Soviet perspective, the associations fulfilled three important functions. First, they served as organizational and informational links with the embassies of the students' home countries. Second, they offered academic and social assistance that the Soviets were often unable to deliver. Third, they were self-regulatory bodies, where the students learned to monitor and discipline each other's behavior. Yet by ordering the foreign students to form associations comprising their compatriots, the Soviet authorities also paved the way for behaviors that could be construed as isolationist— and even nationalist. A 1950 Soviet report complained that foreign students in Leningrad "spend all their free time . . . in the zemliachestvo."[59] This report also alleged that the Hungarian, Czechoslovak, Albanian, and Polish student associations were being run by these countries' party organizations without any input from Soviet organizations: "[They] are working in isolation from our social organizations [and thus] negatively affect our work. The party organizations accept new members, carry out purges in their ranks, [and] recall students to the motherland without the knowledge or advice of the [Soviet] administrative and social organizations."[60]

School for Scandal

In the fall of 1951, representatives from the Soviet political organizations at MGU began to complain about the conduct of members of the Czechoslovak student association. A campus party leader named Voronkov advised members that because their organization was made up of "young Communists" they should invite representatives from the Soviet social organizations to monitor their meetings. According to a Soviet report, while the Czechoslovak students agreed, in private they complained that Voronkov's request was evidence of his "distrust of the Czechoslovak Communists, of the Czechoslovak zemliachestvo."[61]

Voronkov and other Soviet leaders on campus were also troubled by their communications with the Czechoslovaks concerning the wall newspapers the exchange students created for the anniversaries of the October Revolution and the Red Army's liberation of Czechoslovakia. The Soviets routinely checked these newspapers for "grammatical, stylistic, and political mistakes." The Czechoslovaks always thanked them for their help. "However," Soviet authorities on campus claimed, "this was not all done sincerely." They accused Mlynář, the head of the Czechoslovak zemliachestvo at MGU, of privately complaining that this Soviet "assistance" was in fact "censorship and impermissible interference in their affairs," and they claimed that he "sharply objected to those students and graduate students who pointed out the necessity of the examination."[62]

Finally, the MGU officials accused the Czechoslovak students of making a series of anti-Soviet remarks. These statements reveal the Czechoslovak students' feelings of superiority in relation to the Soviet Union, on the grounds that their country was more industrialized and thus better positioned to achieve socialism. They reveal that Czechoslovak elites continued to chafe against Soviet hegemony in the friendship project after the 1948 coup. "We will build socialism in Czechoslovakia earlier than in the USSR," one student declared. This student also touted Czechoslovakia's economic advantage over the USSR, claiming it was able to manufacture more goods per person than the Soviet Union. Another student asserted, "The USSR has no role in building socialism in a mature industrialized country [i.e., Czechoslovakia], which exports machines to the other people's democracies and to the USSR."[63] The students also complained that Czechoslovakia was not getting a fair deal in its "friendship" with the Soviet Union. A student named Vladimír Matula, for instance, "even though he had studied in the USSR for four years, lapsed into nationalist tendencies to such an extent that he said, 'In the sphere of Czechoslovak-Soviet friendship, Czechoslovak boxers in Moscow get it straight in the jaw' [*v rámci čs.-sov. přátelství dostanou čs. boxeři v Moskvě přes hubu*]." Matula also declared that "'Czechoslovakia has learned from the Soviet Union to send old people to the festival of youth,'" a possible reference to the predominance of middle-aged functionaries in the Komsomol's leadership, as well as a gibe at the general lack of dynamism in Soviet society.[64] The Czechoslovak students had been brought to the USSR to learn from the Soviet experience; these statements indicate that they had begun to question whether the Soviet example was in fact worth following.

The Czechoslovak students in Moscow launched an investigation, which revealed that these offensive behaviors had spread to their compatriots in other parts of the Soviet Union.[65] In Leningrad, two students had recently been expelled from the USSR, one for making "slanderous utterances about Soviet culture" and the other for "spreading slander about the Soviet Union" while back home in Czechoslovakia. As the scandal among the Czechoslovak students in Moscow intensified, the Leningrad zemliachestvo began to scrutinize the behavior of its current members, including Selucký, whom it accused of "abusing the good name of the Czech students in the Soviet Union, insulting the [Czechoslovak Communist] Party and the USSR . . . and [of being] a source of corruption."[66] Selucký's anti-Soviet statements included accusing the USSR of robbing Czechoslovakia of uranium and complaining that the exchange rate between the ruble and the Czechoslovak crown was disadvantageous for his country. In Sverdlovsk, Czechoslovak students denounced the head of their student organization, Ivo Petrman, for his bourgeois class origins and "dictatorial" leadership style.[67] They accused him of "persistently spreading among his students and graduate students a notion about the darkness and cultural backwardness of the peoples of the Soviet Union."[68]

A Tale of Two Stalinisms

The scandal in the Czechoslovak student community in the Soviet Union was shaped by political events in Moscow and Prague, thus highlighting the transnational structure of the Stalinist empire. In the Soviet Union, the Zhdanovshchina and the other state-sponsored xenophobic campaigns influenced the scandal. During the course of their studies in the USSR, the Eastern European students discovered that their Soviet peers could interpret what they had dismissed as offhand remarks and innocent actions as sinister political machinations. "If a student is mistaken in his thoughts, people scream at him, accuse him of Trotskyism," a Czechoslovak student complained. "They do not try to persuade him from scientific positions, but accuse him, as if he had intentionally distorted the party's policies."[69]

In Czechoslovakia, the arrest of Rudolf Slánský, the KSČ's general secretary, and thirteen other high-ranking party officials in 1951–1952 also had a profound impact on the Czechoslovak students in the USSR and on the Czechoslovak officials responsible for monitoring them. The Slánský case followed a wave of purges of high-level Communist Party officials across the Eastern bloc, which began after the Stalin-Tito split in 1948. These purges are often understood as having been directed by the Soviet government, in an attempt to ensure the Eastern bloc Communist Parties' loyalty to Stalin and the USSR. These purges were also connected with the anti-cosmopolitan campaigns in the USSR. A disproportionate number of the accused were Jews, including Slánský. In the fall of 1952, after a carefully rehearsed show trial—the largest in the Eastern bloc—Slánský and eleven of his codefendants were executed as traitors to the socialist cause.[70]

Referring to the Slánský case, Mlynář wrote in his memoirs, "The wave of suspicion and the witch hunt for 'class enemies and agents of imperialism' that was beginning to rage at home spread to those of us [students] in Moscow as well."[71] The Slánský case was of particular relevance to the Czechoslovak students in the USSR because two of the defendants, Otto Šling and Bedřich Geminder, had played prominent roles in the foreign student program. Šling had been the KSČ's secretary in Brno, the Moravian capital, where he had been responsible for selecting students from the surrounding region to study in the USSR, including Selucký.[72] Geminder had been the head of the KSČ's International Department, and had been responsible for organizing many aspects of the students' lives in the Soviet Union, including the zemliachestvo's activities.[73] The Slánský case also affected the Czechoslovak students in the USSR because the defendants were accused of being anti-Soviet, among a host of other crimes. On April 25, 1951, an article appeared in *Rudé právo* (Red Right), the KSČ's daily, titled "The Great Significance of the Union of Czechoslovak-Soviet Friendship." Referring to the recent arrest of Šling and two other KSČ officials, the article declared that they had been "united by a deadly hatred for the USSR. They hated the Soviet Union because it is the main force for peace, because it impedes . . . the American imperialists' plans for worldwide hegemony, because it is the lighthouse and hope of all the exploited and oppressed [people] in the entire world." The article went on to warn Czechoslovak readers that they should be "vigilant to the smallest expressions of anti-Soviet moods, to distrust, wavering, insincere relations toward the USSR, to anything that disrupts our work in the field of Czechoslovak-Soviet friendship."[74] Speaking of the Slánský case in 1952, KSČ secretary František Pexa declared, "[Our] relationship to the Soviet Union is the cornerstone of proletariat internationalism." He added that anyone who was against the USSR was also a "deadly enemy" of Czechoslovakia.[75] From this perspective, the Soviets' accusations against the Czechoslovak students at MGU, and the latter's refusal to correct them, potentially constituted treason at home and criminal behavior in the Soviet Union.

The Zemliachestvo

In the spring of 1952, members of the Czechoslovak zemliachestvo at MGU stopped ignoring Soviet criticism and instead began applying it to one another.

They singled out the leaders of the association, especially Mlynář, its head, for stringent criticism. On the advice of university officials, the students held meetings on March 19 and 21, dedicated to explaining their "expressions of bourgeois nationalism and undignified pronouncements in address to the Soviet Union." These meetings ran late into the night; the students employed Stalinist rituals of criticism and self-criticism to expiate their anti-Soviet thoughts and behaviors.[76] They also elected three students to serve as an "investigative committee." This committee, along with a newly elected triumvirate interim leadership of the zemliachestvo, wrote a letter to Gottwald detailing the Soviets' accusations: "Rejecting the help of representatives of the Soviet social organizations, slander of the Soviet Party and Komsomol activists and perversion of their statements . . . aiding in the appearance of bourgeois-nationalist views and expressions, challenging the leading roles of the VKP/b [All-Union Communist Party] and the Komsomol in the zemliachestvo's work, and incorrect relations with the USSR."[77]

These accusations were not unusual in the context of the broader foreign student community in the USSR at the time.[78] Patryk Babiracki has described how the Soviet authorities accused Polish students in the USSR of making similar anti-Soviet comments.[79] What distinguishes the Czechoslovak case is how the students responded to these accusations, and what their responses reveal about their relationship to Soviet power and to Stalinism—as practiced in the USSR and in Czechoslovakia. Babiracki argues that the Polish students' anti-Soviet remarks indicate that they experienced an ideological transformation in the USSR, from pro- to anti-Soviet, from believers to "heretics."[80] In contrast, while the Czechoslovak students initially brushed off the Soviets' complaints about their behavior, they ultimately used these complaints to assimilate Stalinist political practices—including criticism, self-criticism, and denunciation.

Scholars have argued that criticism and self-criticism were integral to the construction of individual and collective forms of Soviet identity during Stalinism. J. Arch Getty contends that in the 1930s, Soviet Communist Party members employed self-criticism at the Central Committee as a tool of self-construction.[81] Similarly, Juliane Fürst's work on youth in the postwar Stalinist period argues that the Komsomol used criticism as a tool of Soviet state building. For instance, it was acceptable for members of the Komsomol to accuse their superiors of shortcomings, and this criticism was seen as a means of defending the organization's ideals and of legitimizing the state's power.[82]

In the late 1940s and early 1950s, these practices of criticism and self-criticism crossed the borders of the new European socialist world, becoming important tools that the KSČ and other Czechoslovak government institutions employed to "build" Communism along the lines of the "Soviet model." Marci Shore, for example, has shown that criticism and self-criticism became extremely important for members of the Czechoslovak Writers' Union during this period, resulting in "a certain vocabulary, one that was dominated by such terms as 'mistakes' (*chyby*), 'errors' (*omyly*), 'insufficencies' (*nedostatky*), and 'overcoming' (*překonání*)."[83] At the same time, the Czechoslovak press set out to explain the importance of criticism and self-criticism for rank-and-file party members. In the winter of 1951, *Rudé právo* reprinted an article from the Cominform's journal, *For a Lasting Peace, For a People's Democracy!* informing Czechoslovak readers, "Comrade Stalin teaches that one of the most characteristic features of a revolutionary, Marxist party is its critical relationship to its own shortcomings and mistakes, the education of cadres in the spirit of criticism and self-criticism—open and fundamental criticism, which does not tolerate compromise."[84]

For the Czechoslovak students at MGU, employing criticism and self-criticism became a means to recast their ideological errors as necessary steps on the path to political enlightenment. They thus had to reinterpret what they had initially framed as harmless mistakes—such as refusing the "assistance" of their Soviet peers—as potential political crimes. "I [initially] assumed that the Soviet comrades did not have the 'right' to interfere with our internal affairs (some of the issues they wanted to interfere with were political, and some were related to cadres)," Mlynář confessed at the students' first meeting at MGU on March 19, 1952, "I use the word 'interfere' intentionally, because at that time I baselessly [*bezdůvodně*] looked upon the Soviet comrades as having the tendency to interfere, not to advise or help. . . . At that time I did not understand; however, today I see it clearly, that such . . . overconfidence [*sebevědomí*] very dangerously stinks of nationalism, or more precisely, is an insulting expression of nationalism."[85] Mlynář went on to explain that when his peers in the zemliachestvo had initially approached him with concerns about how he was treating the Soviet representatives, he had not understood that this constituted a political issue. He assumed he could simply sit down with the Soviets and work things out. He had failed to understand that these problems needed to be resolved "in the Communist way, that is, by the path of criticism and self-criticism."[86] Another student,

Brezinová, alleged she had felt caught between the Soviets and her fellow Czechoslovak comrades, who claimed that the MGU party leader Voronkov and the Komsomol representative Sokhin had overstepped their authority by inspecting the students' contributions to the wall newspapers as well as their speeches. At the time, Brezinová admitted that she had agreed with her compatriots that the Soviets should not be present at the zemliachestvo meetings. But she now claimed to realize that this kind of thinking was the result of "political immaturity" and that she should have spoken to Mlynář and tried to convince him to change his behavior. Her mistake was not realizing that "silence signifies agreement."[87]

Friend or Model?

In the course of their criticism sessions, the Czechoslovak students raised concerns about their relationships with their Soviet peers and their integration into Soviet society. The scandal in the zemliachestvo had begun when the Soviets had censured the Czechoslovak students for rebuffing their political "assistance." At one level, the solution to this problem was obvious: the students should seek closer contact with their Soviet peers and the leaders of the political organizations at MGU. Olma, a leader of the student association, confessed, "I committed very serious political mistakes, which came about on the basis of my personal mistakes. . . . I think that it would do me good to be able to be more closely connected with the Soviet comrades, to live in the Soviet collective, to be connected with more Soviet functionaries, in order to eliminate the habits that I had in my work, to get rid of the mistakes that I spoke about."[88] Another student declared with characteristic verve, "It is necessary to liquidate our isolation from the Soviet collective." He argued that existing efforts to introduce the foreign students to Soviet life were insufficient. They should get to know the USSR "not only by trips down the Moscow-Volga canal but also by daily work in the Soviet collective."[89] He called for the zemliachestvo to make a resolution requiring its members to attend Soviet party and Komsomol meetings, and he chastised his compatriots for their superficial approach to Soviet life. "We have not put emphasis on getting to know the Soviet Union, but have only succeeded on the path of onetime actions, cultural ventures, organizing trips, outings to the theater, and so on."[90]

Yet as this chapter has shown, the Soviets were in fact responsible for preventing the foreign students from truly "getting to know" the country. How could these students get to know the USSR when Soviet officials prevented them from learning about local industry or treated their romantic relationships with Soviet peers as criminal behavior? "In every plan we have placed getting to know the Soviet Union in one of the most important places," Krempa, one of the Czechoslovak students, declared at the second criticism session the zemliachestvo held at MGU on the night of March 21. "[But] how *should* we get to know the Soviet Union?" he asked. "What are the paths that lead to that?" Krempa offered familiar solutions: "direct daily contact [with the Soviets], participation in the work of the faculty."[91] But his question could well have been existential. The foreign students' sojourn to the Soviet Union exposed a key paradox in the Soviet-Eastern European friendship project: it was impossible for the Soviet Union to be both "friend" and "model" to the citizens of its satellite states. These roles were inherently incompatible: the former necessitated closeness, and the latter, distance. Mlynář highlighted this paradox in one of his self-criticism statements describing how he felt when he first came to study in the Soviet Union: "I had a clear relationship of love for the Soviet Union; when I got on a trolleybus I took pleasure in it being better than ours. But gradually I began to look at some things as ordinary [*jako na věci všední*]; I sometimes ceased to see a Soviet person [instead I thought] there's Serjoža, there's Miša. This was one of the reasons that I could say that Voronkov was wrong. . . . I forgot that Comrade Voronkov was a representative of the VKP/b."[92] In other words, Mlynář's mistake had been to see his Soviet acquaintances (in particular Voronkov, the campus party leader) as potential friends, rather than as paragons of socialist new men.

Babiracki argues that the Polish exchange students in the USSR made anti-Soviet remarks as a form of resistance. "By articulating their grievances, resentments and—increasingly—demands . . . [they] challenged the empire from the center."[93] Likewise, the Czechoslovak students' anti-Soviet remarks and behaviors that triggered the scandal at MGU in 1952 might appear as acts of resistance to Soviet hegemony. But the students instead used the criticism sessions that ensued to *assimilate* their position of subjugation vis-à-vis the Soviets. The scandal in the zemliachestvo was thus not an example of the breakdown of the Soviet empire in Eastern Europe, but of its construction. It reveals how the actions of ordinary people—in this case, students—were integral to the formation of the Eastern bloc. The scandal was thus a microcosm of the broader shift in Soviet relations with Eastern Europe that occurred in the late 1940s and early 1950s, when the USSR employed purges in Sofia, Budapest, and Prague to signal that it would not tolerate "national paths to Communism," and the Eastern European Communist Parties responded by actively transforming their societies in accordance with the Soviet model.

A Sickness from Home

For the Czechoslovak exchange students, the scandal in Moscow was also more than a way to accommodate Soviet hegemony. It was a means of learning Stalinist tactics of discipline and survival—tactics that became especially important as the Slánský affair rocked the political establishment back home. Initially the students blamed their ideological errors on "political immaturity" or personality flaws. (Mlynář, for example, referred to himself as "stubborn" several times during his self-criticism session.) But before long, the students shifted blame for their actions from the personal to the political. Toward the end of Mlynář's long statement of self-criticism on March 19, he suggested that Geminder's role in overseeing the affairs of the Czechoslovak exchange students might help to explain the outbreak of anti-Soviet behavior in the zemliachestvo.[94] After all, Geminder had been arrested in 1951 and declared an enemy of the people. Another student, Kolář, took this line of reasoning a step further, "It is a saboteur's work that is not helping us to go home to be Soviet specialists, Soviet people."[95] The Slánský affair is usually portrayed as one of the most egregious examples of Soviet imperialism in postwar Eastern Europe: Stalin's attempt to cow the Czechoslovak government into abject loyalty by exporting the Soviet model of political terror to Prague. The scandal in the community of Czechoslovak students in Moscow highlights the didactic effect of the Slánský affair on Czechoslovak citizens. The students drew on the events unfolding in Prague to explain their ideological errors in Moscow. The Slánský affair allowed them to shift the blame for the scandal from their own personal failings and lack of political expertise to "a sickness that may well have its root in what has been going on at home."[96] The Slánský case thus became an opportunity for these students to prove themselves as loyal Communists by engaging in mutual surveillance and denunciation.

In order to find and unmask the enemies in their midst, the students decided to investigate the actions and backgrounds of the officials at the Czechoslovak embassy responsible for overseeing their exchange program and all the Czechoslovak students studying in the USSR. The students wrote to Gottwald:

> If we take into account all of the facts, we cannot disregard the possibility that a deliberately organized activity is going on / this suspicion was expressed at the meeting by a series of comrades / the goal of which is to hinder and thwart the education of highly qualified and politically conscious cadres in the USSR and to cause grave harm to our party and country. . . .
>
> We believe further, that it is necessary to improve the social composition of the Czech scholarship recipients sent to study in the USSR. A great number of the scholarship recipients have petit bourgeois origins; among them are even comrades from kulak families, wholesalers, policemen from the First Republic, from the so-called Slovak state, and so on.[97]

Denunciations

"Before long," Mlynář recalled of the scandal in his memoirs, "letters from strict Stalinists [i.e., among the Czechoslovak students in Moscow] began arriving at party headquarters in Prague warning that I too was very likely one of the 'wreckers in the party.'"[98] One of the members of the zemliachestvo privately approached Soviet Komsomol officials with a series of accusations about Mlynář: he had been a longtime friend of an official at the Czechoslovak embassy in Moscow who had been dismissed from his post in connection with the Slánský affair; Mlynář and the other leaders of the zemliachestvo had unlawfully spent the members' dues on travel around the Soviet Union; Mlynář's father had been a gendarme during the First Republic; Mlynář's mother had been fired from a position in the National Committee in Czechoslovakia; and Mlynář himself had worked for the Czechoslovak secret police after 1945, but had been dismissed from his position. The student alleged that after Mlynář was fired from the secret police, he had betrayed state secrets. A Soviet report about these accusations concluded by suggesting that Mlynář had been involved in a conspiracy. "Rumors have reached us by chance that Mlynář, Zlingová, and some of the other zemliachestvo leaders met several times somewhere near Moscow."[99] At the end of the second criticism session on March 21, the students in the Czechoslovak zemliachestvo at MGU held a vote unanimously dismissing Mlynář as the head of their organization.[100]

Throughout the USSR, the Czechoslovak students became increasingly active in investigating each other's lives, down to the pettiest details. In Leningrad, students denounced each other for frivolously spending money on ice cream or for going on a date. ("There is a war in Korea and you were thinking about sex?" one of the students admonished another.)[101] Selucký, then in the third year of his studies in Leningrad, found himself under attack, both for his connection to Šling and for making a series of anti-Soviet remarks. During his time in the USSR, Selucký had become disillusioned with Stalinism (though he remained, in his own words "a Leninist"), largely as a result of conversations with Soviet friends, who had told him about the horrors of collectivization and the purges.[102] By his own account, he was incapable of "withholding ironic remarks, which were the result of my new knowledge." He told his fellow students that he doubted whether the USSR would ever achieve Communism, and he rejected the official claim that the proletariat in capitalist countries was impoverished. Most damningly, he questioned the very premise of the Stalinist friendship project between the Soviet Union and the other socialist countries, "I expressed doubt about the idea that the annexing of various European and Asian countries to Russia was a progressive historical action, and I did not leave anyone in doubt that I interpreted proletarian internationalism as the complete equality of the various Communist countries and peoples, but not at all, however, as the subordination of their national interests to the Soviet Union's."[103] An investigative report by his fellow students concluded, "Comrade Selucký has not learned during his three-year stay in the USSR how to free himself from individualism, capriciousness, undervaluing of others, lack of discipline."[104] When Selucký was ordered to produce a statement of self-criticism, he made the mistake, in his retrospective estimation, of approaching it "logically." For instance, in response to the students' accusation that he had been sent to the Soviet Union by Šling, who had been unmasked as an enemy of the people, he argued that "everyone who was from the Brno region must have been sent to the USSR by Šling, who at that time held the post of leading regional secretary, just as everyone who was approved by the Prague Central Secretariat must have first been nominated by Bedřich Geminder; according to this logic everyone should have been returned to Czechoslovakia as traitors." This "logic" failed to convince either his fellow students in Leningrad or the Czechoslovak authorities of his innocence. "Naturally that and similar answers were rejected as entirely unacceptable, as an expression of my arrogance toward the party," he recalled. Selucký's fellow students recommended his expulsion from the KSČ and from the USSR. At the end of the spring 1952 semester, he was forced to return to Czechoslovakia.[105]

Denouement

The scandal in the zemliachestvo at MGU reached its apex on May 4, 1952, when the Czechoslovak students held yet another meeting to discuss their ideological errors. This meeting was attended by all the members of the umbrella Czechoslovak student union in Moscow—a total of 138 exchange students from universities and institutes across the city. A representative from the Soviet Ministry of Higher Education was also present, along with Voronkov, the Soviet Communist Party leader at MGU, and three officials from the Czechoslovak embassy in Moscow. The meeting began at 9:30 A.M. and adjourned at 1 A.M. the following day.[106] According to the memo announcing the meeting that students at MGU sent the embassy, the meeting was supposed to begin with a report about the criticism sessions they had held in March. Afterward all the students assembled were to be given the opportunity to criticize the zemliachestvo's work and to make suggestions for improving it.[107]

The chargé d'affaires at the Czechoslovak embassy in Moscow, who attended the meeting, concluded that the students "understood correctly" that their main mistake had been to isolate themselves from their Soviet comrades and the Soviet party and Komsomol organizations. He agreed with them that it would be a good idea to launch an investigation into all the Czechoslovaks studying in the Soviet Union. But he also warned the Czechoslovak Ministry of Foreign Affairs that the students' criticism and self-criticism sessions were threatening to spiral out of control: "The procedure of self-criticism from several of the accused students produces the impression that they assume they are risking everything, that this concerns their further existence [*že jde o jejich další existenci*]. This kind of technique could cause panic, nervousness, from which it would not be possible to distinguish a real intention from stupidity and ignorance."[108]

The embassy official's observation highlights the striking fact that the Czechoslovak students' fervor regarding the scandal in their ranks had surpassed that of both the Soviet officials who initiated it, and the Czechoslovak officials who monitored its course. In both countries, these officials forwarded details about the scandal to the highest ranks of their respective governments, but they appear to have concluded that the whole affair had been properly resolved after the criticism and self-criticism rituals had been completed. On the Soviet side, Sokhin, the MGU Komsomol representative, reassured the students, "Your organization is a strong, healthy organization, which knows how to resolve issues correctly in principle and in a political sense . . . to reveal mistakes and the reasons for them."[109] On the Czechoslovak side, the reaction from party officials was more surprising. At a time when these officials were engaged in a deadly hunt for enemies in their ranks, they took special care not to let the students' healthy Communist criticism lead to a full-blown purge—perhaps because they feared being swept up.[110] In December 1952—a month after Slánský and ten of his codefendants (including Šling and Geminder) were sentenced to death for treason—Czechoslovak prime minister Antonín Zápotocký and deputy prime minister Viliam Široký came to Moscow to speak with the students at MGU. They announced that it was time for the students to stop making accusations against one another. Mlynář recalled that Zápotocký spoke on behalf of Gottwald and admonished the students that "[they] were not to go around suspecting one another but rather to trust each other and study." In response to the students' anti-Soviet remarks that had precipitated the scandal, he said, "'Living here you can see for yourselves that our people could not nor would not want to live in the conditions the Soviet people live in. So don't make a problem of it when discussing it among yourselves, but try to understand it and arrive at a reasonable solution.'"[111]

Even Selucký, who appears to have been the only student expelled from the USSR in connection with the scandal, concluded in retrospect, "Fate was relatively lenient toward me." He was never arrested, and after a few years of doing odd jobs and a stint in the army, was allowed to resume his studies in Prague. He concluded that in the spring of 1952, the party apparatus in Czechoslovakia was too busy with the Slánský case "to deal with a student from Leningrad."[112]

Mastering the Art of Soviet Scholarship

Given the host of obstacles the young Czechoslovaks faced in the USSR—ranging from the material, to the intellectual, to the social—the foreign student program would appear to have failed in its mission to transfer the Soviet model to the new satellite states. The Czechoslovak students often did not learn what they had expected to learn in the Soviet Union, such as how to build Soviet-style factories or how to run Komsomol meetings. Their assimilation into Soviet social life was severely hampered by the ban on marriages with foreigners as well as by the general climate of xenophobia in the country. But paradoxically, it was these very points of exclusion that provided the students with the unexpected opportunity to construct themselves as loyal subjects of Stalin's new empire. The marriage ban hampered their intimate relationships with Soviet citizens, but offered them practice in mutual surveillance. The zemliachestvo was perhaps a poor substitute for the Komsomol or the Soviet Communist Party, but it provided the students with a ready-made framework to investigate and critique each other's behavior. Most dramatically, the events of the spring of 1952 taught the young Czechoslovaks not only how to "speak Bolshevik,"[113] but how to *act* Bolshevik—by denouncing and investigating each other, by searching for enemies in their ranks, by employing criticism and self-criticism to correct their ideological errors. The Soviets suggested that learning these lessons was in fact the real point of their education in the USSR. "You are fulfilling your duty put before you by the party and the government and by Comrade Gottwald to master [*ovladet'*] Soviet scholarship, to master the experience of building socialism in the USSR with honor," Sokhin, the Komsomol representative at MGU, congratulated the students.[114] Stephen Kotkin has used the term "speaking Bolshevik" to describe how the Soviet citizens who built the city of Magnitogorsk in the 1930s acquired "political literacy" alongside industrial skills. He argues that this political literacy was essential to the formation of a uniquely Soviet proletariat.[115] Through their experiences in the Soviet Union in the late 1940s and early 1950s, the Czechoslovak students acquired their own political literacy skills that allowed them to assimilate into the new Communist system back home and to survive Stalinism—in both the USSR and Czechoslovakia—at its most turbulent moment.

The fact that the students learned how to act Bolshevik does not mean that their Soviet sojourn succeeded in transforming their subjectivity, in turning them into "Soviet people"—the goal some had expressed when they first came to the USSR. In Selucký's summation, the political practices the Czechoslovak students were exposed to in the USSR divided them into two groups, "future functionaries and future screwups."[116] According to this categorization, Selucký, Mlýnář, and Reiman went on to become "screwups" in the sense that they became political reformers in the mid-1960s, bent on developing a new type of socialism that rejected the Manichean politics they had experienced in the USSR. After the Soviet invasion of Czechoslovakia in 1968, all three became political exiles in the West.

In contrast, other Czechoslovak students who studied in the USSR in the late Stalinist period, such as Vladimír Blažek and Dušan Spáčil, went on to become high-ranking functionaries in the Czechoslovak government during the era of "normalization" that followed the crushing of the Prague Spring—Blažek as minister of transport and Spáčil as ambassador to the United States. In a memoir that he wrote after the collapse of Communism, Spáčil, who served as the head of the Czechoslovak zemliachestvo in Kiev in the spring of 1952, claimed that his organization saw none of the "spying and snitching to the party and security organizations in Czechoslovakia" that Mlynář detailed in his memoirs. "In my time we were all committed Communists and friends of the Soviet Union," he declared. Yet he also boasted that through his work in the zemliachestvo he had learned critical lessons about proper Communist behavior. If he and his peers discovered "a student whose behavior, whether from a moral standpoint or the standpoint of [his] political views did not correspond to what was considered worthy for a Czechoslovak student who was sent to the [Soviet] Union, we discussed his 'case' within the framework of the zemliachestvo, sometimes, in absolutely exceptional cases, and upon recommendation from the center, he was removed [from the USSR]."[117]

The Czechoslovak students' experiences in the USSR during the late Stalinist period thus played an important role in shaping their future relationships to Soviet politics and the international Communist system. But surprisingly, even for those students who were directly involved in the scandal at MGU, these experiences did not disrupt their contributions to the broader friendship project between Czechoslovakia and the USSR. Reiman became a well-known historian of the Soviet Union, the author of books on the Russian Revolution and Stalinism.[118] In the mid-1960s, Selucký returned to the USSR to write a series of articles on the Soviet economy commissioned by

Svět sovětů (World of the Soviets), the official journal of the Union of Czechoslovak-Soviet Friendship. After his graduation from MGU, Mlynář remained in close contact with his Soviet friend Gorbachev—in 1993, the two men published a book of conversations comparing the Prague Spring and perestroika.[119] Matula, one of the Czechoslovak students at MGU whom the Soviets had singled out in 1952 for his anti-Soviet remarks and "nationalist tendencies" became a leading scholar of Slovak and Slavic history, who returned to the USSR on academic fellowships in 1966–1968 and in 1972–1974. When he died in 2011, he was eulogized by the Russian Academy of Sciences as "a true friend of Russia" whose "friendly relations with Russian scholars were not interrupted even after the 'Velvet Revolution' and the collapse of the USSR."[120]

Chapter 3

The Legacy of the Liberation

There is no greater reward for a soldier who served at the front than the
love of the people he spilled his blood for and risked his life liberating. . . .
It is this love that helped me and my parents survive the heavy grief
that befell us during the May days of 1945.

—Sergei Osipov, Red Army veteran and brother of a Red Army
soldier killed during the Soviet liberation of Czechoslovakia

"I can briefly express my relationship to your country in this way: I am in
love with your people, with your wonderful country," M. E. Votintsev, a Red
Army veteran from the Perm region, wrote in a letter to the Czechoslovak
people, reminiscing about his role in the liberation of their country. "Why?
Your people did so much for me. I can't describe it all. It's enough to say that
three times I almost died in Czechoslovakia, and three times your wonderful people resurrected [voskreshali] me with their care, love, warmth.[1]

In 1965, the same year that Votintsev wrote this paean, Marshall Ivan
Konev, the former commander of the First Ukrainian Front, which had led
the liberation of Prague, published a book about the Red Army's war effort in
Czechoslovakia. In the book, Konev drew a straight line from the Soviet
liberation of Czechoslovakia to the contemporary friendship project. "Soviet-
Czechoslovak friendship, strengthened and tempered in the battles with
fascism, became the unshakable basis for the cooperation between our peoples
in the postwar period."[2] The book's cover further emphasized the liberation's enduring imprint on Czechoslovakia with an inset of the Soviet tank

monument in Prague against the backdrop of the medieval towers on the city's Old Town Square.

Votintsev's letter and Konev's book reveal how the legacy of the Soviet Army's liberation of Czechoslovakia was central to shaping the development of the postwar friendship project. The construction of this legacy was transnational: the result of exchanges of media, tourists, and veterans across the Soviet-Czechoslovak border. The liberation's legacy was also—like the broader friendship project it supported—shaped by forces from above and below: by government officials, journalists, and filmmakers as well as by Red Army veterans and the Czechoslovak civilians they encountered in 1944 and 1945. Examining the legacy of the liberation reveals the stakes that ordinary citizens of the superpower and its satellite had in their countries' alliance and shows how they drew on their experiences during the war to shape the friendship project.

The liberation was memorialized by fixed symbols: statues of Soviet soldiers, gravestones adorned with red stars, monuments of tanks and other heavy weaponry. But its legacy was also fluid, changing in tandem with the broader political background of the Soviet-Czechoslovak alliance. This chapter will examine how the legacy of the liberation, and the mythology it created, evolved from the end of World War II until the late 1960s. In the immediate postwar years, Czechoslovaks constructed monuments and memorials to the Red Army as genuine expressions of friendship with the USSR, and as a way to blot out their experiences of the German occupation. During the Stalinist period in Czechoslovakia, the Soviet government employed the liberation, including the specter of the approximately 140,000 Soviet soldiers who perished, as an imperialist trope justifying its power over the new satellite state. Czechoslovak Communists also capitalized on the legacy of the liberation, using it to rationalize their grandiose cult of the Soviet Union. Meanwhile, in the Soviet Union, the mythology that developed around the legacy of the liberation in Czechoslovakia and the other countries of Eastern Europe had a very different function: it served as a laboratory of remembrance of the war, at a time when Joseph Stalin sharply curtailed commemorations of the conflict in the USSR.

In the decade and a half between Stalin's death in 1953, and the Prague Spring in 1968, the legacy of the liberation took on a new function. Votintsev's letter demonstrates how, during these years, veterans' personal memories of the liberation highlighted Czechoslovaks' heroism and bravery, and thus implicitly challenged the Soviet domination of its satellite state. This more personal approach to the legacy of the liberation was connected with the development of more nuanced commemorations of World War II in the Soviet Union, during the period of reforms that began in the mid-1950s, known as the Thaw. Meanwhile, in Czechoslovakia, testimonies by civilians who had sheltered and cared for Red Army soldiers in 1944–1945 similarly helped reverse the Stalinist hierarchy of liberator over liberated. The new legacy of the liberation that took shape in the 1950s and 1960s created a new mythology of the Soviet Army's actions in the country that reinvigorated the friendship project while glossing over its darker side.

Empire of Liberation

In the first years after the war, Soviet propaganda portrayed Eastern Europeans as indebted to the USSR for the massive casualties sustained by the Red Army, and for providing the foundation for the construction of Communism in their countries. War memorials and Victory Day commemorations in Eastern Europe provided the iconography for this new "empire of liberation."[3]

In 1945, memorials honoring the Red Army were constructed in the capital cities throughout Central and Eastern Europe, including Bucharest, Budapest, Vienna, and Warsaw. Soviet authorities often initiated these memorials while local architects and builders presided over their design and construction, in order to lend credence to the mythology of indigenous gratitude toward the USSR.[4] The 1949 construction of the most famous Red Army memorial in the region, at Treptow Park in Berlin, was an exception to this pattern. The Soviet Military Administration in Berlin was both mastermind and executor of the vast memorial complex. Its centerpiece—a towering statue of a Red Army soldier cradling a young German girl in his arms, while crushing a swastika with his foot—emphasized the USSR's humanitarian mission, ideological resolve, and military power. A series of sarcophagi were erected beneath the statue, decorated with scenes from the war, including a tableau of Eastern Europeans thanking their Soviet liberators.[5]

In Czechoslovakia in the summer and fall of 1945, while Red Army troops remained in the country, local groups began constructing monuments commemorating the Soviet liberation. One of the first memorials to the Red Army in the country was the Monument to the Soviet Tank Crews in Prague, discussed in the introduction of this book. Although many of the initial monuments to the war in Czechoslovakia were ostensibly erected as expressions of gratitude toward the USSR, they also celebrated the Czechoslovak national triumph over the country's German minority. In Czechoslovakia, Nancy Wingfield argues, "The Communists interpreted the Second World War as a 'Great Patriotic War,' a Slavic war against the age-old German enemy."[6] In many Czechoslovak villages, locals used commemorations of the Soviet liberation to erase the German legacy by disinterring occupation soldiers and replacing them with the bodies of recently fallen Red Army fighters.[7]

In November 1945, a special section of the seventeenth-century Olšanské cemetery in Prague was dedicated to the Red Army to house the graves of several hundred Soviet soldiers. The centerpiece of the section was a statue by the Czech sculptor Jaroslav Brůha of two Red Army soldiers standing guard over their fallen comrades. The monument's inscription portrayed the Soviet troops as pan-Slavic liberators:

ETERNAL GLORY

TO THE SOLDIERS OF THE RED ARMY

WHO FELL IN THE BATTLE FOR THE INDEPENDENCE

OF THE SOVIET POWER

AND OF THE LIBERATION OF THE SLAVIC PEOPLES FROM FASCISM.[8]

A year later, at a celebration in Prague to honor the first anniversary of the liberation, Dr. J. Fiala, rector of Saint Jakub's church, "Pointed to the eternal struggle of our people with Germandom and stressed the need for all the Slavic peoples to cooperate," with the USSR, regardless of their religious or political affiliation.[9]

By the fall of 1946, the bodies of Red Army soldiers had been laid to rest in twenty-one central cemeteries in Czechoslovakia.[10] Volunteers from pro-Soviet organizations, such as the Communist Party of Czechoslovakia's (KSČ's) Union of Friends of the USSR, maintained these burial sites and also tried to establish connections with the soldiers' families in the USSR by sending them photographs of their loved ones' graves.[11] In the initial postwar period, celebrations and commemorations of the Soviet liberation in Czechoslovakia thus served several functions: they were demonstrations of nationalism and pan-Slavism, and at a time when the vast majority of Czechoslovaks supported a close alliance with the USSR, they were also often genuine expressions of gratitude toward the Red Army and friendship with the Soviet Union.

In the late 1940s, as the Cold War intensified, the Soviet government made the legacy of World War II a cornerstone of its foreign policy. Soviet officials employed the memory of the war to unify the new Eastern bloc, and to showcase its alleged moral superiority over the capitalist West. In 1947, in a famous speech at the first conference of the Cominform, Andrei Zhdanov proclaimed the division of the world into "two camps": Western/capitalist and Soviet/socialist. In Zhdanov's estimation, the major divide between these two camps pivoted on their different approaches to the legacy of World War II. Zhdanov excoriated the Western camp as "imperialist," a supporter of "reactionary and anti-democratic pro-fascist forces," which were ready to betray their "wartime allies." By contrast, he lauded the Soviets' camp as consisting of "anti-fascist," forces. Its goal was to "resist the threat of new wars and imperialist expansion, to strengthen democracy and to extirpate the vestiges of fascism."[12] The Soviet government thus attempted to use the legacy of the liberation to unite Central and Eastern Europeans to avert a new world war—a war launched by the United States and its Western European allies. At the dedication of the Treptow memorial on May 8, 1949, General Aleksandr Kotikov, the commander of the Soviet forces in Berlin, used the occasion to warn attendees about the threat posed by Western "'arsonists of a new war.'"[13]

After the KSČ took power in Czechoslovakia in February 1948, the legacy of the liberation developed into a highly politicized myth to justify the Soviet Union's hegemony over its new satellite state. Both the Soviet and Czechoslovak governments drew on the memory of the liberation to rationalize the imbalance of power between their countries. The Czechoslovak government stressed the need for the country's citizens to be grateful to their former liberators. Prague, in particular, increasingly reflected this iconography of gratitude. In 1950, a statue called "Fraternization," by the Czech sculptor Karel Pokorný, depicting a Soviet soldier and a Czech male civilian embracing during the liberation, was unveiled on Prague's Old Town Square in front of the town hall.[14] In the early 1950s, the memorial complex on Prague's Vítkov Hill (which had been constructed during the interwar period to pay homage to the Czech legionnaires whose service in World War I had paved the way for Czechoslovak independence from the Habsburg Empire) was expanded to include a memorial hall for the Red Army.[15] In 1953, Štefánik Square in Prague was renamed "The Square of the Soviet Tank Crews" to honor the tank monument that had been unveiled eight years earlier, which had become the country's most iconic symbol of the liberation.

In 1955, the infamous Stalin monument in Prague—the largest statue of the Soviet leader ever constructed anywhere in the world—was unveiled on the top of Letná hill, overlooking Prague's Old Town. The ill-fated monument is often portrayed as marking the apotheosis of the Czechoslovak version of what Nikita Khrushchev dubbed "the cult of personality." The statue depicted Czechoslovak workers and peasants gazing gratefully up at the massive stone figure of the Soviet leader. But the monument was also the apex of the Stalin-era cult of the liberation of Czechoslovakia. The monument's inscription read: "To Our Liberator, from the Czechoslovak People." Less than a year after the monument was unveiled, Khrushchev gave his "secret speech" in Moscow denouncing Stalin's crimes. Monuments to Stalin were subsequently demolished across the USSR, and the Stalin statute in Prague thus increasingly became a source of embarrassment to the Czechoslovak government. In 1961, the KSČ ordered the statue to be dynamited.[16]

In the Stalinist period, holidays also played an important role in the construction of the Soviet empire of liberation in Eastern Europe. In Czechoslovakia during the Third Republic, the National Front government designated May 5—the anniversary of the Prague Uprising against the German occupation—the official holiday commemorating the war. In 1951, the Communist government instituted a new state holiday in honor of the war: May 9, "Day of the Liberation of Czechoslovakia by the Soviet Army."[17] This new holiday explicitly usurped the role Czechoslovaks had played fighting the Nazis, and further entrenched the Soviets' chronology of the conflict. The holiday marked the German surrender, which was signed at 11:00 P.M. on May 8, 1945, Central European time—May 9, Moscow time. In the early 1950s, the May 9 holiday was adopted throughout the Eastern bloc, thus becoming another example of the USSR's attempts to use the legacy of the liberation to buttress its power in the region. In the German Democratic Republic, the holiday, which had previously been called "Victory Day," was renamed "Liberation Day," in 1950, symbolizing the alleged shift in the USSR's role in the country, from occupier to "friend."[18] In Romania, the

Communist government used the celebration of May 9 to deflect from the country's wartime alliance with Nazi Germany.[19]

In Stalinist Czechoslovakia, the liberation holiday became an occasion for Czechoslovaks to publicly perform their gratitude and indebtedness toward their Soviet "friends." On the anniversary of the liberation in May 1951, a Czech woman wrote a recollection for a national magazine. The piece demonstrated many of the common tropes at the time concerning the Soviet victory: thankfulness, obligation, friendship, and veneration of Stalin. She recounted how in 1945 mothers had lifted their children up to see the Red Army troops and announced: "'Look, these are [our] truest friends. They saved our lives.'" She claimed that after watching a Soviet soldier die in the Prague offensive, she asked herself, "Will we be capable of being grateful enough to the great Soviet Union and to dear Stalin?"[20]

The descriptions of the liberation that were published in the Czechoslovak press during the Stalinist years were highly sanitized. This was also true regarding the portrayals of World War II in the Soviet Union and throughout the Eastern bloc. Denise Youngblood has noted that even in Soviet cinematic depictions of World War II from this period, "combat scenes lack emotion and tension."[21] Reuben Fowkes has observed that across Eastern Europe, monuments to the Red Army rarely focused on soldiers' suffering. For instance, the grandiose monument the Romanian government erected to the Red Army in Bucharest in 1953 consisted solely of joyous, stylized depictions of the liberation.[22] In Czechoslovakia, reminiscences published about the liberation during the early 1950s are notable for how they gloss over the typical emotional and physical experiences of war: exhaustion, hunger, pain, injury, fear, and grief. Ivan Razdin, a Soviet veteran and mechanic in Moscow, recounted his experience of the liberation in a May 1951 article in the Czechoslovak magazine *Svět sovětů* (World of the Soviets) using the heroic, triumphant language of socialist realism. "The advance of the Soviet forces was swift, inexorable. We broke the resistance of the Hitlerites and liberated the brother people." The only challenging moment in Razdin's narrative comes when the victorious Soviet troops struggle to maneuver through the cheering crowds in Prague.[23] Such cartoonish accounts of the liberation served not only to glorify Soviet power in Czechoslovakia: they were also Cold War tropes designed to mobilize Czechoslovaks for the impending conflict with the "imperialist" West. In the same issue of *Svět sovětů*, another Soviet veteran, Vladimir Markov, hailed the friendship between the

Soviet and Czechoslovak people as essential for the "fight" for peace "against the agitators for a new war."[24]

Unsurprisingly, these glorified accounts of the liberation in Czechoslovakia glossed over the crimes Soviet soldiers had committed in Slovakia and the Czech lands, including widespread looting and incidents of rape and murder. Instead, Czechoslovak propagandists engaged in transference: a book published in Prague in 1951, tellingly titled, *The Shameful Role of the American Occupiers in the Western Czech Lands in 1945*, accused American soldiers of a litany of crimes, including theft, murder, and rape. "In Mariánské Lázně a mob of American gangsters in uniform assaulted several Czech girls. When the girls sought refuge at the SNB [police] station, the Americans burst in on them and beat up the SNB officer."[25] Czechoslovak propagandists borrowed from the Soviets this tactic of shifting blame for the Red Army's violent acts to American soldiers. As Tony Shaw and Denise Youngblood note, the 1949 Soviet film *The Meeting on the Elbe* (Grigorii Aleksandrov), portrays American soldiers in occupied Germany as responsible for committing the mass rapes of German women that the Red Army had in fact perpetrated.[26]

Throughout Eastern Europe in the Stalinist period, the Soviet Union used the legacy of World War II to construct an empire of liberation. In Czechoslovakia, monuments, Liberation Day, and reminisces about the war published in the press combined to mythologize the liberation as an encounter between brave, selfless Soviet soldiers and grateful, adoring Czechoslovak civilians. This mythology justified the Soviet Union's exercise of power over its satellite state.

Laboratory of Remembrance

Studies of the legacy of the Soviet liberation in Eastern Europe—which focus almost exclusively on monuments and memorials to the Red Army—have centered on the Soviets' imperialist ambitions in the region. Fowkes writes, "The first wave of war memorials was erected for primarily geo-political reasons. They acted to mark on the map the area of Europe liberated by the Soviets, and to claim that territory as part of the Soviet zone of influence."[27] Anders Åman argues, "The monuments had a message over and above that conveyed by their inscriptions: Soviet influence was to endure. A victorious army does not erect stone and bronze monuments to itself in places where it proposes to relinquish control."[28] As the previous sections of this chapter have shown, the legacy of the liberation certainly functioned to buttress Soviet imperial ambitions in the region. But from the Soviet perspective, the legacy also served another, more unexpected purpose: as a laboratory for remembrance of the war.

Amir Weiner has argued that the Soviet Union's victory in World War II became a new national myth for the country and the basis for its postwar identity, superseding even the October Revolution and the Bolsheviks' triumph in the Civil War.[29] Other historians have described how the Soviet authorities constructed a "cult" of World War II to commemorate the catastrophic losses the country had suffered during the conflict and to instill patriotism in the generations born after the war.[30] But the Soviet cult of World War II only developed after Stalin's death in 1953 and did not reach its apex until the Brezhnev years in the late 1960s and 1970s.

In the Stalinist period, official memory of the war in the Soviet Union was highly circumscribed, showcasing Stalin's role in guiding the country to victory. Geoffrey Roberts notes that in a book Marshall Kliment Voroshilov wrote about Stalin and the Soviet Army in 1951, "In the section on the Great Patriotic War, Soviet military success was presented as entirely due to Stalin."[31] Few Soviet films were made about World War II while Stalin was alive. Those that were, such as the epic *Fall of Berlin* (Mikhail Chiaureli, 1950), paid scant attention to the experiences of ordinary civilians and soldiers, and instead mythologized Stalin as the war's true hero.[32] Soviet veterans, unlike their counterparts in the United States and Western Europe, were denied special privileges by their government and were not even allowed to form their own organization until 1956.[33] In Leningrad, where approximately 800,000 civilians perished during the Germans' brutal three-year siege during the war, the postwar government shut down grassroots efforts to commemorate the tragedy and excised discussions of it from official histories.[34]

The scale and panoply of the celebrations of the liberation in Stalinist Eastern Europe thus contrast starkly with the Soviet government's largely silent approach to the legacy of the war at home. Although monuments to the Red Army were constructed across Eastern Europe in the first years after the war, most World War II memorials in the USSR were not erected until the 1960s.[35] The anniversary of the Soviet victory on May 9 was celebrated as a state holiday in Czechoslovakia and the other countries in the Eastern bloc beginning in the early 1950s, yet in the Soviet Union, Victory Day was not an official holiday from 1947 to 1964, and Soviet workers were not even given the day off. Although reminisces (however highly stylized) by Soviet veterans of the liberation were widely published in the Czechoslovak press during the Stalinist period, in the USSR, veterans' memoirs were suppressed.[36]

What explains the stark differences between how the war was commemorated in the land of the liberator and the countries of the liberated? Despite the Soviet Union's ultimate victory in the war, the incredible loss and destruction the country had suffered did not easily lend itself to heroic narratives. Between twenty-six million and twenty-seven million Soviet citizens perished during the war: seven to eight million Soviet soldiers, and roughly nineteen million civilians.[37] The Germans had occupied a full third of the country, where collaboration, genocidal violence against the Jewish population, and infighting between partisan units ensued.[38] In the first years after the war, it was thus easier for the Soviet state to construct a heroic narrative about the conflict in Eastern Europe than it was at home. This narrative rationalized Soviet casualties as noble sacrifices that enabled the oppressed people of the region, who had suffered under the successive tyrannies of first the bourgeoisie and then the Nazis, to build socialism. During the Stalinist period, the commemoration of the Soviet liberation of Czechoslovakia and the other Eastern bloc countries thus functioned as a way for the Soviet state to mark the trauma of the war abroad, when it was not yet ready to do so at home.

The Soviet Union's empire of liberation in Eastern Europe can thus be seen as a laboratory for remembrance of the war: the incubator of the domestic cult of the conflict that would become so prominent in the Soviet Union in the 1960s and 1970s, and which continues to define post-Soviet Russia.[39] After Stalin's death, Soviet veterans, architects, and planners drew on the legacy of the liberation in the Eastern bloc to develop their own practices of memorialization. When the Soviet Committee for War Veterans was first formed in the mid-1950s, it studied the methods used in Czechoslovakia to preserve soldiers' graves.[40] In the 1960s, when Soviet architects and planners first began to construct World War II monuments and memorials on a broad scale, they used memorials to the liberation in Eastern Europe as examples. One of the most grandiose war memorials constructed in the USSR was the monument to the Soviet victory at Stalingrad, which was completed in 1967. The architect of the Stalingrad memorial was Yevgenii Vuchetich, who had designed the Red Army memorial at Treptow Park in Berlin almost two decades earlier. Vuchetich's first designs for the Stalingrad complex borrowed heavily from his earlier work on the memorial in Berlin.[41] These are concrete examples of how the legacy of the liberation fueled the construction of the cult of World War II in the post-Stalinist Soviet Union. On a broader level, during Stalinism, the Soviet government had sought to use the liberation's legacy to forge cohesion in the Eastern bloc; after Stalin's death it attempted to employ memory of the war to create unity at home.

Photographic Memory

In the photograph (see illustration 5), a middle-aged man with a mustache is standing, holding a baby. They are indoors, likely in a private residence (there is a sink in the background and what appears to be a calendar on the wall). The man is smiling tenderly, looking not at the camera in front of him, but at the baby, who is crying. Even though the man is not the baby's father, he is attempting to soothe the infant by putting a pacifier in its mouth.

The photograph was taken during the Soviet liberation of Prague. The man it depicts was a private in a Red Army guards' unit, and the baby was a local Czech child. The photographer was probably an amateur: the lighting is darker than it should be; a shadow from what appears to be the window's mullion slopes over the man's face; his hand holding the pacifier is a little blurry.[42] The photographer may have been the baby's father. Whoever it was evidently felt comfortable enough with the soldier to continue taking the picture despite the child's tears.

In 1954—almost a decade after the picture was taken—someone submitted it to a contest organized by the Union of Czechoslovak-Soviet Friendship (SČSP) for the best photograph from the liberation. By the time the contest was held, a Red Army soldier holding a young child had become an iconic image of the Soviet liberation of Eastern Europe. Vuchetich immortalized this image in his 1949 Treptow Park memorial in Berlin. This image was likewise featured in a statue to the Red Army unveiled in 1951 in the Southwestern Moravian town of Slavonice (see illustration 6).

The image of a Soviet soldier embracing a Czech child was also popularized in other formats, such as in a 1950 Russian-language textbook for Czechoslovak fifth-graders, which included a text children were supposed to read in preparation for the May 9 holiday. "When the Soviet Army came

Figure 5. A private in a Red Army guard's unit with a Czech baby, Prague, May 1945.
Credit: Národní archiv, f. 1329 [OČRA-1945], Miloslav Beran, inv. č. 3/1.

to us I was five years old. . . . The Soviet tanks drove down the street. All the people waved flowers. Suddenly one tank stopped in front of us. Soviet soldiers got out. I gave one of them the bouquet of flowers and he took me in his arms."[43] But the 1945 photograph of the Soviet private holding the Czech baby differs from its subsequent propaganda versions. The indoor setting, the baby's tears, the soldier's efforts to soothe the child, and the amateur quality of the picture combine to reveal a much more human and intimate vision of the encounter between liberator and liberated.

The fact that someone submitted the photograph of the private and the baby to the SČSP's contest in 1954 is indicative of a significant shift in the legacy of the liberation that began after Stalin's death the previous year. Nina Tumarkin has referred to the Thaw as "the formative stage" of the Soviet "cult" of the war. During the mid- to late 1950s and early 1960s, commemorations of the war increased in the Soviet Union and became more nuanced. Red Army veterans published a wave of memoirs about the conflict, highlighting the experiences of ordinary soldiers, rather than Stalin's heroics. A series of famous films about the war were produced, including *The Cranes Are Flying* (Mikhail Kalatozov, 1957), *Ballad of a Soldier* (Grigorii Chukhrai,

Figure 6. Monument to the Red Army in Slavonice, erected in 1951.
Credit: Author's photograph.

1959), and *Ivan's Childhood* (Andrei Tarkovsky, 1962), which depicted the war years in a more realistic and morally complex manner than those made during the late Stalinist period.[44] As commemorations of the war became more nuanced in the Soviet Union, so did the legacy of the liberation in Czechoslovakia.

Changes in the liberation's legacy were also linked to changes in the broader friendship project. In the aftermath of Stalin's death, the USSR's relations with its Eastern European satellite states changed dramatically, from a more traditional empire, in which the Soviet Union promoted itself up as an explicit model for the bloc countries, to an empire of friends, in which transnational contacts between ordinary citizens in the realm of everyday life were supposed to augment socialist unity.[45] The combination of the new openness about the war in the USSR, and the de-Stalinization of the friendship project (discussed in greater detail in the next chapter), transformed the transnational cult of the Soviet liberation of Czechoslovakia and the rigid hierarchy that had defined the friendship project in the Stalinist period. During Stalinism, official depictions of the liberation had stressed Soviet power over Czechoslovakia: in the 1950s and 1960s, they emphasized the ongoing friendship between the liberators and the liberated, and even Czechoslovak citizens' leverage in this friendship. This new trope of the liberation-as-friendship privileged the personal memories of Soviet veterans and the Czechoslovak civilians they had encountered at the end of the war. During this period, the liberation's legacy was also shaped by a significant expansion of transnational contacts between Soviet and Czechoslovak citizens, including mass tourism, the activities of friendship societies, and veterans' relations.

The SČSP's 1954 photography contest was a harbinger of this new, more populist and nuanced approach to the legacy of the liberation. The contest was open to professional and amateur photographers in Czechoslovakia. The pictures people submitted revealed important features of the liberation that had been excluded from the hagiographic narrative of the Stalinist years. One of these was romance between Soviet soldiers and Czechoslovak women. During Stalinism, official depictions of the liberation had portrayed the relationship between the Soviet soldiers and the people they liberated in strictly paternal, fraternal, or friendly terms. By contrast, romance is a recurring theme in the photographs submitted to the SČSP. One photograph, for example (not included here), depicts a Red Army soldier kissing a local woman, who is holding a bouquet of flowers in her hand.[46] In another image, three

Figure 7. Red Army soldiers and local women during the liberation of Prague, May 1945.
Credit: Národní archiv, f. 1329 [OČRA-1945], Bedřich Bermann, inv. č. 4/2.

Soviet soldiers and two young Czech women sit beneath a patch of wild-flowers, somewhere on the outskirts of Prague. Four of the young people are paired off, and the third soldier serenades them with an accordion. The Soviet soldier in the center of this group has his arm around a blonde girl. She's grinning broadly, while he looks protective, even smug.

In a third photograph (illustration 8), two teenagers lie next to each other on the grass. One is a Red Army soldier, with medals decorating his slim chest. The other is a Czech girl in a dark flowered dress, smiling at the camera.

During the Stalinist period it had been taboo to draw attention to trans-national romances between Soviet soldiers and Czechoslovak civilians, not only because of the xenophobic campaigns then taking place in the USSR

Figure 8. Red Army soldier and a local woman during the liberation of Prague, May 1945.
Credit: Národní archiv, f. 1329 [OČRA-1945], Bedřich Bermann, inv. č. 4/20.

but also because the 1947 Soviet marriage law (discussed in chapter 2) had effectively rendered such romances illegal. In Czechoslovakia, memories of the rapes committed by Soviet soldiers during the liberation may also help to explain the official silence during the Stalinist years about these romances. In the post-Stalinist period, however, romance became an important part of the new mythology of the liberation.

During the Stalinist years, the legacy of the liberation was largely one-sided, emphasizing Czechoslovaks' admiration and gratitude toward the Soviet soldiers. By contrast, the photographs submitted to the SČSP reveal that the Soviet-Czechoslovak encounter had made an indelible impression on both liberators and liberated. The images show that Red Army soldiers were

Figure 9. A wounded Red Army soldier poses with Prague residents, May 1945.
Credit: Národní archiv, f. 1329 [OČRA-1945], Josef Kulhánek, inv. č. 47/3.

keen to preserve the liberation for posterity. One picture depicts a grinning Red Army soldier with a machine gun tucked under his arm standing among a group of Czechs of various ages. A young woman holds his arm. In the soldier's bandaged hand he holds up souvenirs of the liberation: a photograph or large postcard of Prague and a sprig of lilacs. Another picture shows a Red Army soldier taking a photograph of a group of Czech women who are posing for him (see illustration 10).

The pictures submitted to the SČSP's contest thus construct a more down-to-earth, intimate account of the liberation than the hagiographic Stalinist version. These photographs exemplify the new, more reciprocal, and populist legacy of the liberation that developed after Stalin's death.

May Stars

The Soviet and Czechoslovak media played leading roles in promoting the post-Stalinist version of the liberation. Newspaper and magazine articles told

Figure 10. A Red Army soldier takes a photograph of women in Prague, May 1945.
Credit: Národní archiv, f. 1329 [OČRA-1945], Rostislav Novák, inv. č. 61/3.

the stories of friendly encounters that had occurred between Soviet soldiers and Czechoslovak civilians during the war. These narratives, in keeping with Stalinist-era tropes, often emphasized the Czechoslovak people's indebtedness to their Soviet liberators as well as the Czechoslovak state's dependence on Soviet support. But in a departure from the Stalinist years, they depicted Red Army soldiers and Czechoslovak civilians as individuals, rather than as national composites. The articles also took pains to portray the liberation not as a fixed historical moment, but as an ongoing part of the postwar friendship project between the countries; they highlighted recent meetings between Soviet veterans and the Czechs and Slovaks they had first encountered during the war.

An article by a Soviet journalist, published in 1958 in *Svět sovětů*, described a friendship that had developed during the war between two inmates in Ravensbrük, the German concentration camp: Nora Smirnova, a teenage Red Army soldier, and Marie Váňová, a middle-aged Czech housewife. Despite her youth, Smirnova emerges as the story's heroine for having saved Váňová s life. The article described how Smirnova used her skills as a nurse to attend to Váňová after she collapsed while working at the camp's warehouse. The article also depicted Smirnova as Váňová's political mentor. During their captivity, Smirnova entertained the older woman with stories about the Soviet Union: about her father, "an old revolutionary," who had once escaped from a tsarist penal colony, and her mother, who had run away from her bourgeois family to become a village schoolteacher. The article concluded by relating how, at the end of the war, Váňová, inspired by Smirnova's example, joined the KSČ.[47] Smirnova thus saved Váňová's life a second time: by setting her (and more broadly the Czechoslovak nation) on the path to Communism.

Articles about the liberation in the Soviet and Czechoslovak press also emphasized that the transnational friendships forged between Red Army soldiers and local civilians in 1944–1945 continued to flourish in the postwar period. An article in *Sotsialisticheskaia Chekhoslovakiia* (Socialist Czechoslovakia, a Russian-language magazine founded in Czechoslovakia in 1953 for distribution in the Soviet Union) told the story of a Soviet Army doctor, Aleksei Glebov, who had been billeted with a Czech family in Ostrava in May 1945, and had assisted at the birth of their son Ivan.[48] The article highlighted Glebov's ongoing friendship with Ivan and his family in the postwar period, explaining that in 1963 he had traveled to Ostrava to meet the teenage Ivan and his parents, and that Ivan and his family were planning to travel to the Soviet Union for the twentieth anniversary of the liberation in 1965.[49]

The centerpiece of the media's effort to highlight the liberation as an act of friendship was the 1959 film, *May Stars* (*Maiskie zvezdy/Májové hvězdy*), a Soviet-Czechoslovak coproduction. The film was directed by the Soviet director Stanislav Rostotskii and was based on a collection of short stories by the Czech writer Ludvík Aškenazy, who had served in the Red Army during the war. The film consists of a series of vignettes about the liberation, each highlighting a friendly encounter between Soviet soldiers and Czechoslovak civilians during the first two days of the Red Army's advance into Prague and its environs. The film's internationalist spirit was reflected in its cast, a mix of Czechoslovak and Soviet actors, including the young Czech actress Jana Brejchová and the Soviet actor Viacheslav Tikhonov, who would go on to feature in a number of Soviet productions about the war, most famously the 1973 television series, *Seventeen Moments of Spring*.

The opening shots of *May Stars* show a series of iconic images associated with the Soviet liberation of Czechoslovakia and the Nazi occupation: the memorial to the Red Army at Prague's Olšanské cemetery; the town of Lidice,

burned to the ground by German soldiers in 1942; and finally, the Monument to the Soviet Tank Crews in the Czechoslovak capital. This last image
serves as a bridge to the present. The camera lens widens from the monument to reveal children playing in a sandbox at its base. A little boy holds up
a toy tank and explains to his playmate, "The soldiers came on these cars in
the war and shot." "And when was the war?" the little girl asks. "I don't know,"
he admits. "We weren't alive then." This scene explains one of the film's main
goals: to highlight the importance of the liberation for the postwar Soviet-
Czechoslovak friendship project, including for those too young to remember
the war.

Each of the film's four episodes portrays the liberation as having forged
an emotional bond between the Soviet soldiers and the Czechoslovak civilians
they encountered. In a departure from the Stalinist period in Czechoslovakia, when Red Army soldiers had been depicted solely as valiant heroes, the
film portrays them—in the words of one Czechoslovak reviewer—as "ordinary Soviet people."[50] In the first episode, which builds on the trope of
friendship between Soviet soldiers and children in the countries they liberated, a Soviet general befriends a young Czech boy who reminds him of his
own son, who was killed by the Nazis. The second episode aligns with the
new, post-Stalinist attention to romantic encounters during the liberation. It
depicts a brief flirtation between a soldier, Lieutenant Andrei Rukavichkin
(Tikhonov) and a village schoolteacher, Jana (Brejchová), on the outskirts of
Prague. The third episode follows a Czech inmate who has just returned to
Prague from Auschwitz, on his quest to recover his old apartment. He discovers that a Sudeten German has taken over his apartment. A young
Soviet soldier comes to the inmate's defense: he kills the German, sacrificing
his own life in the process. In the final episode, a Soviet soldier, who had been
a tram conductor in Kiev before the war, convinces a Prague conductor to
let him drive his tram through the capital's streets—the passengers cheer.

In addition to its plot, the film employs language to promote friendship
between the Soviet and Czechoslovak peoples. The Czechoslovak actors
speak Czech and the Soviet actors Russian, yet this linguistic divide turns
out not to be a barrier to mutual understanding. In the scene between the
schoolteacher, Jana, and the Soviet lieutenant Rukavichkin, romantic attraction plus the affinity between their countries enables them to communicate
with each other. Rukavichkin tries to guess Jana's name by writing a series
of common Czech women's names (in Latin script) on the blackboard. Jana

then solves the mystery by writing her name for him in Cyrillic. The scene thus indicates that superficial cultural differences, such as language, are not an obstacle to transnational friendship—particularly between Slavic peoples.

Liberation Tourism

Mass tourism, which began between the Soviet Union and Czechoslovakia in 1955, was the largest form of transnational, person-to-person exchange in the post-Stalinist period of the friendship project.[51] The legacy of the liberation significantly shaped tourism between the two countries. When Soviet tour groups visited Czechoslovakia, they were almost always taken to see battlefields where Red Army soldiers had fought and war memorials such as the Monument to the Soviet Tank Crews and the Olšanské cemetery. By visiting these sites, Soviet citizens became active participants in the construction of the legacy of the liberation, and in the broader empire of friends.

"In Prague we visited the national monument on Vítkov hill and the cemetery of the Soviet heroes," the leader of a group of workers from Moscow reported in 1966. "Our tourist group and the Czech comrades accompanying us laid fresh flowers on the graves of the Soviet heroes, and we honored their memory with a moment of silence. The cemetery of Soviet heroes is kept in wonderful condition; you can feel the great care that the party and the government as well as the people of Czechoslovakia pay to the memory of the fallen Soviet heroes."[52] While this account has a rote quality, Soviet tourists' visits to sites of the liberation in Czechoslovakia could be highly emotional. In 1965, the trip leader of a group from Soviet Belorussia, organized by Sputnik, the Soviet youth tourist agency, reported that a visit to Olšanské cemetery had been particularly wrenching for two young men, whose fathers had died during the liberation of Czechoslovakia.[53] In 1967, a group from the Komi Republic in Northern Russia made a special stop so that one of the women on the trip could visit her son's grave.[54] Such visits reveal how, following Stalin's death, Czechoslovakia evolved from a laboratory of remembrance in the USSR to an actual site of memorialization for Soviet citizens.

Tourism to Czechoslovakia in the 1950s and 1960s involved Soviet travelers in the construction of their country's empire of liberation. As they toured the country, they were presented with living tableaux of grateful locals, who personally thanked them for their freedom.[55] A tourist group from the Tula region, visiting Bratislava on a holiday commemorating the Soviet liberation in 1964, observed, "The whole city came to the hill to lay flowers at the monument to the liberators. We . . . could not hold back tears from emotion. At the hill there was even an improvised meeting with children, who presented us with albums and asked for autographs."[56] A group from Crimea traveling with Sputnik reported proudly that Czechoslovaks "see Soviet youth above all as the representatives of a nation of liberators."[57]

These florid descriptions of Czechoslovaks' gratitude toward the USSR should not simply be dismissed as examples of Soviet tourists dutifully performing the language of the empire of liberation. Anatolii Cherniaev, for example, a Soviet Communist Party functionary (and at times a sharp critic of Soviet relations with Czechoslovakia) who lived in Prague in the early 1960s, recalled in his memoirs that the Czechs he met "simply idolized Soviet people out of gratitude for the liberation from fascism and the restoration of [Czechoslovak] independence."[58]

A New Myth of the Liberation

In the mid- to late 1950s, Red Army veterans and the Czechoslovak civilians they had met during the liberation began to attempt to reestablish their relationships, which had been disrupted during the Stalinist period. Social organizations in Czechoslovakia, including the SČSP, the Union of Women, and the Union of the Fighters against Fascism began inviting Soviet veterans to visit the towns they had helped liberate and the relatives of fallen Soviet soldiers to visit their graves. In 1959, Marie Kafková, a member of the Women's Committee in Slavkov u Brna, sent a letter to the widow of a Soviet soldier who had died in her town, describing the care she devoted to maintaining her husband's grave and the local monument to the Red Army:

> It will no doubt seem strange to you, when after fourteen long years you receive this letter from familiar Czechoslovakia. In our town's Women's Committee [Union] we have talked many times about what a joy it would be to meet with the families of the fallen heroes-Soviet soldiers, to inform you about the love and care the dear residents of Slavkov are [expending] looking after their graves. As a member of this committee, I took upon myself the responsibility to search for the place of residence of the families of the fallen soldiers whose remains are buried in a fraternal grave in our town.[59]

In a subsequent letter, Kafková attempted to establish a more intimate connection with the soldier's widow. She described how she was studying Russian through the People's Russian Courses for adults, and how she maintained a pen-pal correspondence with a woman in Penza. She also told the soldier's widow about her family life: her husband, who was the caretaker for a local castle, and her eight year-old grandson. Kafková's letters to the soldier's widow thus exemplify how the legacy of the liberation in the 1950s and 1960s helped form new relationships between Czechoslovak and Soviet citizens.[60]

That same year, Vitalii Aleksandrovich Maslov, a former captain in the Red Army, wrote to the Union of Soviet Friendship Societies asking for help locating Rudolf Kolář, a Czech who had housed him in his apartment in the town of Votice during the liberation.[61] Around the same time, a Czech woman from the small town of Týn nad Vltavou in Southern Bohemia wrote to the Soviet army's newspaper, *Krasnaia zvezda* (Red Star), "Our family often remembers our dear guest, the Soviet lieutenant Andrei Larin. He left us a photograph without an address. My mother says, 'He was a cheerful and dear boy.' . . . Can you imagine what a joy it would be to find out after so many years what he is doing and how he is living?"[62]

When Czechoslovak organizations and individuals tried to reestablish contacts with Soviet veterans, they frequently cited a desire to involve the younger generation in the legacy of the liberation and, by extension, the friendship project. In 1960, the local National Committee in a village near the Slovak city of Banská Bystrica invited a Soviet veteran named Mikhail Glider to attend the unveiling of a monument to the liberation. As a reward for his heroism during the war, the village had made Glider an honorary citizen. The committee stressed the importance of Glider's visit as a way to make history come alive for schoolchildren, who had learned about his heroic exploits in the classroom.[63] In 1965, a Czech woman wrote to the Soviet Committee for War Veterans asking for help finding a Soviet soldier who had stayed with her family during the liberation. She explained that she had corresponded with the soldier for a year after the liberation: her eighth-grade daughter had recently found the letters and wanted to know if the Soviet veteran had children her age she could write to.[64]

Czechoslovak civilians' and Soviet veterans' attempts to reestablish wartime contacts reveal that ordinary citizens in both countries interpreted the idea of "friendship" differently from state and cultural officials. In 1964, the editors of *Sotsialisticheskaia Chekhoslovakiia* reported that they had run out of resources to help Soviet veterans reestablish contacts with Czechoslovaks they had met during the liberation. "Probably it would be better to make new friendships," the editors proposed. They suggested that tourism between the USSR and Czechoslovakia offered the perfect opportunity to forge a new generation of friends.[65] The magazine's readers, by attempting to reestablish their wartime contacts, defined friendship in terms of intimate relations between specific individuals. By contrast, the editors characterized friendship in the broader, more impersonal language of socialist internationalism.

As ordinary citizens in the superpower and its satellite began to participate more actively in the friendship project, they disrupted its Stalinist hierarchy. The contacts between Soviet veterans and Czechoslovak civilians that began to develop in the mid-1950s challenged the USSR's superiority over its satellite by creating a new myth of the liberation that recast the very idea of friendship. In newspaper articles and letters to friendship societies and veterans' organizations, Czechoslovaks reframed the legacy of the liberation to emphasize their own bravery and heroism. In 1962, František Skotnica wrote to the Soviet embassy in Prague to ask for help finding the addresses of two escaped Soviet prisoners of war (POWs) his family had hidden for three months during the conflict. In his letter, he stressed the risks his family had taken to care for the soldiers, explaining that if the Germans had found out what they were doing, the family would have been executed. "Everyone in our house experienced great joy that at the very least [*khotia by takim obrazom*] we were able to help our liberator—the Red Army." With this deceptively humble sentence, Skotnica turned the Stalinist language of Czechoslovak gratitude toward the Soviet Union on its head, instead emphasizing the role his family had played in the liberation.[66]

By highlighting their work feeding, sheltering, and providing medical care to Soviet soldiers and POWs, Czechoslovak citizens transformed themselves from the passive position of "occupied" or "liberated," to people with agency. A 1958 article in *Svět sovětů* told the story of the Harmáček family, who had taken care of two Soviet POWs in April 1945, after they escaped from a concentration camp. The piece provides a stark contrast to an account of the liberation the same journal had published seven years earlier by the Soviet veteran, Ivan Razdin (described earlier in this chapter). Razdin's account sanitized the liberation whereas the 1958 article openly described Soviet soldiers' physical suffering. It detailed how a neighbor had found the Soviet POWs in the Harmáčeks' barn. They were "exhausted," dressed in old military coats, shod in "ruined boots." "They were both shivering and burning as if with fever." Razdin's account highlighted the decisiveness and bravery of the Soviet soldiers. In the 1958 story, it is Miroslav Harmáček, a Czech farmer, who is decisive and brave: "[The POWs] had been on the run for 18 days, without food or a roof over their heads, in constant danger of being captured. They couldn't run any further. Their fate lay in the hands of unfamiliar Czech people. Would they desire to risk their lives to save the lives of two Soviet soldiers? Miroslav Harmáček felt their tense glances. He didn't ponder over the decision."[67]

In the years after Stalin's death, Soviet veterans also began to openly express *their* gratitude toward Czechoslovaks for saving their lives in 1944–1945. They thus challenged the notion of Soviet superiority over the Czechoslovak people—the hierarchy that lay at the center of the friendship project. In 1965, a former Soviet partisan described in an article in *Svět sovětů* how a group of Czechs had rescued him after he injured himself parachuting into the Drahanské highlands in Moravia in March 1945. For days he wandered alone in the woods, until he encountered a small band of Czech lumberjacks who gave him coffee and a hat and directed him toward the local village, Protivanov. When he fell ill, some local peasants took him in and spent six weeks caring for him. Fifteen years later, the former partisan still remembered the names of the doctor who had treated him and the peasants who had sheltered him. He emphasized how the assistance these Czechs had offered him had enabled him to physically survive the war and maintain a sense of dignity while he was injured. "Throughout my entire stay in Protivanov my Czech friends showered me with care and love, thus I did not feel powerless and lonely. I only feared for them and their families, about what would happen to them if the Gestapo were to find me."[68]

The partisan's reminiscence (and others like it) highlighted the vulnerability Soviet soldiers had experienced during the war, which had been completely concealed in Stalinist accounts. More important, such reminiscences reversed the notion of "gratitude," which played such a prominent role in discourse about the liberation in Czechoslovakia in the late 1940s and early 1950s. The story of a former Red Army pilot, V. T. Alekseev, is a particularly striking example of this phenomenon. In a private letter Alekseev wrote to Khrushchev in 1963, he recounted how a Czech family had saved his life after his plane crashed over Nazi-occupied territory. He had grown so close to the family that he had even begun to refer to the matriarch as his "Czech mother." Eventually, the Germans discovered that the family was hiding him, and sent them to a concentration camp. Although the family survived, eighteen years later Alekseev remained guilt-ridden. Rather than hail the Soviet people as the liberators of Czechoslovakia, he asked Khrushchev to issue an official declaration of gratitude to the Czechoslovak people.[69]

Soviet veterans' and Czechoslovak civilians' personal memories thus provided a more complex picture of the liberation and its significance than the stone monuments to the Red Army or the cheering crowds in Prague every May 9. In the 1950s and 1960s, the legacy of the liberation became more than an imperialist trope: it developed into an opportunity for ordinary, nonelite citizens in both countries to participate in the friendship project and to renegotiate the terms of the empire of friends. A photograph in a 1965 issue of *Sotsialisticheskaia Chekhoslovakiia* even showed a Red Army veteran who had been wounded in the Prague offensive on a visit to Czechoslovakia for the twentieth anniversary of the liberation, kissing the hand of the Czech nurse who had taken care of him.[70] Personal reminisces about the war by Czechoslovaks and Soviets alike paralleled the broader changes that occurred in Soviet relations with all the Eastern bloc countries during this period: a new focus on bilateralism and an emphasis on the power of personal connections to shape international relations.

The Limits of Memory

In the 1950s and 1960s, a new, transnational legacy of the liberation developed that was more nuanced and inclusive than the Stalinist version. But this new legacy was still marked by conspicuous silences about the darker aspects of the liberation and the postwar friendship project. Most significantly, accounts of the liberation continued to ignore the violence Soviet soldiers had committed against Czechoslovak civilians in 1945. There are a couple of possible explanations for this silence. First, it was taboo to discuss such crimes in the media and even in private letters to veterans' committees. Second, fifteen to twenty years after the liberation, looting and even rape may have appeared the inevitable by-products of war, crimes that would have been committed by a small percentage of troops from any army.[71] Third, official and private accounts of the Soviet liberation of Czechoslovakia in the 1950s and 1960s tended to emphasize the personal heroism and kindness of individual Soviet soldiers rather than the conduct of the Soviet army as a whole. By focusing on these intimate encounters, such accounts underscored the importance of "personal diplomacy" to transnational relations in the socialist bloc, and avoided the darker side of the Soviet army's actions.

The new mythology of the liberation also left unexplained why contacts between Soviet soldiers and Czechoslovak civilians had been disrupted after the war. One explanation, of course, was that the xenophobia of the late Stalinist period in the Soviet Union proscribed all types of informal contacts with foreigners (even foreigners from "friendly" countries). A second explanation is that attitudes toward the war in the Soviet Union changed during the Thaw: the new Soviet-Czechoslovak contacts of the late 1950s paralleled the rise of the Soviet veterans' movement, which worked to re-form connections among former combatants.[72] A third explanation, however, points to the limits of the post-Stalinist friendship project. Although this version of the project succeeded in bringing far more Soviet and Czechoslovak citizens together than had been possible in the first postwar decade, it could never fully re-create the level of spontaneity or intimacy between them that had existed during the heady time of the liberation.

Surprisingly, the film *May Stars* hints at the idea that the intimate friendship between Soviets and Czechoslovaks forged in war would not survive the peace. In the movie's most famous scene (the only episode in the film not included in Aškenazy's original story), Lieutenant Rukavichkin has come to a village schoolhouse near Prague looking for chalk to mark cleared mines. He and the teacher Jana engage in a brief flirtation, which culminates in a kiss. But their romance is fleeting; Rukavichkin has to leave to return to his army unit. He uses the chalk Jana has given him to write his address in Moscow for her on the blackboard. But later on in the day, when Jana returns to the classroom, she discovers that the director of the school has erased it.

In both the Soviet Union and Czechoslovakia, the era of de-Stalinization was defined by a search for the "truth" about the past. In the case of Soviet-Czechoslovak relations, I would argue that citizens in both countries worked to uncover the "truth" about their encounter during the liberation and, in the process, strengthened the friendship between their countries. They also, however, willingly suspended their memories of the violence and xenophobia that had been entwined with this friendship since its inception. Popular memories of the liberation in the 1950s and 1960s thus refined the Stalinist myth about the liberation, but did not deflate it. The new myth of the liberation that developed in this period highlighted the stakes that both Soviets and Czechoslovaks had in the friendship project. It rejuvenated friendship after the Stalinist years, but also continued to gloss over the coercive side of this relationship.

Chapter 4

Socialist Internationalism with a Human Face

Together with the Soviet Union and the other countries of the socialist
camp we are a big Leninist family, in which we are all equals, in which
the spirit of the complete equality of rights thrives, the spirit of the principles
of proletariat internationalism.

—Jaromír Vošahlík, Czechoslovak ambassador
to the Soviet Union, 1958

The spirit of socialist internationalism reached a small town in Siberia's
Altai region one night in 1963, when the local house of culture staged a
"Czech ball." Visitors arrived to find the building adorned with images
celebrating Czechoslovakia's cultural monuments. They were then invited
to tour a "miniature museum" of souvenirs that Soviet travelers had
brought back from the satellite state, including "hotel brochures, stickers,
theater programs and cafeteria menus, Czech crowns," even "tiny hotel
soaps." A variety show followed: locals, including a student, telegraph op-
erator, and the house of culture's artistic directors performed Czech and
Slovak songs and dances. The highlight of the evening came, however,
when one of the artistic directors struck a piñata, and Czech beer labels
rained on the audience. "Unfortunately [the beer served at the ball] wasn't
Czech, but our Zhigulëvskoe," one participant later wrote in an account to
the magazine *Sotsialisticheskaia Chekhoslovakiia* (Socialist Czechoslovakia),
but the labels nevertheless "served as souvenirs for everyone who came to
the party . . . I wanted to inform you," the letter writer added, "that here in

far-off Siberia you [Czechoslovakia] have made many real and sincere friends."[1]

The "Czech ball" in Siberia marked an important new phase in the friend-ship project between the USSR and its Eastern bloc satellites. In the mid-1950s, in a dramatic shift from Stalinist isolationism, the European socialist countries opened their newsstands, shops, and borders to one another on a broad scale. Their citizens, in turn, began to share their personal lives, by joining friendship societies, engaging in pen-pal correspondences, and visit-ing each other's countries as tourists. This chapter examines the evolution of the friendship project between the Soviet Union and Czechoslovakia in the decade and a half between Joseph Stalin's death and the Prague Spring, against the backdrop of the broader transformation of the Soviet empire in Eastern Europe. During Stalinism, the Soviet-Czechoslovak friendship project had mainly involved elites, such as artists and writers, and the young Czechoslovak exchange students in the USSR. The primary goal of the friendship project had been to augment Soviet supremacy. After Stalin's death, the Soviet and Czechoslovak governments expanded the friendship project to include all citizens, with the new goal of creating a cohesive "socialist world."[2]

Soviet relations with the Eastern bloc in the 1950s and 1960s have tradi-tionally been examined through a lens of "crisis," focusing on the dramatic rebellions against Soviet hegemony that broke out in Poland and Hungary in 1956 and on the Prague Spring in Czechoslovakia in 1968.[3] This chapter shows that the Soviet Union's relations with its satellite states in the 1950s and 1960s cannot be understood solely through a framework of crisis. The events of 1956 and 1968 took place within a broader context of increased eco-nomic, military, and cultural integration in the Eastern bloc. During these years, contacts between the Soviet Union and its satellite states actually became more pervasive than they had been during the Stalinist period, and the lives of ordinary Soviet and Eastern European citizens became more intertwined. The new version of the friendship project that developed in this period en-compassed bilateral treaties on cultural relations, the founding of friendship societies in the USSR, the introduction of mass tourism, the expansion of pen-pal correspondences, and the trade of mass media and consumer goods. In the case of the Soviet-Czechoslovak friendship project, the rise of con-tacts between the two countries was also connected with the legacy of the

Soviet liberation of Czechoslovakia (discussed in chapter 3), and included local celebrations of foreign culture, like the Siberian "Czech ball."

Taken as a whole, these new transnational contacts between the socialist countries amount to a little-examined soft-power side of the post-Stalinist Eastern bloc, which paralleled the more widely known military and economic alliances of the Warsaw Pact. This post-Stalinist version of socialist friendship succeeded in augmenting the bloc's cohesion on an everyday level. But it also inadvertently laid seeds that would eventually undermine the bloc's political stability, by revealing officials' continued fears over their citizens' contacts with foreigners, cultural differences between the bloc countries, and the superpower's decline as a political, economic, and cultural model for its satellites.

The evolution of socialist internationalism in the 1950s and 1960s was linked to—and yet distinct from—the more famous Soviet engagement with the West that occurred during the Khrushchev-era Thaw.[4] In both cases Soviet officials—like their counterparts on the other side of the Iron Curtain— employed transnational contacts as an integral part of their systemic struggle for supremacy in the Cold War.[5] Yet while the "government-sponsored opening to the West" ranks among the "unprecedented shifts" of the Thaw, as the previous chapters of this book have shown, the USSR had never been truly *closed* to contacts with Eastern Europe.[6] Thus while Soviet policy toward Eastern Europe changed dramatically after Stalin's death, it nevertheless operated on a continuum from the early postwar period.

The Soviets also had different goals for expanding contacts with the West than with Eastern Europe. Western contacts were instrumental. The Soviets wagered that cultural and scientific exchanges with the capitalist world would provide them with access to technology that they could use to "overtake" their ideological adversaries.[7] Contacts within the Eastern bloc were more utopian. Exchanges of people, cultures, and goods were supposed to help build a transnational socialist community, which would serve as both a counter to and competitor with the capitalist West. Socialist internationalism was a concept that governed relations between geographical neighbors and ostensible political allies. Ordinary citizens in the Soviet Union and its satellite states were thus permitted (and in fact encouraged) to engage in more intimate contacts across national borders within the Eastern bloc than they were with a distant and ideologically alien West.

Socialist Internationalism in the 1950s and 1960s

In the mid- to late 1950s and 1960s, the friendship project between the Soviet Union and Czechoslovakia underwent a dramatic transformation, which paralleled changes in international relations between the USSR and its other Eastern bloc satellites. Soviet-Czechoslovak friendship became more reciprocal (privileging exchange over Sovietization); more populist (encompassing the broad participation of "ordinary" citizens in both countries); and more modern (becoming intertwined with new practices of leisure and consumption). "The Soviet people have expressed a great interest in the life of the Czechoslovak people and display deep sympathy and friendship toward them," a librarian from Saratov claimed in 1960, using language that contrasted sharply with the Stalinist period. "They familiarize themselves with life in Czechoslovakia through newspapers, books, magazines, movies, theater performances, television programs, at exhibitions, on tourist trips, by corresponding and exchanging experiences with Czechoslovak friends, and so forth."[8] The librarian's comment illustrates how the Stalinist expectation that friendship required Czechoslovakia to imitate the Soviet model was gradually replaced by a new emphasis on mutual understanding. For the first time, not only was the superpower feted by its satellite, but the satellite was celebrated by the superpower.

Soviet officials explained this new reciprocity as stemming from Czechoslovakia's alleged transition to a mature socialist society.[9] "It was entirely natural, that in the first days after the introduction of the popular democratic system [the Communist Party of Czechoslovakia's (KSČ's) coup in February 1948] the Czechoslovak comrades, embarking on the construction of socialist culture, turned to the Soviet Union for help and advice," I. Volenko, the first secretary at the Soviet embassy in Czechoslovakia explained in the late 1950s. During the initial phase of Czechoslovakia's transition to socialism, he continued, cultural ties between the superpower and its new satellite were of necessity based on "acquainting Czechoslovak organizations, institutions, and individuals with the experience of the Soviet Union, on acquainting the Czechoslovak people with the USSR's cultural achievements. But soon these ties began all the more to assume the character of the mutual exchange of experience and cultural achievements."[10]

In reality, the Soviets' new approach to cultural relations with Czechoslovakia and the other countries of the Eastern bloc in the mid-1950s was the result of de-Stalinization in the USSR. Following Stalin's death, the Soviets began to trumpet reciprocity as the new hallmark of relations between the socialist countries.[11] With regard to the Eastern bloc, Soviet officials in the 1950s and 1960s claimed that they were creating "a new socialist type of international relations, [one that] exists on the basis of complete equality."[12] The Czechoslovak government supported this vision: according to the Czechoslovak embassy in Moscow, the goal of propaganda among socialist countries was "to facilitate rapprochement [*sbližování*] by broadening and deepening mutual knowledge of the past and the present."[13] Such optimistic declarations of equality were naturally intended to provide an explicit contrast to Western (especially American) Cold War foreign policy. But they also offered an implicit contrast to *socialist* international relations during Stalinism.

In 1961, Nikita Khrushchev defined "the world socialist system" as "a new type of economic and political relations between countries"—relations based on similar economies and political structures, Marxist-Leninist ideology, and the common goal of attaining Communism.[14] In the previous decade, the Eastern bloc countries' militaries and economies had become more closely integrated. In 1955, the Warsaw Pact was founded as the bloc's counterweight to NATO. In the late 1950s, the Council for Mutual Economic Assistance (founded in 1949) had taken further steps to coordinate the bloc countries' economies by constructing a pipeline that transmitted oil from the Soviet Union to its satellite states, and a unified electrical grid.[15] This military and economic integration was accompanied by a parallel project aimed at social convergence. The lives of ordinary Soviet and Eastern European citizens became increasingly intertwined through mass tourism, membership in friendship societies, pen-pal correspondences, cultural exchange, and the consumption of each other's mass media and consumer goods.

This "soft" integration had two goals: to create an autarkic, transnational, socialist community that would counter the West in the Cold War, and (especially after 1956) to function as a "carrot" to bolster Soviet power in an increasingly tumultuous Eastern Europe.[16] As Soviet actions in Hungary in 1956 and Czechoslovakia in 1968 demonstrated, the USSR continued to rely on hard power to maintain its hegemony in Eastern Europe after Stalin's death. But it also employed soft power to prevent cleavages in the bloc and to try to repair them when they did occur.[17]

A New Reciprocity

The new reciprocity in Soviet-Czechoslovak relations was signaled most clearly by two developments: in 1956, the countries signed their first bilateral cultural exchange agreement, and in 1958, the Society for Soviet-Czechoslovak Friendship (OSChD) was founded in Moscow.

On June 1, 1956, the Soviet and Czechoslovak governments signed an agreement pledging to further develop cultural relations between their countries. This agreement provided for direct contacts between Soviet and Czechoslovak cultural organizations, including both countries' creative unions (of writers, composers, artists, and filmmakers) and publishing houses.[18] In the Soviet Union, the Ministry of Culture and the Committee for Cultural Contacts with Foreign Countries were responsible for maintaining cultural exchanges with Czechoslovakia.[19] In Czechoslovakia, the Ministry of Culture, and its successor, the Ministry of Schools and Culture, oversaw cultural exchanges with the USSR. The 1956 agreement was significant for two reasons: first, it enshrined reciprocity as a cornerstone of the friendship project. For every visit by a Soviet cultural delegation to Czechoslovakia, there would be a similar trip by a Czechoslovak delegation to the USSR. Second, the agreement formalized and regulated cultural relations between the two countries.

The new, bilateral cultural relationship that developed between the Soviet Union and Czechoslovakia was based on annual exchange agreements, which detailed the specific Soviet and Czechoslovak theater groups, dance troupes, orchestras, and art exhibitions that would visit the other country. For instance, the 1958 Soviet-Czechoslovak cultural agreement stipulated that in the field of theater and music alone, the two countries would initiate at least four exchanges, involving puppet theaters, ballet troupes, and orchestras. The agreement was also notable for its geographic reach: exchanges were to take place not only between the capitals but also between Kiev and Bratislava, and the Krasnodar and Košice regions.[20] These new cultural exchange agreements were thus a dramatic shift from the Stalinist period, when Soviet cultural exports to Czechoslovakia had far outstripped Czechoslovak culture in the USSR. In the late 1950s, an official from the Soviet embassy in Prague boasted, "At the present time there is not a single area of culture, science, and art in which the most lively contacts between [our] two countries are not being conducted."[21]

The new reciprocity between the superpower and its satellite was further cemented in 1958 through the founding of the OSChD in Moscow. The society was one of eight founded in 1957–1958 by the Union of Soviet Friendship Societies (SSOD), which had replaced the All-Union Society for Foreign Cultural Ties (VOKS) the previous year as the main Soviet organization responsible for maintaining cultural contacts with foreign countries.[22] The very act of creating these friendship societies was intended to signal the new importance of personal contacts on a mass level in Soviet international relations.[23] VOKS had been responsible for administering cultural relations between Soviet and foreign (generally leftist) elites. By contrast, SSOD was supposed to be a populist organization, founded, according to its chairwoman, Nina Popova, on the initiative of "workers and collective farmers, cultural and scientific figures, writers and journalists."[24]

In the case of relations with Czechoslovakia, the OSChD was as an important symbol of the USSR's new commitment to bilateralism. In Czechoslovakia, two friendship societies with the USSR had been founded in the 1920s and 1930s. During the early postwar period, the absence of a sister friendship society in the USSR had served as an awkward reminder for Czechoslovaks about the limits of transnational friendship. When a Czech reader wrote to *Svět sovětů* (World of the Soviets) in 1947, inquiring why a similar organization did not exist in the USSR, the journal ostensibly turned to a Soviet veteran, who supplied the unconvincing explanation, "There is no Union of Friends of Czechoslovakia here because we are all friends of the ČSR [Czechoslovak Republic]."[25]

The OSChD's official mission was "the further development and strengthening of brotherly friendship and cooperation" with Czechoslovakia. Its goals included establishing cultural ties with the satellite state as well as familiarizing Soviet society "with the successes of the Czechoslovak people."[26] The society lobbied the Soviet media to expand coverage of Czechoslovakia, maintained contacts with a series of Czechoslovak social organizations (most importantly the SČSP [Union of Czechoslovak-Soviet Friendship]), helped organize Czech and Slovak language classes in the Soviet Union and the translation of literature from these languages, arranged events with visiting Czechoslovak cultural delegations, and planned celebrations throughout the USSR of important dates in Czechoslovak history.[27] By 1960, the society had branches in Moscow, Saratov, Stalingrad, Novosibirsk, and Irkutsk, as well as in the Soviet Socialist Republics of Ukraine and Georgia.[28]

The creation of the OSChD involved three different interest groups: lead-ing Soviet military, governmental, industrial, and cultural figures; people with a professional interest in Czechoslovakia; and ordinary citizens with a range of personal ties to the satellite state. The board of governors included luminaries such as Konstantin Vasil'evich Ostrovitianov, vice president of the Soviet Academy of Sciences; Roman Andreevich Rudenko, prosecutor gen-eral of the USSR; and Serafim Romanovich Zakharov, director of the Len-ingrad shoe factory Skorokhod.[29] These luminaries were presumably selected for the prestige and connections they would bring to the fledgling society, rather than for any deep personal ties to Czechoslovakia. In contrast, the 120 people SSOD invited to attend a founding meeting of the society included translators of Czech and Slovak; artists, writers, and factory workers who had traveled to Czechoslovakia; academics specializing in the country; Soviet foreign correspondents to Czechoslovakia; and political figures, including Valerian Zorin, the Soviet minister of foreign affairs, who had served as ambassador to Czechoslovakia from 1945 to 1947.[30] Finally, at a more popu-list level, the OSChD was inundated with letters from ordinary Soviet citi-zens who wanted to join. The majority of these people had personal ties with Czechoslovakia; many were veterans of the Soviet liberation in 1945. Boris Samoilovich Frenkel' wrote that as a soldier during the liberation of Prague, "I became acquainted with the wonderful, hardworking Czech people, who made a deep impression on me. Therefore, having learned about the Society for Soviet-Czechoslovak Friendship, my wife and I, lawyers by pro-fession, sustaining [*pitaia*] sincere feelings of love and respect for the Czech people, have decided to become members of the society, in order to make our modest contribution to the business of developing friendship between the Soviet and Czechoslovak peoples."[31] Other Soviet citizens requested membership in the OSChD as a way to continue personal contacts they had established with Czechoslovaks through pen-pal correspondences, mass tourism, medical and spa treatments in the satellite state, encounters at the 1957 World Youth Festival in Moscow, and friendships with exchange stu-dents in the Soviet Union.[32] A final category of letter writers professed a professional or scholarly interest in the satellite state.[33] Taken as a whole, these letters indicate that the new face of socialist internationalism in the Soviet Union was not simply a state-run project, projected from the top down, but was also a product of ordinary citizens' personal interests and expe-riences. This populist shift matched the new contours of the Soviet system under Khrushchev; the government became more responsive to its citizens' desires, while also making, in turn, "concerted efforts to reinvigorate mass political activism."[34]

The new bilateralism between the superpower and its satellite states after Stalin's death, with its accompanying emphasis on "citizen diplomacy,"[35] also found expression in the expansion of pen-pal correspondences between Soviet and Eastern bloc citizens. During the Stalinist period, the KSČ had seized on pen-pal exchanges as a way to inculcate Czechoslovaks—especially schoolchildren—in Soviet values and as evidence of the country's often-touted "great friendship" with the Soviet Union. The kind of correspondence the party envisioned, however, had more in common with articles in its dailies than with what we might think of as normal exchanges between friends. Pen-pal letters between Czechoslovaks and Soviets were often written collectively (for instance, by an entire class of schoolchildren) and, if not, were read aloud at schools or factories, thus ensuring that they were largely devoid of intimate or controversial details. The purpose of such correspondence was the mutual enforcement of socialist values. "We are happy for you that you are living well and joyfully. We want all children in the world to live as beautifully as we do, and we believe that day is coming," proclaimed one letter, written by a class of schoolchildren from Chelyabinsk, and held up as a model by Czechoslovak officials.[36] The KSČ's hopes that pen-pal correspondences would further friendship with the Soviet Union were, however, stymied by a lackluster Soviet response. In private, the party's functionaries complained that the Soviets did not respond adequately to their efforts to stimulate letter-writing campaigns. In 1950, for instance, Czech children sent 4,158 letters to Soviet schools, but only received a handful of replies.[37]

During the Thaw, the Soviet government began to actively promote pen-pal correspondences between its citizens and their counterparts in Czechoslovakia and the other satellite states. In a further change, individuals were now encouraged to become pen pals—in contrast not only to Stalinist practices but also to Soviet contacts with the West during this period.[38] Within a year after the OSChD's founding, it received 1,500 letters from Czechoslovaks and Soviets looking to correspond with each other.[39] That same year, the People's Russian Courses (LKR), the Czechoslovak network of Russian-language courses for adults, began teaching students to correspond with Soviet pen pals in Russian.[40] Requests for pen pals were also routinely published in each country's press.

The development of pen-pal correspondences—similar to the new contacts between Soviet veterans and Czechoslovak citizens in this period, described in chapter 3—revealed that ordinary citizens and Soviet and Czechoslovak cultural officials often interpreted transnational "friendship" very differently. "I would very much like to visit my friend, to get to know her and her family better, and also her Republic, even if only a little," Galia Kudriavtseva, a sixteen-year-old working on a collective farm in the Pskov region wrote to SSOD in 1959, seeking advice on traveling to Czechoslovakia. "I love her and she loves me as well, even though we have never seen each other."[41] Kudriavtseva's letter emphasized the personal nature of her correspondence: her primary reason for wanting to travel to Czechoslovakia was to meet her friend. Becoming acquainted with the country was an afterthought. SSOD's response to Kudriavtseva's letter and others like it was of necessity negative (before 1965, Soviet citizens were not allowed to travel abroad to visit people who were not relatives or to invite them to the USSR).[42] The agency's responses also show that Soviet cultural officials were less concerned with the development of intimate relationships across borders, and more with using pen-pal letters for educational or propaganda purposes at home. In response to a similar letter from another teenage girl, Pronin, the head of SSOD's department for the European socialist countries, lauded her political contribution, "It is very good that you are corresponding with a girl from Czechoslovakia. . . . Such a correspondence results in an even greater strengthening of friendship between our peoples [and] augments the strength of the entire socialist camp." Pronin suggested that the girl use information she had learned about Czechoslovakia from her pen pal to inform local collective farmers about life in the satellite state.[43]

As Soviet and Czechoslovak officials promoted private friendships between their citizens, they tried to influence them to match state goals. A Czechoslovak-produced handbook from the mid-1960s on corresponding with Soviets is a good illustration of the contradictions that resulted. The handbook served as both a Russian-language textbook (the overwhelming majority of pen-pal correspondences were conducted in Russian) and as an etiquette guide for pen-pal exchanges. Its authors argued that pen-pal correspondences should be more than "a formal affair [comprising] the exchange of a few greetings"; instead, they were to be "a source for the exchange of experience, a source of genuine friendship, and an important factor in fostering socialist internationalism."[44] Yet at the same time, the authors offered what was, in effect, a script for "genuine friendship," in the form of a series of stilted set phrases in Russian that correspondents could copy, covering topics ranging from international affairs ("Our whole country has experienced a magnificent event—the group flight of the Soviet cosmonauts") to Soviet-Czechoslovak friendship ("Soviet tourists are always welcome guests here") to personal interests and health ("I very much love music and have decided to learn to play the piano"; "We have all gotten over the flu. Mama got sick twice").[45]

The founding of the OSChD and the expansion of pen-pal correspondences between Soviet and Czechoslovak citizens exposed the limits of the new program for international socialist relations. In March 1958, SSOD decided—in a policy that extended to all the new friendship societies—that membership would only be considered on a collective basis. In other words, entire schools, factories, and institutes could join, but not individuals. Eleonory Gilburd has argued that the Soviet Union's engagement with the West in the mid-1950s "combined exuberant populism and information hierarchy, conspicuous new openness and gnawing suspicions."[46] These same contradictions emerged in socialist internationalism, evidence that even after Stalin's death, the countries of the socialist world continued to fear influences not only from the West but also from each other. "In corresponding with friends beyond the borders of our land, you must always keep in mind that our letters serve as our calling cards abroad," the Czechoslovak correspondence handbook warned would-be pen pals. "Therefore, pay increased attention to both the content and the formal aspect of your letters."[47]

Mutual Understanding through Magazines

In the 1950s and 1960s, the magazines *Sotsialisticheskaia Chekhoslovakiia* and *Svět sovětů* were two of the most important vehicles for promoting the friendship project to ordinary Soviet and Czechoslovak citizens. *Sotsialisticheskaia Chekhoslovakiia*, which was founded in 1953, was published in Russian and distributed in the USSR whereas *Svět sovětů* was published in Czech for readers in the Czech lands.[48] Remarkably, both magazines were produced in Czechoslovakia by the SČSP. This continued a pattern that had begun in the late 1940s: the Soviet government outsourced much of the production of pro-Soviet propaganda aimed at Czechoslovak citizens to

Czechoslovak organizations. The SČSP had far greater resources than the OSChD, which was, after all, only one of several friendship societies founded in the USSR in the late 1950s. The OSChD received relatively little financial support from the Soviet government and only employed two staff members. These factors also explain why the SČSP and the Czechoslovak embassy in Moscow produced the majority of the lectures, brochures, and articles that promoted Czechoslovakia to Soviet citizens in the 1950s and 1960s.[49]

Sotsialisticheskaia Chekhoslovakiia was not strictly designed for the Soviet reader alone: versions in English, German, and French promoted Czechoslovakia throughout the world. The Russian edition, however, differed from the others in more than just language. In addition to pieces on Czechoslovak politics, the economy, cultural events, and fashion, it also contained a section of letters from Soviet readers, Czech language lessons for Russian speakers, and articles on Czechoslovak-Soviet relations clearly written with Soviet audiences in mind. In 1964, *Sotsialisticheskaia Chekhoslovakiia* had a circulation of 87,500 in the Soviet Union, although the Czechoslovak Ministry of Foreign Affairs estimated that it was actually read by many more people, as readers commonly accessed it through libraries, rather than personal subscriptions, and shared copies with friends and neighbors. The ministry claimed the magazine was very popular and that only Soviet quotas prevented it from being more widely read.[50] This claim was backed up by Soviet readers' complaints that the magazine was often stolen from reading rooms.[51]

Svět sovětů, the magazine responsible for promoting Czechoslovak-Soviet friendship in the Czech lands, was first published by the KSČ in 1932.[52] It came out weekly, and in 1967 had a circulation of 300,000.[53] During Stalinism, it mainly served as a vehicle for praising all aspects of Soviet life. By the late 1950s, it became a socialist version of *Life* magazine, with oversize formats and glossy color photographs. On its pages, the poster children for Czechoslovak-Soviet friendship evolved from the shockworkers and ruddy peasants of late Stalinism to young women in bikinis, men on motorcycles, film stars, and cosmonauts. Articles highlighting the socialist "politics of peace" and Soviet (and Eastern bloc countries') technological and economic achievements were printed alongside features on youth, tourism, consumer goods, fashion, and cultural trends, as well as Russian lessons, and even the occasional Russian recipe.[54] The magazine's makeover was part of a broader trend in the Eastern bloc during this period, as heavy-handed socialist realist propaganda began to give way to more Western-style images promoting the socialist version of "The Age of Affluence."[55]

As *Sotsialisticheskaia Chekhoslovakiia* and *Svět sovětů* introduced readers to a foreign country, they sought to further the goal of transnational socialist friendship by creating a sense of intimacy with their readers. For instance, a popular feature in *Sotsialisticheskaia Chekhoslovakiia* called, "May I Introduce You?" (*Znakom'tes'*) highlighted the lives of "ordinary" Czechoslovaks. It profiled a different citizen in each issue (including a tour guide, student, actor, and housewife) and offered detailed descriptions of their daily activities. Soviet readers responded to such features by describing their relationship with the magazine as a form of friendship. A student at a pedagogical institute in Saratov attested, "When we open this magazine, flip through its pages, we feel something akin to meeting a dear, old friend, who tells you about [what has happened in] his life since the time of your last meeting, who informs you about his news, who talks with you, sometimes arguing, sometimes laughing cheerfully, sometimes sad, remembering the past, or somberly telling tales about the bitter days of the past war. His life becomes close to you, even though he lives in another country."[56]

The two magazines were part of a broader effort to encourage mutual understanding between Soviets and Czechoslovaks by teaching them about life in the other country. Quizzes and contests became an important part of this effort. In 1957, for instance, the SČSP held a quiz show on Czechoslovak state television called "How We Know the USSR." The contestants were workers from an automobile manufacturing factory in Prague, a pipe (*truboprakatnyi*) factory in Ústí nad Labem, and a metallurgical factory in Ostrava. For four nights they were grilled on their knowledge of three aspects of Soviet/Russian culture: "Leningrad-Moscow: centers of the Great October Socialist Revolution"; Pushkin's *Eugene Onegin*; and songs from Soviet films. The grand prize for the best display of Soviet cultural fluency was an all-expenses-paid, two-week trip to the Soviet Union. The runner-up received a Soviet-manufactured camera, and the third-place contestant a leather briefcase.[57] Not long after the quiz show aired, Soviet workers were invited to participate in their own contest, "To See Prague," organized by the trade unions. Contestants vied to win a trip to the Central European capital by answering a series of questions that tested their ideological maturity and knowledge of Czechoslovak geography, culture, and politics. Questions included: "Why is there no unemployment in Czechoslovakia?" "Which countries does Czechoslovakia border?" "Who among Czechoslovak schol-ars, artists, and sportsmen do you know?"[58]

The friendship magazines and the quizzes and contests linked the Soviet Union and Czechoslovakia into an "imagined" transnational, socialist com-munity.[59] This community was united by the goal of building Communism; the cult of the Red Army's liberation of Eastern Europe; the celebration of May Day and Victory Day; and membership in similar political, labor, and youth organizations. The pages of *Sotsialisticheskaia Chekhoslovakiia* and *Svět sovětů* advanced the idea that differences between the USSR and its satellite state were superficial, confined to such benign realms as geography, language, distant history, and cuisine.

By the 1960s, however, this patina of similarity began to wear off. Histo-rians have often argued that Eastern Europe functioned as a clandestine "window to the West" for Soviet citizens during this period: a halfway house for Western intellectual movements, cultural trends, and consumer goods, as well as a source of homegrown political reform.[60] In the context of Soviet-Czechoslovak relations, however, both countries' propagandists deliberately portrayed Czechoslovakia as a more cosmopolitan country than the USSR, with a more advanced consumer sector, in order to bolster support for the friendship project. *Sotsialisticheskaia Chekhoslovakiia* sought to attract Soviet readers by describing self-service shops in Prague, Czech-manufactured tex-tiles and furniture, and local big beat bands. The journal even included positive reviews of Miloš Forman's New Wave films, *Black Peter* (1964) and *Loves of a Blonde* (1965),[61] which at the time Soviet authorities considered un-suitable for release in the USSR.[62] Soviet readers' letters to the journal, ask-ing it to publish more information on interior design,[63] as well as on Czech pop stars and actors, dance, film, and books, are proof that they found these differences alluring.[64] Yet their interest did not necessarily translate into ac-ceptance of the official socialist internationalist project. The Russian writer and former dissident Sergei Iur'enen has recalled that during the mid- to late 1960s he never missed an issue of *Sotsialisticheskaia Chekhoslovakiia* because it included stories and excerpts from novels that were otherwise inaccessible in the Soviet Union. For him, though, this encounter with an alternative cul-ture actually became a way of envisioning an alternative political future. "Prague," he remembered, "was associated with freedom."[65]

In the mid-1960s, Czechoslovak officials confronted the problem of how to attract young people to the cause of friendship with the Soviet Union.[66]

"At the present time the generation that liberated Prague is dying out [*ukhodit*]," a Czechoslovak education minister warned a visiting Soviet delegation in 1966, "We need to think about passing on the revolutionary tradition, about the succeeding generation."[67] In response, *Svět sovětů* became hipper and more irreverent, publishing articles on what American men thought of Soviet women and on Czech big beat bands touring the Soviet Union, as well as features that ostensibly had little to do with advancing socialist friendship—for example, on Ernest Hemingway and on the James Bond movies. The magazine also began to include photographs of topless women and contests for trips not only to the USSR, but also to Cuba, France, and Scandinavia. Paradoxically, these changes at the magazine may have done more to foster nationalism than internationalism among its Czech readers. When readers wrote to the magazine inquiring whether Soviet women wore miniskirts, the subtext was whether they were as fashionable as women in Czechoslovakia.[68] An article entitled "The First Big Beat in the USSR" highlighted a tour of the Soviet Union by Karel Duba and his band, and predicted, slyly, that the performance of the lead singer, Josef Laufer, would impact Soviet audiences like a "bomb," as his "rhythmic movements and jumps . . . are unusual even for us."[69]

The Cultural Challenge

The expansion of Soviet-Czechoslovak cultural relations, which began with the first bilateral cultural exchange agreement the countries signed in 1956, also posed new challenges to the friendship project. The first challenge stemmed from the new geography of cultural relations in the socialist world. During Stalinism, the Soviet Union had been the main supplier of foreign culture to its satellite states, which maintained few cultural contacts with the West. In the mid- to late 1950s, however, both the Soviet Union and the Eastern bloc countries began to establish independent cultural relations with the Western capitalist countries as well as with the "developing countries" in Asia, Africa, and Latin America. By the late 1950s, the Soviet Union had established cultural relations with fifty-four countries.[70] The expanded scope of Soviet and Czechoslovak cultural contacts with foreign countries raises the question of what made the cultural side of the friendship project unique in this period.

Soviet cultural contacts with the West began on a small scale in 1955, and expanded dramatically in 1958, when the USSR signed cultural exchange agreements with the United States and Great Britain.[71] The travels of the celebrated Soviet violinist David Oistrakh illustrate the geographic shift in Soviet cultural diplomacy that occurred from the late 1940s to the mid-1950s, from the Eastern bloc to the capitalist West. In the first few years after the end of World War II, the Soviet authorities restricted Oistrakh's performances abroad to Eastern Europe. (He made visits to Czechoslovakia in 1946, 1947, 1949, and 1950.) His first postwar performance in a capitalist country was in Finland in 1950. It was only after Stalin's death that the Soviet authorities allowed Oistrakh to perform widely in Western Europe. In 1955–1956, he performed in the United States for the first time.[72]

The Czechoslovak government also began to (re)initiate cultural contacts with the West in the mid-1950s, and to allow greater Western influence in the domestic cultural scene. In 1955, for the first time since the coup, the Czechoslovak journal *Výtvarné umění* (Visual Arts) reprinted more images by Western artists than it did by artists from the Eastern bloc.[73] During the 1958 World's Fair in Brussels, the Czechoslovak government sent 262 employees from the Ministry of Consumer Industry to Belgium to study local industrial design and consumer culture.[74] Czechoslovak cultural contacts with the West expanded further in the aftermath of the 1962 Cuban Missile Crisis, in light of the superpowers' increased desire for peaceful cooperation. Čestmír Císař, the Czechoslovak minister of schools and culture at the time, later boasted that during this period, "Czechoslovakia and Prague once again appeared on the map of the world as a cultural region of international significance."[75] In the mid-1960s, the country became an important stop on the global cultural circuit by hosting international events such as a major UNESCO conference, the Second International Television Festival in 1965 in Prague, and the annual film festival in Karlovy Vary.[76]

By the 1960s, Western popular culture had gained a strong foothold in Czechoslovakia. Widespread access to television brought Austrian shows into Czech living rooms.[77] In 1965, a Radio Prague survey revealed the startling news that nearly 100 percent of ninth-graders admitted to listening to music programs broadcast by Radio Free Europe.[78] That same year, the American beat poet Allen Ginsberg visited Prague, and local students crowned him the "King of May." "Everywhere . . . 'big beat' is flourishing [and] Czechoslovaks are bowing before Western fashion," a disgruntled Czech artist complained to the Soviet embassy in Prague.[79]

This new, diverse cultural scene in Czechoslovakia harkened back to the more cosmopolitan atmosphere that had existed in the country in the interwar period, and again, briefly, during the Third Republic. In the early postwar years, access to Western culture had a deleterious impact on Czechoslovaks' interest in Soviet imports. In the 1960s, the revival of Western cultural imports had a similar effect: Czechoslovaks became increasingly reluctant to read Soviet books and to watch Soviet films and television shows. From 1962 to 1967, sales of all genres of Soviet literature, with the exception of textbooks and children's books, declined.[80] As the New Wave film movement revitalized Czechoslovakia's domestic film industry, and American, British, French, and Italian films became widely available, Soviet films became marginalized. In 1965, Western films in Czechoslovakia earned almost ten times more money than Soviet films.[81] By 1967, 51 percent of Czechoslovak viewers were watching Western films, while only 9.3 percent were going to Soviet movies.[82] Of all the forms of Soviet culture exported to Czechoslovakia in the 1960s, television shows fared the worst. In 1965, in order to counteract the influence of the Austrian television serials then popular in Czechoslovakia, the Soviet Union sponsored a week of Soviet television in the country in honor of the annual month of Soviet-Czechoslovak friendship. Viewers called the shows "boring," "mediocre," and "banal," and one added, damningly, "The most skillful enemy from the West could not have caused such harm to Soviet culture, in the eyes of the Czechoslovaks, as your own television programming."[83]

Officials at the Soviet embassy in Prague blamed the decline in interest in Soviet culture on Western competition and the failure of Soviet cultural organizations to tailor their exports to meet the specific needs of Czechoslovak audiences. Officials complained that Soviet cultural organizations "are not taking into consideration the changes going on in the political and economic life of the ČSSR [Czechoslovak Socialist Republic], and corresponding to this, are not changing their forms and methods of approach to distributing works of literature and film in the republic."[84] Notably, their anxieties echoed the complaints Czechoslovaks had made about Soviet cultural imports in 1945–1948, during the Third Republic, when they had protested that Soviet film and art were too ideologically tendentious and parochial to appeal to Czechoslovak audiences. The difference in the 1950s and 1960s was that Soviet officials worried that their country's cultural exports in Czechoslovakia had become too oriented toward *Western* audiences. Reports from the Soviet embassy in Moscow complained, for example, that Soviet soloists touring Czechoslovakia played too many works by Western composers, at the expense of those by Soviets or Czechoslovaks.[85] "The lack of success of our cultural actions in the ČSSR can be explained [by the fact] that our organizations are not taking into consideration the psychology of the Czechoslovak people, their traditions and habits," Stepan Chervonenko, the Soviet ambassador to Czechoslovakia, concluded in 1966.[86]

The geographic expansion of the USSR's foreign cultural relations during this period helps explain why Soviet theater troupes, ballet dancers, and musicians failed to tailor their repertoires to conform to the tastes of Czechoslovak audiences. After the Soviet Union began to engage in cultural exchange with the West on a broad scale in 1958, Czechoslovakia was rarely the primary destination of a Soviet cultural tour abroad. For logistical and financial reasons, individual Soviet performers or groups often stopped in the satellite state on their way to or from visits to the West or "the developing countries."[87] Czechoslovak officials in fact actively encouraged this practice as a way to boost the number of Soviet artists visiting their country. They urged the Soviet Ministry of Culture, for instance, to arrange for the Borodin Quartet to make a stopover in Czechoslovakia on its way home from a tour of West Germany, and for the Georgian ballet to do the same on its way back to the USSR from Latin America.[88] But the result of these new itineraries was that Soviet artists tended to give the same performances in Czechoslovakia as they did elsewhere abroad, and their cultural repertoires were often designed to appeal to Western audiences. The new global scope of Soviet cultural diplomacy thus increasingly came at the expense of the friendship project with Czechoslovakia.

The geographic expansion of socialist cultural relations was the first challenge that affected the friendship project after Stalin's death; the second challenge concerned the significance of socialist exchange at a time of rapid cultural change in both the superpower and its satellite. In the Soviet Union, the new culture of the Thaw, with its greater emphasis on the fate of the individual, diversity of artistic forms, and willingness to tackle previously taboo topics, challenged the monolith of socialist realism.[89] In Czechoslovakia, the New Wave film movement, avant-garde plays, and Alfréd Radok's Magic Lantern theater, which premiered at the Czechoslovak pavilion at the 1958 World's Fair in Brussels, represented a break from the didactic culture of the Stalinist years.[90] During Stalinism, Soviet cultural exports in Czechoslovakia had served a clear purpose: they were harbingers of the future, transmitters of socialist realism, and models for political development. After Stalin's death, culture evolved in both countries to become less explicitly ideological and more experimental and heterogeneous. The result was that the purpose of Soviet cultural exports in Czechoslovakia became less clear.

In Czechoslovakia, party officials who were opposed to cultural reform or liberalization began to look at Soviet cultural exports not as beacons of the radiant future, but as a firewall to protect against the threats posed by Western culture and domestic experimental movements in the arts. In 1963, Josef Urban, a representative from the Czechoslovak musical theater agency Pragokoncert, asked Soviet officials to send a dance collective to Czechoslovakia to "actively intervene in the composition of dance music [in Czechoslovakia]; to set dance culture along the correct channel." He hoped that the exchange of dance troupes between the USSR and Czechoslovakia would "cleanse" dance culture in Czechoslovakia of the "cacophony and the accretion of bourgeois culture," and would thus "ennoble and educate thousands of people in good taste."[91] The following year, in preparation for a Soviet art exhibition in Prague, Mikhail Zimianin, the Soviet ambassador to Czechoslovakia, reported that "The Czechoslovak comrades" were very anxious that the exhibit be a success because "socialist realist art in the ČSSR has many opponents." Zimianin further noted that officials at the Czechoslovak Ministry of Schools and Culture stressed "it was highly important for the exhibition of Soviet painting to be an outstanding event in the cultural life of Czechoslovakia [which would] help [our] friends in [their] struggle against abstractionism in the fine arts."[92] For Czechoslovak officials in the mid-1960s worried about their country's cultural gravitation toward the West, the Soviet Union had become a kind of anti–avant-garde: a source not of progress, but of obstruction.

While Czechoslovak hard-liners hoped that traditional Soviet dance and art might stem the pace of cultural change in their country, Czechoslovak youth and the intelligentsia were attracted by Soviet Thaw culture: iconoclastic young poets like Yevgeny Yevtushenko and Bella Akhmadulina, experimental theater troupes including the Sovremennik and the Taganka, and avant-garde jazz musicians like Konstantin Orbelian. When a lecturer from the Soviet Knowledge Society (*Znanie*) traveled to Czechoslovakia in 1964, locals bombarded him with questions about Alexander Solzhenitsyn's novel *One Day in the Life of Ivan Denisovich*, and the reception of other Thaw-era writers in the USSR, including Yevtushenko, Andrei Voznesensky, and Viktor Nekrasov.[93] When Orbelian and his twenty-member big beat band performed in Prague in 1966, a local newspaper review noted that "it is not easy to quickly win over the sympathies of Prague viewers, who are spoiled in part by the high level of our dance music. . . . It must be said, that the reception of the Armenian guests is a flattering demonstration of the fact that [they] achieved real success."[94]

Soviet Thaw culture also became incorporated into Czechoslovakia's own experimental cultural scene. In Prague, screenings of short films by the young New Wave feminist director, Věra Chytilová, were accompanied by local residents reading poems by Yevtushenko and Voznesensky.[95] The self-proclaimed "young intelligentsia's weekly," *Student*, founded in 1967, published articles praising the innovative qualities of the Soviet sculptor Ernst Neizvestny, the conceptual artist Ilya Kabakov, and the late author Mikhail Bulgakov (recommended as "a Soviet writer who is not studied in our schools"), even as it broadly criticized Soviet human rights policy.[96]

Reform-minded Czechoslovak intellectuals and officials sympathetic to their point of view complained that cultural organizations in the USSR largely excluded this more daring, experimental side of Soviet culture from official exchanges between the countries. In 1963, R. Klein, the cultural attaché at the Czechoslovak embassy in Moscow, complained to Soviet officials that while "our artists are strongly attracted to modernism," Soviet bookstores in Czechoslovakia only carried reproductions of paintings by the nineteenth-century painter Ivan Shishkin and other Russian artists "who have already long gone out of fashion."[97] On a trip to Czechoslovakia in December 1965, E. S. Romanova, the vice-chairwoman of the Foreign Commission of the Union of Writers of the USSR, heard frequent complaints from intellectuals that the Soviet Union was sending its leading cultural figures to the West, rather than the satellite state. "We followed in the French press what a success a group of your poets had in Paris. Staggering. But why, tell me, do you send such brilliant groups of poets [to the West], but you can't to us?"[98] Czechoslovak intellectuals accused the USSR of demonstrating a "disdainful relationship toward the export of Soviet culture to the socialist countries in general, in particular to Czechoslovakia." They complained, for instance, about the Sovremennik theater troupe's infrequent visits to their country.[99]

Romanova responded to these complaints condescendingly. When Czechoslovak writers told her poets like Voznesensky and Akhmadulina were the only Soviet literary figures likely to draw large audiences in their country "without special preparations," she admonished them for having too narrow a conception of contemporary Soviet literature. She explained that the poets in question had long ago been scheduled to visit other countries and that besides, "writers have to sit down at their desks at some point to write."[100] Soviet diplomats in Prague, who were more closely attuned to the situation in the satellite state than functionaries in the USSR, pleaded with the Central Committee to "implement our cultural relations policies [with Czechoslovakia] more flexibly and to respond more actively to the Czechoslovak intelligentsia's interest in this or that [Soviet] cultural trend." But their requests went largely unheeded.[101]

In the 1960s, Czechoslovak intellectuals, in addition to feeling sidelined by Soviet cultural policy, also expressed resentment at what they perceived as the Soviets' silence over their own experimental culture. The Soviets' reluctance to import Czechoslovakia's New Wave films emerged as a particular source of tension. During this period, Czechoslovakia's experimental films became famous around the world, yet Soveksportfil'm refused to purchase many of them, on the grounds that they were too risqué and too disconnected from socialist ideals.[102] In the mid-1960s, Soveksportfil'm only purchased between 30 percent and 50 percent of the total number of films offered by Czechoslovakia.[103] Even Soviet filmmakers warned that the failure to import New Wave films would have a negative effect on the USSR's relations with Czechoslovakia and on the USSR's broader struggle for cultural supremacy in the Cold War. In 1963, a group of Soviet filmmakers noted, "Czechoslovak films are shown widely on all the continents," and warned, "where we don't show interest and attention, others will. . . . Simple inattention can turn into serious errors in the ideological struggle."[104]

Soviet filmmakers and cultural officials lobbied the Committee for Cultural Contacts with Foreign Countries and the Ministry of Culture to broaden contacts with young Czech and Slovak filmmakers, playwrights, artists, and novelists, yet tended to couch these requests in imperialist language that belied the alleged equality in the post-Stalinist friendship project. After meeting with Chytilová in Prague in 1963, a group of Soviet filmmakers concluded condescendingly, "It seems to us that comradely discussions with V. Chytilová, serious critical analysis of her films, and lastly, simply attention to her [creative] quest, could help her grow into an important artist."[105] On her trip to Czechoslovakia in 1965, Romanova concluded that Soviet contacts with another young experimental Czech artist might benefit the friendship project—and the artist himself: "In Prague the playwright Václav Havel is said to be very talented. His second play, *The Memorandum* is being performed at the popular small theater 'Na zábradlí'—the play sharply satirizes bureaucratism with open hints [*namekami*] that this bureaucratism is propagated from on high. . . . Nonetheless, people in the [Czechoslovak Writers'] Union told me that it would be very useful to organize a trip for Havel to the Soviet Union—there is the chance that the trip could have a beneficial influence on him. He is truly exceptionally talented."[106]

In the Stalinist period, despite the restrictions that had existed in cultural relations between the Soviet Union and Czechoslovakia, the ideological significance of those contacts had been clear. After Stalin's death, the expansion of both countries' foreign cultural relations as well as the growth of new, experimental movements in the arts at home revitalized their respective domestic cultural scenes. At the same time, this revitalization posed new challenges to the friendship project.

The Price of Friendship

After Stalin's death, Soviet and Czechoslovak officials not only continued to grapple with challenges in cultural relations that had existed since the 1940s; they also faced a new test in the realm of consumption. In the mid-1950s, trade between the Soviet Union and the other socialist countries—touted in propaganda as evidence of friendship—expanded from a focus on raw materials and heavy industry to include consumer goods. Soviet citizens could now purchase overcoats from Czechoslovakia and Hungary, furniture from the Eastern bloc countries, and Chinese-made "bath towels, woolen and feather quilts, silk bedspreads, tablecloths and napkins and scarves."[107] In 1956, 70 percent of the Soviet Union's foreign trade was with the socialist countries, with 50 percent (of overall trade) coming from (in descending order) China, the German Democratic Republic, Czechoslovakia, and Poland.[108] Ten years later, a Czechoslovak government report noted that Soviet youth's main connection to the ČSSR was with Czechoslovak consumer goods, along with radio, television, film, music, sports, and tourism.[109]

Soviet and Czechoslovak officials embraced consumer culture to a surprising degree in their efforts to promote the friendship project. The trope of consumption as friendship is evident in the prizes offered to the winners of the magazine and TV contests held to test Soviets' and Czechoslovaks' knowledge of each other's country. Although the grand prize was always a trip to the USSR or Czechoslovakia, runners-up received Soviet- and Czechoslovak-made products, including Soviet cameras and leather goods and Czechoslovak electric grills and transistor radios.

Friendship propaganda in the 1950s and 1960s portrayed Czechoslovakia as a socialist consumer paradise. A 1961 article in *Sotsialisticheskaia Chekhoslovakiia* advised Soviet readers, "When you come to Prague, make sure you stop at the 'White Swan'!" The new, six-story department store was described gushingly as "filled from morning until night with the sound of a human stream," where "the sparkle of the glass display windows, the smell of leather, the rustle of nylon, the china, beckons, calls at you, draws you in, captivates [and] tempts you."[110]

In the 1960s, as Western culture became more prevalent in Czechoslovakia, so did Western consumer products. In Karlovy Vary, whose famous spas and proximity to West Germany made it a magnet for capitalist overtures, a West German firm held an exhibition of consumer goods, complete with a fashion show.[111] In Bratislava, the Italian company Cinzano organized vermouth tastings in the city's streets and squares, yet another example of what local Communists saw as how "troublesome the imperialists are with their propaganda."[112]

How could the Soviets compete with West German fashions and Italian spirits for the affections of Czechoslovak consumers—and ultimately, for their friendship? Czechoslovak officials suggested the only solution was for the Soviets to beat the West at its own game by promoting their goods more intensively. In response to the West German fashion show in Karlovy Vary, an SČSP official suggested that "it would be a great form of counterpropaganda" if the Soviets organized a similar exhibition in the city. He envisioned a grand array of Soviet-made consumer goods: "electrical devices, electric razors, the most recent transistors, cigarettes, chocolate, medical instruments, books, souvenirs, vodka, cognac, liquors, and so on," as well as a cafeteria serving Russian dishes such as pirozhki and borscht, and a fashion show. All this would demonstrate to the city's residents that "in the Soviet Union they put out [*vypuskat'*] goods for the population no worse than in the countries of the West."[113] To counteract the allure of Italian vermouth in Bratislava, friendship society officials reminded the Soviets that they had been waiting for "specialized" exhibitions of Soviet goods for three years, including exhibitions devoted to cosmetics and household appliances. "If we had asked this of the Americans . . . they would have sent us this material quickly," the director of the Soviet house of culture in Bratislava added bitterly.[114]

The Soviets' responses to these kinds of requests were stymied by disorganization and bureaucratic protocol. Just as in the Stalinist years Soviet officials had refused to adapt their films to align with the tastes of Czechoslovak viewers, in the 1960s they demonstrated an unwillingness (or inability) to tailor foreign trade to meet the needs of Czechoslovak consumers. Yet while in the Stalinist period this refusal to change Soviet films had stemmed from ideological conviction, in the 1960s Soviet officials' rejections of changes to trade with Czechoslovakia more likely stemmed from structural problems in the Soviet bureaucracy and economy. Officials from the USSR explained that while they were planning several upcoming exhibitions of "mechanical engineering" for Czechoslovakia, featuring Soviet manufactured products, such as cameras, they could only hold broader exhibitions of consumer goods like the kind imagined by the Karlovy Vary official once every several years. Furthermore, they preferred to organize exhibitions around a single type of product, such as furs, clocks, carvings from Dagestan, and Ukrainian ceramics.[115]

What explains the fact that consumerism became a key part of the project to construct a transnational, socialist community founded on anti-materialist ideals? The Cold War context is crucial for beginning to make sense of this contradiction. As the competition between the blocs became centered on the question of which system could provide a higher standard of living and better access to consumer goods, governments across Eastern Europe attempted to gain their citizens' loyalty—and ward off rebellion—by improving consumption.[116] Both the Soviet and Czechoslovak governments thus promoted consumer goods from the other country not only to benefit the Eastern bloc economy as a whole but also to provide their citizens with ideologically acceptable alternatives to Western products.

The Soviets, for instance, tried to offset the impact of the most famous Cold War consumer challenge from the West—the 1959 American National Exhibition in Moscow—by hosting a simultaneous exhibition of Czechoslovak glass creations. A Czechoslovak newsreel about the event showed crowds of well-dressed Soviet citizens admiring vases, wineglasses, and chandeliers in "classical and modern" styles, and boasted that the "entire Soviet Union" had exclaimed, "Your exhibition is a thousand degrees better than the American one. Good job Czechs!"[117] This self-congratulatory statement was of course hyperbole. Before the exhibition had even opened, František Krajčír, the Czechoslovak minister of foreign trade, had privately warned, "It is not possible to compare our narrow specialized exhibition with a general exhibition of the USA's modern technology." He set a more prosaic goal: "acquainting the broad public with the importance of glass and glass products for raising the cultural and living standards of the people in the socialist community."[118] Nonetheless, the symbolism of the dueling exhibitions was important. Susan Reid has argued that both the U.S. and the Soviet authorities framed the American National Exhibition as a contest between systemic values: freedom as exemplified by individual enrichment and consumer choice, versus freedom as the satisfaction of basic needs in a welfare state. Many of the Soviet visitors to the exhibition, rather than be dazzled by the pots and pans and cars on display, as the Americans had expected, defended the Soviet system as a "different model of consumer society that included collective consumption, welfare, and social justice."[119] Within this framework, the tendency of the Soviet and Czechoslovak governments to promote each other's products as evidence of their "great friendship" makes more sense. As Reid argues in another article, "In modern Soviet society consumption was . . . a symbolic as much as an instrumental activity."[120] The same was true for Cold War consumer competition: much more was at stake than the production of specific goods. Both superpowers, for example, claimed to want to provide their citizens with vacuum cleaners and washing machines. What mattered was what these goods symbolized about their respective political systems. As Krajčír suggested, Czechoslovak products were supposed to be indicative of "raising the cultural and living standards of the people in the socialist community." Thus, for Soviet citizens, these products—unlike those from capitalist countries—were nonthreatening and could theoretically be admired (or procured) guilt free.

For Czechoslovakia, commercial trade with the USSR became a means of national self-definition and of reversing Stalinist hierarchy. "Perhaps the most famous [products] in the Soviet Union are Czechoslovak shoes," *Svět sovětů* reported in 1961. "You ask about Czechoslovak products?" the manager of a Minsk department store replied to the reporter, "When we receive a new shipment of shoes from Czechoslovakia we already know from the start that there will be a line [for them]. And textiles. Take a walk around the city in the evenings, or on Sundays. Look at the children. If you see them wearing clothes that you like, they are definitely from Czechoslovakia. Czech furniture? No one is sorry to wait in line. . . . We often tell our workers from the textile and shoe factories: 'You should take this as a model. All the more because it's from a friend.'"[121]

A Czechoslovak reporter who traveled to Moscow in 1964 noted Soviet praise for the shoes, dresses, stockings, candy, and sewing machines manufactured in her country, as well as the popularity of the Czech restaurants Praga and Plzeň, as evidence of the "great friendship" between Czechoslovakia and the USSR.[122] The magazine also reported with obvious pride that Soviets stopped "randomly" on the street in the USSR in 1966 and quizzed about their knowledge of Czechoslovakia gave positive reviews to Czechoslovak shoes, cosmetics, perfume, undergarments, and glassware.[123]

The Czechoslovak press claimed that friendship through consumption worked both ways. One article described the ubiquity of Soviet products in Czechoslovaks' daily lives: "We eat Soviet canned fish, we bake pastries from Soviet flour, we read Russian books and magazines, we shave with the 'Kharkov' razor, in the evening we sit down before the television 'Temp' and on Sundays we head out for rides in the gleaming [car] 'Moskvich.'" Among the most common Soviet products in Czechoslovakia were cameras, wristwatches, and televisions. There was even a club for Czechoslovak owners of Soviet cars, where they exchanged experiences with Soviet owners of the same models.[124]

The conflation of socialist internationalism with consumption eventually proved problematic for the Soviet Union and Czechoslovakia, although in different ways. In the post-Stalin era, the Soviet government struggled to find a balance between attempting to satisfy its citizens' growing desires for consumer goods and preserving some semblance of the ascetic ideals of the Bolshevik revolution.[125] Its task was no less difficult in the case of relations with Czechoslovakia. Soviet officials walked a fine line between promoting Czechoslovakia's new department stores, for instance, and reducing the image of the "brother country" to one of them. Beyond the glossy pages of *Sotsialisticheskaia Chekhoslovakiia*, encounters between Soviets and Czechoslovaks during this period, especially on tourist trips, were often characterized by illegal, or semilegal exchanges of goods, which took place without the patina of strengthening socialist friendship. Soviet speculators frequently approached Czechoslovak tourists in the USSR with offers to purchase their personal effects, such as shoes, sweaters, and women's blouses.[126] Meanwhile, Soviet tourists in Czechoslovakia were routinely caught selling their watches and transistor radios to locals in order to obtain more foreign currency to buy Czechoslovak goods.[127] For some Soviet citizens, Czechoslovakia's greatest allure became the superior range of products available.[128]

For Czechoslovak officials, the friendship through consumption model raised a different set of problems. After World War II, Czechoslovak citizens' support for the Soviet Union had been based on the promise of egalitarian socialism. By the mid-1960s, as the Czechoslovak government began to enact the economic and political reforms that eventually became the basis for the Prague Spring, many citizens ceased to view the Soviet Union as the vanguard of a socialist society. This, combined with the fact that Czechoslovaks now had access to an array of products from both sides of the Iron Curtain, raised the question of how the Soviet Union could ever compete for their friendship on the sheer quality of its consumer goods alone. Even official Czechoslovak publications did not bother to pretend that Soviet consumer items were more popular than local products or those from other countries. A *Svět sovětů* article readily admitted, for instance, that there were problems with the finish on "the gleaming" Moskvich cars and that Soviet televisions sold poorly compared to Czechoslovak brands. While Soviet cameras were not bad, the German Zeiss brand was at least as good, and also available.[129] As a result, the advantages to consuming Soviet, as opposed to Western products, were primarily political. In honor of the fiftieth anniversary of the October Revolution in 1967, Soviet products were featured at the White Swan department store in Prague. Czechoslovak officials exhorted their citizens to purchase these products, not because of their inherent value or quality, but as a token of their gratitude toward the USSR for its contribution to the existence of the Czechoslovak state.[130] Consuming Soviet products thus became a patriotic performance not unlike "Buy American" campaigns (although aimed at bolstering a transnational, rather than a domestic community)—an act of citizenship in a broader socialist world.

Friendship's New Frontiers

The friendship project expanded and modernized after Stalin's death. The establishment of the OSChD and the circulation of *Sotsialisticheskaia*

Chekhoslovakiia and *Svět sovětů* involved greater numbers of ordinary Soviet and Czechoslovak citizens in socialist internationalism. The new cultural exchange agreements between the two countries, and the trade of consumer goods, highlighted a new reciprocity and a new vitality in Soviet-Czechoslovak relations. At the same time, these expanded contacts revealed fears that both countries had about foreign influences—even from friends. Paradoxically, as the Soviet Union and Czechoslovakia expanded cultural contacts with the West and developed more experimental cultural scenes at home, the ideological significance of the friendship project became less clear. The friendship project would soon face an even greater threat, as Czechoslovakia embarked on a series of political reforms, culminating in the 1968 Prague Spring.

Chapter 5

Tourists on Tanks

It is very alarming, after chanting slogans about eternal friendship over
and over, how small in fact our intimate knowledge of each other is.

—*Svět sovětů*, March 1968

In a 1967 interview, Jan Zelenka, editor of the popular Czechoslovak magazine *Květy* (Flowers), and the Soviet ambassador to Czechoslovakia, Stepan
Chervonenko, discussed the current state of relations between their countries.
Zelenka argued that despite the long history of Czechoslovak-Soviet friendship,
"a space for human relations" was still missing. He suggested that tourism
was one of the areas in which this new space might be created.[1]

Of all the new forms of exchange between the USSR and Czechoslovakia
that developed after Stalin's death, mass tourism offered the greatest number
of people from each country the opportunity to meet in person.[2] Tourism
was supposed to advance rapprochement between the countries by emphasizing their political and cultural similarities. Yet, as Zelenka went on to
complain in the 1967 interview, the structure of tourism, whereby Soviet
and Czechoslovak participants were forced to join carefully planned pack-
aged tours organized by the state travel agencies Intourist and Čedok, was
"over-organized" and "too confined by defined boundaries." He argued that

given the depth of friendship between Czechoslovakia and the USSR, "tourism between our countries [should be] much more."[3]

Zelenka's remarks are indicative of how, in the mid-1960s, Czechoslovak and Soviet citizens began to openly chafe against the bureaucratic, formal structure of both tourism and the broader friendship project between their countries. They drew on friendship propaganda to argue that the goal of tourism should be more than merely to introduce travelers to famous landmarks. Instead, tourism should become a means for the citizens of the superpower and its satellite to truly get to know one another by making new friendships or strengthening existing ties. In 1965, Soviet officials did make some changes to the structure of tourism, but in general they proved resistant to allowing more casual, spontaneous forms of travel.

In 1968, the Prague Spring experiment in reform socialism dramatically disrupted the staid script governing tourism between the Soviet Union and Czechoslovakia—as well as the broader friendship project. Czechoslovak travelers, journalists, and government officials built on the reform movement's broader goals of creating a less bureaucratic and more "human" form of socialism, to argue for less regulated, more individual forms of tourism with the USSR. They believed that reforming tourism would thus help to reform the broader Czechoslovak-Soviet alliance, from the current system of "official, cold, 'delegation' friendship," to one based on "close, individual [friendships]."[4]

Not only did the rhetoric about tourism change during the Prague Spring, so did the experiences of Soviet and Czechoslovak tourists. In 1968, Soviet tourists to Czechoslovakia became eyewitnesses to the reform movement that their government tried to conceal from them. Czechoslovak tourists to the Soviet Union became missionaries, proselytizing the political changes in their country. Czechoslovak journalists wrote travel articles about the USSR that exposed the hypocrisy of friendship propaganda by emphasizing the poverty and backwardness they encountered; as a result, they undermined the Soviet Union's position as the vanguard of the international Communist system. Tourism thus became a reflection of the larger political tensions that rocked Soviet-Czechoslovak relations in 1968; but in the process, it also inadvertently became a means for citizens of both countries to try and shape the broader friendship project.

On the night of August 20–21, 1968, the Soviet government launched a massive invasion of Czechoslovakia to crush the Prague Spring. Yet in the following months, tourism between the countries continued: it became a way for Soviet officials to try to restore friendship with the wayward satellite, and for Czechoslovaks to demonstrate against the invasion. The Soviet government selected tourists on the basis of their political reliability and instructed them to explain the official rationale for the invasion to locals they met on their travels. On the Czechoslovak side, officials in the tourism industry and other citizens who came into contact with Soviet tourists protested the invasion by openly critiquing the Soviets' actions and by adding sites highlighting the damage caused by the military intervention to the tourists' itineraries.

While the friendship project was thus severely tested during the Prague Spring and the initial post-invasion period, it also became more honest and intimate. During the Prague Spring, Soviet tourists and their Czechoslovak hosts engaged in wide-ranging debates about politics and the future of their countries' alliance—debates that were unprecedented in over twenty years of friendship. These debates continued even after the invasion, in the fall of 1968 and throughout 1969. In what was otherwise the nadir of the friendship project, tourism thus become an unlikely space for "human relations" in the empire of friends.

The Structure of Tourism

Tourism between the Soviet Union and Czechoslovakia began in 1955, the same year that the Soviet government initiated agreements on tourism with the other European socialist countries. In the mid- to late 1950s, between 7,800 and 11,000 Soviet tourists traveled to Czechoslovakia annually. In the following decade, these numbers more than doubled; in 1967, for example, 29,900 Soviet tourists visited the satellite state.[5] Similar numbers of Czechoslovaks visited the USSR. In 1961, 24,000 Czechoslovak tourists were projected to travel to the Soviet Union.[6] Four years later, the number had risen to 30,000.[7]

According to a joint protocol issued by the Soviet and Czechoslovak trade unions in 1965, the foremost goal of tourism between their countries was "broadening contacts and strengthening brotherly friendship between the trade unions and the workers of the USSR and the Czechoslovak Socialist Republic."[8] Tourism offered Soviet and Czechoslovak citizens the opportunity to learn about each other in more detail than other forms of post-Stalinist exchange, such as the circulation of friendship publications and the trade of consumer goods. In 1958, a Soviet tourist to Czechoslovakia framed his travels in revelatory terms, "I went to that country as a tourist, acquainted with it from books, the stories of comrades, newspapers, and magazine articles. I returned a sincere friend of that country, its people."[9] In the early years of Soviet-Czechoslovak tourism, some tourists did find their trips eye-opening. But more typically, tourism operated according to a staid script, which served to reinforce existing tropes of the friendship project—most importantly, the idea that the development of socialism in both countries would foster mutual understanding. In the mid-1960s, as Czechoslovakia embarked on the reforms that would culminate in the 1968 Prague Spring, this script was upended and tourism truly became a revelatory experience for citizens of the superpower and its satellite.

This chapter is weighted toward the experiences of Soviet tourists in Czechoslovakia, because the relevant archival records on Czechoslovak tourists to the Soviet Union, from Čedok, the Czechoslovak state travel agency, and the Revolutionary Trade Union Movement (ROH) are unavailable. My analysis of Soviet tourism to Czechoslovakia is largely based on reports filed by the leaders of tour groups who traveled under the auspices of the USSR's trade unions' Tourism Councils, and Sputnik, the Komsomol's travel agency. The tourists who traveled with these agencies came from across the Russian Soviet Federative Socialist Republic (RSFSR) and from every republic in the USSR.

It is difficult to determine the social makeup of Soviet tour groups to Czechoslovakia because most of the trip reports only provide information on the tourists' geographic origins. Anne Gorsuch, in her study of Soviet tourism to the Eastern bloc in the mid- to late 1950s and early 1960s, concludes that the majority of Soviet tourists were members of the technical and creative intelligentsia, including "academics, cultural workers, factory managers, party functionaries."[10] Zbigniew Wojnowski classifies Soviet travelers to the Eastern bloc as "the Soviet aspirational middle class."[11] The notion that Soviet foreign tourism was predominantly the domain of the well-educated and relatively well-to-do makes sense because Soviet tourists paid for their trips, and they were expensive. For instance, as Diane Koenker has noted, in 1960, the cost for a twelve-day Soviet tour to Czechoslovakia leaving from Moscow was 1,250 rubles; roughly 50 percent more than a Soviet worker's average monthly wage, which was 800 rubles.[12] The trip reports on tours to

Czechoslovakia that do specify the tourists' professions corroborate Gorsuch's contention that most were white-collar workers.[13]

Foreign travel was also a privilege in Soviet society reserved for the politically reliable. A prospective tourist thus encountered a complex application process. Applicants first had to apply to their trade union or Komsomol cell, which forwarded their applications on to the regional (*oblast'*) level. Among the documents they had to submit were character references, personal questionnaires, and medical forms.[14] Each Soviet tour group abroad also included a trip leader, who was often a party or Komsomol member or a trade union activist. These people were expected to be more politically conscious than the tourists they led; in some cases they even held positions in the city or regional party branches. In Vologda, RSFSR, candidates for trip leader for tours run through the local Tourism Councils were selected from local managers (*khoziaistvenniki*) and trade union leaders twenty days prior to the date of departure, and were then interviewed by the Trade Union Council before being confirmed by the union's presidium. Before going abroad, the trip leaders participated in preparatory "discussions" with the tourists, run by the trade unions.[15]

The trip leader was responsible for writing a final report about the group's experiences abroad, which was sent on to the organization responsible for organizing the tourist excursion. Such reports provide a range of information. In 1965, for instance, leaders on Sputnik trips to Czechoslovakia were asked to address the following points in their reports: a day-by-day account describing how the trip's "program" was fulfilled, an assessment of the work of the local guide/translator, the organization of accommodation and food, the organization of transport, critical remarks and suggestions relating to the composition of the group, and general conclusions about the trip itinerary and activities.[16] Not all reports responded to all these questions, however, and their styles vary, from brief lists of daily activities to more detailed accounts that sometimes read like guidebooks with long descriptions of all the sights seen.

One of the limitations of the trip leaders' reports is that their authors presumed to speak for the experiences of the entire group, even though they held positions of authority over the other tourists.[17] This discrepancy may account for some of the pro-Soviet political and cultural views expressed in the reports. In addition, trip leaders, like other people who wrote to the Soviet authorities, had to be cautious of the views they expressed, both to avoid getting into trouble, and to ensure that they would not lose the privilege of being able to travel abroad in the future. As Gorsuch has noted, "Each trip leader had to fulfill the multiple, and sometimes untenable, roles of cultural guide, political leader, and informant."[18] As I try to show in this chapter, there was a large variation in trip reports about Soviet tours to Czechoslovakia, particularly in the period after the invasion, despite the fact that at that time the tourists were supposed to have been better prepared politically than in previous years.

In Search of the Familiar

A 1963 guidebook to Karlovy Vary, the historic spa town in Czechoslovakia, advised Soviet tourists, "A tour of the city-resort usually begins from V. I. Lenin square. This square is located several hundred meters from the hotel 'Moscow.' In the center of the square is the hotel 'Central' where in 1936 the writer Aleksei Nikolaevich Tolstoi and his wife lived."[19] Why did the guidebook portray this Central European city, where European luminaries such as Johann Wolfgang von Goethe and Edward VII had taken the waters, as so Soviet? In an article on Soviet domestic tourism in the postwar Stalinist period, Gorsuch argues that the Soviet government used tourism as a form of nation-building. Travel to the different republics, familiarization with the local terrain, and visits to sites of socialist achievement were supposed to transform Soviet tourists into patriots. The title of her article, "There's No Place Like Home," sums up the feelings of pride in one's homeland and sense of superiority that Soviet tourism was supposed to inspire. Gorsuch argues, "Postwar tourism was decidedly not about forming 'new impressions' but about internalizing official ones." Quoting Linda Ellerbee, she describes Soviet domestic tourism under Stalin as a "'ritual of reassurance.'"[20]

This description appears to fit the Soviet tours of Czechoslovakia designed jointly by Intourist and Čedok. In addition to the country's traditional landmarks and natural wonders, such as the Prague castle and the Macocha gorge near Brno, itineraries highlighted sites with Russian/Soviet associations, such as Soviet war memorials and cemeteries, the Vladimir Lenin museum in Prague, the house where Maxim Gorky had lived in Mariánské Lázně, and the bust of Peter I in Karlovy Vary. Soviet tourists were frequently billeted in hotels named after Soviet cities. For entertainment they attended dinners with Czechoslovak comrades in honor of significant occasions in Soviet life such as Nikita Khrushchev's seventieth birthday or performances of Russian ballets.[21]

By attempting to make the foreign feel familiar, Soviet tourists' itineraries in Czechoslovakia might appear to have been designed to augment the USSR's imperial aspirations in its satellite state—to prove that contemporary Czechoslovakia was developing in accordance with the Soviet model. A report by the leader of a Soviet tour group from the Moscow region exclaimed, "The wonderful stadiums, parks, and stores [in Prague] reminded us of the capital of our homeland, and the river Vltava—of our native Moscow River."[22] Yet such statements about the similarities between the two countries were also a common feature in contemporaneous Czechoslovak travel writing about the Soviet Union. The author of a 1964 travel article about Kiev, for instance, stressed how much the Ukrainian capital reminded her of Prague. Her explanation for this alleged similarity emphasized the theme of rapprochement. The correspondence between the two cities was "clear proof that our brother countries are close to each other not just in the figurative sense of the word."[23] Another Czechoslovak travel article, tellingly titled "A Variation on a Prague Theme," described how the streets of Vilnius, in Soviet Lithuania, resembled Prague's Old Town. "This illusion was so strong, that we would not have been taken aback if we had suddenly heard a passerby speaking Czech. We felt so immensely good here, almost like at home, where, as the proverb says, it is best."[24]

These examples show that the theme of similarity between the two countries was more than a Soviet imperialist trope. The idea that Soviet tourists felt at home in Czechoslovakia and that Czechoslovak tourists experienced a similar sensation in the USSR was supposed to serve as proof of the countries' great friendship. Travelers' accounts extolling the similarity between the Soviet Union and Czechoslovakia thus mirrored official goals for Soviet-Czechoslovak relations in the 1950s and 1960s by deemphasizing cultural and political differences. Instead, these accounts stressed the unifying power of socialism.

In Search of "Socialist Czechoslovakia"

Tourism was supposed to bolster the friendship project. Yet, even before the political upheaval of the Prague Spring, it unwittingly exposed tensions between nationalism and internationalism that threatened the project's viability. A recurrent source of friction between the Soviet tourists and Czechoslovak tourist agencies was the inclusion of landmarks from Czechoslovakia's pre-socialist past in Soviet tourists' itineraries, particularly churches and castles. A trip leader from Arkhangelsk protested, "The group wasn't as interested in the life of barons who lived 200–300 years ago, who even many people in Czechoslovakia don't know much about, as they were in the contemporary life in this country: how people work, spend their leisure time, how workers study, what their interests are."[25] A group from Kemerovo complained that their Czech guides had taken them to see too many churches and monasteries, where they were shown "dried out corpses of priests." They also objected when their guide in Prague, a member of the local trade union, suggested taking them to see the city's Jewish cemetery instead of the Lenin museum.[26] "We are interested in modern [life], not religious-church [*bogomol'no-kostël'naia*] Czechoslovakia, but socialist Czechoslovakia," a trip leader from Lipetsk wrote in his report to Sputnik.[27] Soviet officials appealed to Čedok to show Soviet tourists more sites associated with "socialist Czechoslovakia," such as industrial enterprises, cooperatives, and new housing.[28]

Soviet tourists' complaints about being shown too many castles and churches in Czechoslovakia might appear ideologically motivated, evidence of the tourists' strong socialist values. Yet in the USSR, the Soviet government had preserved Romanov palaces as museums for the public after the Bolshevik Revolution.[29] Similarly, in Czechoslovakia after 1948, the socialist government transformed castles and aristocratic homes into public museums precisely to educate citizens about the corrupt old order.[30] It is thus likely that Soviet tourists' complaints about their exposure to Czechoslovakia's historic landmarks were grounded less in socialist convictions than in imperialist sentiments. Friendship propaganda portrayed life in Czechoslovakia before and after the Soviet liberation of Czechoslovakia in 1945 and the Communist coup three years later as a binary between feudalist/capitalist repression and socialist progress.[31] For Soviet tourists, visits to cultural landmarks in Czechoslovakia that had been constructed centuries before the liberation thus challenged their preconceived notions about backwardness and progress before and after 1945—as well as their confidence in Soviet superiority. The churches and castles that they were shown belonged to the unique history of the Czech lands and Slovakia, and predated any Russian/Soviet contacts. The controversy over the inclusion of these landmarks in Soviet tourists' itineraries thus highlights the ongoing struggle between Soviet and Czechoslovak forms of nationalism that continued to lurk beneath rhetoric of international friendship after Stalin's death. In the 1960s, as Czechoslovakia grew more politically independent from the Soviet Union, Soviet-Czechoslovak tourism increasingly became a battleground between competing visions of national and transnational identity.

A "More Civilized" Country

Not all Soviet travelers to Czechoslovakia were upset to discover that friendship propaganda about "rapprochement" masked important differences between the countries. For some tourists and other long-term visitors to the satellite state, it was in fact Czechoslovakia's political and cultural differences from the Soviet Union that made it an attractive destination. Their accounts of life in Czechoslovakia tended to praise what Gorsuch calls "the 'cultured' behaviors of modernity that had long been positively associated with the 'West,'"[32] such as the cleanliness of cities and villages, the orderliness and politeness of the Czechoslovak people, and the attention given to the aesthetic environment. Tourists' praise for such qualities serves as another example of how the Stalinist hierarchy of Soviet superiority and Czechoslovak subordination was partially reversed after Stalin's death. This praise also functioned as an implicit critique of life in the Soviet Union. A Soviet architecture student who traveled to Czechoslovakia in the summer of 1956 suggested that there was much that Soviet citizens could learn from the satellite, "above all . . . the organization and culture of production, the care for natural resources, relations to national traditions and architectural monuments, refined aesthetic tastes and [knowledge of] foreign languages."[33] Another Soviet tourist who traveled to Czechoslovakia around the same time noted, "The first thing that struck me were the roads. Wonderful, asphalted roads . . . lined with fruit trees." She described Czechoslovakia as a more humane country than the Soviet Union, noting that in parks, unlike at home, no one tried to attack the squirrels and birds, and children even fed them.[34] When the director of a high school in Kherson returned home from a trip to Czechoslovakia in 1962, she gave a public lecture praising "the cleanliness and orderliness in the cities and villages of Czechoslovakia, the upbringing of children, people's honesty, the high culture of manufacturing and trade."[35]

The impressions of Soviet expatriates in Czechoslovakia in the 1950s and 1960s provide another lens to evaluate how Soviet citizens viewed the satellite state. During this period, Czechoslovakia was home to a small "colony" of Soviet expatriates, including embassy officials and trade representatives, foreign correspondents, the staff of the Soviet journal *Problemy mira i sotsializma* (Problems of Peace and Socialism), and Soviet citizens married to Czechoslovaks. Many of these expatriates also judged Czechoslovakia to be more "cultured" than the USSR. In 1957, El'vira Filipovich (the young Soviet woman mentioned in chapter 2, whose romance with a Czech student had been imperiled by the 1947 marriage law), moved to Czechoslovakia with her husband Ivo and their young daughter. Filipovich described her arrival in Prague in her diary: "It was already evening but there were so many lights on everywhere! We walked down a broad street. On this street there were stores and display windows in practically every building, like I never saw in Moscow. The mannequins stood as if they were alive: women, men, and children. The clothes they wore were fashionable, beautiful." Her daughter was "unable to tear herself away" from the window displays of children's clothing. But it was not only the consumer culture in Prague that impressed Filipovich; she was also amazed by the Czechs' good manners and cheer, as well as by how attentively they followed rules, "Everyone on the street was well-dressed, and they were all smiling, even though today is a workday. They follow the traffic rules very carefully: they cross [the street] only on the green light. I was about to go on the red, but Ivo grabbed me by the hands [and said] 'that's not polite here, look, people wait.'"[36] Vladlen Krivosheev recalled how Czechoslovakia felt like another world compared to the USSR when he worked as a correspondent for the Soviet newspaper *Izvestiia* (News) in Prague in the mid-1960s. "I fell in love with Prague and Czechoslovakia right away. It was a magnificent country; everything was beautiful and clean. I was struck by the contrast with the gloomy Soviet environment." He mocked the slogans used to propagandize the Soviet Union in Czechoslovakia, "'The Soviet pencil—our model.' 'The Soviet restaurant—our model.' I had to laugh. To compare the magnificent Czech restaurants with their [refined] dining culture with the Soviet variety was a bad joke."[37]

Chapter 4 described how friendship propaganda in the 1960s deliberately portrayed Czechoslovakia as having a more cosmopolitan cultural scene and a more advanced consumer sector than the USSR. This portrayal was meant to attract Soviet citizens to the friendship project, while instilling national pride in Czechoslovaks. Accounts by former Soviet expatriates provide a different perspective on Czechoslovakia as a "Window on the West":[38] they contend that life in the satellite state expanded their political imaginations and their ideas about what constituted a "civilized" society. This was especially true for the staff of *Problemy mira i sotsializma*, which was founded by the Communist Party of the Soviet Union (KPSS) in 1958 as a forum for the international Communist movement, and had its headquarters in Prague. In the decade before the Prague Spring, the journal served as an incubator for a generation of reform-minded Soviet academics and politicians, including the philosopher Merab Mamardashvili, the sociologist Boris Grushin, and the future advisers to Mikhail Gorbachev: Georgii Shakhnazarov, Georgii Arbatov, and Anatolii Cherniaev. Following the collapse of the Soviet Union, former *Problemy* staff described the journal's Prague office as an "oasis of creative thinking," "an intellectual bridge between the twentieth Party Congress of the KPSS and perestroika,"[39] and as a place where "an extraordinarily free atmosphere reigned."[40]

According to Mamardashvili, life in Prague amounted to a "gilded emigration" for *Problemy*'s Soviet staff not only because of the unique working conditions at the journal, but due to their experiences in the capital.[41] Cherniaev claimed in his memoirs, "It was daily life [*byt*] in Prague that played an important role in transforming the journal's employees from communists into humanists." He maintained that Czechs' orderliness, their modest habits, as well as the higher standard of living in Prague served as positive influences on Soviet citizens. "We could not, of course, assimilate the Czechs' manner of living, but coming into contact with it daily, we became accustomed to its formal, outward merits, and we became 'more civilized.'"[42]

Tourism was supposed to highlight the similarities between the superpower and its satellite, in the interests of promoting mutual understanding between their citizens. What unites the Soviet tourists who complained about being shown too many monuments from Czechoslovakia's pre-socialist past, and the Soviet tourists and expatriates who praised life in the satellite state, is that both groups challenged the idea of tourism as a tool of rapprochement.

Tourism with a Human Face: Debates in the Mid-1960s

In the years leading up to the Prague Spring, Soviet-Czechoslovak tourism became a focal point in debates over how to modernize the friendship project.

Until 1965, the Soviet government did not allow its citizens to travel to Czechoslovakia on private visits to visit nonfamily members, and vice versa. This meant that Soviet and Czechoslovak pen pals, for example, could only meet in person by traveling on official tourist groups.[43] It also meant that when Soviets and Czechoslovaks formed friendships while visiting each other's countries as tourists, they had little chance of ever meeting again. In 1957, a young woman named Tania traveled to Czechoslovakia on a tourist excursion and fell in love with a Czech man, Jaroslav. She wrote to the Society for Soviet-Czechoslovak Friendship despairing that she would never see him again; she had attempted to book a ticket on another Soviet tour to Czechoslovakia, but had been rejected on the grounds that Soviet tourists could not visit the same country twice. She had then tried to invite Jaroslav to the Soviet Union, but this application, too, had been rejected, because the young man was not a relative. An official at the Union of Soviet Friendship Societies (SSOD) explained that if she wanted to see Jaroslav again, her only option was to marry him.[44] Soviet tourists found their government's restrictions on travel in Czechoslovakia humiliating. A trip leader from the Kalinin region wrote in his report to the Tourism Councils:

> In the future, in order to develop friendly relations between our peoples, it would be expedient . . . to give the most morally stable and politically literate people the right to take trips around the country individually, so that the Soviet person could freely visit his Czech friend, and Czechs their Soviet friends. The existing limitations cause harm to the business of strengthening friendship. . . . We were bombarded with questions: why can the Germans, the Americans, the English freely travel to visit their Czech friends, and why can't our best, dearest friend—the Russian—travel to visit a Czech?[45]

In Czechoslovakia, advocates of closer ties to the Soviet Union argued that restrictions on tourism threatened the health of the larger friendship project. In 1963–1964, the celebrated Czechoslovak travel writers Jiří Hanzelka and Miroslav Zikmund spent over a year traveling around Siberia, the Soviet Far East, and Central Asia. In an account of their journey, which they sent to leading members of the Czechoslovak government, as well as to Leonid Brezhnev, they complained about the obstacles Soviets and Czechoslovaks faced establishing truly intimate ties, including in the realm of tourism. They noted that while Western governments were beginning to ease passport and visa restrictions, making it easier for people to travel freely within the capitalist world, in the socialist world, "the barriers between [countries] are much higher, and each ordinary citizen feels this firsthand."[46]

In 1965, the Soviet Union signed an agreement to open up visa-less travel with Bulgaria, Czechoslovakia, Poland, and East Germany—a policy designed to allow Soviet citizens to visit nonrelatives. Nonetheless, a variety of bureaucratic obstacles remained in place.[47] The inviting party had to issue his guest an invitation, which, for trips to Czechoslovakia, had to be reviewed by both the Soviet and Czechoslovak police. In addition (as the Czechoslovak embassy in Moscow complained) the Soviets did not advertise the terms of the new agreement in public, or even to Intourist and other tourism agencies. Soviet officials responded to the Czechoslovak government's complaints by saying they had no intention of broadly publicizing the rules for visa-less travel. In frustration, the Czechoslovak embassy in Moscow concluded, "Tourism between the ČSSR [Czechoslovak Socialist Republic] and the USSR is an area of contact that does not completely correspond to the level of political, economic, and cultural ties between our countries."[48] "It is much easier to go to the USA than to the USSR," a Czechoslovak official despaired.[49]

In the mid-1960s, Czechoslovakia became a mecca for Western travelers. As a result, Czechoslovak officials' concerns about restrictions on tourism with the Soviet Union increased. In 1965, 2.8 million foreign tourists visited Czechoslovakia. Of these, only 23,000, or 7 percent came from the Soviet Union. The Soviet government's restrictions on receiving foreign tourists, including the bureaucratic obstacles involved in allowing Soviet citizens to invite personal guests, kept the numbers of Czechoslovaks going to the USSR similarly low. Czechoslovak officials worried, as they did about the influx of Western films and consumer goods in this period, that the onslaught of tourists from capitalist countries constituted a dangerous new front in the Cold War, which would have a deleterious impact on the friendship project.[50]

Swinging Czechoslovakia

The influx of foreign tourists to Czechoslovakia in the mid-1960s contributed to what Czechoslovak party officials retrospectively dubbed the "erosion of the Iron Curtain."[51] To Western eyes, Prague, in particular, was transformed from yet another "gray" Eastern bloc city into the unofficial capital of cosmopolitan

activity—and 1960s culture—in the region. In 1967, a young American traveled to the Czechoslovak capital after spending the year in Moscow as an exchange student, and found the atmosphere there in comparison "refreshingly
relaxed and almost Western in spirit."[52] At the Prague castle, "All possible
languages are heard," *Sotsialisticheskaia Chekhoslovakiia* (Socialist Czechoslovakia) bragged, "Russian, German, English, Italian, Spanish—even Esperanto
and Japanese."[53] A *New York Times* article from May 1968 enthused, "Prague
is a throbbing city. Something close to hand-to-hand combat is required to
conquer a table at a restaurant after the evening's activities, and taxis are as
elusive after dark as the strains of music in the night air."[54]

The contrast between the fervent Czechoslovak capital and staid Soviet
cities was readily apparent to Soviet observers. For some, including reform-
ist members of the intelligentsia and members of the Soviet colony in Prague,
this difference was exciting. "Prague exuded inspiration," Sergei Iurskii, a
Soviet actor who visited Czechoslovakia in the spring of 1968 remembered.[55]
Artemy Troitsky, the future rock critic, who spent his adolescence in Czechoslovakia, where his parents worked for *Problemy mira i sotsializma*, recalled:

> In Prague everything was simple. There were several clubs in the centre of
> the city . . . and every week there were concerts by beat groups. The Mata-
> dors played like The Yardbirds, The Rebels played "West coast," Framus-5
> played r'n'b and The Olympics sang in Czech in the Beatle style. . . . My
> favourite book at the time was, of course, *The Catcher in the Rye* and for
> want of a red hunter's cap I walked around Prague in a yellow chequered
> cotton cap with a long visor, eyeing all the stunning grown-up girls in mini-
> skirts, inhaling other people's tobacco smoke while standing in line for con-
> cert tickets, running "Crystal Ship" through my head over and over again.[56]

For many Soviet tourists, however, encounters with this heady atmosphere
amounted to culture shock. Many of the new trends on display in Czechoslovakia fell outside the purview of what was officially acceptable in Soviet
society. Soviet tourists frequently expressed anger and bewilderment when
describing their exposure to these new phenomena, including nonrepresen-
tational art, 1960s counterculture, and the sexual revolution. "During a visit
to the picture gallery in the city of Bratislava we were told that they didn't
have a building to display classical art," the trip leader of a group from Kemerovo reported. "A building, however, had been found for abstract 'art'

where for the most part naked women are 'drawn' in the strangest poses. Our mood was spoiled after seeing these 'masterpieces.'"[57] Similarly, a group from Soviet Belorussia described their confusion upon encountering abstract art at the National Gallery in Prague, "The accompanying translator Ženja Kudritská and our guide tried their best to justify the abstract art paintings, to prove that abstract art has a great future. . . . Unfortunately, almost no one in our group knew that in Czechoslovakia for a long time there has been a discussion going on in the press about socialist realism as an outmoded method of art, and that abstract art has many admirers in the ČSSR. For all the members of the group that was unexpected."[58]

Such comments reveal Soviet tourists' discomfort on realizing that they no longer represented a cultural vanguard in the eyes of their Czechoslovak hosts. On the contrary, they found themselves relegated to the role of provincial cousins in Czechoslovakia's swinging cities. Tourists from Sverdlovsk were shocked by the capital's hippies: "Groups of young men with messy hair down to their shoulders, and barefoot girls roam the streets of Prague, evidently without any real occupation."[59] The leader of a Komsomol tour group appears to have been simultaneously attracted and repelled by pictures of "girls in miniskirts, and even a series of postcards of naked women and girls" for sale at city kiosks. The leader concluded, "We saw much that was good and wonderful in golden Prague, but that kind of thing and similar occurrences . . . left an unpleasant aftertaste of disappointment in the soul."[60]

Even more unsettling for Soviet tourists was the behavior of their local guides. In Prague these guides were freelancers who led tourist excursions in their spare time; they represented a cross-section of Czechoslovak society, "students, housewives, pensioners, civil servants," as well as "young historians," who worked the tourist circuit as a form of professional training. In addition to extensive training in the history of the city's monuments, the guides were expected to be fluent in the languages of the groups they led.[61] Interestingly, probably due to the latter requirement, many of the guides for Soviet tour groups were Russian émigrés or their children.[62]

A group from Kyrgyzstan in 1965 complained that its guide's "ideological-political level does not fulfill the requirements for working with foreigners. It wasn't pleasant for us to hear praise for abstractionism, the standard of living in the FRG [West Germany], and that in the [Soviet] Union, 'everything is done under pressure.'"[63] Two years later, a group from Yaroslavl accused their guide, a student at an institute of higher education, of "disrespect to our country" because he "constantly tried to prove that we are incorrectly informed by our press about the state of affairs in the West, and so on." The group suggested that guides for Soviet tourists should be more experienced and better "prepared politically."[64] Instead of potential friends, Soviet tourists increasingly viewed all Czechoslovaks as provocateurs. A Komsomol group complained, "In a series of instances several Czech citizens tried to turn completely neutral conversations into discussions of complex political problems, asking provocative questions, purposefully giving incorrect commentary on issues of Soviet domestic and foreign policy." Of their three Czech guides, they added, "only Miroslav Adamec was sufficiently erudite and prepared for work with Soviet tourists, however, even he made attempts to tell anti-Soviet jokes and to sing forbidden songs."[65]

Springtime for Friendship

Alexander Dubček's promotion to first secretary of the Communist Party of Czechoslovakia (KSČ) in January 1968 marked the beginning of the Prague Spring. During the next eight months, victims of the Stalinist terror in Czechoslovakia were rehabilitated, small-scale private enterprises were permitted, censorship was first relaxed and then lifted entirely, and a variety of political clubs were formed, leading to talk that the country might even embrace a multiparty system for the first time since 1948.[66] The relaxation of censorship, in particular, led to a public reexamination of Czechoslovakia's past two decades under Communism. This new openness also caused Czechoslovak politicians, intellectuals, journalists, and the public at large to reevaluate their country's political alliance with the Soviet Union, as well as the friendship project.

From the perspective of Soviet officials, the permissive atmosphere of the Prague Spring precipitated an unprecedented, dangerous rise in anti-Soviet sentiment in the satellite.[67] With increasing alarm, the Soviet embassy in Prague and other Soviet agencies with contacts in the country reported a series of events that just a few months before would have been unthinkable in friendly Czechoslovakia. In February, two Prague residents were arrested for defacing 50 Soviet flags. In March, a demonstration in Brno, attended by 6,000 people, included the sign, "For the Russians—Lenin, for us—[Tomáš] Masaryk."[68] That same month, graffiti appeared in a Slovak village warning, "We will become a Russian colony."[69] In May, 150,000 people held a demonstration at the grave of Milan Štefánik (a leader in the 1918 Czechoslovak independence movement) in Slovakia, during which youths shouted anti-Soviet slogans.[70] Tourism, too, became a target of anti-Soviet sentiment. In Prague, "hooligan" youth entered Intourist's office "shouting threats addressed at the Soviet Union, and pasting leaflets on the glass windows."[71] Dubček repeatedly assured Soviet leaders that "fraternal friendship and firm alliance with the Soviet Union are not a question for individuals in our party," stating that "in my new post I will act, as I always have up until now, to do my utmost to assist the efforts of our party's Central Committee to seek the further consolidation of our fraternal friendship."[72] Nevertheless, other high-ranking members of the KSČ openly displayed anti-Soviet sentiments. In June, the first secretary of the regional party committee in Eastern Slovakia told a visiting delegation from Ukraine that the party had been mistaken to follow the Soviet example, and that as a result, "the past twenty years have been a wasted opportunity."[73]

Against this volatile backdrop, Czechoslovaks began to openly debate the tenets of the friendship project with the Soviet Union for the first time in twenty years. These debates were, in effect, a sequel to the wide-ranging discussions about Soviet culture, and the terms of Czechoslovakia's alliance with the USSR, that had flourished in 1945–1948, during the Third Republic. Like these earlier discussions, the 1968 debates about the future of the friendship project concerned fundamental issues, including the role of nationalism versus internationalism, the Soviet Union's leadership in the socialist world, and the participation of ordinary citizens in international politics.

Svět sovětů (World of the Soviets) played a leading role in these debates. In a series of articles, editors and journalists critically examined the history of the Czechoslovak-Soviet alliance and discussed how the friendship project could be improved. The magazine's reexamination of Czechoslovak-Soviet relations served partially as a form of self-criticism for its role in having extolled all aspects of Soviet life during the past two decades. Journalists apologized for "distorting" and "embellishing reality" about life in the USSR.[74] They argued that Dubček's reforms were paving the way for an improvement in Czechoslovakia's relations with the entire socialist camp, and they suggested that *Svět sovětů* could contribute to this effort by becoming a platform for "the truth" about the Soviet Union and Czechoslovak-Soviet relations: "If through all the distortions on both of our sides, the majority of our people have maintained heartfelt relations to the Soviet Union, if they have weathered the period of varnished and half-truth, then the truth cannot be of harm to them. On the contrary, it can only restore them."[75] This optimistic idea, that truth about the Stalinist years could reinvigorate contemporary politics, was a central tenet of the Prague Spring. Czechoslovak reformers, in fact, adopted this notion from the earlier experience of de-Stalinization in the Soviet Union. Jiří Pelikán, one of the leaders of the Czechoslovak reform movement, later argued that in his country in 1968, "the scrutinizing of the political system . . . represented, in essence, an effort to complete the job that the Soviet Twentieth [Party] Congress had left unfinished."[76] Czechoslovak writers and intellectuals fervently examined the past twenty years of their country's history, highlighting events that their government had tried to gloss over, such as the political repressions of the 1950s.[77] For their part, Czechoslovak proponents of the friendship project hoped to reinvigorate their country's alliance with the USSR by exposing what they saw as the "truth" about the Soviet Union and the countries' relations. When Jiří Hájek became Czechoslovak foreign minister in April 1968, he declared at his first press conference that "he hoped free discussion of attitudes toward Russia would repair the damage done to Czechoslovak-Soviet friendship by 'twenty years of uncritical exaltation of everything Russian' and 'stupid pro-Soviet propaganda.'"[78]

One of *Svět sovětů*'s foremost conclusions was that Czechoslovak-Soviet relations had become too formulaic to elicit genuine enthusiasm among the Czechoslovak people. The magazine's journalists thus built upon earlier complaints by Soviets and Czechoslovaks about the structure of tourism between the countries. *Svět sovětů* claimed that the Czechoslovak people craved direct, unfettered contacts with Soviet citizens, rather than stale, ritualistic ties. The post-Stalinist version of the friendship project had been designed to foster a sense of intimacy between Soviets and Czechoslovaks through new forms of interpersonal contacts, such as tourism and pen-pal correspondences. Yet the journal's writers judged these efforts to have been unsuccessful. They asked how much the Soviet people really knew about life in Czechoslovakia, and vice versa. "It is very alarming," one article declared, "that after chanting slogans about eternal friendship over and over, how small in fact our intimate [*důvěrná*] knowledge of each other is; that is factual and unsentimental knowledge, including various weaknesses and shortcomings. . . . Results, not words, must become the measure of our friendship."[79]

The *Svět sovětů* journalists proposed an array of solutions for how to foster "factual and unsentimental knowledge" between ordinary Czechoslovaks and Soviets. These solutions effectively amounted to a more intimate, honest, and less bureaucratic version of the existing friendship project. In a forum the magazine held with prominent Czechoslovak cultural figures on the future of Czechoslovak-Soviet relations, the travel writer Hanzelka advocated for "an informal path to friendship. . . . For us to visit each other, to be perfectly free to marry one another, to send [our] children on exchanges." In Hanzelka's view, the problem with many Soviet functionaries in charge of maintaining relations with Czechoslovakia was their "lack of faith in deep, human ties."[80] A *Svět sovětů* journalist similarly suggested that mutual understanding could be achieved through student and work exchanges, and by sending Soviet and Czechoslovak children on homestays in the other country.[81] These suggestions echoed those of functionaries from the Union of Czechoslovak-Soviet Friendship (SČSP) who made "persistent requests" in 1968 for "the expansion of personal and group contacts between Soviet and Czechoslovak citizens."[82]

During the Prague Spring, the angry demonstrators marching with anti-Soviet signs, and the more cerebral *Svět sovětů* journalists critiquing relations with the USSR were united by the belief that the political reforms represented a turning point in the Czechoslovak-Soviet alliance. The demonstrators called for Czechoslovakia to distance itself from the Soviet Union, but the writers in *Svět sovětů* took an entirely different view, arguing that the Czechoslovak and Soviet people needed to become closer, to engage in more open, honest dialogue about the differences between their countries and the future of their friendship. They looked to personal contacts between Czechoslovak and Soviet citizens, including tourism, to strengthen the friendship project.

Tourists on the Front Lines

In the heat of the Prague Spring, Soviet-Czechoslovak tourism became a crucible of the broader friendship project. Tourism came to highlight the very political and cultural differences that it had previously been designed to conceal. Soviet tourists had once complained about the inclusion of too many churches and castles on their tours to Czechoslovakia; the scenes they witnessed in 1968 appeared truly heretical. A group of schoolteachers observed May Day celebrations in Prague and declared themselves "shocked": "The city was poorly prepared for the holiday, the show was absolutely disorganized, there were no flowers. . . . A group of students from the medical faculty marched with slogans in support of Israel. Others marched with portraits of Masaryk. And no one stopped [them]. And when we asked why this was so, the answer was: we have democracy; everyone is allowed to express his own opinion."[83] A group from Sverdlovsk that visited Prague in July noted, "Meetings were going on in the central streets from morning until late in the evening. A collection of signatures was organized in support of the liquidation of the people's militia [the armed wing of the KSČ], moreover [these petitions] were signed by tourists from the FRG, England, and so forth. Portraits of Masaryk [and Edvard] Beneš were displayed in kiosks and shop windows, but there were none of the leaders of the Communist movement."[84]

The reform movement also transformed how Czechoslovaks depicted the Soviet Union. During the Prague Spring, the country's travel writers sought to undermine the USSR's official, sanitized image, especially its role as the model for Czechoslovakia's political development, by highlighting contradictions between Soviet propaganda and the reality of daily life in the USSR. Instead of an exemplary society, they depicted the Soviet Union as a country of contrasts, caught between success and failure: for instance, the model urban planning of the New Arbat district in Moscow versus the destruction of the city's historic neighborhoods. "It is . . . a land whose people make unbelievably perfect rockets and spaceships [and] transplant artificial organs, yet bungle the simplest skilled handicrafts."[85]

Most damningly, Czechoslovak travel accounts implicitly questioned the Soviets' success in building socialism by highlighting the persistence of religious beliefs and poverty in the USSR. *Svět sovětů*'s Moscow correspondent, for instance, alleged that the elderly women waiting in line to pay their respects at the Lenin mausoleum on Red Square were the same women who had filled the churches on Orthodox Easter the day before.[86] A travel article about the Golden Ring town Vladimir, served as an exposé of poverty in provincial Russia.[87] Other accounts highlighted the Soviet service industry's failings: anecdotes about rude taxi drivers and salespeople belied the myth of the USSR as a land of "friends."[88]

Travel writing about the Soviet Union during the Prague Spring, instead of emphasizing similarities between Soviet and Czechoslovak society, argued that mutual understanding between the two countries should be predicated on respect and tolerance for their fundamental differences. In reevaluating relations with the Soviet Union, *Svět sovětů* wrote, "It will be necessary to emphasize more often that the Soviet Union is not Czechoslovakia, that we cannot apply our standards to it, that the mentality of the Soviet people is not the same as ours. . . . This is natural, logical and could not be otherwise." This new attitude undermined a central aspect of the friendship project between the USSR and Czechoslovakia: the idea that socialism alone could provide the basis for rapprochement. "We all [the Soviet and Czechoslovak people] agree on a common socialist program and we have definitely put an end to capitalism. But otherwise each [country] is different [*každý jinak*]."[89]

The new political differences between Czechoslovakia and the USSR put a strain on tourism. Politics had, of course, always been central to tourism between the countries, but before the Prague Spring it had served as a unifying factor, since both sides were engaged in building the same type of socialism. Soviet tourists traveled to Czechoslovakia as ambassadors of socialism; Czechoslovak tourists went to the Soviet Union to see a vision of their own future. In 1968, however, the two countries' conceptions of socialism radically diverged. For Czechoslovaks, their new ability to express political as well as cultural differences with the Soviet Union was liberating, even intoxicating. It represented a fundamental reversal in the balance of power between the superpower and its satellite. Iurskii, the Soviet actor who traveled to Prague in the spring of 1968, observed this imbalance in interviews led by local reporters: "These were strange interviews. The interviewers asked me little, instead they talked more, [they] breathlessly described their [country's] changes."[90]

For most Soviet tourists as well as the Soviet guides who worked with Czechoslovak tourists in the USSR, this reversal in the political status quo was disturbing. The revival of Czechoslovak autonomy represented an attack on Soviet hegemony. In accounts written by Soviet guides and translators for Czechoslovak tour groups to the USSR, the Prague Spring transformed previously friendly and deferential Czechoslovaks into arrogant, aggressive proponents of their country's new political path. "From the very first day of their arrival in our country, this group differed radically from all the previous Czech groups I've worked with," a Komsomol interpreter reported. He complained that the tourists were disrespectful to the Soviet Union: they denigrated Siberia and Central Asia as impoverished and laughed at a brochure about class conflict they found on a train, claiming "capitalist exploitation no longer exists."[91]

During the Prague Spring, Czechoslovaks not only sought to undermine the Soviet Union's historic role as the leader of the international Communist movement, they also fashioned themselves as missionaries for reform vis-à-vis their Soviet friends. "We were filled with hopes that this time we would be the ones who would shift development further, and that this would benefit [people] in the Soviet Union as well," Petr Pithart, a Prague Spring activist, later recalled, "[People] felt and thought and even said that in Prague they were also fighting for Moscow."[92] Many Soviet intellectuals, and members of the small, nascent dissident movement were receptive to this idea. "The entire Moscow intelligentsia was preoccupied with Prague Spring," former Soviet dissident Ludmilla Alexeyeva later claimed.[93] For Soviet intellectuals, the Czechoslovak reforms seemed to be the true realization of Communism; in Czechoslovakia, the people and the party appeared to be genuinely united. The Czechoslovak reforms also demonstrated the kind of respect for the value and autonomy of individuals that Soviet intellectuals were searching for in the 1960s, after decades of Stalinist (and Khrushchevian) collectivism.[94] "We were hoping that Czechoslovakia's reformers would develop—and that our government would import—a form of socialism that people like us could accept," Alexeyeva wrote.[95]

Czechoslovak proponents of the Prague Spring also tried to use tourism to educate the broader Soviet public about the reform movement, which the Soviet press largely refrained from covering.[96] A Soviet guide for a group of Czechoslovak teenage pioneers and their leaders visiting the USSR complained about the travelers' attempts to spread their politics, "According to the leaders of the group, none of the members had received special instructions before their trip to the Soviet Union, but every citizen of the ČSSR knew that the group was . . . 'asked to tell the truth about the events in Czechoslovakia.' It must be said that the leaders of the group continually fulfilled this request."[97] Soviet tourists to Czechoslovakia also described themselves as targets of Czechoslovak political propaganda. One group reported on its Czech guide: "Věra Březinová, a student from the political economy faculty, fulfilled her responsibilities conscientiously. But during the trip there were many debates on political subjects. She extolled the process of democratization taking place, the establishment of freedom of speech, the press, broadcasting." The trip leader added, with obvious relief, "In these discussions the tourists showed the steadfastness of [their] Communist convictions, their political preparation and devotion to the ideals of our party."[98] A group from the Kuibyshev region reported hearing complaints about the Soviet Union, such as, "We have lived for twenty years under Moscow's yoke and now we have freedom and democracy . . . you, the USSR, have led us, the ČSSR, in unequal trade, you have forbidden us to trade with the Western countries." Czechoslovaks additionally complained that it was harder for them to travel to the USSR than to West Germany or Austria, and that the Soviet press was paying insufficient attention to events in Czechoslovakia.[99] One Soviet trip leader reported, "During the [train] journeys from Chop-Prague, Prague-Brno, Brno-Olomouc . . . several representatives of the Czechoslovak young intelligentsia and students tried to foist upon [*naviazyvat'*] the tourists of our group political discussions, they tried to propagandize the political platform laid out in 'Two Thousand Words.'"[100]

Soviet tourists' tendency to portray themselves as unwillingly drawn into political disputes with heretical Czechoslovaks may have been an attempt to shield themselves from accusations by the authorities of showing sympathy with their Czechoslovak interlocutors. Czechoslovaks were eager to use Soviet tourists as witnesses to refute claims in the Soviet press about counterrevolutionary activity in their country. One Soviet Sputnik trip leader reported how a Prague TV correspondent had stopped him as his group visited the Prague castle in July 1968 and asked whether he had seen anything on his trip to corroborate "'rumors abroad that things are not calm in our country.'" The leader answered in the negative. In his report back to the Komsomol shortly after the Soviet invasion of Czechoslovakia, however, he claimed, "Now I am very displeased with my answer. If this question had been asked when I read the announcement by the five Communist parties [about the invasion] and had spent even two more weeks in the country, then the answer would have had to have been different."[101]

To avoid such faux pas, officials in the Soviet tourism industry tried to prepare Soviet tourists for encounters with their evermore-troublesome Czechoslovak "friends." At least some Soviet tourist groups received lectures on the political situation in Czechoslovakia, including decisions issued by the KSČ's Presidium and Central Committee, and the contents of the "Two

Thousand Words Manifesto," written by Ludvík Vaculík, detailing support
for the political reforms. Shortly before the invasion, one group even met with
Soviet delegates returning from the World Youth festival in Sofia, who reported on the "moods" of the Czechoslovak youth they had encountered.[102]

Occupation Tourism

On the night of August 20–21, 1968, the Soviet government launched a massive invasion of its erstwhile friend. To put an end to the Prague Spring,
300,000–350,000 Soviet troops, along with an additional 50,000 soldiers from
Bulgaria, East Germany, Hungary, and Poland, occupied Czechoslovakia.[103]
That night, a Komsomol tour group from Chita was in Karlovy Vary: "The
town was clean and quiet; the well-designed shop window displays sparkled
with cleanliness. In the evening twilight the lights burned at the hotels 'Vol-
gograd' and 'Moscow.' In the cozy little square our Lenin stood on a short
pedestal. . . . In the morning we woke up to the terrifying howl of the loud-
speaker. In tones reaching a howl, radio station announcers reported . . . the
occupation of Czechoslovakia by the Warsaw Pact forces." When the group
ventured out of their hotel they witnessed two men across the street chop-
ping down a sign with a slogan by former Czechoslovak president Klement
Gottwald, "With the Soviet Union for eternity."[104] The report's jarring jux-
taposition between the "clean and quiet," "cozy" Czechoslovakia before August 20 and the chaos the Soviet tourists awoke to the next morning serves
as a useful metaphor for how the invasion transformed Soviet tourism to
Czechoslovakia. What little remained of the ritual of reassurance came to a
dramatic end. Soviet tourists were no longer welcomed as friends and "liberators." Instead, they came to be treated by both Czechoslovaks and their
own government as representatives of an occupying regime.

With the invasion, Soviet tourists' entire experience in Czechoslovakia
changed. Guides refused to take them to the sites traditionally included on
their itineraries, such as the Lenin museum and landmarks associated with
World War II or Soviet-Czechoslovak friendship. When a group from the
Penza region passed the Monument to the Soviet Tank Crews in Prague,
their Czech guide remained notably silent, and instead directed their attention to a nearby "modern vegetable store."[105] Other guides even replaced the
traditional landmarks celebrating Soviet power with new ones designed to

flaunt its oppression, such as the facade of the National Museum in Prague riddled with bullets from Soviet tank fire, and the square named after Jan Palach, the Czech student who burned himself to death to protest the invasion.[106]

Soviet tourists now faced a range of humiliations during their travels. Locals excoriated them as "fascists," "Asians," or simply yelled at them to get out of the country.[107] A series of (empty) Soviet tour buses were vandalized.[108] Workers refused to meet them, passersby denounced them as "occupiers," and the tourists complained that while Western newspapers were widely available, it was impossible to obtain the Soviet press.[109] Many of their Čedok guides made no attempt to conceal their antipathy toward the Soviet Union. In 1969, a group from Kalinin complained that at a ceremonial dinner sponsored by Čedok on the anniversary of the October Revolution they were mysteriously presented with calendars from 1968 and tourist brochures titled "Prague in August 1968." The Čedok guide for a group from Ukraine told them, "You should not make your conclusions from the speeches of those demagogues who have been telling you about the friendship and brotherhood of our peoples. All of that is idle talk. The feeling of friendship must be in people's hearts, and we have absolutely none [of this left] after August 1968."[110] Intourist officials complained to Čedok about the Czechoslovak guides and were told that indeed, many of them were "reactionaries."[111] "The group's general opinion about the trip is difficult to express in two words," a trip leader from Kuibyshev concluded. "Almost no one expressed regret about the trip, however, the trip also brought little joy."[112]

Why did the Soviet government continue to promote tourism to Czechoslovakia after the invasion, at a time when even the secretary of the Central Committee of the SČSP estimated that only 20 percent of the population "firmly support cooperation with the USSR"?[113] The Soviet authorities did suspend Sputnik groups from traveling to Czechoslovakia immediately following the invasion, but they reinitiated them in mid-October 1968.[114]

One reason that Soviet authorities may have wanted to continue tourism is that exposing Soviet citizens to anti-Soviet attitudes and behaviors in Czechoslovakia probably helped augment support for the invasion in the USSR. The Soviet government justified the invasion (which it referred to euphemistically as the "bringing in" [*vvod*] of Soviet troops) to Soviet citizens by arguing that the Czechoslovak government and Central Committee had appealed for its assistance to put down "reactionary, anti-socialist elements, backed by international imperialism," which had threatened to start a civil war.[115] For Soviet tourists, confrontations with angry Czechoslovaks could serve as living proof that the invasion had been necessary, underscoring their government's explanation that loyal Czechoslovakia had been taken over by "rightist forces" in the pocket of Western imperialists.[116] This was the conclusion that a group from Kaliningrad came to: "The events which took place in Czechoslovakia once again reminded us that we must be vigilant, that the forces of imperialists and worldwide counterrevolution do not slumber and do everything to estrange the brother peoples of the socialist countries."[117]

At the same time, Soviet officials saw tourism as a key element of their policy of "normalization" in post-invasion Czechoslovakia: the attempt to return both internal Czechoslovak politics, and Soviet-Czechoslovak relations, to the pre-1968 status quo.[118] In the fall of 1968 and throughout 1969, Soviet tourists became ambassadors of normalization, called upon to defend Soviet actions to the Czechs and Slovaks they met on their travels.[119] For such tourists, the pleasures of travel now took the backseat to political duty. The composition of the tourist groups changed accordingly: they now included more "propagandists" and other party functionaries. In the Sverdlovsk region, for instance, the regional committee of the KPSS decreed that each tourist group to Czechoslovakia should include at least three propagandists, who were to conduct "explanatory work" in the country.[120] A group from Penza that traveled to Czechoslovakia in December 1968 included eight propagandists.[121] Ambassador Chervonenko argued that the quantity of Soviet tourists traveling to Czechoslovakia was less important than "the quality of their ideological and moral preparation." He urged Sputnik, in particular, to select tourists for these trips carefully. The ideal candidates were "politically prepared Communists and Komsomol members who will be able to lead discussions [with the Czechoslovak people] and explain the policies of the KPSS and the Soviet government in relation to Czechoslovakia."[122] The Soviet government also sent groups of World War II veterans who had taken part in the liberation of Czechoslovakia in 1945 on tours to Czechoslovakia, to meet with Czechoslovak veterans.[123] Soviet tourists sometimes met with Soviet troops stationed in the country, in an attempt to boost their morale.[124]

In the aftermath of the Soviet invasion of Czechoslovakia, political protest jokes proliferated in the country. One joke took the form of a wanted advertisement: "Looking for lodging for half a million Soviet tourists . . . an extra bed needed for tanks, heavy artillery, and machine guns." Another joke mocked promotional materials by Intourist, "Free trip to the USSR by tank! 'Tanktourist' is receiving applications."[125] The persistence of Soviet-Czechoslovak tourism after the invasion once again revealed the thin line between friendship and violence in the empire of friends. The Soviet government's policies on tourism after the invasion blurred the distinction between pleasure and politics, tourists and tank drivers. The image of "tourists on tanks" that circulated in post-invasion Czechoslovakia was not just black humor—it exposed the interconnection between tourism and occupation, and between coercion and comity that would characterize normalization.[126]

As Soviet tourists became complicit in their government's occupation of Czechoslovakia, the real occupiers—Soviet troops—also became tourists. In Northern Moravia, where many Soviet soldiers were stationed, the local branch of the SČSP ordered its members to guide the occupiers on tourist "excursions." Much like Soviet civilians visiting Czechoslovakia, the soldiers and their families were supposed to be shown a mix of socialist sites and traditional landmarks, "factories and agricultural cooperatives, and also well-known [*pamiatnye*] historical places on the territory of our region, so that they will feel as if they are among their own [*rodnykh*] brothers."[127]

Soviet tourists were mixed in their assessments of whether their trips were successful at reestablishing friendly ties with Czechoslovakia. Several divided the Czechoslovak population into categories based on their support for the Soviet Union. One group, for instance, suggested three categories: those in their forties and fifties, who related well to Soviet tourists, twenty-five to forty year olds who were "reserved," and youth (under twenty-five) who expressed negative attitudes toward the USSR.[128] Czechoslovak war veterans were the most likely to show support for the Soviets. A group of Soviet tourists visited Slovakia in May 1969 and attended a memorial ceremony with Czechoslovak veterans at the site of the battle of the Dukla Pass in Prešov, which they described in terms similar to the standard, pre-1968, liberation narratives: "The older generation begged [us] not to consider the events [of 1968] their fault, [and said] that nonetheless friendship and brotherhood will be restored. During the delivery of souvenirs to the Slovak officers and expressions of thanks for preserving the memorials to the soldiers, some of the residents and officers of the Czechoslovak army cried."[129]

Other groups were more equivocal. "An unfriendly mood toward the Soviet people still reigns among some citizens of the ČSSR.... Healthy-minded people say that a lot of time is required in order to restore a normal position."[130] Still other groups gave more pessimistic accounts of their missions to convert Czechoslovaks to the path of normalization. One reported that although they were all members of the regional or city branches of the Moscow Komsomol, they still felt ill prepared when they heard statements such as "we want to find our own path, like in Yugoslavia." In order for discussions with locals to "have some kind of useful outcome," they suggested that future tourist groups should be given handouts with typical questions and arguments that the Czechoslovaks might advance, along with possible answers and counterarguments from the Soviet perspective.[131] Another group simply concluded, "Contacts with the local population were of no consequence. We did not meet with any warm relations from the side of the Czechs and Slovaks."[132]

"A Space for Human Relations"?

In the late 1950s and early 1960s, Lily Golden, the daughter of an interracial American Communist couple who had moved to the USSR in the 1930s, took advantage of the new opportunities for socialist foreign tourism, and traveled on Soviet package tours to Bulgaria, East Germany, Hungary, and Czechoslovakia. She soon became disillusioned with the Soviet tourist experience: "I wanted to be free to go where I desired and to talk to whomever caught my fancy. I believed that the experience of being abroad meant walking the streets of an unknown city, maybe even getting lost and finding one's own way out, to spend an evening in someone's home, to discover what people thought about their lives. These 'socialist trips' provided none of those satisfactions."[133]

The Prague Spring and the subsequent Soviet invasion of Czechoslovakia marked the nadir of Soviet-Czechoslovak relations, yet these dramatic developments also amounted to a unique moment in the friendship project between the two countries. The events of 1968–1969 disrupted the friendship project's formal "script." The volatile political situation in Czechoslovakia, combined with the temporary suspension of censorship in the Czechoslovak media, resulted in a degree of openness between Soviets and Czechoslovaks that was unprecedented and would not be repeated until 1989. Nowhere was this openness more apparent than in the realm of tourism. The conviction of both Soviet tourists in Czechoslovakia and Czechoslovak tourists in the Soviet Union that they were on a mission to tell each other "the truth" about current events led for the first time to real conversations and arguments touching on such previously taboo subjects as freedom of the press, travel, and the advantages of socialism as compared to Western democracy. Ironically, it took the crises of the Prague Spring and the Soviet invasion to bring a measure of openness and spontaneity to the "socialist trips," that Golden complained about.

This new openness between Soviets and Czechoslovaks began during the Prague Spring. What is especially surprising is that it continued in the first year after the invasion. A Czech guide's denunciation of a group from Kazakhstan as "occupiers," in April 1969 led to a spirited argument about the meaning of the term.[134] A group from Sverdlovsk stayed up until four in the morning arguing with their Czech guides about the invasion, Czechoslovak history, and the Vietnam War. "The discussions ended in a stalemate," the Sverdlovsk group concluded.[135] Later the group met two students on a train, who volunteered to act as their guides around Prague. Despite the political tensions, the Soviet tourists and the Czechoslovak students seem to have developed some affection for one another. "During our walks, when we noticed an anti-Soviet slogan on a wall, one of the guys turned his back to us. They were both embarrassed."[136] A Komsomol group traveling to Czechoslovakia in February 1969 concluded after a chance meeting with some local youth, "Despite the fact that at times [our] arguments were very heated and critical, we were able to reach normal human relations with them; we met again, and with the guys from Prague we will to some degree even remain friends in the future. . . . This was all despite the fact that neither we nor they succeeded at changing the opinions of the other."[137] The crises of the Prague Spring and the invasion thus unexpectedly created a version of the "space for human relations" in the friendship project that both Czechoslovaks and Soviets had begun advocating for in the mid-1960s.

Chapter 6

THE NORMALIZATION OF FRIENDSHIP

[The Soviets] want to strengthen friendship with bullets.
—CZECH CITIZEN, OCTOBER 1968

In the winter of 1971–1972, the Soviet House of Science and Culture in Prague hosted a series of festivities to "educate children in the glorious traditions of proletarian internationalism." Two thousand young Czechs came to the building in groups of 150 to 200 for special New Year's celebrations, complete with a Soviet New Year's tree. The children had the opportunity to admire the tree, decorated with Russian toys, and they received gifts from the Soviet Union. Children from the Soviet embassy's school in Prague also attended. The celebrations were organized by the embassy and the House of Culture and were supported by the Czechoslovak state, including the Union of Czechoslovak-Soviet Friendship (SČSP), the Ministry of Education, and the Socialist Union of Youth. The organizers hoped that the festivities, in addition to winning Czech children over to the cause of friendship with the Soviet Union, would not "fail to make a definite impression on [their] parents." Soviet officials judged the New Year's celebrations a great success.[1]

While the Soviet House of Culture was hosting the New Year's festivities in Prague, the Soviet Army was maintaining an occupation force of roughly

75,000 troops in garrisons across Czechoslovakia.[2] Soviet troops would remain in the country until 1990. Historians often depict the Soviet invasion and occupation of Czechoslovakia as the end of an era. In his history of postwar Europe, Tony Judt writes that the invasion marked the moment when "the soul of Communism . . . died" on the continent.[3] The Russian cultural historians Pëtr Vail' and Aleksandr Genis argue that the invasion not only triggered the Prague Spring's demise, but the end of the 1960s reform era in the USSR.[4] Logically, the Soviet occupation of Czechoslovakia should have also been the death knell for the friendship project. In fact, as this chapter will show, the friendship project survived the invasion and played a central role in the occupation. In Czechoslovakia, both protesters and proponents of the Soviets' actions drew on the friendship project's central tropes to reinforce their respective positions. They thus transformed the project and, paradoxically, helped it to endure.

In 1968–1969, Czechoslovak opponents of the invasion used the friendship project's central symbols, themes, and tools to shape their resistance: they appropriated the mythology of the Red Army's 1945 liberation of their country to shame Soviet soldiers; they organized a yearlong boycott of Soviet films; and they reworked official newsreel footage celebrating Soviet-Czechoslovak relations into anti-Soviet propaganda. At the same time, the friendship project influenced efforts by Soviet officials and their allies in the Czechoslovak government to "normalize" relations between their countries. Immediately after the invasion, the Soviet government turned to tourism, friendship societies, and even its soldiers to restore relations with Czechoslovakia. Beginning in April 1969, when Leonid Brezhnev forced Alexander Dubček to resign from his position as first secretary of the Communist Party of Czechoslovakia (KSČ) and appointed Gustáv Husák to take his place, the Soviet and Czechoslovak governments worked together to use the friendship project to rebuild their political and military alliance.

The very venue for the New Year's celebrations in Prague demonstrates the extent to which the two governments considered the friendship project essential to restoring relations after the invasion. Throughout the winter months of 1971, five hundred construction workers labored intensely, seven days a week, to turn a building that had once housed a monastery in the center of Prague's Old Town into a showcase of Soviet soft power. On May 28, 1971, the House of Soviet Science and Culture opened, in time for the fiftieth anniversary of the founding of the KSČ.[5] Brezhnev traveled to Prague for the opening ceremonies, which were also attended by Husák, and the Czechoslovak president, Ludvík Svoboda. The mayor of Prague, Zdeněk Zuska, gave a speech, declaring that the House of Culture "will not only be an integral part of Prague's cultural politics, but will contribute to the development of the friendship of our people."[6] The House of Culture perfectly encapsulated the cultural and commercial aspirations of the friendship project: by the mid-1970s it included a store selling Soviet products, a restaurant offering food from the Soviet republics, and a filial of the Pushkin Institute, which promoted Russian-language teaching.[7] By building the House of Culture, the two governments sought to rebuild their empire of friends.

In studies of Communist Czechoslovakia, "normalization" is usually understood as a domestic policy put in place by Husák's government to return the country to the pre-1968 status quo. Normalization entailed scaling back Dubček's reforms and purging the Czechoslovak Communist Party and other state organizations of his most ardent supporters. "Normalization" has also become a synonym for the last two decades of Communist rule in Czechoslovakia.[8] Yet as this chapter will show, normalization had still another function: it was a transnational policy designed to restore the Soviet-Czechoslovak alliance in both countries to its pre-1968 vigor, along with the friendship project that supported it.

From "Liberators" to "Occupiers"

The legacy of the Red Army's liberation of Czechoslovakia from German occupation in 1945 shaped the Soviet decision to invade in 1968, and the Czechoslovak resistance that followed. As chapter 3 explained, following the KSČ's 1948 coup, Czechoslovak and Soviet officials and propagandists fashioned the legacy of the liberation into a foundational myth for friendship between their countries. In the mid-1960s, however, Czechoslovak citizens began to question this myth, which focused solely on the Red Army's heroism. In 1965, at a public event in Prague about the history of the war, participants asked why the Czechoslovak government and media only highlighted the Soviet army's role in the liberation, while ignoring the fact that the U.S. Army had liberated Western Bohemia.[9] As censorship relaxed in 1967 and 1968, the Czechoslovak press began to examine previously prohibited questions about the war, such as why Prague had been liberated by the Soviet

Army, when the U.S. Army had been closer to the capital in early May 1945, and thus could have aided the Prague Uprising sooner.[10] In a forum *Svět sovětů* (World of the Soviets) held in 1968 about the future of Czechoslovak-Soviet friendship, the travel writer Jiří Hanzelka even made a passing reference to the crimes Red Army soldiers had committed in Czechoslovakia, which he delicately termed "excesses." Hanzelka mentioned Soviet soldiers' notorious propensity for looting, even as he emphasized the sacrifices they had made liberating his country, "Just as there were soldiers here who said, 'give up your watches,' there were also soldiers here who gave everything they had."[11]

From the Soviet government's perspective, this new scrutiny of the history of World War II in Czechoslovakia posed a threat to the USSR's broader empire of liberation in Eastern Europe. In July 1968, when Brezhnev held a meeting in Warsaw with the leaders of Poland, Bulgaria, the German Democratic Republic, and Hungary to discuss what he saw as the mounting political crisis in Czechoslovakia, he spoke out against "attacks" on the Soviet Union in the Czechoslovak media, including "offensive remarks about the Soviet troops that had liberated Czechoslovakia."[12] The resulting letter, sent by the leaders of the five countries to the Czechoslovak Central Committee protesting the Prague Spring, portrayed the reform movement as a threat to the legitimacy of the socialist world. It reminded the Czechoslovaks of the gratitude they were supposed to feel toward the USSR on account of the Soviet people's sacrifices during the war, "The peoples of our countries won a victory over Hitlerite fascism at the price of immense sacrifices. They have won freedom and independence and the opportunity to advance on the road of progress and socialism. The borders of the socialist world have been transferred to the center of Europe, to the Elbe and the Šumava mountains." The letter then went on to warn the KSČ, "We can never agree that these historic gains of socialism and independence and security of all our peoples should be threatened. We can never agree that imperialism should break through the socialist system by peaceful or violent means, from within or from without, and change the balance of power in Europe to its advantage."[13]

As tensions between the USSR and Czechoslovakia increased, the KGB reinforced the idea that the Czechoslovak reforms were threatening the security of the Soviet empire of liberation. In the summer of 1968, reports the KGB compiled for the Communist Party of the Soviet Union about Soviet popular opinion of the "events" in Czechoslovakia—likely designed to encourage an invasion—depicted the satellite's citizens as having betrayed the sacred legacy of the liberation. Students at Uzhgorod State University chastised the Czechoslovaks for having "forgotten . . . that without the help of the Soviet Army, Czechoslovakia could not have existed independently."[14] A manager from Azerbaijan declared that it was necessary to "take immediate measures, including military interference, in order not to allow the capitalist order to be restored under the flag of democracy in brother Czechoslovakia, for which the Soviet people spilled so much blood."[15] A veteran of the Soviet liberation of Czechoslovakia, now a worker in Chelyabinsk, urged the Soviet authorities to "act more decisively, including bringing Soviet forces to Czechoslovakia." He added, "The use of troops is an extreme measure, but it would be justified, and the Czechoslovak people would support such a step."[16] These remarks indicate that twenty-three years after the end of World War II, Soviet citizens still viewed the liberation's legacy as legitimizing the USSR's power over its satellite state.

Following the invasion, Czechoslovaks, too, drew on the legacy of the Soviet liberation—to protest the Soviets' actions. They singled out the ubiquitous memorials to the Red Army in their country as targets. The morning after the invasion, a crowd of at least one thousand people in Karlovy Vary tore down the monument to the Red Army in front of the central post office. In Trutnov, protesters torched the local Soviet tank memorial and tore the hammer and sickle off its pedestal. A similar incident occurred in Slovakia, in Humenné. In the Moravian town of Kroměříž, protesters destroyed the wreaths adorning the local monument to the Red Army.[17]

These assaults on Soviet war memorials were clearly meant to protest not only the invasion, but the very legacy of the liberation and the broader friendship project. This connection was most clearly demonstrated in Mělník, where protesters defaced the local tank monument to the Red Army with anti-Soviet graffiti, including a swastika, and destroyed the town's obelisk to Czechoslovak-Soviet friendship.[18] The use of swastikas as symbols of protests—which Czechoslovaks not only painted on World War II monuments, but on the actual Soviet tanks moving through their towns—was an especially caustic attack on the friendship project's central trope: the Soviet Union's self-appointed role as the savior of Europe from fascism.[19] By using Nazi symbols to protest the invasion, Czechoslovaks accused the Soviets of having become akin to the very enemies they had vanquished in 1945. "We outlived Hitler, we'll outlive Brezhnev!" an anonymous flyer taped to a mailbox in Prague proclaimed.[20]

Czechoslovaks' comparisons of Soviet soldiers to Nazis would appear to mark the decisive end to the twenty-three-year-old transnational mythology of the liberation, and thus the friendship project it supported. But another, simultaneous line of protest demonstrates this was not the case. Czechoslovaks also opposed the invasion by setting up a contrast between what they depicted as the Soviet Army's benevolence in 1945 with its violent aggression in 1968. In letters to the Soviet authorities, graffiti, and street demonstrations, Czechoslovaks labeled the Soviet military's actions in 1945 a "liberation" and in 1968 as an "occupation." "Twenty-three years ago, when the soldiers of the Soviet army came to us, they were welcomed by the people of Czechoslovakia as [our] dearest friends, as liberators, as the guardians of the freedom and independence of our people," workers from a transport factory in Plzeň wrote to the Soviet embassy in Czechoslovakia. "We are deeply shocked by the reality that today, Soviet forces are again in our country, not as friends, but as occupiers."[21] Members of the National Committee in Litoměřice sent a letter of protest to Marshal Ivan Konev and other Soviet military leaders who had participated in the liberation of Czechoslovakia, lamenting, "Now . . . the sons of our liberators have entered [our] town with guns and bullets aimed at peaceful residents."[22] These sentiments were also reflected in visual imagery protesting the invasion. In Prague one poster showed a Soviet soldier in 1945 holding a young Czech boy in his arms next to a picture of his "son," a Soviet soldier in 1968, pointing a gun at a map of Czechoslovakia.[23] In Bratislava, graffiti appeared on the Slavín War Memorial to the Red Army, "The father was a liberator—the son is an occupier."[24] On October 28, 1968, the fiftieth anniversary of the founding of the Czechoslovak Republic, several thousand young people gathered on Wenceslaus Square in Prague to protest the Soviet occupation, yelling slogans that included "1945—yes, 1968—no!"[25]

For Czechoslovak protesters, creating such a stark dichotomy between the Soviet Army's heroic behavior in 1945 and its violent aggression in 1968 was a deliberate strategy of resistance, designed to shame their Soviet "friends." Yet this strategy had an unintended consequence. By constructing a binary between the 1945 liberation and the 1968 occupation, protesters reinforced the core myth of the friendship project: that the Soviet Army had acted

Figure 11. Memorial to the Red Army in Brno, August 1968.
The protest sign attached reads, "I am a liberator, but you are an aggressor!"
Credit: Česká tisková kancelář.

benevolently and selflessly in 1945. In this way, even as they protested the Soviet invasion, Czechoslovaks helped restore the empire of friends.

Boycotting Friendship

Another strategy Czechoslovaks developed to protest the invasion was to target the cultural side of the friendship project, especially Soviet films. During the Third Republic, Soviet films in Czechoslovakia had served as a particular source of contention in the countries' alliance. Following the 1968 invasion, Czechoslovakia's movie theaters once again became critical battlegrounds over the future of Czechoslovak-Soviet friendship.

For a year after the invasion, the Czechoslovak film industry presided over a de facto boycott of Soviet films, as well as films from the other Warsaw Pact countries that had sent troops to suppress the Prague Spring.[26] In November 1968, for instance, only one Soviet film was playing in Prague's seventy-two movie theaters, compared to fifteen French films, nine American, eight British, five Yugoslav, and four Romanian. (Romania was the only Warsaw Pact country that did not participate in the invasion.) The screening of the single Soviet film, *Ordinary Fascism*, Mikhail Romm's 1965 documentary about Nazi Germany, was in and of itself an act of protest, designed to elicit a comparison with the Soviet invasion.

The film boycott represented a significant reversal in Czechoslovak-Soviet relations. Ever since the early postwar period, Czechoslovak cultural officials had gone to extraordinary lengths to promote Soviet films; in 1968 and 1969 they took equally extreme measures to avoid showing them.[27] A pro-Soviet Prague resident described in disgust how Soviet films were being substituted with poor quality copies of forty-year-old American movies, such as a Buster Keaton feature from the 1920s. Calling this "sabotage," he added, "I have no doubt that they don't even show [this film] in America. But our cultural workers buy it for big dollars (the Americans are probably laughing)."[28]

Soviet officials complained that when their films were shown in Czechoslovakia, they were relegated to second-rate theaters on the outskirts of cities, and were screened at unpopular times, such as at nine-thirty in the morning. Furthermore, most of these films were ten to fifteen years old, and did not represent "the best side of Soviet cinematography." Many were not dubbed, as was customary for foreign films in Czechoslovakia, but were instead accompanied by poor-quality subtitles. To make matters worse, in the few instances when Soviet films were shown, the screenings were sometimes interrupted by "hooligans" from the audience who covered up the screens with curtains.[29]

In February 1969, six months after the invasion, the majority of foreign films being shown in Prague were American, British, and West German, and there were no Soviet, Bulgarian, or Polish films on offer. To make matters worse for the Soviets, the Western films that were shown were the very antithesis of what they considered to be healthy socialist cinema: "trashy hit films, sexual films, horror films, and the like," complained a report by the Soviet embassy, which concluded darkly, "It is becoming apparent that the leading employees of Czechoslovak film, under the leadership of Alois Poledňák, are using the political situation to reorient the Czechoslovak people in a direction that they find advantageous."[30]

Officials at Czechoslovakia's state film agency, Státní film, claimed by contrast that the reason they were screening few Soviet movies had nothing to do with politics, but merely reflected their desire to take market considerations and Czechoslovak viewers' tastes into account. "Previously, the commission for film selection sometimes had to submit to various pressures, but the result was usually that the viewers of such films were absolutely uninterested in them," an agency report claimed in the spring of 1969. "For the past twenty years," the report continued, Czechoslovak film organizations had done everything in their power to get viewers to see films from the USSR and the other socialist countries, including "[removing] films from all other countries; . . . organizing visits by schools, social organizations, and institutions; holding contests for office workers and viewers; and even subsidizing ticket sales." The report asked, rhetorically, "How can this contribute to the knowledge of the culture of these countries, how does this help us show support for friendly relations? The experience of the past twenty years—not just from the past year—shows completely definitively, that some types of administrative measures aimed at forming movie theaters' programs (and by the way, in the [sphere] of culture as a whole) lead in practice to the opposite result." Officials at Státní film proposed that rather than determine film imports based on political considerations, as had been the practice throughout the Communist period, they should select movies on the basis of their potential to "excite, entertain, and make [the viewer] think." The agency argued that politics should play only a secondary role in selecting which films to import, and that the foreign films shown in Czechoslovakia should reflect the best cinema had to offer from both sides of the Iron Curtain: "All the great personalities should be represented in our repertoire—Bergman and Wajda, Tarkovsky and Antonioni, Jancsó and Kubrick."[31] In making this argument, Státní film was, in effect, reviving arguments cultural critics had raised in Czechoslovakia during the Third Republic about the necessity of having access to world culture, as opposed to exclusively Soviet/Eastern bloc culture. The Prague Spring reformers were cosmopolitans, who sought to return Czechoslovakia to the "world stage."[32] After the invasion they recoiled against the prospect of their country being once again confined to the socialist world.

By the winter of 1969, Soviet officials had become increasingly frustrated by what they saw as Státní film's intransience regarding their film exports. In January, Solovei, a secretary at the Soviet embassy in Prague, had a remarkable confrontation with Poledňák, the head of Státní film. The two officials argued heatedly about the role of cultural relations between their countries and about the broader friendship project. Solovei argued that Státní film, by withholding Soviet movies from the Czechoslovak market, was engaging in political sabotage. He reminded Poledňák of the pledge the KSČ had made at its November 1968 plenum, "to develop and strengthen friendship with the Soviet Union and other socialist countries, to wage a permanent war against anti-Soviet and anti-socialist forces." Poledňák claimed that he and his colleagues were not prejudiced against Soviet films, but that the question of their popularity with Czechoslovak viewers was another matter. For instance, he noted that only twelve people had attended a recent screening of *Ordinary Fascism*, a number so small that the director of the movie theater had wondered whether it was even worth it to show the film. Poledňák argued—in a departure from over two decades of practice in the friendship project—that Státní film could not force Czechoslovak citizens to see Soviet movies.[33]

Solovei responded that Czechoslovak policies regarding Soviet films, including poor advertising, were to blame for their unprecedented unpopularity, and that these policies "do not answer the interests of our Communist parties." In a not so subtle jab at the Soviet invasion, Poledňák retorted, "But do your policies really always answer the interests of our brother countries?"[34] Poledňák drew on the rhetoric of the friendship project to insist that Státní film's position on the import of Soviet movies was not motivated by anti-Sovietism. He claimed, "Many of my colleagues and I know the USSR well, we've been there several times," and cited his personal friendships with Soviet film directors, including Stanislav Rostotskii (director of the 1959 joint Soviet-Czechoslovak production about the Soviet liberation of Czechoslovakia, *May Stars*), before concluding, "I don't think there are any grounds for particular concern. Czechoslovak film is now on an upswing; in recent years our films have received worldwide recognition. The government of the ČSSR (Czechoslovak Socialist Republic) highly values the work of our films. I think that everything on our end is going well." In his report about this meeting, Solovei voiced skepticism about Poledňák's claim, "I said to Poledňák that, unfortunately, I could not completely share the opinion that 'everything is going well' in Czechoslovak film, but that I want to believe that everything can and should change for the better. We, Soviet people . . . sincerely desire that Czechoslovak film help its Communist party, its people, in fulfilling the great tasks outlined in the November plenum of the Central Committee of the Czechoslovak Communist Party."[35]

The turning point in the crisis over Soviet films came in the spring of 1969. On March 28, after the Czechoslovak hockey team beat its Soviet rival at the World Ice Hockey Championships in Stockholm, at least a 100,000 protesters took to the streets in Prague chanting anti-Soviet slogans. In Wenceslaus Square, protestors directed their rage at a symbol of the friendship project, storming the office of Aeroflot, the Soviet airline. In the town of Ústí nad Labem, 5,000 demonstrators broke into the office of the representative of the Soviet forces, smashing windows and cutting the phone lines.[36] The Soviet government used the unrest as a pretext to finally force Dubček to resign as first secretary of the KSČ, replacing him with the more pliant Husák. The day after the hockey protests, officials at the Soviet embassy in Prague celebrated the successful screening of Aleksandr Zarkhi's film *Anna Karenina* (1967) in Brno. The movie was the first Soviet film shown in the city in six months; to the embassy officials' surprise and relief, all 1,000 seats in the theater were filled.[37]

The celluloid version of Lev Tolstoy's novel from the 1870s had little explicit ideological significance for the construction of socialism, yet the embassy officials portrayed its debut as a key step in rebuilding the friendship project. They judged Zarkhi's movie important simply because it was a Soviet work of culture, and its screening would, they hoped, help restore the Soviet Union's standing in its satellite. On the Czechoslovak side, the film's (negative) symbolic importance can be deduced from the efforts taken to block its release: local actors attempted to sabotage the dubbing,[38] and the Czech official who organized the premiere in Prague received threats and even had his phone line cut.[39]

Státní film's boycott of Soviet movies, and the energy Soviet officials expended to break it, demonstrate the extent to which culture and politics remained intertwined in Soviet-Czechoslovak relations after the invasion, but also the extent to which their significance—and that of the broader friendship project—had changed. In the Stalinist period, the friendship project had been intended to transmit an explicit ideological program to Czechoslovakia, which was supposed to transform the satellite in accordance with the Soviet model. In the decade and a half after Stalin's death, friendship was supposed to lead to mutual understanding between Soviets and Czechoslovaks; this understanding was, in turn, viewed as a precondition for the construction of a unified socialist world. During normalization, however, the ideological substance of both Soviet films in Czechoslovakia and the friendship these films symbolized became less clear. The Soviet government now viewed its films primarily as symbols of its geopolitical power, rather than as transmitters of specific ideological messages. The friendship project with Czechoslovakia also became first and foremost a geopolitical symbol: designed to convince citizens of the Soviet Union, Czechoslovakia—and their adversaries in the West—that the Soviet Union's control over Eastern Europe was not grounded in military force, but in the soft power of cultural and interpersonal contacts.

Fighting with Film

In the year after the invasion, Czechoslovak film personnel not only organized a boycott of Soviet films, they also tried to turn their country's cinemas into centers of active resistance against the occupation, by screening short films critical of the USSR before feature films. These short films were spin-offs of traditional newsreels (Soviet documents refer to them as "film magazines" [*kinozhurnaly*]). They were produced by splicing together images from documentary footage, often from old newsreels, and adding a new voice-over. Soviet officials were particularly incensed by these films, which, they charged, "tendentiously show and comment on [current] events."[40]

Two versions of these short films circulated in Czechoslovakia. One version, which was shown in movie theaters in Prague, where Soviet citizens might be in attendance, contained oblique critiques of the USSR. The other version, shown in the provinces, consisted of "more outright anti-Soviet propaganda."[41] Soviet officials found some of these short films objectionable because they depicted the Prague Spring in a positive light. For example, one film contrasted images of the violent police response to student unrest in Western countries in 1968 with Czechoslovak authorities' sympathetic reactions to student protests in Prague.[42] Soviet officials judged other films offensive because they criticized the Communist system as a whole: one film, for example, suggested that the United States would be the first country to reach the moon; another showed images of empty stores in Prague, and of people waiting in long lines for goods. The voice-over asked rhetorically, "Probably there's no need to explain to viewers why this has all turned out this way?"[43] Most troubling of all to the Soviets and their allies in the Czechoslovak government were films that used Soviet footage to depict the USSR in a negative light, such as one that juxtaposed images of the signing of the 1938 Munich Agreement, which had effectively allowed Adolf Hitler to invade Czechoslovakia, with the Moscow Protocol that the Soviet government pressured Dubček to sign after the invasion, and which sanctioned the presence of Soviet troops in the country. "It is amazing," a disgruntled Czech viewer wrote to the Soviet embassy in Prague, "they use government money to show anti-Soviet propaganda! I think it would be correct for the public prosecutor to occupy himself with the activities of these film workers."[44]

The short film that most angered Soviet authorities was produced in the fall of 1968 by the Czechoslovak Army's documentary film unit. Entitled *On That Green Meadow* (*Na tý louce zelený*, Milan Růžička) the eight-minute film was shot with a hidden camera at an airbase near Prague in September. It highlighted the plight of pilots in the Czechoslovak Army who had been displaced by the Soviet troops.[45] A Soviet report assailed the film as "anti-Soviet to a loathsome extent. To the melody of a popular Russian song it captures various episodes from the daily lives of the [Soviet] soldiers and officers located at the airdrome, while in the background the soldiers' underwear is hanging out to dry. [The creators of the film] try and depict the Soviet soldiers and officers as clodhoppers, slovenly occupiers, who have come from the uncivilized steppe. In the background they show the handsome, smart,

Czechoslovak pilots longing for flight, threatened by the [Soviet] military fighter pilots."[46] Soviet officials considered this film particularly toxic because it attempted to turn the Soviet Army, which was supposed to be a symbol of Soviet honor and strength, into an object of ridicule and derision. Their antipathy toward the film may have also stemmed from the fact that it was a "'hit'" with Czechoslovak audiences, who responded to its mocking depiction of the Soviet troops "'with . . . salvos of laughter.'"[47] Soviet military commanders complained that the film contradicted statements the Czechoslovak government had made "about the importance of improving and strengthening friendly relations with the Soviet Union." By March 1969, presumably as a result of pressure from the Soviet military, the offending film had been removed from both army and civilian cinemas.[48]

Soviet officials were not as successful removing short films on nonmilitary topics from Czechoslovak cinemas. In his January 1969 meeting with Poledňák, Solovei, the secretary at the Soviet embassy in Prague, singled out one film that he found particularly offensive because it "tries to prove that the USSR has acted from a position of force in its relations with the socialist countries." The film in question established a pattern of Soviet aggression toward the Eastern bloc satellites by comparing footage from Poland and Hungary in 1956 with Czechoslovakia in 1968. A sequence of images showed the Soviet government signing an agreement with Poland in 1956 on the "temporary" stationing of Soviet forces in the country, then showed a similar scene from Hungary after the 1956 uprising, and then moved to footage of Brezhnev greeting both former KSČ general secretary Antonín Novotný and Dubček with kisses. "So what isn't true here?" Poledňák asked. "These are only historical images, everyone knows about them." "From my side," Solovei wrote in his account of the meeting, "I expressed astonishment that Poledňák considers all this to be the truth. Frames snatched up from the Western movie chronicles, tendentiously selected and united in one reel, accompanied by a clearly anti-Soviet announcer's text—such examples are usually [only] used by our most irreconcilable enemies."[49]

By the summer of 1969, the Soviet embassy reported a small improvement in the state of Soviet film imports in the country: during the first three weeks of August, there had been a total of eighty-nine screenings of three Soviet films in the capital—albeit at second-rate theaters and with low attendance. The "film magazines" were also becoming more neutral. The embassy attributed these signs of progress to rumors of purges among employees of the

Czechoslovak film industry.[50] At the end of October 1969, the Soviet film *We'll Live until Monday* (Rostotskii, 1968) had a successful premiere in Czechoslovakia. Aided by the fact that censorship had been largely successfully reinstated in the press, the film received positive reviews in major Czechoslovak newspapers. The Soviet embassy hailed this as "a first step on the path to restoring good cooperation between Czechoslovak and Soviet cinematography."[51] This shift did indeed occur against the backdrop of extensive purges and staff changes in the Czechoslovak film industry.[52] In the fall of 1969, Jiří Purš replaced Poledňák as head of Státní film.[53] In 1970, Poledňák was arrested and sentenced to prison on charges of anti-socialist activity. He was released the following year and issued a public self-criticism apologizing for his "deeds and behavior" in 1968 and 1969.[54]

Normalizing Friendship

In June 1969, members of the KSČ's presidium took stock of what they viewed as the massive damage the Prague Spring had caused the party and Czechoslovak society. In particular, they worried about the harm the reform movement had inflicted on the friendship project, "Most dangerous is the appearance of the growth of anti-Sovietism in various forms. This is a mass phenomenon and has hit all strata of the population, including part of the membership of the party. Especially serious is the situation with youth, the intelligentsia, and school children."[55]

   In reality, it was the Soviet invasion, not the Prague Spring, which caused the greatest harm to the friendship project. For example, during the Prague Spring, the leaders of the SČSP, the most important organization in Czechoslovakia for advancing friendship with the Soviet Union, boasted of its ability to remain popular at a time when other mass organizations in the country, such as the Czechoslovak Union of Youth and the trade unions (ROH), were in disarray. In 1968, the SČSP had 1.5 million members.[56] But when Soviet tanks entered Czechoslovakia, the friendship society nearly collapsed.[57] Its chairman, Zdeněk Fierlinger, personally told Soviet representatives he thought the invasion had been a mistake, accusing them of having "sent a half million soldiers to put down a counterrevolution that didn't exist."[58] The SČSP's rank-and-file members demonstrated their anger at the Soviet Union by turning in their membership cards en masse.[59] The local branch in

Ústí nad Labem "was virtually paralyzed": all nine of its "collective" institutional members resigned, as did the majority of its individual members.
Even the custodian and driver at the branch's headquarters quit.[60] In
Gottwaldov, membership in the SČSP plunged from 18,000 to 2,000.[61] To
add to the SČSP's troubles, the editors of its journal, *Svět sovětů*, which had
played a central role in promoting friendship with the USSR, and which in
1967 boasted a circulation of 300,000, refused to continue publishing after the
invasion.[62] The editor, whom Soviet colleagues described as a "good Communist," defended the journal's actions by explaining, "The arrival of Soviet
troops aroused a natural feeling of protest."[63]

Contacts between the SČSP and its sister organization in the USSR, the
Society for Soviet-Czechoslovak Friendship (OSChD), also broke down after
the invasion. Between August 21 and the beginning of September, the two
friendship societies stopped exchanging delegations and communicating with
one another. The OSChD thus temporarily reframed its mission to explain
to the Soviet people their government's decision to invade Czechoslovakia,
and to try to support "healthy forces within the SČSP," working to "normalize the political situation in the ČSSR."[64] To accomplish this task, the
society drew on the legacy of World War II. A week after the invasion, the
Dinamo factory in Moscow held a celebration in honor of the twenty-fourth
anniversary of the Slovak uprising against Nazi Germany. On September 6, the House of Unions in Moscow hosted a memorial event in honor
of Julius Fučík, the KSČ member who was executed by the Nazis in 1943 for
his work in the resistance to the German occupation of Czechoslovakia.[65]
The OSChD intended for these events to have a transnational impact: they
hoped Czechoslovaks would learn of them and realize that the Soviet
people harbored no ill-will toward their Central European friends.

The crisis in the SČSP following the invasion, combined with the rash of
anti-Soviet activity in Czechoslovakia—including the attacks on Red Army
memorials, street protests, the boycott of Soviet films, and the screening of
the anti-Soviet "film magazines"—forced Soviet officials and their supporters
in the Czechoslovak government to quickly develop a plan to "normalize" relations between their countries. On August 30, under Soviet pressure, the
Czechoslovak government created the Office for the Press, Radio, and
Television, which tried to reestablish censorship in the country. This move
particularly curtailed the media's authority to critique Czechoslovakia's relations with the USSR. The Czechoslovak media was forbidden "to use the

word 'occupier' or 'occupation,' criticize the Warsaw pact countries or their Communist parties, attack their troops based on Czechoslovak territory, or write about the victims or damages caused by the military intervention."[66] In October, the Soviet and Czechoslovak governments signed an agreement that allowed the USSR to "temporarily" station troops in the country. The agreement effectively amounted to an official sanction of the invasion by the Czechoslovak state and helped to stabilize the political situation.[67]

Yet the pressing question remained of "how to win the hearts and minds of the Czechs," as the Soviet Politburo phrased it.[68] The method the Soviet and Czechoslovak governments chose for this inauspicious task was a familiar one: they employed cultural, interpersonal, and commercial contacts between Soviet and Czechoslovak citizens to rebuild their countries' alliance. Even as Soviet tanks remained in Czechoslovak cities, the two governments thus tried to reestablish the friendship project along the lines of the model that had developed after Stalin's death.

Why did both Soviet officials and Czechoslovaks who supported the goals of normalization stubbornly cling to the tenets of the friendship project after the violence and enmity of the invasion? Were they cynical, naive, or simply lacking imagination? There are four possible explanations. First, Soviet officials' stubborn attachment to the traditional rituals of Soviet-Czechoslovak friendship speaks to the cynicism at the root of Soviet policy in Czechoslovakia, where rhetoric about transnational friendship had from the early postwar years served to sugarcoat imperialist aims. Second, this attachment to the friendship project was connected with the utopianism that developed after Stalin's death, which found its apex in the Prague Spring. This was the fantasy of rapprochement, the idea that the better Soviets and Czechoslovaks came to know each other, the closer the two nations would become: the dream that personal ties between citizens could transcend national differences. It was a notion that remained powerful even after the invasion.

Third, if, as Kieran Williams has suggested, "normalization is primarily about restoring extreme predictability," then efforts to revive the friendship project seem less audacious.[69] Normalization was an antidote to the experimentation and tumult of the Prague Spring. The policy was meant to be uninventive—an attempt to ignore recent history, to turn back the clock to a more static and predictable era of Soviet-Czechoslovak relations.

A fourth and final explanation concerns the realm of international affairs. From its inception, the Soviet-Czechoslovak friendship project had been shaped by tensions between the superpowers. After the invasion, the Brezhnev and Husák governments framed the Prague Spring in Cold War terms: they portrayed the reform movement as a plot by the Soviet Union's enemies in the West to kidnap the formerly loyal satellite state from the socialist world and transform it into a member of the capitalist camp. This was the message of a "documentary" film the Soviet government commissioned about the Prague Spring in 1969, *Czechoslovakia: Year of Trial* (*Chekhoslovakiia, god ispytanii*, Anatolii Koloshin), which was shown in the USSR and Czechoslovakia.[70] The film posited a parallel between what it claimed were Western designs on Czechoslovakia in 1968 and the German annexation of the Sudetenland in 1938.[71] In internal discussions in the spring of 1969, the KSČ also described the Prague Spring as a vast Western-sponsored assault on Czechoslovak society, involving the American, British, and French embassies, foreign broadcasting, foreign correspondents, and tourists.[72] The KSČ singled out the West's use of cultural diplomacy and other forms of soft power in the Cold War—including the West German policy of Ostpolitik—as an attempt to undermine transnational relations in the socialist world. Czechoslovak and Soviet officials believed that Western efforts to woo Czechoslovak citizens with soft power could only be offset by cultural and interpersonal diplomacy between the socialist countries. They wagered that by reviving the friendship project, they would ensure the survival of the larger socialist world.

From Soldiers to Samaritans

As the Soviet and Czechoslovak governments revived the friendship project after the invasion, they largely drew on traditional methods: they renewed Soviet cultural exports to Czechoslovakia; they reinstated mass tourism between their countries; they resuscitated Czechoslovakia's friendship organizations and publications; and they tried to reimpose the pre-1968 mythology of the Red Army's liberation. The Soviet government, however, developed one significant new strategy for the post-invasion version of the friendship project: it drafted its soldiers in Czechoslovakia to make friends with the people they were occupying.

A mere two weeks after the invasion, Soviet officials from the Central Committee's Department of Agitation and Propaganda proposed inviting

Soviet troops in Czechoslovakia to engage in what might be termed outreach work to local communities. They suggested that Soviet generals and officers should give presentations to the Czechoslovak Army and the civilian population explaining the USSR's justification for the invasion. They recommended organizing meetings with Czechoslovaks who had served in the Red Army during World War II to broaden support for the USSR's actions. The department also suggested that Soviet troops could improve relations with Czechoslovaks by assisting with the harvest in rural areas, repairing locals' broken down cars, as well as engaging youth in sports matches and chess games, accompanied by exchanges of pins and souvenirs.[73] Soviet soldiers were thus not only supposed to defend against "counterrevolutionary activity" in Czechoslovakia; they were supposed to be good Samaritans and friends to the local populace.

Why would the Soviet government make this highly risky move to recast its troops occupying Czechoslovakia into "friends" of the local populace? Marie Černá argues that Soviet attempts to establish friendly ties between the soldiers and Czechoslovak civilians should be seen as part of the USSR's larger effort to rewrite the history of the Prague Spring and the invasion during normalization.[74] Much as psychotherapists believe that victims of trauma need to develop a narrative explaining their suffering in order to heal, Soviet authorities believed that in order to restore order in Czechoslovakia they had to work in tandem with the new government in Prague to explain the extraordinary events of 1968. As Paulina Bren writes, "They demanded a retelling of the Prague Spring that would serve as the official collective memory of 1968 as well as an ideological launching pad for normalization."[75] Official Soviet and Czechoslovak accounts argued that the Prague Spring had constituted a "counterrevolution," not a reform movement, and that by crushing it, the Soviet Army was a "savior," not an occupying force.[76] Directing troops to play soccer and chess with local youth was thus an effort to convince the Czechoslovak people that this new, official narrative was correct: that the Soviet Army was indeed a "friend," not an "occupier."

Soviet troops' "friendly" overtures to the Czechoslovak populace were also directed at their compatriots back home in the USSR. While normalization is usually portrayed as primarily a domestic policy in Czechoslovakia, it was in fact a transnational project, directed at the Czechoslovak and Soviet people. Following the invasion, the Soviet government not only faced the task of restoring friendship with Czechoslovakia, it also had to convince its own citizens that the friendship project remained viable. This was important because socialist internationalism continued to play a central role in Soviet ideology. The Soviet Union could not afford to appear as an occupier to its own people, since it had been founded explicitly as an anti-imperialist state. According to Soviet ideology, only imperialists could be occupiers. Yet the task of convincing the Soviet people that Czechoslovaks remained committed to the friendship project was threatened by events on the ground. In the first few months after the invasion, in every city Soviet troops occupied in Czechoslovakia, they encountered crowds of angry locals who wanted to argue about the invasion. The Soviet government struggled to contain the fallout from these unscripted encounters. Soviet propagandists reported anxiously in the fall of 1968, "Literally every tank or armored vehicle positioned in Czechoslovak population centers has been turned into a space for lively discussions, in which every day more and more people from the Czechoslovak population take part, including young workers, university students, and high school students from the upper grades."[77] An intelligence commander in the Soviet Army, who was stationed in a town in Northern Moravia, recalled how troops could not go to restaurants without being set upon by locals wanting to argue about the invasion. "At first it was interesting to enter into discussions with Czechs, but then we got so sick [*tak nadoeli*] of these conversations, that if someone sat down next to us at a table for a 'chat' we either left or chased this 'interlocutor' away."[78] For Soviet officials, these encounters inspired fears about ideological contamination among the troops and about the transmission of "counterrevolutionary" ideas back to the USSR. During a one-month period between October and November 1968, for instance, the KGB confiscated up to one hundred letters a day that Soviet troops had attempted to mail home, containing "anti-Soviet and anti-socialist publications that have fallen into their hands, photographs of anti-Soviet slogans and other politically harmful material, the goal of which is clearly to corroborate the situation they have encountered."[79] The transmission of such "anti-Soviet material" to the USSR threatened to directly contradict the Soviet government's official explanation of its military activity in Czechoslovakia, which was that the Czechoslovak people had invited Soviet soldiers to their country to protect them from "counterrevolutionaries" directed by the West.

To counteract Soviet troops' descriptions of their encounters with angry Czechoslovaks, the Soviet government instructed the editors of the USSR's

leading newspapers to "expand positive information about the life of Czechoslovak workers," in order to "unmask anti-socialist and anti-Soviet pronouncements," and to publish interviews with Soviet soldiers showing that
they were working in cooperation with local organizations in Czechoslovakia.[80] In other words, it was just as important for the Soviet government to
create an official narrative about the invasion for public consumption in the
USSR, as it was in Czechoslovakia. The Soviet government remained intent
on depicting its empire in Eastern Europe as a friendship project. Accounts
in the Soviet press, such as an article in *Izvestiia* (News) in October 1968,
which portrayed Soviet soldiers as selflessly assisting Czechoslovak farmers
with the harvest, were thus intended to convince the Soviet people of the righ-
teousness of their army's actions, and of the positive prospects for continuing Soviet-Czechoslovak friendship.[81] The "friendly" relationship between
Soviet troops and Czechoslovak civilians became a central trope of propaganda in normalized Czechoslovakia, especially in the regions where Soviet
troops were garrisoned.[82] But this trope also had a transnational message,
aimed at the Soviet public.

"With the Soviet Union for Eternity and Never Any Other Way"

In normalized Czechoslovakia, participating in the friendship project became
a way to prove one's loyalty as a citizen of the country, and as a citizen of the
broader socialist world. The Czechoslovak government promoted friendship
with the Soviet Union as a means to simultaneously foster "socialist patriotism and internationalism."[83] This dual and seemingly contradictory effort
involved convincing Czechoslovaks that the security of their country—and
the sanctity of their private lives—was dependent on cultural, interpersonal,
and commercial contacts with the USSR. The Czechoslovak government
therefore strove to present friendship with the Soviet Union as inevitable and
inviolable. It thus implicitly attacked the arguments reformers had made during the Prague Spring about the inherent historical and cultural differences
between the two countries, and the need for each to pursue its own political
path. "To like and dislike the same things is indeed true friendship," *Rudé
pravo* (Red Right) claimed in May 1970, when Czechoslovakia and the USSR
signed a new treaty of "friendship, cooperation, and mutual assistance."[84]

One of the key steps Husák's government took in 1969 to restore order was to institute political screenings for members of the KSČ, the intelligentsia, ideological activists, and people who worked in the mass media. These people were called before party commissions and interrogated about their activities during the Prague Spring and their attitudes toward normalization. The screening process effectively functioned as a way for the state to create a new, healthier socialist community, untainted by the upheaval of 1968–1969. Those who refused to condemn the Prague Spring and to pledge their loyalty to the process of normalization were expelled from the party or fired from their positions. From 1969 to 1972, 653 people were sent to prison.[85]

Bren has stressed the performative side of these screenings, arguing, "The purge . . . forced citizens into dialogue with the regime" and thus helped to legitimize it.[86] Less well-known is the fact that normalization also forced— or at least highly incentivized—Czechoslovaks to engage in the friendship project, thus relegitimizing *it*. In the early 1970s, an SČSP report highlighted the need for the organization to increase its membership; the organization thus invited anyone to become a member who "agrees with the goals and basis of the Union [of Czechoslovak-Soviet Friendship] and who did not behave negatively during the crisis of 1968–1969."[87] Scholars have argued that the majority of Czechoslovak citizens acquiesced to Husák's counterreforms because they saw little chance of successfully resisting the Soviet troops, and because they desired a return to peace, calm, and ordinary life after the upheaval caused by the invasion.[88] Maintaining friendship with the Soviet Union became a way of ensuring this peace. By 1977, the SČSP had 2.24 million members—a roughly 50 percent increase from the preinvasion period.[89] "Whoever was not a member of the Union of Czechoslovak-Soviet Friendship was a nobody," a former member of the organization recalled in a 2009 documentary shown on Czech television.[90]

Over the course of the 1970s, the regime and its citizens worked out a type of social contract. Writing in the late 1970s, the Czech dissident Milan Šimečka argued that the state required Czechoslovaks to "manifest their public assent [for the Husák regime], march on May Day, pay their subscription to the Soviet Friendship Society, raise their hands at meetings and sign resolutions."[91] In return, the Husák government offered Czechoslovaks not only one of the highest standards of living in the Eastern bloc, but the time and space for "self-actualization": for family life, hobbies, and consumption.[92] Involvement in the friendship project thus became one of the ways that

Czechoslovak citizens fulfilled their side of this social contract. In the 1970s and 1980s, participation in this project continued to be a routine aspect of everyday life: from the consumption of Soviet canned goods and technology to the obligatory study of Russian in school.[93] A 1983 Russian textbook for Czech eighth-graders emphasized the language's importance as a conduit of friendship with the USSR; it promoted the language as a means of communicating with visiting Soviet pioneers, corresponding with Soviet pen pals, and participating in "international friends['] club[s]."[94] A new journal promoting friendship with the USSR, called *Svět socialismu* (The World of Socialism) replaced *Svět sovětu*. Tens of thousands of Czechoslovaks traveled to the Soviet Union each year as tourists, and attended Soviet performances in Czechoslovakia.[95]

In the immediate aftermath of the invasion, Czechoslovak protesters had attacked the mythology of the Soviet liberation in 1945, even going so far as to compare the Soviet soldiers riding on tanks through the streets of their cities with the Germans who had occupied their country during World War II. During normalization, the Czechoslovak and Soviet governments used the mythology of the liberation as yet another trope to restore their countries' friendship. In particular, they tried to establish a positive connection between the two times Soviet troops had come to Czechoslovakia. An article in *Rudé právo* in 1970, in the form of a "message" to the Soviet people from the "Czechoslovak working people," expressed "gratitude for [your] selfless fraternal assistance in liberating Czechoslovakia in 1945," and for "the international assistance you extended in August 1968."[96] This was not the first time the Soviet government had tried to use its empire of liberation to restore its empire of friends: after the Soviet Army invaded Hungary in 1956, Nikita Khrushchev attempted to use the legacy of the Red Army's liberation of Hungary at the end of World War II to reestablish Soviet-Hungarian "friendship."[97]

In 1969, the Czechoslovak trade unions began to organize annual trips to the Soviet Union on "friendship trains." These trips further demonstrate how officials in the two countries attempted to employ transnational contacts and the legacy of the liberation to stamp out the remaining embers of the Prague Spring and to restore friendship between their citizens. Like many other Czechoslovak institutions, the ROH, which was the largest mass organization in the country, was thrown into turmoil during the Prague Spring.[98] International contacts had always formed an important part of the trade unions' work. Yet according to institutional reports written during normalization, in 1968–1969, the leaders of the trade unions had gone rogue, adopting their own model for conducting international contacts. The task of the normalized trade unions was thus to reestablish friendship with the Soviet Union as the fundamental principle of their international outreach.[99]

The method the trade unions chose to accomplish this formidable task was to establish an exchange of high-profile delegations with the USSR, which would travel on "friendship trains." Each year a train of between 150 and 300 carefully selected activists from the ROH would be sent on a trip to the Soviet Union, and a Soviet delegation would travel to Czechoslovakia. The Czechoslovak participants on these friendship trains were "experienced and verified [*osvědčených*] functionaries of the ROH." They included members of the people's militia, which had opposed the Prague Spring, members of the secret police, and servicemen in the Czechoslovak Army. In particular, the trade unions' leadership selected people who had actively helped to suppress the Prague Spring, "those who contributed directly to liquidating counterrevolutionary groups and their plans in the August days."[100]

Travel on the friendship trains thus served as a reward for upholding friendship with the Soviet Union in 1968–1969. In 1971, the trade unions called for selecting participants "who have a positive connection to socialist development, and a good [*dobrý*] relationship to the USSR." When the trade unions' Central Committee selected candidates for the trip, it was instructed to include information about the person's "political stance in the years 1968–1969."[101] For example, Marie Bělohubá, an ROH official from Kutná Hora, was recommended on account of what the ROH's Central Committee considered her positive behavior during the Prague Spring and its aftermath. "In the years 1968–69 she distanced herself from rightest influences [*živlů*] and at the present time agrees with the politics of the KSČ." Václav Lapice, another ROH functionary, was nominated for his "rich activity in the trade [unions] and party functions." "In the years 1968–1969 [he] belonged to the healthy nucleus . . . of the KSČ and actively helped with cleansing the party."[102]

In the Stalinist period, Czechoslovaks had framed travel to the Soviet Union as an act of conversion, which transformed visitors into socialists. By contrast, the Czechoslovaks who traveled to the USSR on the trade unions' friendship trains during normalization explained their journeys as acts of penitence for the heresy of the Prague Spring. This was the theme of Václav

Valenta's remarkable account of his experience on the 1971 friendship train. Valenta began his narrative, written for the trade unions' administration, by describing the moment the train crossed into the USSR. In Chop, the Ukrainian border town, Soviet citizens greeted the Czechoslovak delegation with flowers, and the locals and tourists proceeded to dance together. Valenta depicted this encounter as having triggered feelings of guilt and atonement among the group's participants. "We parted from the citizens of Chop in great emotion, gushing over how warm and sincere the reception was. We boarded the train, waved for the last time out the window, wiped our moist eyes, and sat down to meditate over how we could have allowed such a rupture here [i.e., in Czechoslovakia] in the year 1968."[103]

An especially notable theme in Valenta's account is his portrayal of the legacy of World War II as having convinced members of the Czechoslovak delegation that the Prague Spring had been misguided and that Czechoslovakia's future depended on close friendship with the Soviet Union. From Minsk, the friendship train participants visited the nearby village of Khatyn, whose inhabitants had all been murdered by German soldiers in 1943 in retaliation for an attack by local partisans. Valenta described how touched his compatriots were by the visit. "We drove away from this place full of hate and malice toward all the barbarians and fomenters of war. On the other hand, [we experienced] great respect for the heroes who fell, and for those who are still alive and had to survive the fires of battle." And then he suddenly shifted gears, making a surprising analogy between German war criminals and the Prague Spring's reformers. Referencing Ludvík Vaculík's famous manifesto from June 1968 in support of the Prague Spring, and the Club of Engaged Non-Party Members [KAN], one of the new political organizations that had formed that year, Valenta continued, "And then the thought came, what did people at home [*u nás*] really want in 1968? What did all those devotees of the 2,000 words, KAN, and others desire."[104]

Valenta's tendentious analogy between the Germans' massacre of innocent villagers at Khatyn and the Prague Spring's political reformers demonstrates yet another twist in the long legacy of World War II and its role in the friendship project. After the Soviet invasion of Czechoslovakia, angry Czechoslovaks had tried to disrupt the friendship project by accusing Soviet troops of being akin to the very fascists the Red Army had defeated in 1945. Three years later, in his attempt to restore the friendship project, Valenta effectively accused the Prague Spring's *reformers* of acting like the German invaders.

During Stalinism, the Czechoslovak mythology of the Red Army's liberation had been grounded in gratitude for the opportunity to build a socialist society modeled on the USSR. Valenta's travelogue also portrayed his fellow countrymen as indebted to the Soviet Union—but for the benefits of normalization in the private sphere. In Leningrad, the group visited the Piskarëvskoe cemetery, the burial site of the Soviet soldiers who had died defending the city during the siege and the civilian victims of the blockade. Valenta reflected on the sacrifices the Soviets had made for the Czechoslovak people. He contended that the Soviet soldiers had given their lives not for the construction of a new, revolutionary order in Eastern Europe, but so that "we could live freely today, have [our] work and quiet homes."[105]

Moscow was the last stop in the Soviet Union on the 1971 Czechoslovak friendship train. Valenta was among a select group of the travelers who were invited to a reception in honor of the fifty-fourth anniversary of the October Revolution, which Brezhnev himself attended. "This was the most beautiful and precious evening in my life, which I will remember forever," Valenta gushed. The following day, the group received special tickets to the military parade on Red Square.[106] After watching members of the army occupying his country strut across the square, Valenta concluded his report on the friendship train by directly addressing the high-level trade unions' officials it was intended for, "In truth, comrades, it would be hard to look for a better friendship in the world, and therefore I would like to conclude my impressions with the words 'With the Soviet Union for eternity and never any other way.'"[107]

During the Prague Spring, Soviet and Czechoslovak citizens had attempted to use tourism to transform relations between their countries, to make them more spontaneous and informal. By contrast, the friendship trains during normalization were designed to showcase the friendship project as a fixed entity, at once inevitable and inviolable.

The Song of the Tree and the Rose

In the late 1970s, a Soviet engineer arrives in Prague. He is in his early fifties, still handsome, but visibly exhausted. He has been invited to the Czechoslovak capital to assist with the construction of the city's new metro system: his expertise is required to build a tunnel under the Vltava River, connecting the city's Old Town with the Lesser Town. As soon as the engineer steps off the plane at Prague's Ruzyně airport, it becomes clear that this will be no ordinary business trip: he has a flashback to a wartime scene in the city's streets, where a bomb has exploded. The engineer has come to Prague not only to build the metro, but to resolve a personal issue from his past.

The scene described above comes from a 1978 Czechoslovak film by Ladislav Rychman, *The Song of the Tree and the Rose* (*Píseň o stromu a růži*). In the film, the legendary Soviet actor Viacheslav Tikhonov plays the engineer, Vladimir Kuznetsov, who is also a veteran of the Soviet liberation of Czechoslovakia in 1945. The film tells two stories: the first is a conventionally heroic socialist labor narrative about the completion of the metro tunnel, thanks to Kuznetsov's expertise, with long industrial sequences accompanied by dramatic violin music. The second is a much more melancholy, personal narrative. It turns out that Kuznetsov has come to Prague not only on a mission of labor, but on a mission of the heart: he is looking for Věra, a Czech schoolteacher he fell in love with as a young soldier during the liberation.

The Song of the Tree and the Rose, produced as pro-Soviet propaganda in Czechoslovakia, is also a surprisingly revealing document about the limits of the friendship project during normalization. In stark contrast to Valenta's hagiographic account of the friendship train to the Soviet Union, the film portrays Czechoslovak-Soviet friendship in the late 1970s as emotionally fraught, weighed down by the burden of history, and as surprisingly ambiguous. The story about the construction of the metro tunnel depicts friendship between Czechoslovakia and the Soviet Union as mutually beneficial and permanent. By contrast, the narrative about Kuznetsov's search for his long-lost Czech love conveys the underlying frustrations and fragility of this friendship.

In the film, the metro construction headquarters tasks Lenka Panková, a secretary in her early twenties (played by Jelena Šebestová), with showing Kuznetsov around Prague. At first she is annoyed by this assignment: in a conversation with her mother she refers to Kuznetsov dismissively as "some Russian" and she worries that his visit will interrupt her time with her boyfriend, a construction worker on the metro project who moonlights as a jazz musician. Soon, however, Lenka develops a crush on Kuznetsov, thanks to his courtly manners, world-weary air, and ability to speak fluent Czech. When she learns he is looking for Věra, she eagerly tries to help. She succeeds in tracking down the Czech nurse who cared for Kuznetsov in a Prague hospital after he was injured in battle, and she finds the Czech resistance fighter who had convalesced in the bed next to him. She even manages to locate Věra's last known address, by speaking with the administrator of the school where she had taught in 1946. Yet when she and Kuznetsov go to the address, they find that the apartment building has been torn down as part of the metro construction project. Věra remains literally out of reach. The friendship project's technological achievements have inadvertently destroyed its human side.

The Song of the Tree and the Rose, while not a formal sequel to *May Stars*, has obvious parallels with the 1959 Soviet-Czechoslovak coproduction about the liberation, which also starred Tikhonov.[108] In *May Stars*, Tikhonov played a Soviet lieutenant, Andrei Rukavichkin, who came to a schoolhouse on the outskirts of Prague during the liberation looking for chalk to mark cleared mines. He has a brief flirtation with the young schoolteacher, Jana, before he has to leave to return to his unit. In *The Song of the Tree and the Rose*, Tikhonov can be understood as playing the same character nearly two decades later (even though the character has a different name). The Czech semiologist Vladimír Macura has argued that the film portrays the construction of the Prague metro as a sequel to the 1945 liberation.[109] But even as the film conveys a triumphant message about technological cooperation between the superpower and satellite, its message about Czechoslovak-Soviet friendship is far more ambiguous. In *May Stars*, Rukavichkin's romance with Jana was aborted after the head of her school erased his address from the blackboard. In *The Song of the Tree and the Rose*, Tikhonov's character has two failed Czech romances. The first was with Věra in 1945, which is magnified by his inability to find her over three decades later. The second is with Lenka, whom he ultimately concludes is a poor match because of their insurmountable age difference. "There is a wise, old proverb, 'don't attach a rose to an old tree,'" he tells her. The film's ultimate message is that while the official side of Czechoslovak-Soviet friendship, symbolized by the countries' cooperation building the Prague metro is strong, the intimate, personal side of friendship has been irrevocably damaged by the ravages of time.

Friendship in a Time of Occupation

In May 1970, the Czechoslovak government signed a treaty of "friendship, cooperation, and mutual assistance" with the Soviet Union. This was the third such treaty the two countries had signed since 1943, and it represented their formal commitment to normalization. *Rudé právo* devoted an entire edition to the treaty and friendship with the Soviet Union. Alongside the text of the treaty, the newspaper published transcripts of speeches by dignitaries, and appeals of friendship to the Soviet people by Czechoslovak workers. The edition also included reviews of Andrei Konchalovsky's film version of Ivan Turgenev's novel *Nest of the Gentry*, and of a documentary film about the Soviet ballerina, Maya Plisetskaya.[110] The newspaper thus demonstrated the extent to which hard and soft power remained intertwined in the friendship project.

In 1968, the Soviet government had hoped not only that its troops in Czechoslovakia would put an end to Dubček's heretical reforms, but that they would quell the groundswell of anti-Soviet sentiment that had accompanied them. Instead, the specter of Soviet tanks moving through the streets of Prague and other Czechoslovak cities exacerbated anti-Soviet attitudes among ordinary Czechoslovak citizens and resulted in the biggest crisis in the history of the friendship project. Scenes of unarmed Czechoslovaks angrily confronting Soviet tanks became some of the most iconic images of the Cold War.

The invasion was thus the biggest crisis in the friendship project. Yet unexpectedly, the events of 1968–1969 propelled the project forward. Czechoslovaks who protested the invasion drew on the language and tropes of the friendship project to critique the Soviets' actions, thus inadvertently helping the project to endure. The Soviet government and its allies in Czechoslovakia also turned to the friendship project to restore relations between their countries. For the next two decades, the Soviet Union and Czechoslovakia remained committed to maintaining an alliance that relied not only on political and military ties, but on personal, cultural, and commercial contacts.

Yet, as the film *The Song of the Tree and the Rose* unwittingly reveals, the version of the friendship project that developed during normalization lacked the optimism and intimacy of the preinvasion iterations. Friendship between the two countries did indeed become normalized in the 1970s and 1980s, in that it continued to shape the most intimate aspects of Soviets' and Czechoslovaks' lives. Yet this friendship was no longer in service of something greater: the construction of a new, utopian political system, or the creation of a new role for ordinary citizens in international diplomacy. Instead, the friendship project exposed, more than ever before, the incongruity between violence and amity in the Soviet empire of friends.

CONCLUSION

The Tank Turns Pink

In the early hours of the morning on April 28, 1991, David Černý, a twenty-three-year-old art student, and a group of his friends pulled off a daring stunt: they painted the Monument to the Soviet Tank Crews in Prague pink and placed a papier-mâché model of an upright middle finger in its center. For four and a half decades, the tank monument, which commemorated the Red Army's liberation of Czechoslovakia in World War II, had served as the most prominent symbol of Soviet power in Czechoslovakia, and the friendship project that supported it. The pink tank proved to be the final blow to both the Soviet-Czechoslovak friendship project and the USSR's empire of friends.

In the late 1980s, Mikhail Gorbachev declared that the Soviet Union would no longer use military force to prop up the Communist governments in the satellite states. He thus sacrificed the USSR's empire in Eastern Europe in an attempt to save its empire at home.[1] On November 9, 1989, with the threat of Soviet military interference lifted, East Germans breached the Berlin Wall. Later that month, Czechoslovakia's Communist government collapsed, following a wave of peaceful protests that became known as the

Figure 12. The Monument to the Soviet Tank Crews in Prague,
after David Černý painted it pink and added a model of a middle finger, April 1991.

Credit: Česká tisková kancelář/Pavel Hořejší.

Velvet Revolution. After this momentous event, Czechoslovaks began to openly debate the history of Soviet involvement in their country. These debates centered on the future of the tank monument.

The monument's supporters were mostly Communists as well as older people who personally remembered the Soviet liberation in 1945. Both groups argued that the tank should remain in Prague as a symbol of gratitude and respect for the Soviet soldiers who had lost their lives in Czechoslovakia. The monument's detractors were young people. They argued the tank should be taken down. Some claimed that it should be removed because heavy weaponry—symbolic or not—had no place in a city square.[2] Others argued that the problem was that the tank symbolized Soviet imperialism and a transnational "murderous and inhuman ideology."[3]

The pink tank caused an international scandal. In Moscow, where the Soviet state was on the verge of collapse, commentators responded with a mixture of disbelief and sadness. Some dismissed Černý's act as a drunken stunt,[4] while others argued that it was indicative of a broader "shift to the right" in Czechoslovak politics following the Velvet Revolution.[5] The Soviet government lodged a formal protest with Prague, and Černý was briefly arrested for defacing a cultural monument. The authorities in Prague repainted the tank green and removed the offending finger. A few days later, however, a group of members of the Czechoslovak parliament, who enjoyed immunity from prosecution, painted the tank pink again in solidarity with Černý.[6]

For his part, Černý insisted he had not meant to disrespect the Soviet soldiers who had fought in his country during World War II. In some interviews he declared he was protesting against the tank as a symbol of the Soviet invasion in 1968.[7] In others he claimed that he was simply trying to impress a girl.[8] He later concluded, "Of course, it was a political statement and at the same time it was an artistic action. And it was a lot of fun."[9]

Černý's statements highlight the interplay of politics, culture, and personal interests in the very friendship project that his stunt helped end. For Soviet officials and leaders of the Communist Party of Czechoslovakia, the promotion of friendship between their countries was first and foremost a political strategy, designed to create a cohesive, transnational socialist community to counter the West in the Cold War. In this project, cultural contacts and interpersonal relations were supposed to lead to political unity. Yet ordinary Soviet and Czechoslovak citizens participated in the friendship project for a range of reasons, which at times departed from, or even contradicted, the aims of their governments. These reasons included personal involvement in the 1945 liberation, the desire to continue transnational friendships established in other contexts, careerism, a yearning for goods and culture unavailable at home, intellectual interest, and a desire to avoid censure. Even active participation in the friendship project did not necessarily entail endorsement of its official goal of constructing a transnational, socialist community led by the Soviet Union. Alexei Yurchak has argued that in the Soviet Union during the Brezhnev era, identification with the system did not always involve acceptance of state doctrine. "For many, 'socialism' as a system of human values and as an everyday reality of 'normal life' . . . was not necessarily equivalent to 'the state' or 'ideology'; indeed, living socialism to them often meant something quite different from the official interpretations provided by state rhetoric."[10] In the USSR and Czechoslovakia, ordinary people adapted the concept of socialist internationalism to suit their own interests, needs, and aspirations.

During the Cold War, critics of the Soviet Union's relations with its satellites accused the USSR of imperialism. In his well-known 1984 essay "The Tragedy of Central Europe," the Czech writer Milan Kundera argued, "In spite of their linguistic kinship, the Czechs and the Russians have never shared a common *world*: neither a common history nor a common culture." Kundera was contrasting the Czech lands before 1945 with Poland, which had been partitioned and annexed by the Russian Empire. But he also made this contention as part of a broader, provocative argument accusing the Soviet Union of creating a new empire in postwar Central Europe. In Kundera's view, Czechoslovakia, along with Poland and Hungary, had always belonged culturally and spiritually to Western Europe and had been "kidnapped, displaced, and brainwashed" by the USSR after World War II.[11] The Soviet empire that emerged in Kundera's essay was thus a traditional empire, based on military force and political oppression.

In fact, as this book has shown, the citizens of the Soviet Union and its satellite states constituted a new type of empire: an empire of friends. They were connected not only by a political system and military treaties such as the Warsaw Pact but also by a vast network of cultural, interpersonal, and commercial ties. During the Cold War, Soviet and Czechoslovak citizens did thus share a "common world"—a world they built together.

What accounts for the endurance of this empire of friends, which lasted for four and a half decades despite multiple uprisings in the Eastern bloc and

Soviet military interventions? The empire's endurance was anchored in the realm of everyday life. The practices of socialist friendship that developed during the Cold War were so extensive and habitual that it was possible for Soviet and Eastern European citizens to engage in them unselfconsciously. In the case of the Soviet-Czechoslovak friendship project, hundreds of thousands of citizens from both countries participated in student exchanges, mass tourism, pen-pal correspondences, and veterans' relations. Millions more took part in more indirect forms of contact—through the friendship societies and the exchange of culture and consumer goods.

The empire of friends constituted an authoritarian version of internationalism: study abroad programs promoted Stalinist political tactics, tourism was used to justify a military invasion, and an occupying army engaged in personal diplomacy. This empire shaped the most intimate aspects of people's lives not only in Moscow and Prague, but throughout the socialist world.

The Red Army's liberation of Czechoslovakia in 1945 served as the foundation of the postwar empire of friends. And in the spring of 1991, the legacy of the liberation emerged as the empire's final fault line. In May, the correspondent for the Soviet newspaper *Izvestiia* (News) traveled to the village of Ořechov, near Brno, where the Red Army had fought a battle against German forces during World War II. In the local cemetery, 1,452 Soviet soldiers were buried in unmarked graves. The Soviet correspondent described the village's inhabitants as conflicted over the legacy of the liberation, and the friendship project. Since the Velvet Revolution, the village had shut down its museum dedicated to the battle, and at the local school, authorities had removed the sign proclaiming Czechoslovak-Soviet friendship. At the same time, however, a group of local veterans continued to work on identifying the remains of the Soviet soldiers buried in their village. They presented the correspondent with a list of the names of over six hundred Soviet soldiers they had painstakingly identified. The correspondent acknowledged that this was a great accomplishment, but also noted that there remained hundreds of graves left to identify. He decided to give the list to the Soviet embassy in Prague so that it could take over the work of establishing the identity of the rest of the fallen Soviet soldiers. He concluded, "This duty is above all ours, the ancestors and compatriots of those whose lives were cut short in the Czechoslovak land in the spring of 1945."[12] The correspondent thus indicated that the shared legacy of the liberation between the Soviet Union and Czechoslovakia—the foundation of their friendship—had come to an end.

On June 13, 1991, the Czechoslovak government found a solution to the controversy over the tank monument, by transferring the tank to a military museum, where it remains today.[13] The history of Soviet power in Czechoslovakia during the Cold War and the friendship project that supported it thus ended as it had begun, with a tank on the streets of Prague.

NOTES

Introduction

1. "Otkrytie v Prage pamiatnika pavshim sovetskim tankistam," *Pravda*, August 1, 1945; "Odhalení pomníku padlých rudoarmějců," *Rudé právo*, August 1, 1945.

2. Karl Marx and Frederick Engels, *The Communist Manifesto: With Related Documents*, ed. John E. Toews (Boston: Bedford/St. Martins, 1999), 96. See also John Schwarzmantel, "Nationalism and Socialist Internationalism," in *The Oxford Handbook of the History of Nationalism*, ed. John Breuilly (Oxford: Oxford University Press, 2013), 635–654.

3. Jon Jacobson, *When the Soviet Union Entered World Politics* (Berkeley: University of California Press, 1994), 13.

4. Terry Martin, "The Friendship of the Peoples," in *Affirmative Action Empire: Nations and Nationalities in the Soviet Union, 1923–1939* (Ithaca, NY: Cornell University Press, 2001), 432–460.

5. On Czech nationalists' relations with Russia during the nineteenth century, see Karen Gammelgaard, "Were the Czechs More Western Than Slavic? Nineteenth-Century Travel Literature from Russia by Disillusioned Czechs," in *Imagining the West in Eastern Europe and the Soviet Union*, ed. György Péteri (Pittsburgh: University of Pittsburgh Press, 2010), 13–35.

6. Bradley F. Abrams, *The Struggle for the Soul of the Nation: Czech Culture and the Rise of Communism* (Lanham, MD: Rowman and Littlefield, 2000).

7. On Czechoslovak identity vis-à-vis the West in the interwar period, see Igor Lukes, *Czechoslovakia between Hitler and Stalin: The Diplomacy of Edvard Beneš in the 1930s* (New York: Oxford University Press, 1996) and Andrea Orzoff, *Battle for the Castle: The Myth of Czechoslovakia in Europe, 1914–1948* (Oxford: Oxford University Press, 2009).

8. For information on the security services and propaganda units that followed on the heels of the Red Army's liberation of Slovakia, see Jaroslav Hrbek, "Slovensko v závěru války," in *Draze zaplacená svoboda: Osvobození Československa 1944–1945*, vol. 2, ed. Hrbek et al. (Prague: Paseka, 2009), 115, 119.

9. Karel C. Berkhoff, "Hatred with All the Might of the Soul," in *Motherland in Danger: Soviet Propaganda during World War II* (Cambridge, MA: Harvard University Press, 2012), 167–202.

10. Vasily Grossman, *A Writer at War: A Soviet Journalist with the Red Army, 1941–1945*, ed. and trans. Antony Beevor and Luba Vinogradova (New York: Vintage Books, 2005), 325.

11. On crimes committed by the Red Army in Germany and Hungary, see James Mark, "Remembering Rape: Divided Social Memory and the Red Army in Hungary, 1944–1945," *Past & Present* 188, no. 1 (2005): 131–161; Norman Naimark, "Soviet Soldiers, German Women and the Problem of Rape," *The Russians in Germany: A History of the Soviet Zone of Occupation, 1945–1949* (Cambridge, MA: Harvard University Press, 1995), 69–140; Oleg Budnitskii, "The Intelligentsia Meets the Enemy: Educated Soviet Officers in Defeated Germany, 1945," trans. Susan Rupp, *Kritika: Explorations in Russian and Eurasian History* 10, no. 3 (Summer 2009): 629–682; and Peter Kenez, *Hungary from the Nazis to the Soviets: The Establishment of the Communist Regime in Hungary, 1944–1948* (New York: Cambridge University Press), 39–45.

12. See, for instance, Konstantin Simonov, "Pis'ma iz Chekhoslovakii," *Krasnaia zvezda*, April 12, 1945.

13. Instructions issued to the First and Fourth Ukrainian Fronts on October 31, 1944, quoted in Hrbek et al., *Draze zaplacená svoboda*, 113.

14. On the number of Soviet soldiers who died in Czechoslovakia, see Ústav pro soudobé dějiny AV ČR (Institute for Contemporary History of the Academy of Sciences of the Czech Republic), Sbírka dokumentů Komise vlády ČSFR pro analýzu událostí let 1967–1970, inv. č.274, sign. DI/274, k. 7 [Report by General Ogarkov on the destruction of monuments to Soviet soldiers in Czechoslovakia, September, 1968]. This compares to estimates of 7,889 Soviet soldiers who died in Yugoslavia; 69,000 in Romania; 26,000 in Austria; and 140,000 in Hungary. Statistics from Vojin Majstorović, "The Red Army in Yugoslavia, 1944–1945," *Slavic Review* 75, no. 2 (Summer, 2016): 401.

15. Evgenii D. Moniushko, *From Leningrad to Hungary: Notes of a Red Army Soldier, 1941–1946*, ed. David M. Glantz, trans. Oleg Sheremet (London: Frank Cass, 2005), 186–188.

16. Gosudarstvennyi arkhiv Rossiiskoi Federatsii (State Archive of the Russian Federation; hereafter GARF), f. 9576, op. 4, d. 95, l. 196.

17. "Sovětský voják mezi námi," *Česká pravda*, May 13, 1945.

18. See photographs at Národní archiv (National Archive; hereafter NA), f. 1329 [Osvobození Československa Rudou armádou—1945].

19. U.S. National Archives (hereafter USNA), U.S. Embassy in Czechoslovakia, Enclosure to Despatch 1193, "Report on Political Conditions in Czechoslovakia," by John H. Backer, first lieutenant, M. I., October 19, 1945, file 800, Classified General Records, 1945–1957, RG 84 (Records of the Foreign Service Posts of the Department of State).

20. NA, f. 850/2 [Ministerstvo vnitra-Noskův archiv, 1945–1953], inv. č. 161, k. 255 [Report from the Regional National Committee in Kutná Hora]. The U.S. Army also registered Czechoslovaks' complaints about the behavior of Red Army soldiers, including looting and drunkenness. See USNA, Report from the Headquarters of the ninety-fourth Infantry Division Office of Assistant Chief of Staff G-2, R. L. Love Lt. Col. G. S. C., July 6, 1945, file 820.02 G-2, folder "Prague—correspondence, 1945," RG 84.

21. For an overview of crimes committed by NKVD and counterintelligence units traveling with the Red Army in Slovakia and the Czech lands during the liberation, as well as by regular Soviet soldiers, including deportations of local citizens to labor camps in the USSR, arrests of members of the Russian émigré community, and the appropriation of local apartments and factory equipment, see Karel Richter, *Dobývání domova: osvobození Československa bez cenzury a legend*, part 2 (Prague: Ostrov, 2005), 268–278.

22. NA, f. 1261/0/32 [Generální sekretariát, 1945–1951], sv. 63, a.j. 517 [Letter from the Union of Friends of the USSR, September 9, 1945], p. 84.

23. Ibid. [Report from the district secretary of the KSČ in Hustopeče, August 1, 1945], 96.

24. Quoted in Jan Stransky, *East Wind over Prague* (New York: Random House, 1951), 27.

25. Igor Lukes, *On the Edge of the Cold War: American Diplomats and Spies in Postwar Prague* (New York: Oxford University Press, 2012), 37.

26. Arkhiv vneshnei politiki Rossiiskoi Federatsii (Foreign Policy Archive of the Russian Federation) f. 198, op. 22a, d. 16, p. 32, l. 12.

27. On the teaching of Russian, see GARF, f. 5283, op. 17, d. 423, l. 11.

28. See Karel Kaplan, *The Short March: The Communist Takeover of Power in Czechoslovakia, 1945–48* (London: Hurst, 1987); Abrams, *Struggle for the Soul*; and Lukes, *On the Edge of the Cold War.*

29. NA, f. 861 [Ministerstvo informací-dodatky, 1945–1953] inv. č. 632, k. 224 [Report by the Cultural Attaché at the Czechoslovak embassy in Moscow on performances in the Soviet Union by the Czechoslovak artistic ensemble named after Vít Nejedlý, November 21, 1952], 72.

30. Austin Jersild, "The Soviet State as Imperial Scavenger: 'Catch Up and Surpass' in the Transnational Socialist Bloc, 1950–1960," *American Historical Review* 116, no. 1 (February 2011): 116–117; Zbigniew Wojnowski explains how Khrushchev viewed strife between the USSR and its satellites as a threat to the expansion of socialism around the world, *The Near Abroad: Socialist Eastern Europe and Soviet Patriotism in Ukraine, 1956–85* (Toronto: University of Toronto Press, 2017), 75.

31. "Nežiji s hlavou v růžových oblacích," *Student*, March 6, 1968, 3.

32. "Přátelství na věčné časy," produced by the Czech television station "Retro," first aired August 11, 2009. The show can be viewed on the station's website, accessed March 14, 2018, http://www.ceskatelevize.cz/porady/10176269182-retro/209411000360034/.

33. The majority of the post-Communist literature on Soviet-Czechoslovak relations in the postwar period concerns either the establishment of Communism in Czechoslovakia in the 1940s, or the Prague Spring. See, for instance, V. V. Mar'ina, *Sovetskii Soiuz i chekho-slovatskii vopros vo vremia Vtoroi mirovoi voiny: 1939–1945, gg.* (Moscow: Indrik, 2007–2009); Vladislav Moulis, *Podivné spojenectví: k československo-sovětským politickým a hospodářským vztahům mezi dubnem 1945 a únorem 1948* (Prague: Karolinium, 1996); Karel Kaplan, *Sovětští poradci v Československu 1949–1956* (Prague: Ústav pro soudobé dějiny AV ČR, 2003); M. V. Latysh, *"Prazhskaia vesna" 1968 g. i reaktsiia Kremlia* (Moscow: Tipografiia RAN, 1998); G. P. Murashko, T. V. Volokitina, and A. S. Stykalin, eds., *1968 god: "Prazhskaia vesna," istoricheskaia retrospektiva, sbornik statei* (Moscow: ROSSPEN, 2010); and Josef Pazderka, ed., *Invaze 1968: Ruský pohled* (Prague: Ústav pro studium totalitních režimů, Torst, 2011).

34. Hugh Seton-Watson, *The East European Revolution* (London: Metheun, 1952), 383. See also Leland Stowe, *The Story of Satellite Europe: Conquest by Terror* (New York: Random House, 1952).

35. Zbigniew Brzezinski, *The Soviet Bloc: Unity and Conflict*, 2nd ed. (Cambridge, MA: Harvard University Press, 1967), 456–457.

36. John Connelly, *Captive University: The Sovietization of East German, Czech, and Polish Higher Education, 1945–1956* (Chapel Hill: University of North Carolina Press, 2000).

37. V. Pechatnov, "Exercise in Frustration: Soviet Foreign Propaganda in the Early Cold War, 1945–1947," *Cold War History* 1, no. 2 (January 2001): 1–27; A. S. Stykalin, "Propaganda SSSR na zarubezhnuiu auditoriiu i obshchestvennoe mnenie stran zapada v pervye poslevoennye gody (po dokumentam rossiiskikh arkhivov)," *Vestnik Moskovskogo universiteta*, Seriia X: Zhurnalistika (1/1997): 57–70.

38. Naimark, "The Politics of Culture and Education," in *The Russians in Germany*, 398–464; Kenez, "Cinema," in *Hungary from the Nazis to the Soviets*, 239–258.

39. Jan C. Behrends, "Agitation, Organization, Mobilization: The League for Polish-Soviet Friendship in Stalinist Poland," in *The Sovietization of Eastern Europe: New Perspectives on the Postwar Period,* ed. Balázs Apor, Péter Apor, and E. A. Rees (Washington, DC, 2008), 181–198; Alan L. Nothnagle, *Building the East German Myth: Historical Mythology and Youth Propaganda in the German Democratic Republic, 1945–1989* (Ann Arbor: University of Michigan Press, 1999).

40. Patryk Babiracki, *Soviet Soft Power in Poland: Culture and the Making of Stalin's New Empire, 1943–1957* (Chapel Hill: University of North Carolina Press, 2015), 13.

41. The quote is from Behrends, "Agitation, Organization, Mobilization," 194. For a similar argument about East Germany, see Nothnagle, *Building the East German Myth*, 157.

42. Wojnowski, *Near Abroad*.

43. On economic and interpersonal contacts between the Soviet Union and the Eastern bloc countries with China, see Austin Jersild, *The Sino-Soviet Alliance: An International History* (Chapel Hill: University of North Carolina Press, 2014) and Elizabeth

McGuire, *Red at Heart: How Chinese Communists Fell in Love with the Russian Revolution* (New York: Oxford University Press, 2017). On Soviet-Cuban relations, see Anne E. Gorsuch, "'Cuba, My Love,' The Romance of Revolutionary Cuba in the Soviet Sixties," *American Historical Review* 120, no. 2 (April 2015): 497–526. Recent works on Soviet economic and cultural relations with the Third World include David C. Engerman, "The Second World's Third World," *Kritika: Explorations in Russian and Eurasian History* 12, no. 1 (2011): 183–211, and Tobias Rupprecht, *Soviet Internationalism after Stalin: Interaction and Exchange between the Soviet Union and Latin America during the Cold War* (Cambridge: Cambridge University Press, 2015).

44. Stephen Kotkin, "Mongol Commonwealth? Exchange and Governance across the Post-Mongol Space," *Kritika: Explorations in Russian and Eurasian History* 8, no. 3 (Summer 2007): 525; Patryk Babiracki and Austin Jersild, "Editors' Introduction," in *Socialist Internationalism in the Cold War: Exploring the Second World* (Cham, Switzerland: Palgrave Macmillan, 2016), 1; Elidor Mëhilli, *From Stalin to Mao: Albania and the Socialist World* (Ithaca, NY: Cornell University Press, 2017).

45. Mëhilli, *From Stalin to Mao*, 4.

46. Examples of this extensive literature include, Mary Fulbrook, *The People's State: East German Society from Hitler to Honecker* (New Haven, CT: Yale University Press, 2005); Paul Betts, *Within Walls: Private Life in the German Democratic Republic* (Oxford: Oxford University Press, 2010); Paulina Bren, *The Greengrocer and His TV: The Culture of Communism after the 1968 Prague Spring* (Ithaca, NY: Cornell University Press, 2010); Josie McLellan, *Love in the Time of Communism: Intimacy and Sexuality in the GDR* (Cambridge: Cambridge University Press, 2011); and Steven E. Harris, *Communism on Tomorrow Street: Mass Housing and Everyday Life after Stalin* (Baltimore: Johns Hopkins University Press, and Washington, DC: Woodrow Wilson Center Press, 2013).

47. Fulbrook, *People's State*, 12–15.

48. Akira Iriye, *Cultural Internationalism and World Order* (Baltimore: Johns Hopkins University Press, 1997), 1–3.

49. Joseph S. Nye Jr., *Soft Power: The Means to Success in World Politics* (New York: Public Affairs, 2004), x. On the different types of power available to democracies versus authoritarian governments, see ibid., 6. See also Julie Reeves, *Culture and International Relations: Narratives, Natives and Tourists* (London: Routledge, 2004), 41–44.

50. On twentieth-century internationalism as a liberal project, see Daniel Gorman, *The Emergence of International Society in the 1920s* (Cambridge: Cambridge University Press, 2012); and Glenda Sluga, *Internationalism in the Age of Nationalism* (Philadelphia: University of Pennsylvania Press, 2013). On the role of student exchanges in promoting liberalism, see Whitney Walton, *Internationalism, National Identities, and Study Abroad: France and the United States, 1890–1970* (Stanford, CA: Stanford University Press, 2010). On cultural exchange as crucial to the United States' "success" in the Cold War, see Walter L. Hixson, *Parting the Curtain: Propaganda, Culture, and the Cold War, 1945–1961* (New York: St. Martin's Press, 1997); David Caute, *The Dancer Defects: The Struggle for Cultural Supremacy during the Cold War* (Oxford: Oxford University Press, 2003); and Yale Richmond, *Cultural Exchange and the Cold War: Raising the Iron Curtain* (University Park: Pennsylvania State University Press, 2003).

51. Ana Antic, Johanna Conterio, and Dora Vargha, "Conclusion: Beyond Liberal Internationalism," *Contemporary European History* 25, no. 2 (May 2016): 371.

52. On the Eastern bloc as a Soviet empire, see Jane Burbank and Frederick Cooper, *Empires in World History: Power and the Politics of Difference* (Princeton, NJ: Princeton University Press, 2010), 431–433; on Soviet imperial relations with postwar Poland, see Babiracki, *Soviet Soft Power and the Poles*; on applying an imperial paradigm to Soviet relations with Eastern Europe more broadly (including during the Soviet occupation of Eastern Poland in 1939–1941), see Tarik Amar, "Sovietization as a Civilizing Mission in the West," in Apor, Apor, and Rees, *Sovietization of Eastern Europe*, 29–45. Kiril Tomoff argues that during the Cold War, the Soviet Union and the United States each "sought to integrate the world into its own economic, political, and cultural system," and that "This domination by integration constituted a fundamentally new form of empire," *Virtuosi Abroad: Soviet Music and Imperial Competition during the Early Cold War, 1945–1958* (Ithaca, NY: Cornell University Press, 2015), 3.

1. Culture Wars

Epigraph: "Práce s filmem," *Přítel SSSR*, May 25, 1950, 307.

1. The quote is from Jan Masaryk, "K výstavě sovětského malířství," in *Střetnutí sovětské malířství a současné umění*, ed. O. Mrkvička (Prague: Vladimír Žikeš, 1947), 19.

2. "Výstava sovětského malířství: další sblížení sovětské a naší kultury," *Rudé právo*, April 19, 1947.

3. Zdeněk Hlaváček, "Obrazy národních umělců SSSR," *Svět práce*, April 24, 1947, reprinted in Mrkvička, *Střetnutí*, 63.

4. See Kiril Tomoff, "A Pivotal Turn: Prague Spring 1948 and the Soviet Construction of a Cultural Sphere," *Slavonica* 10, no. 2 (November 2004): 157–176.

5. Antoine Baudin, "Why is Soviet Painting Hidden from Us? Zhdanov Art and Its International Relations and Fallout, 1947–53," in *Socialist Realism Without Shores*, ed. Thomas Lahusen and Evgeny Dobrenko (Durham, NC: Duke University Press, 1997), 236.

6. Rossiiskii gosudarstvennyi arkhiv sotsial'no-politicheskoi istorii (Russian State Archive for Social and Political History; hereafter RGASPI), f. 17, op. 133, d. 386, l. 89.

7. Košice program, fourth section, April 5, 1945, *ČSR a SSSR, 1945–1948: Dokumenty mezivládních jednání*, ed. Karel Kaplan and Alexandra Špiritová (Brno: Doplněk, 1996), 23.

8. Karel Kaplan, *The Short March: The Communist Takeover in Postwar Czechoslovakia* (London: Hurst, 1987), 12.

9. "Bez 7. listopadu nebylo by 28. října 1918," *Rudé právo*, December 30, 1947.

10. For a detailed discussion of the political parties that made up the National Front government, see Bradley F. Abrams, "Four Groups of Postwar Intellectuals," in *The Struggle for the Soul of the Nation: Czech Culture and the Rise of Communism* (Lanham, MD: Rowman and Littlefield, 2000), 53–88.

11. Benjamin Frommer, *National Cleansing: Retribution against Nazi Collaborators in Postwar Czechoslovakia* (Cambridge: Cambridge University Press, 2005), 31n101; Maurice Hindus, *The Bright Passage* (Garden City, NY: Doubleday, 1947), 240.

12. Derek Sayer, *The Coasts of Bohemia: A Czech History* (Princeton, NJ: Princeton University Press, 1998), 207.

13. Petr Szczepanik, "Hollywood in Disguise: Practices of Exhibition and Reception of Foreign Films in Czechoslovakia in the 1930s," in *Cinema, Audiences and Modernity: New Perspectives on European Cinema History*, ed. Daniel Biltereyst, Richard Maltby, and Philippe Meers (Abingdon, Oxon: Routledge, 2012), 179. The film came out in the United States in 1937.

14. Joseph Wechsberg, *Homecoming* (New York: Alfred A. Knopf, 1946), 39.

15. Peter Demetz, *Prague in Danger: The Years of German Occupation, 1939–1945: Memories and History, Terror and Resistance, Theater and Jazz, Film and Poetry, Politics and War* (New York: Farrar, Straus and Giroux, 2008), 152–159.

16. Ibid., 193.

17. Wechsburg, *Homecoming*, 5–16.

18. Hindus, *Bright Passage*, 32.

19. Arkhiv vneshnei politiki Rossiiskoi Federatsii (Foreign Policy Archive of the Russian Federation; hereafter AVP RF), f. 198, op. 22a, d. 16, p. 32, l. 12. Soiuzintorgkino became Soveksportfil'm in December 1945.

20. Rossiiskii gosudarstvennyi arkhiv literatury i iskusstva (Russian State Archive of Literature and Art; hereafter RGALI), f. 2918, op. 1, d. 128, ll. 22–23. For the text of the agreement, see Národní archiv (National Archive; hereafter NA), f. 861 [Ministerstvo informací, 1945–1953), inv. č. 506, k. 230 [Film agreements with the Soviet Union].

21. AVP RF, f. 198, op. 22a, d. 16, p. 32, l. 12.

22. Ibid., l.

23. Robert Argenbright, "The Soviet Agitational Vehicle: State Power on the Social Frontier," *Political Geography* 17, no. 3 (March 1998): 253–272.

24. U.S. National Archives (hereafter USNA), U.S. Embassy Czechoslovakia, Ambassador Steinhardt to the Secretary of State, May 22, 1947, "Films Destined to Public Performance in 1937–1946 (up to November)," statistics on Soviet film exports to Czechoslovakia from *Statistical Bulletin of Czechoslovakia* 4, 1947, file 860F.406IMP/6-1647, dec. file 1945–1949, RG 59: General Records of the State Department.

25. "Program pražských biografů," *Rudé právo*, September 7, 1945.

26. "O sovětském filmu," *Přítel SSSR*, May 15, 1946, 7.

27. Peter Kenez, *Cinema and Soviet Society: From the Revolution to the Death of Stalin* (London: I. B. Tauris, 2001), 176–178.

28. "Tvář sovětského filmu," *Tvorba*, August 30, 1945, 94.

29. NA, f. 861 [Ministerstvo informací, 1945–1953], inv. č. 506, k. 230 [letter from F. Bílek of the regional Prague film division of the ROH (Revolutionary Trade Movement) to the Ministry of Information about popularizing Soviet films, January 24, 1946].

30. Chad Bryant, *Prague in Black: Nazi Rule and Czech Nationalism* (Cambridge, MA: Harvard University Press, 2007), 220

31. Gosudarstvennyi arkhiv Rossiiskoi Federatsii (State Archive of the Russian Federation; hereafter GARF), f. 5283, op. 17, d. 423, l. 11.

32. "Ruská symfonická hudba," *Svobodné noviny*, June 12, 1945.

33. "Hudba po zajetí babylonském," *Svobodné slovo*, June 6, 1945.

34. Frommer, *National Cleansing*, 33–35.

35. Vítězslav Nezval, "Sovětský příklad," *Svět v obrazech*, July 13, 1945, republished in Nezval, *Dílo XXVI. Eseje a projevy po osvobození (1945–1958)* (Prague: Československý spisovatel, 1976), 343.

36. In 1937, the Czechoslovak film industry produced forty-nine films, and in 1938, forty-one, Demetz, *Prague in Danger*, 198. On collaboration in the industry, see RGALI, f. 2456, op. 4, d. 96, l. 1.

37. Wechsberg, *Homecoming*, 92. Karl Hermann Frank was a Sudeten German who held high-ranking positions in the Protectorate and the SS. He was executed in Prague for war crimes in May 1946.

38. See listings in *Rudé právo*, September 7, 1945.

39. "Film týdne," *Obzory*, September 1, 1945, 31.

40. "Anglické a francouzské filmy do Československa," *Rudé právo*, October 11, 1945.

41. RGASPI, f. 17, op. 128, d. 105, l. 7

42. Szczepanik, "Hollywood in Disguise," 172.

43. "Film týdne," *Obzory*, September, 1, 1945, 31.

44. See "Proč se dosud u nás nehrají americké filmy?" *Svobodné noviny*, October 12, 1945.

45. Andrea Orzoff, *Battle for the Castle: The Myth of Czechoslovakia in Europe, 1914–1948* (New York: Oxford University Press, 2009), 26–27.

46. Kevin McDermott, *Communist Czechoslovakia: A Political and Social History* (London: Palgrave Macmillan, 2015), 26.

47. Quoted in Hindus, *Bright Passage*, 304. Tomáš Garrigue Masaryk was the first president of Czechoslovakia, from 1918–1935.

48. "Film týdne," *Obzory*, September 1, 1945, 31.

49. USNA, Ambassador Steinhardt "secret paraphrase" of telegram sent to the Secretary of State, August 2, 1945, Entry UD 2378, file 711.9, Prague Correspondence 1945, RG 84. For a similar statement by Ján Papánek, chief of the Czechoslovak Information Service, see Department of State Memorandum of Conversation on "Conditions in Czechoslovakia," November 15, 1945, file 860F.00/11-1545 CS/LE, dec. file 1945–1949, RG 59.

50. GARF, f. 8581, op. 2, d. 158, ll. 61–62.

51. USNA, Department of State Memorandum of Conversation on "Conditions in Czechoslovakia," November 15, 1945, file 860F.00/11-1545 CS/LE, dec. file 1945–1949, RG 59.

52. Igor Lukes, *On the Edge of the Cold War: American Diplomats and Spies in Postwar Prague* (New York: Oxford University Press, 2012).

53. The government also nationalized the National Gallery in Prague and the Czech Philharmonic Orchestra, took control of private theaters, and regulated the book market. See Jiří Knapík, "Czechoslovak Culture and Cinema, 1945–1960," in *Cinema in Service of the State: Perspectives on Film Culture in the GDR and Czechoslovakia, 1945–1960*, ed. Lars Karl and Pavel Skopal (New York: Berghahn Books, 2015), 40.

54. USNA, Steinhardt "secret paraphrase" of telegram sent to the secretary of state, August 2, 1945, Entry UD 2378, file 711.9, Prague Correspondence 1945, RG 84.

55. USNA, Telegram from Byrnes at the Department of State [to Ambassador Steinhardt at the American Embassy in Czechoslovakia], August 23, 1945, file 860F.4061 M.P./8-1545 CS/SMS, dec. file 1945–1949, RG 59.

56. USNA, Department of State, Incoming telegram [from the American Embassy in Czechoslovakia], March 1, 1946, file 860F.4061MP/3-146 CS/VJ, dec. file 1945–1949, RG 59.

57. For details of the MPEA's agreement with Czechoslovakia, see Jindřiška Bláhová, "Hollywood za železnou oponou: Jednání o nové smlouvě o dovozu hollywoodských filmů mezi MPEA a ČSR (1946–1951)," *Iluminace: časopis pro teorii, historii a estetiku filmu* 20, no. 4 (2008): 19–20; on the success of U.S. films in Czechoslovakia after the agreement was implemented in October 1946, see USNA, Ambassador Steinhardt to the secretary of state, May 22, 1947, "Statistics on Films for Public Performance and Attendance," file 860F.406IMP/5-2247, dec. file 1945–1949, RG 59.

58. Norman Naimark, "The Sovietization of Eastern Europe, 1944–1953," in *The Cambridge History of the Cold War*, vol. 1, ed. Melvyn P. Leffler and Odd Arne Westad (Cambridge: Cambridge University Press, 2010), 185–188.

59. USNA, Steinhardt to the secretary of state, June 27, 1947, file 811.42760F/6-2747, dec. file 1945–1949, RG 59.

60. USNA, Steinhardt to the secretary of state, June 16, 1947, file 860F.4061MP /6-167, dec. file 1945–1949, RG 59.

61. RGALI, f. 2918, op. 1, d. 128, l. 105.

62. Frank A. Ninkovich, *The Diplomacy of Ideas: U.S. Foreign Policy and Cultural Relations, 1938–1950* (New York: Cambridge University Press, 1981), 132.

63. USNA, Ambassador Steinhardt to the secretary of state, June 27, 1947, file 811.42760F/6-2747, dec. file 1945–1949, RG 59.

64. USNA, Telegram from State Department to U.S. Embassy in Prague, October 3, 1947, file 811.42760F/7-2247, dec. file 1945–1949, RG 59.

65. USNA, Telegram from Steinhardt to the secretary of state, October 9, 1947, file 811.42760F/10-947, dec. file 1945–1949, RG 59.

66. USNA, Airgram from Lovett at the Department of State to the U.S. Embassy in Prague, April 5, 1948, file 811.42760F/3-348 CS/A, dec. file 1945–1949, RG 59.

67. Ninkovich, *Diplomacy of Ideas*, 147.

68. GARF, f. 8581, op. 2, d. 158, ll. 61–62.

69. Justin Hart notes that the United States has always faced the challenge of reconciling state power abroad with efforts by private citizens and the mass media, *Empire of Ideas: The Origins of Public Diplomacy and the Transformation of U.S. Foreign Policy* (New York: Oxford University Press, 2013), 4.

70. V. Pechatnov, "Exercise in Frustration: Soviet Foreign Propaganda in the Early Cold War, 1945–1947," *Cold War History* 1, no. 2 (January 2001): 1–27. I discuss the anti-Western campaigns launched by Zhdanov in greater detail in the next chapter.

71. RGASPI, f. 17, op. 132, d. 89, l. 47.

72. RGASPI, f. 17, op. 128, d. 105, l. 6.

73. Ibid., 13.

74. Patryk Babiracki, "Postwar Hopes and Promises," in *Soviet Soft Power in Poland: Culture and the Making of Stalin's New Empire, 1943–1957* (Chapel Hill: University of North Carolina Press, 2015), 52–96; John Connelly, *Captive University: The Sovietization of East German, Czech, and Polish Higher Education, 1945–1956* (Chapel Hill: University of North Carolina Press, 2000).

75. RGASPI, f. 17, op. 128, d. 89, l. 31. On the founding of this society, see Jiří Křesťan, "KSČ, Společnost pro hospodářské a kulturní styky s SSSR a obraz Sovětského svazu v prostředí české levicové inteligence (1925–1939)," in *Bolševismus, komunismus a radikální socialismus v Československu*, svazek II., ed. Zdeněk Kárník and Michal Kopeček (Prague: Ústav pro soudobé dějiny AV ČR, Dokořán, 2004), 84–109.

76. GARF, f. 5283, op. 17, d. 426, l. 60.

77. RGASPI, f. 17, op. 128, d. 89, ll. 27–28.

78. Ibid., 28.

79. GARF, f. 5283, op. 17, d. 426, l. 103.

80. RGASPI, f. 17, op. 128, d. 89, l. 30.

81. "Propagujeme sovětské filmy!" *Přítel SSSR*, November 20, 1946, 5.

82. "Tvář sovětského filmu," *Tvorba*, August 30, 1945, 94.

83. "Propagujeme sovětské filmy," *Přítel SSSR*, November 20, 1946, 5.

84. "Film dvou světů," *Rudé právo*, October 15, 1946.

85. "O sovětských filmech," *Svobodné noviny*, November 14, 1945.

86. "Sovětský film versus český divák," *Svobodné noviny*, January 30, 1946.

87. RGASPI, f. 17, op. 132, d. 75, l. 198.

88. Quoted in Matthew Cullerne Bown, *Socialist Realist Painting* (New Haven, CT: Yale University Press, 1998), 141.

89. USNA, The American Embassy in Prague, to the Department of State, April 29, 1947, file, 811.42700(A)/4-2947 CS/A, dec. file, 1945–1949, RG 59.

90. USNA, Steinhardt to Secretary of State, May 6, 1947, file 811.42700(A)/5-647, dec. file, 1945–1949, RG 59.

91. Quoted in Derek Sayer, *Prague, Capital of the Twentieth Century: A Surrealist History* (Princeton, NJ: Princeton University Press, 2013), 26.

92. Ctibor Štolovský, "Obrazy národních a zasloužilých umělců SSSR," *Rudé právo*, April 18, 1947, reprinted in Mrkvička, *Střetnutí*, 32.

93. Zdeněk Hlaváček, "Obrazy národních umělců SSSR," *Svět práce*, April 24, 1947, reprinted in Mrkvička, *Střetnutí*, 65.

94. Ctibor Štolovský, "Obrazy národních a zasloužilých umělců SSSR," *Rudé právo*, reprinted in Mrkvička, *Střetnutí*, 34.

95. NA, f. 861 [Ministerstvo informací-dodatky, 1945–1953], inv. č. 632, k. 226, o. "SSSR-Výstavy, 1946–1952" [excerpts from the exhibition's comment books], 1.

96. Ibid.

97. RGALI, f. 962, op. 11, d. 208, l. 19.

98. Ibid., 17.

99. NA, f. 861 [Ministerstvo informací-dodatky, 1945–1953], inv. č. 632, k. 226, o. "SSSR-Výstavy, 1946–1952" [excerpts from the exhibition's comment books], 2.

100. Ibid., 4.

101. Ibid., 3.

102. Ibid., 1.

103. Mrkvička, introduction to *Střetnutí*, 9–10.

104. Bohuslav Brouk, "Dovětek k ruské výstavě," *Dnešek*, May 15, 1947, reprinted in *Na ztracené vartě Západu. Antologie české nesocialistické publicistiky z let 1945–1948:*

Koželuhová, Skácel, Forman, Tigrid, Kolár, Chudoba, Brouk, Jehlička, ed. Milan Drápala (Prague: Prostor, 2000), 567.

105. On these debates, see Sayer, *Prague, Capital of the Twentieth Century,* 378–383; and Shawn Clybor, "Socialist (Sur)Realism: Karel Teige, Ladislav Štoll and the Politics of Communist Culture in Czechoslovakia," *History of Communism in Europe* 2 (2011): 143–167.

106. NA, f. 861 [Ministerstvo informací-dodatky, 1945–1953], inv. č. 632, k. 226, o."SSSR-Výstavy, 1946–1952" [excerpts from the exhibition's comment books], 3.

107. "Výstava sovětského malířství: další sblížení sovětské a naší kultury," *Rudé právo,* April 19, 1947.

108. Bohulslav Brouk, "K odezvě výstavy sovětského umění," *Dnešek,* May 1, 1947, reprinted in Drápala, *Na ztracené vartě Západu,* 563–565.

109. GARF, f. 5283, op. 22, d. 43, l. reverse side of 140–reverse side 141.

110. Brouk, "K odezvě výstavy sovětského umění," *Dnešek,* May 1, 1947, reprinted in Drápala, *Na ztracené vartě Západu,* 563.

111. Ibid., 565.

112. "Kam s ním?" *Vývoj,* December 7, 1946, 268.

113. "O sovětských filmech," *Svobodné noviny,* November 14, 1945.

114. "Kam s ním?" *Vývoj,* December 7, 1946, 268.

115. A. Zamoshkin, "Vystavka sovetskoi zhivopisi v Prage," *Moskovskaia pravda,* June 6, 1947.

116. See, for instance, issues of *Přítel SSSR,* 1949–1951.

117. Jiří Knapík, *Únor a kultura: sovětizace české kultury, 1948–1950* (Prague: Nakladatelství Libri, 2004), 166.

118. NA, f. 1261/2/28 [ÚV KSČ-oddělení masových organizací, 1945–1956], a.j. 281, o. 2 [Memo on suggestions for expanding the SČSP's cultural activities, no date].

119. NA, f. 1261/2/28 [ÚV KSČ-oddělení masových organizací, 1945–1956], a.j. 282 [Report on the third campaign of the People's Russian Courses, July 10, 1951]. In 1951, an estimated 317,381 people were studying in the LKR—by far the highest number of adults taking Russian courses in an Eastern bloc country, GARF, f. 5283, op. 17, d. 7, l. 10.

120. NA, f. 1261/2/28 [ÚV KSČ-oddělení masových organizací, 1945–1956], a. j. 281, o. 2 [Proposal for creating clubs for reading Soviet literature, no date].

121. *Kulturní besedy Československo-sovětského přátelství,* February 1950, 1.

122. Ibid., 9, 33.

123. Ibid., 14–15.

124. Bláhová, "Hollywood za železnou oponou," 52–54.

125. RGALI, f. 2918, op. 1, d. 128, l. 24.

126. Ibid., 105.

127. "Odpověd na otevřený dopis zplnomocněnce pro dovoz a vývoz filmu J. Elbla," *Obzory,* November 7, 1945, 174–175.

128. Maya Turovskaya, "The 1930s and 1940s: Cinema in Context," in *Stalinism and Soviet Cinema,* ed. Richard Taylor and Derek Spring (London: Routledge, 1993), 44.

129. The term "film hunger" comes from Kenez, *Cinema and Soviet Society,* 187; for statistics on Soviet film releases during late Stalinism, see ibid., 188; and on the reasons for the film shortage, see 189–191.

130. RGASPI, f. 17, op. 132, d. 250, April 4, 1949, l. 42.

131. See for instance, RGASPI, f. 17, op. 132, d. 75, l. 199; Babiracki, *Soviet Soft Power and the Poles*, 83; Peter Kenez, *Hungary from the Nazis to the Soviets: The Establishment of the Communist Regime in Hungary, 1944–1948* (New York: Cambridge University Press, 2006), 255–256; and Norman M. Naimark, *The Russians in Germany: A History of the Soviet Zone of Occupation, 1945–1949* (Cambridge, MA: Harvard University Press, 1995), 421.

132. "Práce s filmem," *Přítel SSSR*, May 25, 1950, 307.

133. "Filmovým referentům," *Sovětským filmem*, January 1952, 17.

134. "Propagujeme sovětské filmy!" *Přítel SSSR*, November 20, 1946, 5.

135. Summary of *Chapaev*, *Sovětským filmem*, January 1952, nonpaginated insert.

136. Bláhová, "Hollywood za železnou oponou," 36–37.

137. "Co děláme pro zvýšení návštěv na sovětské filmy?" *Sovětským filmem*, January 1952, 22.

138. Quoted in Kenez, *Hungary from the Nazis to the Soviets*, 257.

139. RGASPI, f. 17, op. 132, d. 75, l. 199.

2. "The Land of Our Destiny"

Epigraph 1: "Údernice Marta Čistecká vypráví: Viděla jsem Stalina," *Práce* (Labor), January 8, 1950.
Epigraph 2: Archiv ministerstva zahraničních věcí České Republiky (Archive of the Ministry of Foreign Affairs of the Czech Republic; hereafter AMZV), f. TO SSSR-Obyčejně, 1945–1959, k. 17, o. 25 [Transcript of the plenary meeting of the zemliachestvo group Moscow IV, March 19, 1952], [page] 15.

1. "Zájezdy do Sovětského svazu," *Přítel SSSR*, April 20, 1946, 4.

2. For an example of these choreographed visits, see Patryk Babiracki, "The Taste of Red Watermelon: Polish Peasants Visit Soviet Collective Farms, 1949–1952," in *Cold War Crossings: International Travel and Exchange Across the Soviet Bloc, 1940s–1960s*, ed. Babiracki and Kenyon Zimmer (College Station: Texas A&M University Press, 2014), 40–77.

3. Rossiiskii gosudarstvennyi arkhiv noveishei istorii (Russian State Archive for Contemporary History; hereafter RGANI), f. 5, op. 17, d. 431, l. 125.

4. On the Soviet foreign student program with the Eastern bloc in this period, see Patryk Babiracki, "Imperial Heresies: Polish Students in the Soviet Union, 1948–1957," *Ab Imperio* 4 (2007): 199–236 and Benjamin Tromly, "Brother or Other: East European Students in Soviet Higher Education Establishments, 1948–1956, *European History Quarterly* 44, no. 1 (2014): 80–102. On the Soviet foreign student program with the "developing countries" in Africa, Asia, and Latin America, which began in the early 1960s, see, for instance, Julie Hessler, "Death of an African Student in Moscow: Race, Politics, and the Cold War," *Cahiers du Monde russe* 47, no. 1 (2006): 33–64; Sean Guillory, "Culture Clash in the Socialist Paradise: Soviet Patronage and African Students' Urbanity in the Soviet Union, 1960–1965," *Diplomatic History* 38, no. 2 (2014): 271–281; Constantin Katsakioris, "The Soviet-South Encounter: Tensions in the Friendship with Afro-Asian Partners, 1945–1965," in Babiracki and Zimmer, *Cold War Crossings*, 134–165; and Katsakioris,

"Burden or Allies? Third World Students and Internationalist Duty through Soviet Eyes," *Kritika: Explorations in Russian and Eurasian History* 18, no. 3 (Summer 2017): 539–567.

5. Rossiiskii gosudarstvennyi arkhiv sotsial'no-politicheskoi istorii (Russian State Archive for Social and Political History; hereafter RGASPI), f. 17, op. 128, d. 52, l. 103 and RGASPI, f. 17, op. 128, d. 223, l. 45.

6. RGASPI, f. 17, op. 133, d. 237, l. 55.

7. Lisa A. Kirschenbaum, *International Communism and the Spanish Civil War: Solidarity and Suspicion* (New York: Cambridge University Press, 2015), 15–20. See also Elizabeth McGuire, "Sino-Soviet Every Day: Chinese Revolutionaries in Moscow Military Schools, 1927–1930," in *Everyday Life in Russia Past and Present*, ed. Choi Chatterjee, David L. Ransel, Mary Cavender, and Karen Petrone (Bloomington: University of Indiana Press, 2015), 329–349.

8. Národní archiv (National Archive; hereafter NA), f. 1261/0/13 [Sekretariát ÚV KSČ, 1945–1951], sv.19, a.j. 140, b. 18 [draft of pledge for Czechoslovak students studying in the Soviet Union, August 2, 1950].

9. Quotations from the legislation on the Fulbright program taken from Richard Pells, *Not Like Us: How Europeans Have Loved, Hated, and Transformed American Culture Since World War II* (New York: Basic Books, 1997), 59.

10. Frank A. Ninkovich, *The Diplomacy of Ideas: U.S. Foreign Policy and Cultural Relations, 1938–1950* (New York: Cambridge University Press, 1981), 108–110.

11. For example, the USSR did not begin sending Soviet students to study in Czechoslovakia until 1957, Gosudarstvennyi arkhiv Rossiiskoi Federatsii (State Archive of the Russian Federation; hereafter GARF), f. 9518, op. 1, d. 143, l. 41.

12. J. W. Fulbright, "Forward," in *The Fulbright Program: A History*, ed. Walter Johnson and Francis J. Colligan (Chicago: University of Chicago Press, 1965), vii.

13. Ninkovich, *Diplomacy of Ideas*, 145–148, quote from Fulbright on 148.

14. NA, f. 1261/0/13 [Sekretariát ÚV KSČ, 1945–1951], sv. 40, a.j. 189, b. 13 [Ratification of students to the USSR for the school year 1951–1952, June 12, 1951].

15. Giles Scott-Smith has used "interpreters," in reference to the idea in the United States during the Cold War that participants of American exchange programs would transmit American political values back to their home countries. See Giles Scott-Smith, "Mapping the Undefinable: Some Thoughts on the Relevance of Exchange Programs within International Relations Theory," *ANNALS of the American Academy of Political and Social Science* 616 (March 2008): 177.

16. Zdeněk Mlynář, *Nightfrost in Prague: The End of Humane Socialism*, trans. Paul Wilson (New York: Karz, 1980), 7.

17. Michal Reiman, *Rusko jako téma a realita doma a v exilu. Vzpomínky na léta 1968–1990* (Prague: Ústav pro soudobé dějiny AV ČR, 2008), 11.

18. Radoslav Selucký, *Východ je východ* (Cologne: Index, 1972), 7, 10–11.

19. On areas of specialization, see NA, f. 1261/0/13 [Sekretariát ÚV KSČ, 1945–1951], a.j. 189, sv. 40, b. 11, [page] 6 [Report on Czechoslovak students in the USSR, June 12, 1951] and AMZV, f. TO SSSR-Obyčejně, 1945–1959, k. 17, o. 22 [List of specializations of students sent to the USSR in 1952/1953].

20. Mikhail Gorbachev, *Memoirs*, trans. Georges Peronansky and Tatjana Varsavsky (New York: Doubleday, 1996), 42.

21. Mlynář, *Nightfrost in Prague*, 20.

22. RGANI, f. 5, op. 17, d. 431, ll. 53–54.

23. For an overview of these campaigns, see Geoffrey Roberts, "Generalissimo at Home: The Domestic Context of Stalin's Postwar Foreign Policy," in *Stalin's Wars: from World War to Cold War, 1939–1953* (New Haven, CT: Yale University Press, 2006), 329–344. On the Roskin-Kliueva affair, see Nikolai Krementsov, *The Cure: A Story of Cancer and Politics from the Annals of the Cold War* (Chicago: University of Chicago Press, 2002); and on the purge of the Jewish Anti-Fascist Committee and the anticosmopolitan campaigns, see Joshua Rubenstein, "Introduction: Night of the Murdered Poets," in *Stalin's Secret Pogrom: The Postwar Inquisition of the Jewish Anti-Fascist Committee,* ed. Joshua Rubenstein and Vladimir P. Naumov (New Haven, CT: Yale University Press, 2001), 1–64; and Konstantin Azadovskii and Boris Egorov, "From Anti-Westernism to Anti-Semitism: Stalin and the Impact of the 'Anti-Cosmopolitan' Campaigns on Soviet Culture," *Journal of Cold War Studies* 4, no. 1 (Winter 2002): 66–80.

24. Juliane Fürst, *Stalin's Last Generation: Soviet Post-War Youth and the Emergence of Mature Socialism* (Oxford: Oxford University Press, 2010), 71.

25. RGASPI, f. 17, op. 128, d. 223, l. 107.

26. Michael David-Fox, *Showcasing the Great Experiment: Cultural Diplomacy and Western Visitors to the Soviet Union, 1921–1941* (New York: Oxford University Press, 2011), 26.

27. Ludmilla Alexeyeva and Paul Goldberg, *The Thaw Generation: Coming of Age in the Post-Stalin Era* (Boston: Little, Brown and Company, 1990), 38–39.

28. Selucký, *Východ je východ*, 34.

29. Ibid., 32–33.

30. RGANI, f. 5, op. 17, d. 431, l. 23.

31. RGANI, f. 5, op. 17, d. 483, l. 3.

32. RGASPI, f. 17, op. 128, d. 52, l. 114.

33. RGASPI, f. 17, op. 163, d. 1496, ll. 9–11. See also, *Sovetskoe gosudarstvennoe pravo* (Moscow: Iuridicheskoe izdatel'stvo Ministerstva iustitsii SSSR, 1948), 263n2, as well as M. M. Wolff, "Some Aspects of Marriage and Divorce Laws in Soviet Russia," *Modern Law Review* 12, no. 3 (July 1949): 290–296.

34. On the broader push for pronatalist laws in the USSR in response to war losses, see Mie Nakachi, "N. S. Khrushchev and the 1944 Soviet Family Law: Politics, Reproduction, and Language," *East European Politics and Societies* 20, no. 1 (2006): 40–68.

35. *The Soviet Union as Reported by Former Soviet Citizens;* Report No. 2 (Washington D.C.: United States Department of State, February 1952), 2.

36. Norman M. Naimark, *The Russians in Germany: A History of the Soviet Zone of Occupation, 1945–1949* (Cambridge, MA: Harvard University Press, 1995), 93.

37. See Fabrice Virgili, *Shorn Women: Gender and Punishment in Liberation France*, trans. John Flower (Oxford: Berg, 2002); Heide Fehrenbach, *Race after Hitler: Black Occupation Children in Postwar Germany and America* (Princeton, NJ: Princeton University Press, 2005); and Atina Grossmann, *Jews, Germans, and Allies: Close Encounters in Occupied Germany* (Princeton, NJ: Princeton University Press, 2007).

38. Perry Biddiscombe, "Dangerous Liaisons: The Anti-Fraternization Movement in the U.S. Occupation Zones of Germany and Austria, 1945–1948," *Journal of Social History* 34, no. 3 (2001): 616.

39. Selucký, *Východ je východ*, 36.

40. RGASPI, f. 17, op. 133, d. 237, l. 45.

41. El'vira Filipovich, *Ot sovetskoi pionerki do chelnoka-pensionerki (moi dnevnik). Kniga I (1944–1972)* (Podol'sk: Saturn, 2000), entry for February 9, 1953, 55–56.

42. NA, f. 1261/0/13 [Sekretariát ÚV KSČ, 1945–1951], sv. 40, a.j. 189, b. 13 [Ratification of students sent to the USSR for the 1951–1952 academic year, June 12, 1951].

43. Tromly, "Brother or Other?" 93.

44. RGANI, f. 5, op. 17, d. 431, l. 94.

45. Kirschenbaum, "Learning to Be Bolshevik," in *International Communism and the Spanish Civil War*, 15–51.

46. See RGANI, f. 5, op. 17, d. 431, l. 94, as well as Selucký, *Východ je východ*, 37.

47. AMZV, f. TO SSSR-Obyčejně, 1945–1959, k. 5, o. 22 [letter from the Czechoslovak zemliachestvo in Moscow to the Czechoslovak embassy in Moscow, April 18, 1952].

48. Ibid. [Report on the situation with Czechoslovak students in Leningrad]. See also Report on the Czechoslovak students in Leningrad, from the Cultural Attaché at the Czechoslovak embassy in Moscow to the Czechoslovak Ministry of Schools, Science, and Art, April 25, 1952.

49. Tromly writes, regarding Soviet-Eastern European marriages after the ban was lifted in the fall of 1953, "Trans-bloc marriages confirmed that some sort of 'socialist internationalism' within the Soviet bloc, long existing only in rhetoric, had finally become a reality," "Brother or Other?" 94.

50. Filipovich, *Ot sovetskoi pionerki*, entry from May 27, 1954, 64.

51. Ibid., entry from February 13, 1955, 70.

52. Selucký, *Východ je východ*, 37.

53. RGANI, f. 5, op. 17, d. 431, l. 133.

54. Ibid., 73.

55. RGASPI, f. 17, op. 128, d. 52, l. 110.

56. RGANI, f. 5, op. 17, d. 483, l. 6.

57. RGASPI, f. 17, op. 128, d. 52, l. 104.

58. Ibid., 109.

59. RGASPI, f.M-1 (Molodezhnyi arkhiv), op. 46, d. 125, l. 13.

60. Ibid., 15.

61. RGASPI, f. 17, op. 133, d. 237, ll. 26–27.

62. Ibid.

63. AMZV, f. TO SSSR-Obyčejně, 1945–1959, k. 5, o. 25 [Report by Jaroslav Olma, addendum to the transcript of the plenary session of the meeting of the Moscow zemliachestvo on March 19, 1952], 4.

64. Ibid. [Report sent by members of the investigative committee of the Czechoslovak zemliachestvo at MGU to Klement Gottwald, April 4, 1952], 3. I would like to thank Nicholas Rutter for his help interpreting this comment.

65. Ibid.

66. AMZV, f. TO SSSR-Obyčejně, 1945–1959, k. 17, o. 22 [Letter from the Czechoslovak zemliachestvo in Moscow to the Czechoslovak embassy in the Soviet Union, April 18, 1952].

67. AMZV, f. TO SSSR-Obyčejně, 1945–1959, k. 17, o. 25 [Report sent by members of the investigative committee of the Czechoslovak zemliachestvo at MGU to Klement Gottwald, April 4, 1952].

68. RGASPI, f. 17, op. 133, d. 237, l. 29.

69. RGANI, f. 5, op. 17, d. 431, l. 227.

70. On the Slánský affair, see Karel Kaplan, *Report on the Murder of the General Secretary*, trans. Karel Kovanda (Columbus: Ohio State University Press, 1990); Jiří Pelikán, ed., *The Czechoslovak Political Trials, 1950–1954: The Suppressed Report of the Dubček Government's Commission of Inquiry, 1968* (Stanford, CA: Stanford University Press, 1971); Jiří Pernes and Jan Foitzik, eds., *Politické procesy v Československu po roce 1945 a "případ Slánský." Sborník příspěvků ze stejnojmenné konference, pořádané ve dnech 14.–16. dubna 2003 v Praze* (Brno: Kateřina Mikšová-Nakladalství Prius pro Ústav pro soudobé dějiny AV ČR v Praze, 2005); and Kevin McDermott, "A 'Polyphony of Voices'? Czech Popular Opinion and the Slánský Affair," *Slavic Review* 67, no. 4 (Winter 2008): 840–865.

71. Mlynář, *Nightfrost in Prague*, 7.

72. Selucký, *Východ je východ*, 64.

73. See, for instance, NA f. 1261/0/13 [Sekretariát ÚV KSČ, 1945–1951], sv. 21, a.j. 146, b. 14 [Proposal for a work plan for the Czechoslovak zemliachestvo in the USSR for 1950/1951].

74. Article translated into Russian and filed in GARF, f. 5283, op. 22, d. 484, l. 36.

75. NA, f. 1261/2/2 [Ideologické oddělení, 1951–1961], sv. 15, a.j. 86, l. 6 [Report on improving the KSČ's ideological work, 1952].

76. RGASPI, f. 17, op. 133, d. 237, l. 24.

77. AMZV, f. TO SSSR-Obyčejně, 1945–1959, k. 17, o. 25 [Resolution from the plenary meetings of the zemliachestvo group Moscow IV on March 19 and 21, 1952], 3.

78. Ibid. [Report from the Czechoslovak embassy in Moscow on May 7, 1952 to Kopecký at the Soviet Division of the Czechoslovak Ministry of Foreign Affairs, regarding a meeting of the Czechoslovak zemliachestvo in Moscow on May 4, 1952], 2.

79. Babiracki, "Imperial Heresies": 216–219.

80. I am referencing the title of Babiracki's article, "Imperial Heresies."

81. J. Arch Getty, "*Samokritika* Rituals in the Stalinist Central Committee: 1933–38," *Russian Review* 58, no. 1 (January 1999): 56.

82. Fürst, *Stalin's Last Generation*, 108.

83. Marci Shore, "Engineering in the Age of Innocence: A Genealogy of Discourse Inside the Czechoslovak Writers' Union, 1949–67," *East European Politics and Societies* 12, no. 3 (Fall 1998): 403–404.

84. "Kritika a sebekritika—metoda výchovy kádrů," *Rudé právo*, January 13, 1951.

85. AMZV, f. TO SSSR-Obyčejně, 1945–1959, k. 17, o. 25 [Transcript of the plenary meeting of the zemliachestvo group Moscow IV, March 19, 1952], 3.

86. Ibid., 4.

87. Ibid., 3.

88. Ibid., 2.

89. Ibid., 18.

90. Ibid., 20.

91. Ibid., emphasis added.

92. Ibid., 37.

93. Babiracki, "Imperial Heresies," 202.

94. AMZV, f. TO SSSR-Obyčejně, 1945–1959, k. 17, o. 25 [Transcript of the plenary meeting of the zemliachestvo group Moscow IV, March 19, 1952], 4.

95. Ibid., 17.

96. Ibid., 15.

97. AMZV, f. TO SSSR-Obyčejně, 1945–1959, k. 5, o. 25 [Report from April 4, 1952, sent to the political secretary of the ÚV KSČ, Gottwald], 4.

98. Mlynář, *Nightfrost in Prague*, 7.

99. RGASPI, f. 17, op. 133, d. 237, ll. 31–33.

100. AMZV, f. TO SSSR-Obyčejně, 1945–1959, k. 17, o. 25 [Report on the meeting of the zemliachestvo at MGU on March 21, 1952], 42.

101. Selucký, *Východ je východ*, 63.

102. Ibid., 60.

103. Ibid., 62.

104. AMZV, f. TO SSSR-Obyčejně, 1945–1959, k. 17, o. 25 [Letter from the chargé d'affaires at the Czechoslovak embassy in Moscow to Kopecký, May 30, 1952].

105. Selucký, *Východ je východ*, 63–64.

106. AMZV, f. TO SSSR-Obyčejné, 1945–1959, k. 17, o. 25 [Report from the Czechoslovak embassy in Moscow on May 7, 1952 to Kopecký at the Soviet Division of the Czechoslovak Ministry of Foreign Affairs, on the meeting of members of the Czechoslovak zemliachestvo in Moscow on May 4, 1952], 1.

107. Ibid. [Memo from the Czechoslovak embassy in Moscow to the Soviet Division of the Czechoslovak Ministry of Foreign Affairs, including a summons from the zemliachestvo at MGU, April 25, 1952].

108. Ibid. [Letter from the embassy of the Czechoslovak Republic in Moscow to the Ministry of Foreign Affairs, Kopecký, Soviet division, May 7, 1952], 3.

109. Ibid. [Text of Sokhin's statement at the meeting of the zemliachestvo on March 19, 1952, forwarded to I. Kopecký at the Ministry of Foreign Affairs on June 6, 1952. In Russian], 3.

110. From 1948 to 1954, nearly 90,000 Czechoslovak citizens were prosecuted for political crimes, including 278 high-ranking party functionaries, Kevin McDermott, "Stalinist Terror in Czechoslovakia: Origins, Processes, Responses," in *Stalinist Terror in Eastern Europe: Elite Purges and Mass Repression*, ed. McDermott and Matthew Stibbe (Manchester: Manchester University Press, 2010), 109, 100.

111. Quoted in Mlynář, *Nightfrost in Prague*, 9.

112. Selucký, *Východ je východ*, 65–66.

113. Stephen Kotkin, *Magnetic Mountain: Stalinism as a Civilization* (Berkeley: University of California Press, 1995), 220.

114. AMZV, f. TO SSSR-Obyčejně, 1945–1959, k. 5, o. 25 [Text of Sokhin's statement at the meeting of the zemliachestvo on March 19, 1952, forwarded to I. Kopecký at the Ministry of Foreign Affairs on June 6, 1952. In Russian], 3.

115. Kotkin, *Magnetic Mountain*, 220.

116. Selucký, *Východ je východ*, 37–38.

117. Dušan Spáčil, *My z Černína: Paměti československého diplomata* (Prague: Periskop, 1995), 65–66.

118. Michal Reiman, *Ruská revoluce, 23. únor–25. říjen 1917* (Prague: Naše vojsko, 1967) and *The Birth of Stalinism: The USSR on the Eve of the "Second Revolution,"* trans. George Saunders (Bloomington: Indiana University Press, 1987).

119. Mikhail Gorbachev and Zdeněk Mlynář, *Conversations with Gorbachev: On Perestroika, the Prague Spring, and the Crossroads of Socialism*, trans. George Shriver (New York: Columbia University Press, 2003).

120. M. Iu. Dostal' and I. V. Churkina, "Pamiati slovatskogo istorika Vladimira Matuly (1928–2011)," *Slavianovedenie* 5 (2011): 125–126.

3. The Legacy of the Liberation

Epigraph: Archiv ministerstva zahraničních věcí České republiky (Archive of the Ministry of Foreign Affairs of the Czech Republic; hereafter AMZV), f. TO SSSR-Tajné, 1960–1964, k. 8 [Letter from Sergei Osipov to the Czechoslovak Ministry of Foreign Affairs].

1. "Pis'ma chitatelei," *Sotsialisticheskaia Chekhoslovakiia*, April 1965, 28.

2. I. S. Konev, ed., *Za osvobozhdenie Chekhoslovakii* (Moscow: Voennoe izdatel'stvo Ministerstva oborony SSSR, 1965), 296.

3. I would like to thank Michael Geyer for suggesting this term.

4. Reuben Fowkes, "Soviet War Memorials in Eastern Europe, 1945–74," in *Figuration/Abstraction: Strategies for Public Sculpture in Europe, 1945–1968*, ed. Charlotte Benton (Aldershot: Ashgate, 2004), 11–32.

5. Paul Stangl, "The Soviet War Memorial in Treptow, Berlin," *Geographical Review* 93, no. 2 (April 2003): 213–236.

6. Nancy M. Wingfield, *Flag Wars and Stone Saints: How the Bohemian Lands Became Czech* (Cambridge, MA: Harvard University Press, 2007), 275.

7. Ibid., 283–285.

8. Quoted in Irena and Ladislav Michálkovi, *Olšany hrdinské* (Prague, n.p.: 2008), 226–227.

9. "Vzpomínali jsme svého osvobození," *Přítel SSSR*, May 15, 1946, 2.

10. "Hřbitovy příslušníků Rudé armády v ČSR," *Přítel SSSR*, October 5, 1946, 4.

11. Gosudarstvennyi arkhiv Rossiiskoi Federatsii (State Archive of the Russian Federation; hereafter GARF), f. 5283, op. 17, d. 422, l. 124.

12. Andrei Zhdanov, "Report on the International Situation to the Cominform," September 22, 1947, accessed April 9, 2018, http://soviethistory.msu.edu/1947-2/cominform-and-the-soviet-bloc/cominform-and-the-soviet-bloc-texts/report-on-the-international-situation-to-the-cominform/. Translated from *Informatsionnoe soveshchanie predstavitelei nekotorykh kompartii v Pol'she v kontse sentiabria 1947 goda* (s.n.: Gospolitizdat, 1948), 30–35.

13. Quoted in Stangl, "Soviet War Memorial," 227.

14. See Marie Klimešová, "Czechoslovak Public Sculpture and Its Context from 1945 to the 'Realizations' Exhibition, 1961," in Benton, *Figuration/Abstraction*, 36, and

Zdeněk Hojda and Jiří Pokorný, *Pomníky a zapomníky* (Prague: Paseka, 1996), 223. The statue currently stands next to the main train station (Hlavní nádraží) in Prague.

15. Cynthia Paces, *Prague Panoramas: National Memory and Sacred Space in the Twentieth Century* (Pittsburgh: University of Pittsburgh Press, 2009), 177.

16. On the Stalin monument, see Hana Pichova, "The Lineup for Meat: The Stalin Statue in Prague," *PMLA* 123, no. 3 (May 2008): 614–630; and Klimešová, "Czechoslovak Public Sculpture," 36–39.

17. "Změna osvobození," *Mladá fronta Dnes*, May 16, 1991. On the various holidays commemorating the war and the liberation in Czechoslovakia, see also Wingfield, *Flag Wars and Stone Saints*, 271, and accessed April 28, 2018, http://www.fronta.cz/konec-valky-den-osvobozeni-den-vitezstvi.

18. Stangl, "Soviet War Memorial," 228.

19. Maria Bucur, *Heroes and Victims: Remembering War in Twentieth-Century Romania* (Bloomington: Indiana University Press, 2009), 147–158.

20. Bohumila Málková, "Vrátili nám život," *Svět sovětů*, May 4, 1951, 7.

21. Denise J. Youngblood, *Russian War Films: On the Cinema Front, 1914–2005* (Lawrence: University Press of Kansas, 2007), 101.

22. Fowkes, "Soviet Memorials in Eastern Europe," 24.

23. Ivan Razdin, "Na jaře roku 1945 . . ." *Svět sovětů*, May 4, 1951, 6.

24. Vladimír Markov, ibid., 7.

25. K. Bartošek and K. Pichlík, *Hanebná role amerických okupantů v západních Čechách v roce 1945* (Prague: Svoboda, 1951), 27.

26. Tony Shaw and Denise J. Youngblood, *Cinematic Cold War: The American and Soviet Struggle for Hearts and Minds* (Lawrence: University Press of Kansas, 2010), 68.

27. Fowkes, "Soviet Memorials in Eastern Europe," 11.

28. Anders Åman, *Architecture and Ideology in Eastern Europe during the Stalin Era: An Aspect of Cold War History* (Cambridge, MA: MIT Press, 1992), 38.

29. Amir Weiner, *Making Sense of War: The Second World War and the Fate of the Bolshevik Revolution* (Princeton, NJ: Princeton University Press, 2001).

30. See Nina Tumarkin, *The Living and the Dead: The Rise and Fall of the Cult of World War II in Russia* (New York: Basic Books, 1994) and Lisa A. Kirschenbaum, *The Legacy of the Siege of Leningrad, 1941–1995: Myths, Memories, and Monuments* (New York: Cambridge University Press, 2006).

31. Geoffrey Roberts, *Stalin's Wars: from World War to Cold War, 1939–1953* (New Haven, CT: Yale University Press, 2006), 322.

32. Youngblood, *Russian War Films*, 97.

33. Mark Edele, *Soviet Veterans of the Second World War: A Popular Movement in an Authoritarian Society 1941–1991* (Oxford: Oxford University Press, 2008).

34. Kirschenbaum, *Legacy of the Siege of Leningrad*, 116.

35. In Bulgaria, monuments to the Red Army were constructed as early as January 1945, Nikolai Vukov, "'Brotherly Help': Representations or 'Imperial' Legacy: Monuments to the Soviet Army in Bulgaria before and after 1989," *Ab Imperio* 1 (2006): 276. On the construction of Soviet war memorials in Eastern Europe, see Stangl, "Soviet War Memorial," Åman, *Architecture and Ideology*, and Reuben Fowkes, "The Role of Monumental Sculpture in the Construction of Socialist Space in Stalinist Hungary," in

Socialist Spaces: Sites of Everyday Life in the Eastern Bloc, ed. David Crowley and Susan E. Reid (Oxford: Berg Publishers, 2002), 65–84. On World War II monuments in the Soviet Union, see Scott W. Palmer, "How Memory Was Made: The Construction of the Memorial to the Heroes of the Battle of Stalingrad," *Russian Review* 68, no. 3 (July 2009): 373.

36. Tumarkin, *The Living and the Dead*, 104.

37. Statistics from Ronald Grigor Suny, *The Soviet Experiment: Russia, the USSR, and the Successor States* (New York: Oxford University Press, 1998), 333.

38. See, for example, Richard Overy, *Russia's War* (New York: Penguin Books, 1998) and Karel C. Berkhoff, *Harvest of Despair: Life and Death in Ukraine under Nazi Rule* (Cambridge, MA: Harvard University Press, 2008).

39. Elizabeth A. Wood, "Performing Memory: Vladimir Putin and the Celebration of WWII in Russia," *Soviet and Post-Soviet Review* 38 (2011): 172–200.

40. Russian translation of an article in *Hlas revoluce*, "This Is How Our Friends Live: A Discussion with Heroes of the Soviet Union A. P. Mares'ev, F. I. Kravchenko, and B. Sakharov," no date, but likely 1957, filed in GARF, f. 9541, op. 1, d. 114, l. 11. In 1963, a group of Soviet tourists from Gomel' who visited Czechoslovakia also noted how well the Czechoslovaks had preserved monuments to the Red Army, and explicitly stated that this was something the USSR could learn from Czechoslovakia. GARF, f. 9520, op. 1, d. 599, l. 48.

41. Palmer, "How Memory Was Made," 382–385.

42. I would like to thank Brandon Schechter for identifying the soldier's rank.

43. Lesson 52, "Den' osvobozhdeniia," in F. Malíř et al., *Russkii iazyk: učebnice pro 5. postupný ročník národních škol* (Prague: Státní nakladatelství, 1950), 99.

44. See Tumarkin, *The Living and the Dead*, 110–113, quotation on 110; Youngblood, *Russian War Films*, 117–131.

45. Rachel Applebaum, "The Friendship Project: Socialist Internationalism in the Soviet Union and Czechoslovakia in the 1950s and 1960s," *Slavic Review* 74, no. 3 (Fall 2015): 484–507.

46. Národní archiv (National Archive), f. 1329 [Osvobození Československa Rudou armádou-1945], inv. č. 18/3.

47. "Česká matka a ruská dcera," *Svět sovětů*, March 6, 1958, 11.

48. Discussed in greater detail in chapter 4.

49. "Znakom'tes'," *Sotsialisticheskaia Chekhoslovakiia*, May 1965, 15.

50. Jiří Chrbas, "Poiski novogo (Pis'mo iz Pragi)," *Iskusstvo kino*, no. 5 (May 1960), 147. Chrbas was the main editor of the Czechoslovak journal *Film a doba*.

51. I discuss the role of tourism in the friendship project in more detail in chapter 5.

52. GARF, f. 9520, op. 1, d. 1007, l. 10.

53. Rossiiskii gosudarstvennyi arkhiv sotsial'no-politicheskoi istorii (Russian State Archive for Social and Political History; hereafter RGASPI), f. M-5 (Molodezhnyi arkhiv), op. 1, d. 326, l. 75.

54. GARF, f. 9520, op. 1, d. 1131, ll. 49–50.

55. RGASPI, f. M-5, op. 1, d. 326, l. 57.

56. GARF, f. 9520, op. 1, d. 726, l. 105.

57. RGASPI, f. M-5, op. 1, d. 326, l. 57.

58. A. S. Cherniaev, *Moia zhizn' i moë vremia* (Moscow: Mezhdunarodnye otnoshe-niia, 1995), 230.

59. GARF, f. 9576, op. 4, d. 70, ll. 72–73.

60. Ibid., 74.

61. GARF, f. 9576, op. 4, d. 68, l. 168.

62. GARF, f. 9576, op. 4, d. 36, l. 238.

63. GARF, f. 9541, op. 1, d. 584, l. 99.

64. GARF, f. 9541, op. 1, d. 980, l. 104.

65. "Pis'ma chitatelei," *Sotsialisticheskaia Chekhoslovakiia*, May 1964, 30.

66. GARF, f. 9541, op. 1, d. 786, l. 10.

67. "Aleksei Remembers," *Svět sovětů*, May 7, 1958, Russian translation of the article, filed in GARF, f. 9541, op. 1, d. 180, l. 104.

68. "Poděkování partyzána," *Svět sovětů*, April 6, 1960, 19.

69. GARF, f. 9541, op. 1, d. 786, ll. 82–84.

70. "Druzhba naveki," *Sotsialisticheskaia Chekhoslovakiia*, April 1965, 6.

71. Mary Louise Roberts, *What Soldiers Do: Sex and the American GI in World War II France* (Chicago: University of Chicago Press, 2013), 197.

72. Edele, *Soviet Veterans*, 208.

4. Socialist Internationalism with a Human Face

Epigraph: Gosudarstvennyi arkhiv Rossiiskoi Federatsii (State Archive of the Russian Federation; hereafter GARF), f. 9576, op. 2, d. 55, l. 46.

1. "Pis'ma chitatelei," *Sotsialisticheskaia Chekhoslovakiia*, January 1964, 30.

2. In the post-Stalinist period, journalists and officials frequently used the "socialist world" to describe the relationship between the Soviet Union and its satellites. For example, "My i mir v Monreale," *Sotsialisticheskaia Chekhoslovakiia*, September 1967, 9.

3. See, for example, Vladislav M. Zubok, *A Failed Empire: The Soviet Union in the Cold War from Stalin to Gorbachev* (Chapel Hill: University of North Carolina Press, 2007); Jonathan Haslam, *Russia's Cold War: From the October Revolution to the Fall of the Wall* (New Haven, CT: Yale University Press, 2011); Amir Weiner, "Déjà Vu All Over Again: Prague Spring, Romanian Summer and Soviet Autumn on the Soviet Western Frontier," *Contemporary European History* 15, no. 2 (2006): 159–194; and Zbigniew Wojnowski, *The Near Abroad: Socialist Eastern Europe and Soviet Patriotism in Ukraine, 1956–85* (Toronto: University of Toronto Press, 2017).

4. See, for example, Susan E. Reid, "Who Will Beat Whom? Soviet Popular Reception of the American National Exhibition in Moscow, 1959," in *Imagining the West in Eastern Europe and the Soviet Union*, ed. György Péteri (Pittsburgh: University of Pittsburgh Press, 2010), 194–236; Yale Richmond, *Cultural Exchange and the Cold War: Raising the Iron Curtain* (University Park: Pennsylvania State University Press, 2003); Robert D. English, *Russia and the Idea of the West: Gorbachev, Intellectuals, and the End of the Cold War* (New York: Columbia University Press, 2000); Eleonory Gilburd, "Picasso in Thaw Culture," *Cahiers du Monde russe* 47, no. 1–2 (January–July 2006): 65–108; and György Péteri, "Nylon Curtain: Transnational and Transsystemic Tendencies in the

Cultural Life of State-Socialist Russia and East-Central Europe," *Slavonica* 10, no. 2 (2004): 113–123.

5. On the United States' use of cultural contacts with Western Europe to create a unified front in the Cold War, see, for example, Mary Nolan, "Culture Wars," in *The Transatlantic Century: Europe and America, 1890–2010* (Cambridge: Cambridge University Press, 2012), 230–267; Oliver Schmidt, "Small Atlantic World: U.S. Philanthropy and the Expanding Exchange of Scholars after 1945," in *Culture and International History*, ed. Jessica C. E. Gienow-Hecht and Frank Schumacher (Oxford: Berghahn Books, 2003), 125; and Reinhold Wagnleitner, "'No Commodity Is Quite So Strange as This Thing Called Cultural Exchange': The Foreign Politics of American Pop Culture Hegemony," *Amerikastudien/American Studies* 46, no. 3 (2001): 452.

6. Denis Kozlov and Eleonory Gilburd, "The Thaw as an Event in Russian History," in *The Thaw: Soviet Society and Culture during the 1950s and 1960s*, ed. Kozlov and Gilburd (Toronto: University of Toronto Press, 2013), 27.

7. Nigel Gould-Davies, "The Logic of Soviet Cultural Diplomacy," *Diplomatic History* 27, no. 2 (April 2003), 207.

8. GARF, f. 9576, op. 4, d. 100, l. 167.

9. In 1960, the KSČ officially declared that Czechoslovakia had achieved socialism, see Pavel Skopal, "The Cinematic Shapes of the Socialist Modernity Programme: Ideological and Economic Parameters of Cinema Distribution in the Czech Lands, 1948–70," in *Cinema, Audiences and Modernity: New Perspectives on European Cinema History*, ed. Daniel Biltereyst, Richard Maltby, and Philippe Meers (Abingdon, Oxon: Routledge, 2012), 82.

10. GARF, f. 9518, op. 1, d. 143, l. 29.

11. Austin Jersild, "The Soviet State as Imperial Scavenger: 'Catch Up and Surpass' in the Transnational Socialist Bloc, 1950–1960," *American Historical Review* 116, no. 1 (February 2011): 116–117.

12. GARF, f. 9576, op. 2, d. 53, l. 33.

13. Archiv ministerstva zahraničních věcí České republiky (Archive of the Ministry of Foreign Affairs of the Czech Republic; hereafter AMZV), f. TO SSSR-Tajné, 1965–1969, k. 3, o. 5 [Report by the D[iplomatic]C[orps] in Moscow on the promotion of the ČSSR in the USSR.]

14. Programma KPSS priniata XXII s"ezdom KPSS, III. Mirovaia sistema sotsializma (Moscow, 1974), accessed April 10, 2018, http://leftinmsu.narod.ru/polit_files/books/III_program_KPSS_files/019.htm.

15. Zbigniew Brzezinski, *The Soviet Bloc: Unity and Conflict*, 2nd ed. (Cambridge, MA: Harvard University Press, 1967), 456–460.

16. On Hungary as a motivating factor behind Eastern European integration, see ibid., 456.

17. For instance, the USSR attempted to use the 1957 World Youth Festival in Moscow to repair relations with Hungary, see Gilburd, "The Revival of Soviet Internationalism in the Mid to Late 1950s," in Kozlov and Gilburd, *The Thaw*, 386.

18. GARF, f. 9518, op. 1, d. 143, ll. 29–30.

19. The Committee for Cultural Contacts with Foreign Countries operated under the auspices of the Council of Ministers of the USSR. It was founded in 1957 and dissolved ten years later.

20. GARF, f. 9518, op. 1, d. 143, ll. 88–89.

21. Ibid., 28.

22. The other friendship societies were devoted to China, Finland, Hungary, the German Democratic Republic, Poland, Italy, and India. See Eleonory Gilburd, "To See Paris and Die: Western Culture in the Soviet Union, 1950s and 1960s" (PhD diss., University of California, Berkeley, 2010), 35n110.

23. Ibid., 25.

24. On SSOD's replacement of VOKS, see Gilburd, "The Revival of Soviet Internationalism," 373. For Popova's quote, see GARF, f. 9576, op. 4, d. 31, l. 260.

25. "Oč nám jde milý příteli," *Svět sovětů*, January 17, 1947, 7.

26. GARF, f. 9576, op. 2, d. 55, ll. 36–37.

27. Ibid., 62–70.

28. Ibid., 85 and GARF, f. 9576, op. 4, d. 95, l. 196.

29. GARF, f. 9576, op. 2, d. 55, ll. 21–24.

30. Ibid., 8–17.

31. GARF, f. 9576, op. 4, d. 38, l. 28.

32. See letters from people interested in joining the OSChD, in GARF, f. 9576, op. 4, d. 38.

33. Ibid.,19. On scholarly interests, see ll. 77, 105, 138.

34. The quote comes from David Crowley and Susan E. Reid, "Introduction: Pleasures in Socialism?" in *Pleasures in Socialism: Leisure and Luxury in the Eastern Bloc*, ed. Crowley and Reid (Evanston, IL: Northwestern University Press, 2010), 15. See also Mark Edele, *Soviet Veterans of the Second World War: A Popular Movement in an Authoritarian Society 1941–1991* (Oxford: Oxford University Press, 2008), 170; and Gleb Tsipursky, "Having Fun in the Thaw: Youth Initiative Clubs in the Post-Stalin Years," *The Carl Beck Papers in Russian and East European Studies* no. 2201 (Pittsburgh: University of Pittsburgh Press, 2012), 12.

35. Gilburd, "Revival of Internationalism," 363.

36. "Dobrý den, drazí českoslovenští přátelé!" *Svět sovětů,* September 3, 1952, 19.

37. Národní archiv (National Archive; hereafter NA), f. 1261/2/28 [ÚV KSČ-oddělení masových organizací 1945–1956], a.j. 282 [Report on the LKR for the SČSP, December 28, 1951].

38. The prospect of Soviet citizens corresponding with people in the capitalist countries was widely discussed during the Thaw, although the Soviet government was very hesitant about it. Ultimately, most pen-pal correspondences with the West were undertaken on a collective basis, which made them easier for the authorities to control. See Gilburd, "To See Paris and Die," 36–38.

39. GARF, f. 9576, op. 2, d. 55, l. 91.

40. GARF, f. 9576, op. 4, d. 69, ll. 219–220.

41. GARF, f. 9576, op. 4, d. 71, ll. 27–27a.

42. See chapter 5 for more details.

43. GARF, f. 9576, op. 4, d. 68, l. 282.

44. F. Malíř, T. Franková, and A. Lukešová, *Dopisujeme si rusky: Příručka pro kursy ruského jazyka a pro přípravu dopisů do SSSR* (Prague: Svět sovětů, 1965), 10.

45. Ibid., 21, 26, 36, 42.

46. Gilburd, "Revival of Soviet Internationalism," 363.

47. Malíř, Franková, and Lukešová, *Dopisujeme si Rusky*, 10.

48. There was also a separate Slovak magazine, *Svet socializmu* [The World of Socialism].

49. AMZV, f. TO SSSR-Tajné, 1960–1964, k. 3, o. 4 [Report from the Czechoslovak embassy in Moscow on propagating the ČSSR in the USSR, September 1964].

50. AMZV, f. TO SSSR-Tajné, 1965–1969, k. 2, o. 10 [Report on further possibilities for propagating the ČSSR in the USSR, May 1965], 9.

51. GARF, f. 9572, op. 4, d. 100, l. 183.

52. "Čtenáři promluví," *Svět sovětů*, December 27, 1961, 2–3.

53. NA, f. 1261/1/8 [Ideologická komise ÚV KSČ, 1958–1968], sv. 7, a.j. 23, b. 4 [Report by the Ideological Commission of the KSČ's Central Committee on the current state of propaganda of socialist internationalism and the USSR in the ČSSR, and suggestions for improving it, January 14, 1967], 43.

54. See, for instance, a Russian recipe for borscht in *Svět sovětů*, October 12, 1960, 15.

55. *Svět sovětů*'s format sounds very similar to the Romanian women's magazine *Femeia* from the same period, Jill Massino, "From Black Caviar to Blackouts: Gender, Consumption, and Lifestyle in Ceausescu's Romania," in *Communism Unwrapped: Consumption in Cold War Eastern Europe*, ed. Paulina Bren and Mary Neuburger (Oxford: Oxford University Press, 2012), 230–235. "The Age of Affluence," comes from Tony Judt's description of Western Europe from the 1950s–1970s, *Postwar: A History of Europe Since 1945* (New York: Penguin Press, 2005), 324.

56. GARF, f. 9576, op. 4, d. 100, l. 183.

57. GARF, f. 9576, op. 4, d. 31, ll. 66–67.

58. GARF, f. 9576, op. 4, d. 67, l. 141.

59. Benedict Anderson, *Imagined Communities: Reflections on the Origin and Spread of Nationalism* (London: Verso, 2006), 6–7.

60. The quote is from Richmond, *Cultural Exchange and the Cold War*, 200. On intellectual trends, see Richmond, "The Polish Connection," 200–204. On cultural and commercial influences, see Anne E. Gorsuch, "Time Travelers: Soviet Tourists to Eastern Europe," in *Turizm: The Russian and East European Tourist under Capitalism and Socialism*, ed. Gorsuch and Diane P. Koenker (Ithaca, NY: Cornell University Press, 2006), 205–226; and Anne E. Gorsuch, *All This Is Your World: Soviet Tourism at Home and Abroad after Stalin* (Oxford: Oxford University Press, 2011), 80. On home grown political reform, see English, *Russia and the Idea of the West*, 100–115.

61. "Doverie k molodëzhi," *Sotsialisticheskaia Chekhoslovakiia*, May 1964, 20, and "Liubovnye pokhozhdeniia blondinki," *Sotsialisticheskaia Chekhoslovakiia*, October 1965, 20.

62. Rossiiskii gosudarstvennyi arkhiv noveishei istorii (Russian State Archive for Contemporary History; hereafter RGANI), f. 5, op. 36, d. 158, l. 239. *Loves of a Blonde* appears to have eventually been released in the USSR because a Soviet woman named it as her favorite Czechoslovak movie in an interview for *Svět sovětů* the following year. See "Co o nás vědí Moskvané," *Svět sovětů*, November 23, 1966, 13.

63. "Izdeliia iz tekstilia dlia kvartiry," *Sotsialisticheskaia Chekhoslovakiia*, May 1963, 24–25.

64. "Pis'ma chitatelei," *Sotsialisticheskaia Chekhoslovakiia*, January 1965, 28.

65. Interview with Sergei Iur'enen, accessed April 10, 2018, http://archive.svoboda.org/programs/OTB/2003/OBT.033003.asp.

66. AMZV, f. TO SSSR-Tajné, 1965–1969, k. 2, o. 10 [Report on propagating the ČSSR in the USSR, May 1965], 2.

67. RGANI, f. 5, op. 33, d. 234, l. 28.

68. "Ptejte se, APN odpovídá," *Svět sovětů*, April 8, 1968, 13.

69. "První big beat v SSSR," *Svět sovětů*, February 2, 1966, 14–15.

70. Kiril Tomoff, "Agents of Empire: Soviet Concert Tours and Cultural Empire in Eastern Europe, 1945–1958," paper presented at the annual convention of the Association for Slavic, East European, and Eurasian Studies in New Orleans, November 18, 2012.

71. Gilburd, "Revival of Socialist Internationalism," 364–367.

72. Kiril Tomoff, *Virtuosi Abroad: Soviet Music and Imperial Competition during the Early Cold War, 1945–1958* (Ithaca, NY: Cornell University Press, 2015), 117–119.

73. Maruška Svašek, "The Politics of Artistic Identity: The Czech Art World in the 1950s and 1960s," *Contemporary European History* 6, no. 3 (November 1997): 395.

74. Cathleen M. Giustino, "Industrial Design and the Czechoslovak Pavilion at EXPO '58: Artistic Autonomy, Party Control and Cold War Common Ground," *Journal of Contemporary History* 47, no. 1 (January 2012): 210.

75. Čestmír Císař, *Člověk a politik: kniha vzpomínek a úvah* (Prague: ETC, 1998), 329.

76. Ibid., 325–329.

77. RGANI, f. 5, op. 36, d. 156, l. 20. In 1965, two million out of Czechoslovakia's four million television sets were able to receive programming from Austria and West Germany, see RGANI, f. 5, op. 36, d. 216, l. 64.

78. Open Society Archives, Budapest, Hungary, 300-6-2, box 2, Jan 1966–Dec 1967, folder, "1965–1966" [Report on Audience Mail, April 1965]. The Radio Prague poll was broadcast on December 22, 1965.

79. RGANI, f.5, op.36, d.152, l.23.

80. Rossiiskii gosudarstvennyi arkhiv literatury i iskusstva (Russian State Archive of Literature and Art; hereafter RGALI), f. 2918, op. 5, d. 446, ll. 52–53.

81. Ibid., 61

82. Ibid., 53.

83. RGANI, f. 5, op. 36, d. 156, l. 19.

84. RGALI, f. 2918, op. 5, d. 446, l. 53.

85. GARF, f. 9518, op. 1, d. 144, l. 192.

86. GARF, f. 9518, op. 1, d. 148, l. 272.

87. GARF, f. 9518, op. 1, d. 146, l. 76.

88. GARF, f. 9518, op. 1, d. 143, ll. 129–130. Similarly, Czechoslovak officials touted the success of performances by Czechoslovak groups abroad as evidence that these groups would attract large audiences in the USSR. See ibid., 88.

89. On the new emphasis on the individual in Soviet literature during the Thaw, see Katerina Clark, "'Wait for Me and I Shall Return': The Early Thaw as a Reprise of Late Thirties Culture?" in Kozlov and Gilburd, *The Thaw*, 85–101.

90. Peter Hames, *The Czechoslovak New Wave* (Berkeley: University of California Press, 1985), 7, 28–30.

91. GARF, f. 9518, op. 1, d. 146, ll. 76–77.

92. GARF, f. 9518, op. 1, d. 147, l. 263.

93. Ibid., 134.

94. GARF, f. 9576, op. 2, d. 272, ll. 133–34.

95. GARF, f. 9518, op. 1, d. 147, l. 30.

96. See articles in *Student*, "Ďábel v Moskvě," September 12, 1967, 28–29; "Pětaosmdesátimetrový gigant Asuánské přehrady: Ernst Něizvěstnyj," January 10, 1968, 3; and "Volím číslo tři," February 7, 1968, 3. On *Student*'s coverage of the Soviet dissident movement, see, for example, "Sovětský leden," June 5, 1968, 3.

97. GARF, f. 9518, op. 1, d. 146, l. 61.

98. RGANI, f. 5, op. 36, d. 156, l. 20.

99. Ibid.

100. Ibid., 23–24.

101. RGANI, f. 5, op. 59, d. 28, l. 86. See also RGANI, f. 5, op. 36, d. 158, ll. 239–241.

102. RGANI, f. 5, op. 36, d. 158, ll. 239–241.

103. AMZV, f. TO SSSR-Tajné, 1965–1969, k. 2, o. 10 [Report about the propaganda of the ČSSR in the USSR, May 1965], 8.

104. GARF, f. 9518, op. 1, d. 147, l. 41.

105. Ibid., 31.

106. RGANI, f. 5, op. 36, d. 156, l. 34.

107. "Foreign Goods," *Sovetskaia torgovlia*, October 13, 1956, 2, translated and reprinted in condensed form in *Current Digest of the Soviet Press* 8, no. 42 (November 28, 1956): 5–6.

108. "Development of the U.S.S.R. Foreign Trade," *Current Digest of the Soviet Press* 10, no. 6 (1958): 12–15.

109. AMZV, f. TO SSSR-Tajné, 1965–1969, k. 2, o. 10 [Report on propagating the ČSSR in the USSR, May 1965], 2.

110. "Vstretimsia v 'Belom lebede,'" *Sotsialisticheskaia Chekhoslovakiia*, April 1961, 12.

111. GARF, f. 9572, op. 4, d. 295, l. 183.

112. RGANI, f. 5, op. 33, d. 234, l. 30.

113. GARF, f. 9572, op. 4, d. 295, l. 183.

114. RGANI, f. 5, op. 33, d. 234, l. 30.

115. GARF, f. 9572, op. 4, d. 295, l. 184.

116. See, for example, Bren and Neuburger, "Introduction," in *Communism Unwrapped*, 10–11; Susan E. Reid, "This Is Tomorrow! Becoming a Consumer in the Soviet Sixties," in *The Socialist Sixties: Crossing Borders in the Second World*, ed. Anne E. Gorsuch and Diane P. Koenker (Bloomington: Indiana University Press, 2013), 25–65; and Patrick Hyder Patterson, "Risky Business: What was Really Being Sold in the Department Stores of Socialist Eastern Europe?" in Bren and Neuburger, *Communism Unwrapped*, 116–139.

117. Newsreel included in the show "Československé úspěchy," which premiered on ČT24, March 2, 2013, accessed May 22, 2014, http://www.ceskatelevize.cz/ivysilani/10116288585-archiv-ct24/213411058210009.

118. NA f. 1261/0/44, II část [Kancelář tajemníka ÚV KSČ Antonína Novotného (1946) 1951–1967 (1968)], inv. č. 278 [Letter from František Krajčír to the Czechoslovak Ministry of Schools and Culture, March 25, 1959].

119. Reid, "Who Will Beat Whom?" 236.

120. Susan E. Reid, "Khrushchev Modern: Agency and Modernization in the Soviet Home," *Cahiers du Monde russe* 47, no. 1–2 (January–June 2006): 249.

121. "Vyřídíte v Československu," *Svět sovětů*, December 6, 1961, 2.

122. "Nebol'shie zametki o bol'shoi druzhbe," *Sotsialisticheskaia Chekhoslovakiia,* September 1964, 12–13.

123. "Co o nás vědí Moskvané," *Svět sovětů*, November 23, 1966, 13.

124. "Ot 'zari' k 'Moskvichu'," *Sotsialisticheskaia Chekhoslovakiia*, June 1964, 9.

125. Susan E. Reid, "Cold War in the Kitchen: Gender and the de-Stalinization of Consumer Taste in the Soviet Union under Khrushchev," *Slavic Review* 61, no. 2 (Summer 2002): 211–252.

126. AMZV, f. TO SSSR-Tajné, 1960–1964, k.2, o.9 [Report from the General Consulate of Czechoslovakia in Kiev to the Czechoslovak Ministry of Foreign Affairs, on Soviet tourist trips to the ČSSR, June 30, 1961].

127. See, for instance, GARF, f. 9520, op. 1, d. 726, l. 35.

128. Georgii Shakhnazarov, *S vozhdiami i bez nikh* (Moscow: Vagrius, 2001), 94.

129. "Ot 'zari' k 'Moskvichu,'" *Sotsialisticheskaia Chekhoslovakiia*, June 1964, 9.

130. "Beskonechnoe mnozhestvo druzei," *Sotsialisticheskaia Chekhoslovakiia*, October 1967, 11.

5. Tourists on Tanks

Epigraph: "Mluví se o nás," *Svět sovětů*, March 12, 1968, 13.

1. Article published in *Květy*, October 1967; translated into Russian and filed in Arkhiv vneshnei politiki Rossiiskoi Federatsii (Foreign Policy Archive of the Russian Federation; hereafter AVP RF), f. 198, op. 49, r. 113, d. 10, l. 44.

2. On Soviet tourism to Eastern Europe, see Anne E. Gorsuch, *All This Is Your World: Soviet Tourism at Home and Abroad after Stalin* (Oxford: Oxford University Press, 2011); Anne E. Gorsuch, "Time Travelers: Soviet Tourists to Eastern Europe," in *Turizm: The Russian and East European Tourist under Capitalism and Socialism*, ed. Gorsuch and Diane P. Koenker (Ithaca, NY: Cornell University Press, 2006), 205–226; Zbigniew Wojnowski, "Friendship in the Soviet Empire: Salvaging International Socialism in Eastern Europe after 1956," in *The Near Abroad: Socialist Eastern Europe and Soviet Patriotism in Ukraine, 1956–1985* (Toronto: University of Toronto Press, 2017), 70–104; and Rachel Applebaum, "A Test of Friendship: Soviet-Czechoslovak Tourism and the Prague Spring," in *The Socialist Sixties: Crossing Borders in the Second World*, ed. Anne E. Gorsuch and Diane P. Koenker (Bloomington: Indiana University Press, 2013), 213–232.

3. Article published in *Květy*, October 1967, translated into Russian and filed in AVP RF, f. 198, op. 49, r. 113, d. 10, l. 44.

4. "I zde třeba zlepšovat," *Rudé právo*, April 24, 1968.

5. Statistics for 1955–1960 from Archiv ministerstva zahraničních věcí České republiky (Archive of the Ministry of Foreign Affairs of the Czech Republic; hereafter AMZV), f. TO SSSR-Tajné, 1960–1964, k. 2, o. 9 [Report on tourism between the ČSR and the USSR, August 9, 1960]; for 1965, see AMZV, f. TO SSSR-Tajné, 1965–1969, k.

2, o. 6 [Report on the current state of contacts between the ČSSR and the USSR in tourism, and on private visits between Czechoslovak and Soviet citizens, December 10, 1965]; for 1967–1969, see Gosudarstvennyi arkhiv Rossiiskoi Federatsii (State Archive of the Russian Federation; hereafter GARF), f. 9520, op. 2, d. 24, l. 30.

6. AMZV, f. TO SSSR-Tajné, 1960–1964, k. 2, o. 9 [Report from the Czechoslovak embassy in Moscow on tourism, 1961].

7. AMZV, f. TO SSSR-Tajné, 1965–1969, k. 2, o. 6 [Report on the current state of contacts between the ČSSR and the USSR in tourism, and on private visits between Czechoslovak and Soviet citizens, December 10, 1965].

8. GARF, f. 9520, op. 1, d. 913, l. 1.

9. GARF, f. 9576, op. 4, d. 38, l. 5.

10. Gorsuch, *All This Is Your World*, 82.

11. Wojnowski, *Near Abroad*, 72–73.

12. Diane P. Koenker, *Club Red: Vacation Travel and the Soviet Dream* (Ithaca, NY: Cornell University Press, 2013), 241.

13. For instance, a group from Yakutsk traveling in 1961 under the auspices of the Tourism Councils was made up of twenty-nine people: thirteen engineers, eight white-collar professionals (*sluzhashchie*), two students, two lab assistants, and one teacher. GARF, f. 9520, op. 1, d. 410, l. 71.

14. Gorsuch, *All This Is Your World*, 82–83.

15. GARF, f. 9520, op. 1, d. 504, l. 101.

16. Rossiiskii gosudarstvennyi arkhiv sotsial'no-politicheskoi istorii (Russian State Archive for Social and Political History; hereafter RGASPI), f. M-5 (Molodezhnyi arkhiv), op. 1, d. 326, l. 4.

17. The majority of Soviet tourists to Czechoslovakia were not party members. Trip leaders sometimes made references to separate meetings they held with the party members on their tours. For an example, see GARF, f. 9520, op. 1, d. 1344, l. 60.

18. Gorsuch, *All This Is Your World*, 22.

19. Aleksei Kraizinger, *Karlovy Vary: Putevoditel' dlia sovetskikh turistov po gorodu-kurotu* (Prague: Svět sovětů, 1963), 34.

20. Anne E. Gorsuch, "'There's No Place Like Home': Soviet Tourism in Late Stalinism," *Slavic Review* 62, no. 4 (Winter 2003): 784–785.

21. On Khrushchev's birthday, see RGASPI, f. M-5, op. 1, d. 207, l. 150. On ballet, see, for instance, GARF, f. 9520, op. 1, d. 493, l. 28 and f. 9520, op. 1, d. 726, l. 24.

22. GARF, f. 9520, op. 1, d. 1005, l. 25.

23. "Nebol'shie zametki o bol'shoi druzhbe," *Sotsialisticheskaia Chekhoslovakiia*, September 1964, 12–13.

24. "Variace na Pražské téma," *Svět sovětů*, January 24, 1968, 16–17.

25. GARF, f. 9520, op. 1, d. 891, l. 14.

26. GARF, f. 9520, op. 1, d. 1007, l. 61.

27. RGASPI, f. M-5, op. 1, d. 326, l. 331.

28. GARF, f. 9520, op. 2, d. 24, l. 33.

29. Steven M. Maddox, *Saving Stalin's Imperial City: Historic Preservation in Leningrad, 1930–1950* (Bloomington: Indiana University Press, 2014), 34.

30. See Cathleen M. Giustino, "Open Gates and Wandering Minds: Codes, Castles, and Chateaux in Socialist Czechoslovakia before 1960," in *Socialist Escapes: Breaking Away from Ideology and Everyday Routine in Eastern Europe, 1945–1989*, ed. Giustino, Catherine J. Plum, and Alexander Vari (New York: Berghahn Books, 2013), 48–72. Giustino reveals that visitors to castles, and even official tour guides, often interpreted these historical sites differently than the KSČ had intended, 57–61.

31. See, for example, Kraizinger, *Karlovy Vary*, 7.

32. Gorsuch, *All This Is Your World*, 103.

33. GARF, f. 9170, op. 1, d. 50, ll. 1–2.

34. Ibid., 3.

35. GARF, f. 9520, op. 1, d. 504, l. 26.

36. El'vira Filipovich, *Ot sovetskoi pionerki do chelnoka-pensionerki (moi dnevnik). Kniga I (1944–1972)* (Podol'sk: Saturn, 2000), entry for August 5, 1957, 93–94.

37. Josef Pazderka, "Zkoušel jsem s nimi mluvit. Rozhovor s Vladlenem Krivošejevem," in *Invaze 1968: Ruský pohled*, ed. Pazderka (Prague: Ústav pro studium totalitních režimů, Torst, 2011), 181.

38. The phrase is from Yale Richmond, *Cultural Exchange and the Cold War: Raising the Iron Curtain* (University Park: Pennsylvania State University Press, 2003), 201.

39. G. A. Arbatov, *Zatianuvsheesia vyzdorovlenie (1953–1985): Svidetel'stvo sovremennika* (Moscow: Mezhdunarodnye otnosheniia, 1991), 76.

40. Pazderka, "Rok 1968 nás změnil, rozhovor s Vladimirem Lukinem," in Pazderka, *Invaze 1968*, 165.

41. Quoted in Dimitrij Běloševský, "Mediální zákulisí invaze. Osudy (některých) ruských novinářů v srpnu 1968," in Pazderka, *Invaze 1968*, 155.

42. A. S. Cherniaev, *Moia zhizn' i moë vremia* (Moscow: Mezhdunarodnye otnosheniia, 1995), 234–236.

43. For examples of SSOD's responses to Soviet citizens' requests to visit pen pals in Czechoslovakia, see GARF, f. 9576, op. 4, d. 32, ll. 27, 136.

44. GARF, f. 9576, op. 4, d. 32, l. 127.

45. GARF, f. 9520, op. 1, d. 891, l. 62.

46. Jiří Hanzelka and Miroslav Zikmund, *Zvláštní zpráva č. 4: tajné* (Prague: Lidové nakladatelství, 1990), 108.

47. AMZV, f. TO SSSR-Tajné, 1965–1969, k. 2, o. 6 [Secret report from the Ministry of Foreign Affairs on the current state of contacts between the ČSSR and the USSR concerning tourism and private visits between Czechoslovak and Soviet citizens, December 10, 1965].

48. Ibid. [Report on tourism and private visits between Czechoslovak and Soviet citizens after the signing of the protocol on visa-less travel between the ČSSR and the USSR in 1965].

49. Rossiiskii gosudarstvennyi arkhiv noveishei istorii (Russian State Archive for Contemporary History; hereafter RGANI), f. 5, op. 33, d. 234, ll. 27–28.

50. Ibid.

51. Ústav pro soudobé dějiny AV ČR (Institute for Contemporary History of the Academy of Sciences of the Czech Republic; hereafter ÚSD, KV ČSFR), inv. 274,

sign. DI/274, k. 7 [Report from the Presidium of the ÚV KSČ on the struggle against anti-Communist ideology and propaganda in the ČSSR, June 25, 1969], 12.

52. William Taubman, *The View from Lenin Hills: Soviet Youth in Ferment* (New York: Coward-McCann, 1967), 229.

53. "Znakom'tes'," *Sotsialisticheskaia Chekhoslovakiia*, December 1967, 8.

54. "Cultural Life in Prague Is Thriving amid Change," *New York Times*, May 28, 1968.

55. S. A. Iurskii "Zapadnyi ekspress," excerpted in *Praga: Russkii vzgliad: Vek vosemnadstati—vek dvadstat' pervyi* (Moscow: VGBIL, 2003), 287. Originally published as S. A. Iurskii, *Igra v zhizn'* (Moscow: Vagrius, 2002).

56. Artemy Troitsky, *Back in the USSR: The True Story of Rock in Russia* (Boston: Faber and Faber, 1987), 29.

57. GARF, f. 9520, op. 1, d. 1007, l. 61.

58. RGASPI, f. M-5, op. 1, d. 326, l. 73.

59. GARF, f. 9520, op. 1, d. 1238, l. 22.

60. RGASPI, f. M-5, op. 2, d. 87, ll. 186–187.

61. "Znakom'tes'," *Sotsialisticheskaia Chekhoslovakiia*, December 1967, 8.

62. See, for instance, GARF, f. 9520, op. 1, d. 1344, l. 64.

63. RGASPI, f. M-5, op. 1, d. 326, l. 137.

64. GARF, f. 9520, op. 1, d. 1131, l. 2.

65. RGASPI, f. M-5, op. 1, d. 326, l. 59.

66. Mark Kramer, "The Czechoslovak Crisis and the Brezhnev Doctrine," in *1968: The World Transformed*, ed. Carole Fink, Philipp Gassert, and Detlef Junker (Cambridge: Cambridge University Press, 1998), 122–123; Kieran Williams, *The Prague Spring and Its Aftermath: Czechoslovak Politics, 1968–1970* (Cambridge: Cambridge University Press, 1997), 23.

67. For examples of these concerns, see documents in Jaromír Navrátil et al., ed., *The Prague Spring 1968: A National Security Archive Documents Reader*, trans. Mark Kramer, Joy Moss, and Ruth Tosek (Budapest, Hungary: Central European University Press, 1998), including document no. 22, "Cable from Czechoslovak Ambassador Oldřich Pavlovský on a Conversation with Soviet Deputy Foreign Minister Il'ichev, April 17, 1968 (Excerpts)," 101, and document no. 28, "Stenographic Account of the Soviet-Czechoslovak Summit Meeting in Moscow, May 4–5, 1968 (Excerpts)," 114–125.

68. RGASPI, f. M-5, op. 2, d. 87, l. 16.

69. ÚSD, KV ČSFR, inv. č. 5172, sign. Z/S/26 [Report from the Soviet embassy in Prague on "several negative events in the ČSSR," April 17, 1968], 187.

70. ÚSD, KV ČSFR, inv. č. 5294, sign. Z/S/148, k.73 [Report from the Soviet Committee for War Veterans on a trip to Czechoslovakia, June 10, 1968], 93–94.

71. N. P. Semënov, *Trevozhnaia Praga: Vospominaniia sovetskogo vitse-konsula v Chekhoslovakii (1968–1972)* (Moscow: Mezhdunarodnye otnosheniia, 2004), 79.

72. Document no. 8, "Report Submitted to the CPCz CC Presidium on Alexander Dubček's Visit to Moscow, January 29–30, 1968," (Excerpts), in Navrátil et al., *The Prague Spring 1968*, 42.

73. RGANI, f. 5, op. 60, d. 1, l. 89.

74. "Může pravda ublížit?" *Svět sovětů*, March 19, 1968, 20–21.

75. Ibid.

76. Jiří Pelikán, ed., "Preface," in *The Czechoslovak Political Trials, 1950–1954: The Suppressed Report of the Dubček Government's Commission of Inquiry, 1968* (Stanford, CA: Stanford University Press, 1971), 10. On the search for truth during de-Stalinization, see Vladislav Zubok, "Soviet Society in the 1960s," in *The Prague Spring and the Warsaw Pact Invasion of Czechoslovakia in 1968*, ed. Günter Bischof, Stefan Karner, and Peter Ruggenthaler (Lanham: Rowman and Littlefield, 2010), 87.

77. See, for example, Pelikán, *Czechoslovak Political Trials*, and the interviews *Student* conducted with the widows of the defendants in the Slánský trial, March 1968.

78. Alan Levy, *So Many Heroes* (Sagaponack, NY: Second Chance Press, 1972, 1980), 95.

79. "Mluví se o nás," *Svět sovětů*, March 12, 1968, 13.

80. "Kde začíná a kde končí přátelství," *Svět sovětů*, May 14, 1968, 4.

81. "Mluví se o nás," *Svět sovětů*, March 12, 1968, 13.

82. GARF, f. 9576, op. 4, d. 330a, l. 26.

83. RGASPI, f. M-5, op. 2, d. 87, l. 16.

84. GARF, f. 9520, op. 1, d. 1238, l. 22

85. "O Sovětském svazu nově-ale jak?" *Svět sovětů*, May 28, 1968, 3–4.

86. Ibid.

87. "Stará Rus ještě žije," *Svět sovětů*, August 30, 1967, 16.

88. "Kolik tváří má Moskva?" *Svět sovětů*, June 4, 1968, 3.

89. "O Sovětském svazu nově-ale jak?" *Svět sovětů*, May 28, 1968, 3.

90. Iurskii, "Zapadnyi ekspress," 287.

91. RGASPI, f. M-5, op. 1, d. 628, ll. 140–141.

92. Petr Pithart, "Gorbačovovi lidé z pražských Dejvic: Osobní vzpomínka na pražskou redakci *Otázek míru a socialismu*," in Pazderka, *Invaze 1968*, 176.

93. Ludmilla Alexeyeva and Paul Goldberg, *The Thaw Generation: Coming of Age in the Post-Stalin Era* (Boston: Little, Brown, 1990), 210.

94. Pëtr Vail' and Aleksandr Genis, *60-e—Mir Sovetskogo cheloveka* (Moscow: Novoe literaturnoe obozrenie, 1998), 311.

95. Alexeyeva and Goldberg, *Thaw Generation*, 209. On the Prague Spring as a model for Soviet reform, see also Robert D. English, *Russia and the Idea of the West: Gorbachev, Intellectuals, and the End of the Cold War* (New York: Columbia University Press, 2000), 109; and Vail' and Genis, *60-e—*, 311.

96. When a KGB agent arrived in Czechoslovakia in the spring of 1968, he asked *Pravda*'s correspondent why the newspaper was not providing Soviet readers with more information on the Czechoslovak events. "'Do you really want us to print all of the bastards' outrageous escapades?'" the correspondent asked. "'Such information will only harm the normalization of the situation, it will arouse unhealthy moods at home,'" Semënov, *Trevozhnaia Praga*, 76.

97. RGASPI, f. M-5, op. 1, d. 629, ll. 42–43.

98. RGASPI f. M-5, op. 2, d. 87, l. 55.

99. Ibid., 58.

100. Ibid., 54. The "Two Thousand Words Manifesto," by the Czech writer Ludvík Vaculík, and signed by prominent members of Czechoslovak society, expressed support for the Prague Spring reforms. For the text, see Navrátil et al., *Prague Spring 1968*, 177–181.

101. RGASPI, f. M-5, op. 2, d. 87, l. 106.

102. Ibid., 183.

103. The statistics come from Daniel Povolný, "Přijeli jsme splnit úkol: Sovětští vojáci a jejich pohled na invazi," in Pazderka, *Invaze 1968*, 17.

104. RGASPI, f. M-5, op. 2, d. 87, ll. 188–189.

105. GARF, f. 9520, op. 1, d. 1237, l. 3.

106. RGASPI f. M-5, op. 2, d. 129, l. 91.

107. ÚSD, KV ČSFR, inv. č. 5266, sign. Z/S/120, k. 7 [Excerpt from protocol no. 61 9s by the Secretariat of the TsK (Central Committee) KPSS on measures to normalize the situation in the ČSSR and to improve Soviet-Czechoslovak relations, November 26, 1968], 198.

108. AMZV, TO SSSR-Tajné, 1965–1969, k. 7, o. 3 [Aide-mémoire from the Soviet embassy in Prague to the Czechoslovak Ministry of Foreign Affairs, July 31, 1969].

109. On workers not wanting to meet with the tourists, see GARF, f. 9520, op. 1, d. 1344, l. 57; on access to the Soviet press, see ibid., 46 and 70; on being called "occupiers," see GARF, f. 9520, op. 1, d. 1237, l. 3.

110. GARF, f. 9520, op. 1, d. 1344, l. 121.

111. GARF, f. 9612, op. 3, d. 381, l. 5.

112. GARF, f. 9520, op. 1, d. 1237, l. 10.

113. AVP RF, f. 198, op. 50, p. 120, d. 21, l. 38.

114. Ibid., 1. Records from GARF, f. 9520, op. 1, d. 1237 indicate that the Trade Union's Tourism Councils also suspended sending tourists to Czechoslovakia after the invasion but resumed the trips at the end of October 1968.

115. Document no. 114: "*Pravda* Editorial Justifying the Invasion, August 22, 1968 (Excerpts)," translated and reprinted in Navrátil et al., *Prague Spring 1968*, 456.

116. Ibid., 457.

117. GARF, f. 9520, op. 1, d. 1345, l. 25.

118. The term "normalization" was used as early as June 1968 by the Central Committee of the Communist Party of the Soviet Union, in a report about providing assistance to the KSČ to "normalize the situation in the country," RGANI, f. 5, op. 60, d. 1, l. 92. I discuss the use of the term "normalization" in more detail in chapter 6.

119. ÚSD, KV ČSFR, inv. č. 5266, sign. Z/S/120, k. 7 [Excerpt from protocol no. 61 9s by the Secretariat of the TsK KPSS, on measures to normalize the situation in the ČSSR and to improve Soviet-Czechoslovak relations, November 26, 1968].

120. See RGANI, f. 5, op. 61, d. 10, l. 50 and GARF, f. 9520, op. 1, d. 1237, l. 2.

121. GARF, f. 9520, op. 1, d. 1237, l. 2.

122. AVP RF, f. 198, op. 50, p. 120, d. 21, l. 1.

123. GARF, f. 9520, op. 1, d. 1344, l. 3.

124. See, for instance, GARF, f. 9520, op. 1, d. 1345, l. 3.

125. Jindřich Pecka, ed., *Spontánní projevy pražského jara 1968–1969* (Brno: Ústav pro soudobé dějiny AV ČR v nakladatelství Doplněk, 1993), entry 716, page 80.

126. This is the subject of chapter 6.

127. GARF, f. 9576, op. 4 d. 478, l. 123.

128. GARF, f. 9520, op. 1, d. 1344, l. 7.

129. Ibid., 2.

130. Ibid., 88.
131. RGASPI, f. M-1, op. 2, d. 129, l. 52.
132. GARF, f. 9520, op. 1, d. 1237, l. 9.
133. Lily Golden, *My Long Journey Home* (Chicago: Third World Press, 2002), 99.
134. RGASPI, f. M-5, op. 2, d. 129, l. 103.
135. Ibid., 3.
136. Ibid., 5.
137. Ibid., 47.

6. The Normalization of Friendship

Epigraph: Ústav pro soudobé dějiny AV ČR (Institute for Contemporary History of the Academy of Sciences of the Czech Republic; hereafter ÚSD, KV ČSFR), inv. č. 5536, sign. Z/S/190, k. 73 [Report by V. Sel'ianov, editor of *Sovetskaia Rossiia*, about a trip to Czechoslovakia, October 1968], 194.

1. Quotes from Gosudarstvennyi arkhiv Rossiiskoi Federatsii (State Archive of the Russian Federation; hereafter GARF), f. 9576, op. 4, d. 427, l. 240; assessment of the event's success in GARF, f. 9576, op. 4, d. 478, l. 214.

2. During negotiations held in Moscow in October 1968, the Soviet and Czechoslovak governments agreed that the USSR would keep between 70,000 and 80,000 troops in Czechoslovakia. See Document no. 131, "Stenographic Account of Soviet-Czechoslovak Negotiations in Moscow, October 3–4, 1968 (Excerpts)," in Jaromír Navrátil et al., eds., *The Prague Spring 1968: A National Security Archive Documents Reader*, trans. Mark Kramer, Joy Moss, and Ruth Tosek (Budapest: Central European University Press, 1998), 528. On October 16, 1968, the two governments signed a "temporary" treaty ratifying the presence of Soviet troops in Czechoslovakia. See Document no.133, "Bilateral Treaty on the 'Temporary Presence of Soviet forces on Czechoslovak Territory,' October 16, 1968," ibid., 533. When the USSR began to withdraw its troops from Czechoslovakia in February 1990, there were 73,500 Soviet soldiers in the country, Josef Pazderka, "Samozřejmě, že to v člověku vzbuzuje lítost. Rozhovor s generálem Eduardem Vorobjovem," in Pazderka, *Invaze 1968: Ruský pohled* (Prague: Ústav pro studium totalitních režimů, Torst, 2011), 56.

3. Tony Judt, *Postwar: A History of Europe since 1945* (New York: Penguin, 2005), 447.

4. Pëtr Vail' and Aleksandr Genis, *60-e: Mir sovetskogo cheloveka* (Moscow: Novoe literaturnoe obozrenie, 1996), 310. In the Soviet Union, the most famous act of protest against the invasion was the August 25 demonstration on Red Square by seven Soviet citizens, among them Larisa Bogoraz and Pavel Litvinov, activists in the nascent dissident movement. The protestors barely had time to unfurl banners in Russian proclaiming: "Hands off the ČSSR!" "For Your Freedom and Ours!" and one in Czech, "Long Live Free and Independent Czechoslovakia!" before they were arrested by the KGB. Rossiiskii gosudarstvennyi arkhiv noveishei istorii (Russian State Archive for Contemporary History; hereafter RGANI), f. 89, op. 25, d. 32, l. 1. See also, Natal'ia Gorbanevskaia, *Polden'. Delo o demonstratsii 25 avgusta 1968 goda na Krasnoi ploshchadi* (Moscow: Novoe izdatel'stvo, 2017).

5. GARF, f. 9576, op. 4, d. 427, ll. 10, 21. Before becoming the House of Soviet Science and Culture, the building had housed the KSČ's Institute of History; accessed April 17, 2018, http://rsvk.cz/rossijskij-tsentr-nauki-i-kultury-v-prage/.

6. "Dům sovětské vědy a kultury otevřen," *Rudé právo*, May 29, 1971.

7. Accessed April 17, 2018, http://rsvk.cz/rossijskij-tsentr-nauki-i-kultury-v-prage/.

8. On the use of the term "normalization" in the immediate post-invasion period, see H. Gordon Skilling, *Czechoslovakia's Interrupted Revolution* (Princeton, NJ: Princeton University Press, 1976), 802; and Kieran Williams, *The Prague Spring and Its Aftermath: Czechoslovak Politics, 1968–1970* (Cambridge: Cambridge University Press, 1997). On "normalization" as a term denoting the 1970s and 1980s in Czechoslovakia, see Paulina Bren, "Mirror, Mirror on the Wall . . . Is the West the Fairest of Them All? Czechoslovak Normalization and Its (Dis)Contents," *Kritika: Explorations in Russian and Eurasian History* 9, no. 4 (Fall 2008): 831–854; Bren, *The Greengrocer and His TV: The Culture of Communism after the 1968 Prague Spring* (Ithaca, NY: Cornell University Press, 2010); and Milan Šimečka, *The Restoration of Order: The Normalization of Czechoslovakia, 1969–1976*, trans. A. G. Brain (London: Verso, 1984).

9. This was one of the questions raised by attendees at a forum in Prague in April 1965 sponsored by the Society for the Dissemination of Political and Scientific Knowledge, GARF, f. 9518 op. 1, d. 148, l. 78.

10. "Proč neosvobodili Prahu Američané?" *Student*, June 20, 1967, 1–5.

11. "Kde začíná a kde končí přátelství," *Svět sovětů*, May 14, 1968, 4.

12. Document no. 52, "Transcript of the Warsaw Meeting, July 14–15, 1968 (excerpts)," in Navrátil et al., *Prague Spring 1968*, 224.

13. Ibid., Document no. 53, "The Warsaw Letter, July 14–15, 1968," 235.

14. ÚSD, KV ČSFR, inv. č. 5298, sign. Z/S/153, k. 73 [Report from the KGB to the TsK KPSS (Central Committee of the Communist Party of the Soviet Union), July 16, 1968], 59. Vladislav M. Zubok argues that Yuri Andropov, who was the KGB chief in 1968, had been scarred by his experience as Soviet ambassador in Hungary in 1956, and thus deliberately skewed reports to the Politburo about the situation in Czechoslovakia in order to emphasize the need for military action, *A Failed Empire: The Soviet Union in the Cold War from Stalin to Gorbachev* (Chapel Hill: University of North Carolina Press, 2007), 208.

15. ÚSD, KV ČSFR, inv. č. 5298, sign. Z/S/153, k. 73 [Report from the KGB to the TsK KPSS, July 16, 1968], 60. In 1956, during the crises in Poland and Hungary, Soviet citizens used almost identical language about "'spilt blood,'" to urge their government to intervene militarily, Zbigniew Wojnowski, *The Near Abroad: Socialist Eastern Europe and Soviet Patriotism in Ukraine, 1956–1985* (Toronto: University of Toronto Press, 2017), 41.

16. ÚSD, KV ČSFR, inv. č. 5300, sign. Z/S/154, k. 73 [KGB report by Yuri Andropov, July 27, 1968], 67.

17. ÚSD, KV ČSFR, inv. č. 1948, sign. CII/250, k. 46 [Protest by Soviet military representatives against the defacement and destruction of Soviet soldiers' graves and monuments to Soviet soldiers who died in the liberation of Czechoslovakia, September, 1968], 1–3.

18. Ibid.

19. See, for instance, the photograph by Jovan Dezort of swastikas on a Soviet tank in Prague in *1945 . . . Osvobození/Liberation . . . 1968 Okupace/Occupation: Sovětská vojska*

v Československu (Prague: Pražský dům fotografie, 2008), 115. On the legacy of World War II as fodder for Russian triumphalism, see Gregory Carleton, "History Done Right: War and the Dynamics of Triumphalism in Contemporary Russian Culture," *Slavic Review* 70, no. 3 (Fall 2011): 616.

20. Photograph by Miroslav Zajíc in *1945 . . . Osvobození/Liberation . . . 1968 Okupace/Occupation*, 143.

21. GARF, f. 9524, op. 1, d. 51 [Letter 1137].

22. GARF, f. 9524, op. 1, d. 94 [Letter 2115].

23. Photograph by ČTK, *1945 . . . Osvobození/Liberation . . . 1968 Okupace/Occupation*, 178.

24. Ibid., photograph by Pavol Breier, 233.

25. ÚSD, KV ČSFR, 5536 Z/S/190, k. 73 [Report by V. Sel'ianov, editor of *Sovetskaia Rossiia* [Soviet Russia], about a trip to Czechoslovakia in the fall of 1968, filed March 3, 1969], 185–86.

26. RGANI, f. 5, op. 61, d. 89, l. 18.

27. GARF, f. 9576, op. 4, d. 356, ll. 86–87.

28. GARF, f. 9576, op. 4, d. 298, l. 221.

29. GARF, f. 9576, op. 4, d. 356, ll. 162–164.

30. GARF, f. 9576, op. 4, d. 355, ll. 19–20.

31. GARF, f. 9576, op. 4, d. 356, ll. 85–88. This document, "On the import of films from the socialist countries to the ČSSR," was prepared by the Central Committee of the KSČ for Husák sometime in 1969. Excerpts from it were leaked to the Soviet embassy in Prague by a Czech journalist, Jiří Schmidt, in October 1969 and were then translated into Russian.

32. Bren, *Greengrocer and His TV*, 15.

33. RGANI, f. 5, op. 61, d. 89, l. 18.

34. Ibid., 20.

35. Ibid., 22.

36. Document no. 113, "Report on the visit of Ambassador of the USSR to Czechoslovakia S. Chervonenko to the State Secretary for the Ministry of Foreign Affairs of the ČSSR V. Pleskot in connection with the anti-Soviet excesses after the hockey match between the teams of the ČSSR and the USSR," March 29, 1969, in N. G. Tomilina, S. Karner, and A. O. Chubar'ian, eds., *"Prazhskaia vesna" i mezhdunarodnyi krizis 1968 goda: dokumenty* (Moscow: Mezhdunarodnyi fond "Demokratiia," 2010), 409–410. Some Czechoslovaks claimed that the secret police had placed stones in front of the office to provoke the demonstrators, and thus trigger a broader crackdown on what remained of the Prague Spring reform movement. See Bren, *Greengrocer and His TV*, 32.

37. GARF, f. 9576, op. 4, d. 355, ll. 81–82.

38. GARF, f. 9576, op. 4, d. 356, l. 164.

39. RGANI, f. 5, op. 61, d. 89, l. 23.

40. GARF, f. 9576, op. 4, d. 355, l. 23.

41. GARF, f. 9576, op. 4, d. 298, l. 221.

42. GARF, f. 9576, op. 4, d. 355, l. 22.

43. Ibid., 130.

44. GARF, f. 9576, op. 4, d. 298, l. 221.

45. See Alice Lovejoy, *Army Film and the Avant Garde: Cinema and Experiment in the Czechoslovak Military* (Bloomington: Indiana University Press, 2014), 189–190. The film can be viewed online; accessed April 15, 2018, https://www.youtube.com/watch?v=2y9hkA075ao. On tensions between the Czechoslovak and Soviet armies after the invasion, see ÚSD, KV ČSFR, sign. 5536 Z/S/190, k. 73 [Report by V. Sel'ianov, editor of *Sovetskaia Rossiia*, about a trip to Czechoslovakia in the fall of 1968, filed March 3, 1969], 193.

46. GARF, f. 9576, op. 4, d. 355, l. 23.

47. Petr Zvoníček, "Dokumenty jako řemen," quoted in Lovejoy, *Army Film and the Avant Garde*, 189.

48. Arkhiv vneshnei politiki Rossiiskoi Federatsii (Foreign Policy Archive of the Russian Federation), f. 198, op. 50, p. 120, d. 21, l. 48.

49. RGANI, f. 5, op. 61, d. 89, ll. 20–22.

50. GARF, f. 9576, op. 4, d. 355, ll. 203–204.

51. GARF, f. 9576, op. 4, d. 356, ll. 82–84.

52. Ibid., 108–109.

53. Ibid., 162.

54. Quoted in Bren, *Greengrocer and His TV*, 57.

55. ÚSD, KV ČSFR, inv. č. 274, sign. DI/274, k. 7 [Report from the Presidium of the ÚV KSČ on the struggle against anti-Communist ideology and propaganda in the ČSSR, June 25, 1969], 23.

56. ÚSD, KV ČSFR, inv. č.5295, sign. Z/S/149, k. 73 [letter from N. Popova, chairwoman the Presidium of SSOD to the TsK KPSS, July 22, 1968]; for statistics on membership in the SČSP, see GARF, f. 9576, op. 4, d. 330a, l. 2.

57. GARF, f. 9576, op. 4, d. 330a, l. 2.

58. ÚSD, inv. č. 5371, sign. Z/S/225, k. 73 [account by I. A. Cherkasov from the Soviet embassy in Prague of a discussion with Fierlinger on September 6, 1968].

59. GARF, f. 9576, op. 4, d. 330a, l. 8.

60. GARF, f. 9576, op. 4, d. 356, l. 39.

61. GARF, f. 9576, op. 4, d. 355, l. 127.

62. On *Svět sovětů*'s circulation, see Národní archiv (National Archive), f. 1261/1/8 [Ideologická komise KSČ, 1958–1968], sv. 7, a.j. 23, b. 4 [Report by the Ideological Commission of the ÚV KSČ on the current state of the propaganda about socialist internationalism and the USSR in the ČSSR, and suggestions for improving it, January 14, 1967], 43.

63. ÚSD, KV ČSFR, inv. č. 5536, sign. Z/S/190, k. 73 [Report by V. Sel'ianov, editor of *Sovetskaia Rossiia*, about a trip to Czechoslovakia in the fall of 1968, dated March 3, 1969], 192.

64. GARF, f. 9576, op. 4, d. 330a, l. 2.

65. On the OSChD's events honoring the Slovak uprising and Fučík, see ibid., 35. The KSČ had made Fučík into a cult figure in the 1950s. See Nancy M. Wingfield and Lisa A. Kirschenbaum, "Gender and the Construction of Wartime Heroism in Czechoslovakia and the USSR," *European History Quarterly* 39, no. 3 (2009): 471–473.

66. Marie Černá, "From 'Occupation' to 'Friendly Assistance': The 'Presence' of Soviet Troops in Czechoslovakia after August 1968," *Hungarian Historical Review* 4, no. 1 (2015): 123.

67. Document no. 133, "Bilateral Treaty on the 'Temporary Presence of Soviet Forces on Czechoslovak Territory,' October 16, 1968," in Navrátil et al., *Prague Spring 1968*, 533.

68. Document no. 135, "The Soviet Politburo's Assessment of the Lessons of Operation 'Danube' and the Tasks Ahead, November 16, 1968," in Navrátil et al., *Prague Spring 1968*, 551.

69. Williams, *Prague Spring and Its Aftermath*, 41.

70. GARF, f. 9576, op. 4, d. 356, l. 40.

71. Accessed April 16, 2018, https://csdfmuseum.ru/films/91/.

72. ÚSD, KV ČSFR, inv. č. 274, sign. DI/274, k. 7 [Report from the Presidium of the ÚV KSČ on anti-Communist ideology and propaganda in the ČSSR, June 25, 1969], 8–15.

73. RGANI, f. 5, op. 60, d. 37, l. 30.

74. Černá, "From 'Occupation' to 'Friendly Assistance,'" 116.

75. Bren, *Greengrocer and His TV*, 63.

76. Černá, "From 'Occupation' to 'Friendly Assistance,'" 116.

77. RGANI, f. 5, op. 60, d. 19, l. 204.

78. O. F. Zhemaitis, "Vospominaniia: Chekhoslovatskii dnevnik (1968–1972)," *Voprosy istorii* 8 (1999): 90.

79. ÚSD, KV ČSFR, inv. č. 5347, sign. Z/3-201, k. 73 [KGB report to the TsK KPSS, November 19, 1968], 125.

80. ÚSD, KV ČSFR, inv. č. 5266, sign. Z/S/120, k. 7 [Excerpt from TsK KPSS protocol no. 61, 9s, "On measures to normalize the situation in the ČSSR and to improve Soviet-Czechoslovak relations," November 26, 1968], 194–196.

81. "Report from Czechoslovakia: Encounters on Route," *Izvestiia*, October 2, 1968, condensed, translated, and reprinted in *Current Digest of the Soviet Press* 23, no. 40 (October 23, 1968): 5.

82. Černá, "From 'Occupation' to 'Friendly Assistance,'" 133.

83. GARF, f. 9576, op. 4, d. 427, l. 48.

84. "Mít přítele znamená být přítelem," *Rudé právo*, May 7, 1970.

85. Bren, *Greengrocer and His TV*, 36–60; the statistic on the number of people sent to prison is on page 59.

86. Ibid., 60.

87. GARF, f. 9576, op. 4, d. 427, l. 50.

88. Bren, *Greengrocer and His TV*; Šimečka, *Restoration of Order*.

89. GARF, f. 9576, op. 4, d. 1942, ll. 20–24

90. "Přátelství na věčné časy," produced by the Czech TV station Retro, first aired August 11, 2009, accessed March 14, 2018.

91. Šimečka, *Restoration of Order*, 144.

92. Bren, "Mirror, Mirror on the Wall."

93. On the extent to which the friendship project was entwined with ordinary life in Czechoslovakia in the 1970s and 1980s, see "Přátelství na věčné časy."

94. Václav Cícha [on behalf of the collective], *Ruský jazyk pro 8. ročník základní školy* (Prague: Státní pedagogické nakladatelství, 1983), 46, 99–100, 103.

95. *Svět socialismu* was founded in the fall of 1968 and had a circulation of 142,422 in 1971. From 1973 to 1978, over 1.5 million Czechoslovaks attended concerts by Soviet

performers, including several hundred performances by the musical ensemble of the Central Group of Soviet Forces in Czechoslovakia. From 1972 to 1978, 143,442 Czechoslovaks traveled to the USSR as tourists under the auspices of the SČSP; GARF, f. 9576, op. 4, d. 1942, ll. 20–24.

96. "Na věčné časy a nikdy jinak!" *Rudé právo*, May 7, 1970.

97. Andrew Felkay, *Hungary and the USSR: 1956–1988: Kadar's Political Leadership* (New York: Greenwood Press, 1989), 116–118. See also Wojnowski, *Near Abroad*, 79.

98. In 1971, the ROH had 5.5 million members, Všeodborový archiv Českomoravské konfederace odborových svazů (hereafter VA-ČMKOS), k. Vlak družby 1971 [Report on the 1971 Friendship Train to the USSR by Václav Valenta], 4.

99. Ibid. [Ammendment 1: Political evaluation of the 'Friendship Train' of Soviet trade unionists to the ČSSR and its contribution to consolidating and strengthening ties between the Czechoslovak and Soviet trade unions], 1.

100. VA-ČMKOS, k. Vlak družby 1970 [Amendment 1: Friendship Train to the USSR on the occasion of the fifty-second anniversary of the October Revolution].

101. VA-ČMKOS, k. Vlak družby 1971 [Letter from July 27, 1971, outlining the selection criteria for participants on the Friendship Train], 1–2.

102. Ibid. [Biographical data and political evaluation of participants on the Friendship Train], 1.

103. Ibid. [Notes on the 1971 Friendship Train to the USSR by Václav Valenta], 2.

104. Ibid., 6.

105. Ibid., 9.

106. Ibid., 13.

107. Ibid., 15.

108. See chapter 3.

109. Vladimír Macura, "The Metro," in *The Mystifications of a Nation: "The Potato Bug," and Other Essays on Czech Culture*, ed. and trans. Hana Pichová and Craig Cravens (Madison: University of Wisconsin Press, 2010), 82.

110. "Turgeněv znovu ve filmu," *Rudé právo*, May 7, 1970; "Pro milovníky klasického baletu," *Rudé právo*, May 7, 1970.

Conclusion

1. Mark Kramer argues that Gorbachev actively tried to promote perestroika and glasnost in the Eastern bloc countries to avoid an outbreak of violence along the lines of the 1956 Hungarian uprising or the Tiananmen Square massacre in Beijing in June 1989, "The Collapse of East European Communism and the Repercussions within the Soviet Union (Part I)," *Journal of Cold War Studies* 5, no. 4 (Fall 2003): 185–190.

2. "Causa tank," *Mladá fronta Dnes*, May 4, 1991.

3. On the tank as an imperialist symbol, see "Růžová kulturní památka," *Mladá fronta Dnes*, May 2, 1991; on the tank as a symbol of the oppressive, transnational, Communist system, see the letter to the editor from Dr. Petr Kolář, *Mladá fronta Dnes*, "Růžový tank," May 14, 1991.

4. "Ot chego pokrasnel Pan Uchitel'," *Izvestiia*, May 7, 1991.

5. "Kren vpravo?" *Pravda*, June 4, 1991.

6. "Parlament v akci," *Mladá fronta Dnes*, May 17, 1991. See also Jenelle Davis, "Marking Memory: Ambiguity and Amnesia in the Monument to Soviet Tank Crews in Prague," *Public Art Dialogue* 6, no.1 (2016): 37–57.

7. Pavla Horáková, Radio Prague, August 5, 2005, accessed April 25, 2018, http://www.radio.cz/en/section/curraffrs/the-complicated-history-of-pragues-tank-no-23/.

8. David Černý interview with RFE/RL, April 11, 2010, accessed April 25, 2018, http://www.rferl.org/content/Provocateur_Artist_David_Cerny_I_Painted_Tank_Pink_To_Get_A_Girl/2008892.html.

9. Horáková, Radio Prague, August 5, 2005.

10. Alexei Yurchak, *Everything Was Forever Until It Was No More: The Last Soviet Generation* (Princeton, NJ: Princeton University Press, 2005), 8.

11. Milan Kundera, "The Tragedy of Central Europe," trans. Edmund White, *New York Review of Books*, April 26, 1984, 33–34.

12. "Ot chego pokrasnel Pan Uchitel'," *Izvestiia*, May 7, 1991.

13. "So Smikhova—v muzei," *Pravda*, June 15, 1991.

Works Cited

Archives

Czech Republic

Archiv ministerstva zahraničních věcí České republiky (Archive of the Ministry of Foreign Affairs of the Czech Republic)
Teritoriální odbory SSSR (Territorial divisions—USSR):
1945–1959 (Obyčejné/ordinary); 1960–1964 (Tajné/secret); 1965–1969 (Tajné)

Národní archiv (National Archive)
Fotodokumentace 1897–1981 (Photo documentation)
F. 1329 Osvobození Československa Rudou armádou—1945 (The liberation of Czechoslovakia by the Red Army)
F. 850/2 Ministerstvo vnitra-Noskův archiv 1945–1953 (Ministry of Interior)
F. 861 Ministerstvo informací 1945–1953 (Ministry of Information)
F. 861 Ministerstvo informací–dodatky 1945–1953 (Ministry of Information, appendixes)
F. 1261/0/32 Generální sekretariát 1945–1951 (General Secretariat)
F. 1261/0/44 Kancelář tajemníka ÚV KSČ Antonína Novotného, II část (1946) 1951–1967 (1968) (Office of Antonín Novotný, Secretary of the Central Committee of the KSČ, Part II)

F. 1261/1/8 Ideologická komise ÚV KSČ 1958–1968 (Ideological Commission, Central Committee of the KSČ)
F. 1261/2/2 Ideologické oddělení 1951–1961 (Ideological Division)
F. 1261/2/28 Oddělení masových organizací 1945–1956 (Division of Mass Organizations)
F. 1261/0/13 Sekretariát ÚV KSČ, 1945–1951 (Secretariat, Central Committee of the KSČ)

Ústav pro soudobé dějiny AV ČR (Institute for Contemporary History of the Academy of Sciences of the Czech Republic)
Sbírka dokumentů Komise vlády ČSFR pro analýzu událostí let 1967–1970 (Collection of documents compiled by the Government Commission of the Czechoslovak Federal Republic for the Analysis of the Events of the Years 1967–1970. The collection includes documents originating from the Soviet and Czechoslovak archives)

Všeodborový archiv Českomoravské konfederace odborových svazů (Archive of the Trade Unions in the Czech Lands and Moravia)
Materials on the Trade Unions' friendship trains to the USSR, 1970 and 1971

Hungary

Open Society Archives
Radio Free Europe/Radio Liberty Research Institute/Media and Opinion Research Department/East Europe Area and Opinion Research

Russia

Arkhiv vneshnei politiki Rossiiskoi Federatsii (Foreign Policy Archive of the Russian Federation)
F. 198 Posol'stvo SSSR v Chekhoslovakii (Embassy of the USSR in Czechoslovakia)

Gosudarstvennyi arkhiv Rossiiskoi Federatsii (State Archive of the Russian Federation)
F. 5283 Vsesoiuznoe obshchestvo kul'turnoi sviazi s zagranitsei (All-Union Society for Cultural Contacts Abroad, VOKS)
F. 8581 Sovetskoe informatsionnoe biuro (Soviet Information Bureau)
F. 9170 Redaktsiia zhurnala Slaviane (Editorial Office of the magazine *Slaviane*)
F. 9524 Kollektsiia pisem Czekhoslovatskikh grazhdan i organizatsii, poluchennykh posol'stvom SSSR v Chekhoslovakii, 1968–1969 (Collection of letters from Czechoslovak citizens and organizations, received by the Soviet Embassy in Czechoslovakia, 1968–1969)
F. 9541 Sovetskii komitet veteranov voiny (Soviet Committee for War Veterans)
F. 9547 Vsesoiuznoe obshchestvo "Znanie" (The All-Union Knowledge Society)
F. 9518 Komitet po kul'turnym sviaziam s zarubezhnymi stranami pri Sovete Ministrov SSSR (Committee for Cultural Contacts with Foreign Countries, under the auspices of the Council of Ministers)

F. 9576 Soiuz sovetskikh obshchestv druzhby i kul'turnoi sviazei s zarubezhnymi stranami (The Union of Soviet Friendship Societies, SSOD)

F. 9520 Tsentral'nyi sovet po turizmu i ekskursiiam VTsSPS, 1936–1991 (The Trade Union's Central Council for Tourism and Excursions)

F. 9612 Uchrezhdeniia po rukovodstvu inostrannym turizmom v SSSR, 1929–1991 (Institution for Managing Foreign Tourism in the USSR, Intourist)

Rossiiskii gosudarstvennyi arkhiv literatury i iskusstva (Russian State Archive of Literature and Art)

F. 962 Komitet po delam iskusstv pri Sovete Ministrov SSSR (Committee for Artistic Affairs under the auspices of the Council of Ministers of the USSR)

F. 2456 Ministerstvo kinematografii (Ministry of Cinematography)

F. 2918 Soveksportfil'm (Soviet Export Film)

Rossiiskii gosudarstvennyi arkhiv noveishei istorii (Russian State Archive for Contemporary History)

F. 5 Apparat TsK KPSS (Apparatus of the Central Committee of the Communist Party, post-1953)

F. 89 (Collection of documents declassified by the Special Archival Commission under the auspices of the President of the Russian Federation, 1992–1994)

Rossiiskii gosudarstvennyi arkhiv sotsial'no-politicheskoi istorii (Russian State Archive for Social and Political History)

F. 17 Tsentral'nyi komitet KPSS (Central Committee of the Communist Party, pre-1953)

Rossiiskii gosudarstvennyi arkhiv sotsial'no-politicheskoi istorii, Molodezhnyi arkhiv (Russian State Archive for Social and Political History, Youth Archive)

F. M-1 Tsentral'nyi komitet VLKSM (Central Committee of the Komsomol)

F. M-5 Biuro molodezhnogo mezhdunarodnogo turizma (Office of the International Organization for Youth Tourism, "Sputnik")

United States

United States National Archives, College Park, Maryland

Record Group 59 General Records of the Department of State

Record Group 84 Foreign Service Posts of the Department of State

II. Periodicals

Czechoslovakia

Česká pravda

Katolík

Kulturní besedy Československo-sovětského přátelství

Květy

Literární listy

Mladá fronta Dnes
Obzory
Práce
Přítel SSSR
Rudé právo
Sotsialisticheskaia Chekhoslovakiia
Sovětským filmem
Student
Svět sovětů
Svobodné noviny
Svobodné slovo
Tvorba
Vývoj

Soviet Union
Iskusstvo kino
Izvestiia
Krasnaia zvezda
Moskovskaia pravda
Pravda

United States
Current Digest of the Soviet Press
New York Times

III. Collections of Documents and Newspaper Articles

Drápala, Milan, ed. *Na ztracené vartě Západu. Antologie české nesocialistické publicistiky z let 1945–1948: Koželuhová, Skácel, Forman, Tigrid, Kolár, Chudoba, Brouk, Jehlička.* Prague: Prostor, 2000.

Kaplan, Karel, and Alexandra Špiritová, eds. *ČSR a SSSR, 1945–1948: Dokumenty mezivládních jednání.* Brno: Doplněk, 1996.

Mrkvička, O., ed. *Střetnutí Sovětské malířství a současné umění.* Prague: Vladimír Žikeš, 1947.

Navrátil, Jaromír, Antonín Benčík, Václav Kural, Marie Michálková, and Jitka Vondrová, eds. *The Prague Spring 1968: A National Security Archive Documents Reader.* Translated by Mark Kramer, Joy Moss, and Ruth Tosek. Budapest: Central European University Press, 1998.

Pecka, Jindřich, ed. *Spontánní projevy pražského jara 1968–1969.* Brno: Ústav pro soudobé dějiny AV ČR v nakladatelství Doplněk, 1993.

Tomilina, N. G., S. Karner, and A. O. Chubar'ian, eds. *"Prazhskaia vesna" i mezhdunarodnyi krizis 1968 goda: dokumenty.* Moscow: Mezhdunarodnyi fond "Demokratiia," 2010.

IV. Memoirs and Published Interviews

Alexeyeva, Ludmilla, and Paul Goldberg. *The Thaw Generation: Coming of Age in the Post-Stalin Era*. Boston: Little, Brown, 1990.

Arbatov, G. A. *Zatianuvsheesia vyzdorovlenie (1953–1985 gg.) Svidetel'stvo sovremennika*. Moscow: Mezhdunarodnye otnosheniia, 1991.

Cherniaev, A. S. *Moia zhizn' i moë vremia*. Moscow: Mezhdunarodnye otnosheniia, 1995.

Císař, Čestmír. *Člověk a politik: kniha vzpomínek a úvah*. Prague: ETC, 1998.

Filipovich, El'vira. *Ot sovetskoi pionerki do chelnoka-pensionerki (moi dnevnik). Kniga I (1944–1972)*. Podol'sk: Saturn, 2000.

Golden, Lily. *My Long Journey Home*. Chicago: Third World Press, 2002.

Gorbachev, Mikhail. *Memoirs*. Translated by Georges Peronansky and Tatjana Varsavsky. New York: Doubleday, 1996.

Gorbachev, Mikhail, and Zdeněk Mlynář. *Conversations with Gorbachev: On Perestroika, the Prague Spring, and the Crossroads of Socialism*. Translated by George Shriver. New York: Columbia University Press, 2003.

Gorbanevskaia, Natal'ia. *Polden'. Delo o demonstratsii 25 avgusta 1968 goda na Krasnoi ploshchadi*. Moscow: Novoe izdatel'stvo, 2017.

Hindus, Maurice. *The Bright Passage*. Garden City, NY: Doubleday, 1947.

Iurskii, S. A. "Zapadnyi ekspress." Excerpted in *Praga: Russkii vzgliad: Vek vosemnadtsatyi—vek dvadtsat' pervyi*, edited by S. V. Nikol'skii and Iu. G. Fridshtein, 287–294. Moscow: VGBIL, 2003. (Originally published as S. A. Iurskii, *Igra v zhizn'* [Moscow: Vagrius, 2002.])

Levy, Alan. *So Many Heroes*. Sagaponack, NY: Second Chance Press, 1972, 1980.

Mlynář, Zdeněk. *Nightfrost in Prague: The End of Humane Socialism*. Translated by Paul Wilson. New York: Karz, 1980.

Moniushko, Evgenii D. *From Leningrad to Hungary: Notes of a Red Army Soldier, 1941–1946*. Edited by David M. Glantz. Translated by Oleg Sheremet. London: Frank Cass, 2005.

Pazderka, Josef. "Rok 1968 nás změnil, rozhovor s Vladimirem Lukinem." In Pazderka, *Invaze 1968*, 160–172.

———. "Samozřejmě, že to v človeku vzbuzuje lítost. Rozhovor s generálem Eduardem Vorobjovem." In Pazderka, *Invaze 1968*, 42–61.

———. "Zkoušel jsem s nimi mluvit. Rozhovor s Vladlenem Krivošejevem." In Pazderka, *Invaze 1968*, 180–185.

Pithart, Petr. "Gorbačovovi lidé z pražských Dejvic: Osobní vzpomínka na pražskou redakci *Otázek míru a socialism*." In Pazderka, *Invaze 1968*, 174–179.

Reiman, Michal. *Rusko jako téma a realita doma a v exilu. Vzpomínky na léta 1968–1990*. Prague: Ústav pro soudobé dějiny AV ČR, 2008.

Selucký, Radoslav. *Východ je východ*. Cologne: Index, 1972.

Semënov, N.P. *Trevozhnaia Praga: Vospominaniia sovetskogo vitse-konsula v Chekhoslovakii (1968–1972)*. Moscow: Mezhdunarodnye otnosheniia, 2004.

Shakhnazarov, Georgii. *S vozhdiami i bez nikh*. Moscow: Vagrius, 2001.

The *Soviet Union as Reported by Former Soviet Citizens*. Report No. 2. Washington, DC: United States Department of State, February 1952.

Spáčil, Dušan. *My z Černína: Paměti československého diplomata*. Prague: Periskop, 1995.

Stransky, Jan. *East Wind over Prague*. New York: Random House, 1951.

Taubman, William. *The View from Lenin Hills: Soviet Youth in Ferment*. New York: Coward-McCann, 1967

Wechsberg, Joseph. *Homecoming*. New York: Alfred A. Knopf, 1946.

Zhemaitis, O. F. "Vospominaniia: Chekhoslovatskii dnevnik (1968–1972)." *Voprosy istorii* 8 (1999): 86–97.

V. Other Primary Sources

Cícha, Václav [on behalf of the collective]. *Ruský jazyk pro 8. ročník základní školy*. Prague: Státní pedagogické nakladatelství, 1983.

Grossman, Vasily. *A Writer at War: A Soviet Journalist with the Red Army, 1941–1945*. Edited and translated by Antony Beevor and Luba Vinogradova. New York: Vintage Books, 2005.

Hanzelka, Jiří, and Miroslav Zikmund. *Zvláštní zpráva č. 4: tajné*. Prague: Lidové nakladatelství, 1990.

Kraizinger, Aleksei. *Karlovy Vary: Putevoditel' dlia sovetskikh turistov po gorodu-kurotu*. Prague: Svět sovětů, 1963.

Malíř, F., M. Chaloupková, K. Vlastníková, V. Schmitt, K. Hanuš, and M. Cipro. *Russkii iazyk: učebnice pro 5. postupný ročník národních škol*. Prague: Státní nakladatelství, 1950.

Malíř, F., T. Franková, and A. Lukešová. *Dopisujeme si Rusky: Příručka pro kursy ruského jazyka a pro přípravu dopisů do SSSR*. Prague: Svět sovětů, 1965.

Marx, Karl, and Frederick Engels. *The Communist Manifesto: With Related Documents*. Edited by John E. Toews. Boston: Bedford/St. Martins, 1999.

Nezval, Vítězslav. *Dílo XXVI. Eseje a projevy po osvobození (1945–1958)*. Prague: Československý spisovatel, 1976.

1945 . . . Osvobození/Liberation . . . 1968 Okupace/Occupation: Sovětská vojska v Československu. Prague: Pražský dům fotografie, 2008.

Pecka, Jindřich, ed. *Spontánní projevy pražského jara 1968–1969*. Brno: Ústav pro soudobé dějiny AV ČR v nakladatelství Doplněk, 1993.

Sovetskoe gosudarstvennoe pravo. Moscow: Iuridicheskoe izdatel'stvo Ministerstva iustitsii SSSR, 1948.

VI. Secondary Sources

Abrams, Bradley F. *The Struggle for the Soul of the Nation: Czech Culture and the Rise of Communism*. Lanham, MD: Rowman and Littlefield, 2000.

Åman, Anders. *Architecture and Ideology in Eastern Europe during the Stalin Era: An Aspect of Cold War History*. Cambridge, MA: MIT Press, 1992.

Amar, Tarik. "Sovietization as a Civilizing Mission in the West." In Apor, Apor, and Rees, *Sovietization of Eastern Europe*, 29–45.

Anderson, Benedict. *Imagined Communities: Reflections on the Origin and Spread of Nationalism*. London: Verso, 2006.

Antic, Ana, Johanna Conterio, and Dora Vargha. "Conclusion: Beyond Liberal Internationalism." *Contemporary European History* 25, no. 2 (May 2016): 359–371.

Apor, Balázs, Péter Apor, and E. A. Rees, eds. *The Sovietization of Eastern Europe: New Perspectives on the Postwar Period*. Washington, DC: New Academia Publishers, 2008.

Applebaum, Rachel. "The Friendship Project: Socialist Internationalism in the Soviet Union and Czechoslovakia in the 1950s and 1960s." *Slavic Review* 74, no. 3 (Fall 2015): 484–507.

——. "A Test of Friendship: Soviet-Czechoslovak Tourism and the Prague Spring." In Gorsuch and Koenker, *Socialist Sixties*, 213–232.

Argenbright, Robert. "The Soviet Agitational Vehicle: State Power on the Social Frontier." *Political Geography* 17, no. 3 (March 1998): 253–272.

Azadovskii, Konstantin, and Boris Egorov. "From Anti-Westernism to Anti-Semitism: Stalin and the Impact of the 'Anti-Cosmopolitan' Campaigns on Soviet Culture." *Journal of Cold War Studies* 4, no. 1 (Winter 2002): 66–80.

Babiracki, Patryk. "Imperial Heresies: Polish Students in the Soviet Union, 1948–1957." *Ab Imperio* 4 (2007): 199–236.

——. *Soviet Soft Power in Poland: Culture and the Making of Stalin's New Empire, 1943–1957*. Chapel Hill: University of North Carolina Press, 2015.

——. "The Taste of Red Watermelon: Polish Peasants Visit Soviet Collective Farms, 1949–1952." In Babiracki and Zimmer, *Cold War Crossings*, 40–77.

Babiracki, Patryk, and Austin Jersild, eds. "Editors' Introduction." In *Socialist Internationalism in the Cold War: Exploring the Second World*, 1–16. Cham, Switzerland: Palgrave Macmillan, 2016.

Babiracki, Patryk, and Kenyon Zimmer, eds. *Cold War Crossings: International Travel and Exchange across the Soviet Bloc, 1940s–1960s*. College Station: Texas A&M University Press, 2014.

Bartošek, K., and K. Pichlík. *Hanebná role amerických okupantů v západních Čechách v roce 1945*. Prague: Svoboda, 1951.

Baudin, Antoine. "Why Is Soviet Painting Hidden from Us? Zhdanov Art and Its International Relations and Fallout, 1947–53." In *Socialist Realism without Shores*, edited by Thomas Lahusen and Evgeny Dobrenko, 227–256. Durham, NC: Duke University Press, 1997.

Behrends, Jan. "Agitation, Organization, Mobilization. The League for Polish-Soviet Friendship in Stalinist Poland." In Apor, Apor, and Rees, *Sovietization of Eastern Europe*, 181–198.

Běloševský, Dimitrij. "Mediální zákulisí invaze. Osudy (některých) ruských novinářů v srpnu 1968." In Josef Pazderka, ed., *Invaze 1968: Ruský pohled*, 150–158.

Benton, Charlotte, ed. *Figuration/Abstraction: Strategies for Public Sculpture in Europe, 1945–1968*. Aldershot: Ashgate, 2004.

Berkhoff, Karel C. *Harvest of Despair: Life and Death in Ukraine under Nazi Rule*. Cambridge, MA, Harvard University Press, 2008.

——. *Motherland in Danger: Soviet Propaganda during World War II*. Cambridge, MA: Harvard University Press, 2012.

Betts, Paul. *Within Walls: Private Life in the German Democratic Republic*. Oxford: Oxford University Press, 2010.

Biddiscombe, Perry. "Dangerous Liaisons: The Anti-Fraternization Movement in the U.S. Occupation Zones of Germany and Austria, 1945–1948." *Journal of Social History* 34, no. 3 (Spring 2001): 611–647.

Biltereyst, Daniel, Richard Maltby, and Philippe Meers, eds. *Cinema, Audiences and Modernity: New Perspectives on European Cinema History*. Abingdon, Oxon: Routledge, 2012.

Bláhová, Jindřiška. "Hollywood za železnou oponou. Jednání o nové smlouvě o dovozu hollywoodských filmů mezi MPEA a ČSR (1946–1951)." *Iluminace: časopis pro teorii, historii a estetiku filmu* 20, no. 4 (2008): 19–62.

Bown, Matthew Cullerne. *Socialist Realist Painting*. New Haven, CT: Yale University Press, 1998.

Bren, Paulina. *The Greengrocer and His TV: The Culture of Communism after the 1968 Prague Spring*. Ithaca, NY: Cornell University Press, 2010.

——. "Mirror, Mirror on the Wall . . . Is the West the Fairest of Them All? Czechoslovak Normalization and Its (Dis)Contents." *Kritika: Explorations in Russian and Eurasian History* 9, no. 4 (Fall 2008): 831–854.

Bren, Paulina, and Mary Neuburger, eds. *Communism Unwrapped: Consumption in Cold War Eastern Europe*. Oxford: Oxford University Press, 2012.

——. "Introduction." In Bren and Neuburger, *Communism Unwrapped*, 3–19.

Bryant, Chad. *Prague in Black: Nazi Rule and Czech Nationalism*. Cambridge, MA: Harvard University Press, 2007.

Brzezinski, Zbigniew. *The Soviet Bloc: Unity and Conflict*. 2nd ed. Cambridge, MA: Harvard University Press, 1967.

Bucur, Maria. *Heroes and Victims: Remembering War in Twentieth-Century Romania*. Bloomington: Indiana University Press, 2009.

Budnitskii, Oleg. "The Intelligentsia Meets the Enemy: Educated Soviet Officers in Defeated Germany, 1945." Translated by Susan Rupp. *Kritika: Explorations in Russian and Eurasian History* 10, no. 3 (Summer 2009): 629–682.

Burbank, Jane, and Frederick Cooper. *Empires in World History: Power and the Politics of Difference*. Princeton, NJ: Princeton University Press, 2010.

Carleton, Gregory. "History Done Right: War and the Dynamics of Triumphalism in Contemporary Russian Culture." *Slavic Review* 70, no. 3 (Fall 2011): 615–636.

Caute, David. *The Dancer Defects: The Struggle for Cultural Supremacy during the Cold War*. Oxford: Oxford University Press, 2003.

Černá, Marie. "From 'Occupation' to 'Friendly Assistance': The 'Presence' of Soviet Troops in Czechoslovakia after August 1968." *Hungarian Historical Review* 4, no. 1 (2015): 114–143.

Clark, Katerina. "'Wait for Me and I Shall Return': The Early Thaw as a Reprise of Late Thirties Culture?" In Kozlov and Gilburd, *The Thaw*, 85–101.

Clybor, Shawn. "Socialist (Sur)Realism: Karel Teige, Ladislav Štoll and the Politics of Communist Culture in Czechoslovakia." *History of Communism in Europe* 2 (2011): 143–167.

Connelly, John. *Captive University: The Sovietization of East German, Czech, and Polish Higher Education, 1945–1956*. Chapel Hill: University of North Carolina Press, 2000.

Crowley, David, and Susan E. Reid. "Introduction: Pleasures in Socialism?" In *Pleasures in Socialism: Leisure and Luxury in the Eastern Bloc*, edited by Reid and Crowley, 3–51. Evanston, IL: Northwestern University Press, 2010.

David-Fox, Michael. *Showcasing the Great Experiment: Cultural Diplomacy and Western Visitors to the Soviet Union, 1921–1941*. New York: Oxford University Press, 2011.

Davis, Jenelle. "Marking Memory: Ambiguity and Amnesia in the Monument to Soviet Tank Crews in Prague." *Public Art Dialogue* 6, no. 1 (2016): 37–57.

Demetz, Peter. *Prague in Danger: The Years of German Occupation, 1939–1945: Memories and History, Terror and Resistance, Theater and Jazz, Film and Poetry, Politics and War*. New York: Farrar, Straus and Giroux, 2008.

Dostal', M. Iu., and I. V. Churkina. "Pamiati slovatskogo istorika Vladimira Matuly (1928–2011)." *Slavianovedenie* 5 (2011): 125–126.

Edele, Mark. *Soviet Veterans of the Second World War: A Popular Movement in an Authoritarian Society 1941–1991*. Oxford: Oxford University Press, 2008.

Engerman, David C. "The Second World's Third World." *Kritika: Explorations in Russian and Eurasian History* 12, no. 1 (2011): 183–211.

English, Robert D. *Russia and the Idea of the West: Gorbachev, Intellectuals, and the End of the Cold War*. New York: Columbia University Press, 2000.

Fehrenbach, Heide. *Race after Hitler: Black Occupation Children in Postwar Germany and America*. Princeton, NJ: Princeton University Press, 2005.

Felkay, Andrew. *Hungary and the USSR, 1956–1988: Kadar's Political Leadership*. New York: Greenwood Press, 1989.

Fowkes, Reuben. "The Role of Monumental Sculpture in the Construction of Socialist Space in Stalinist Hungary." In *Socialist Spaces: Sites of Everyday Life in the Eastern Bloc*, edited by David Crowley and Susan E. Reid, 65–84. Oxford: Berg Publishers, 2002.

——. "Soviet War Memorials in Eastern Europe, 1945–74." In Benton, *Figuration/Abstraction*, 11–32.

Frommer, Benjamin. *National Cleansing: Retribution against Nazi Collaborators in Postwar Czechoslovakia*. Cambridge: Cambridge University Press, 2005.

Fulbright, J. W. "Foreword." In *The Fulbright Program: A History*, edited by Walter Johnson and Francis J. Colligan, vii–ix. Chicago: University of Chicago Press, 1965.

Fulbrook, Mary. *The People's State: East German Society from Hitler to Honecker*. New Haven, CT: Yale University Press, 2005

Fürst, Juliane. *Stalin's Last Generation: Soviet Post-War Youth and the Emergence of Mature Socialism*. Oxford: Oxford University Press, 2010.

Gammelgaard, Karen. "Were the Czechs More Western Than Slavic? Nineteenth-Century Travel Literature from Russia by Disillusioned Czechs." In *Imagining the West in Eastern Europe and the Soviet Union*, edited by György Péteri, 13–35. Pittsburgh: University of Pittsburgh Press, 2010.

Getty, J. Arch. "*Samokritika* Rituals in the Stalinist Central Committee: 1933–38." *Russian Review* 58 (January 1999): 49–70.

Gilburd, Eleonory. "Picasso in Thaw Culture." *Cahiers du Monde russe* 47, no. 1–2 (January–July 2006): 65–108.

——. "The Revival of Soviet Internationalism in the Mid to Late 1950s." In Kozlov and Gilburd, *The Thaw*, 362–401.

——. "To See Paris and Die: Western Culture in the Soviet Union, 1950s and 1960s." PhD diss., University of California, Berkeley, 2010.

Giustino, Cathleen M. "Industrial Design and the Czechoslovak Pavilion at EXPO '58: Artistic Autonomy, Party Control and Cold War Common Ground." *Journal of Contemporary History* 47, no. 1 (January 2012): 185–212.

——. "Open Gates and Wandering Minds: Codes, Castles, and Chateaux in Socialist Czechoslovakia before 1960." In *Socialist Escapes: Breaking Away from Ideology and Everyday Routine in Eastern Europe, 1945–1989*, edited by Giustino, Catherine J. Plum, and Alexander Vari, 48–72. New York: Berghahn Books, 2013.

Gorman, Daniel. *The Emergence of International Society in the 1920s*. Cambridge: Cambridge University Press, 2012.

Gorsuch, Anne E. *All This Is Your World: Soviet Tourism at Home and Abroad after Stalin*. Oxford: Oxford University Press, 2011.

——. "'Cuba, My Love': The Romance of Revolutionary Cuba in the Soviet Sixties." *American Historical Review* 120, no. 2 (April 2015): 497–526.

——. "'There's No Place Like Home': Soviet Tourism in Late Stalinism." *Slavic Review* 62, no. 4 (Winter, 2003): 760–785.

——. "Time Travelers: Soviet Tourists to Eastern Europe." In *Turizm: The Russian and East European Tourist under Capitalism and Socialism*, edited by Anne E. Gorsuch and Diane P. Koenker, 205–226. Ithaca, NY: Cornell University Press, 2006.

Gorsuch, Anne E., and Diane P. Koenker. *The Socialist Sixties: Crossing Borders in the Second World*. Bloomington: Indiana University Press, 2013.

Gould-Davies, Nigel. "The Logic of Soviet Cultural Diplomacy." *Diplomatic History* 27, no. 2 (April 2003): 193–214.

Grossmann, Atina. *Jews, Germans, and Allies: Close Encounters in Occupied Germany*. Princeton, NJ: Princeton University Press, 2007.

Guillory, Sean. "Culture Clash in the Socialist Paradise: Soviet Patronage and African Students' Urbanity in the Soviet Union, 1960–1965." *Diplomatic History* 38, no. 2 (2014): 271–281.

Hames, Peter. *The Czechoslovak New Wave*. Berkeley: University of California Press, 1985.

Harris, Steven E. *Communism on Tomorrow Street: Mass Housing and Everyday Life after Stalin*. Baltimore: Johns Hopkins University Press, and Washington, DC: Woodrow Wilson Center Press, 2013.

Hart, Justin. *Empire of Ideas: The Origins of Public Diplomacy, and the Transformation of U.S. Foreign Policy*. New York: Oxford University Press, 2013.

Haslam, Jonathan. *Russia's Cold War: From the October Revolution to the Fall of the Wall*. New Haven, CT: Yale University Press, 2011.

Hessler, Julie. "Death of an African Student in Moscow: Race, Politics, and the Cold War." *Cahiers du Monde russe* 47, no. 1 (2006): 33–64.

Hixson, Walter L. *Parting the Curtain: Propaganda, Culture, and the Cold War, 1945–1961*. New York: St. Martin's Press, 1997.

Hojda, Zdeněk, and Jiří Pokorný. *Pomníky a zapomníky*. Prague: Paseka, 1996.

Hrbek, Jaroslav, Vít Smetana, Stanislav Kokoška, Vladimír Pilát, and Petr Hofman, *Draze zaplacená svoboda: Osvobození Československa 1944–1945*. Vol. 2. Prague: Paseka, 2009.

Iriye, Akira. *Cultural Internationalism and World Order*. Baltimore: Johns Hopkins University Press, 1997.

Jacobson, Jon. *When the Soviet Union Entered World Politics*. Berkeley: University of California Press, 1994.

Jersild, Austin. *The Sino-Soviet Alliance: An International History*. Chapel Hill: University of North Carolina Press, 2014.

———. "The Soviet State as Imperial Scavenger: 'Catch Up and Surpass' in the Transnational Socialist Bloc, 1950–1960." *American Historical Review* 116, no. 1 (February 2011): 109–132.

Judt, Tony. *Postwar: A History of Europe since 1945*. New York: Penguin, 2005.

Kaplan, Karel. *Report on the Murder of the General Secretary*. Translated by Karel Kovanda. Columbus: Ohio State University Press, 1990.

———. *The Short March: The Communist Takeover in Postwar Czechoslovakia*. London: Hurst, 1987.

———. *Sovětští poradci v Československu, 1949–1956*. Prague: Ústav pro soudobé dějiny AV ČR, 1993.

Katsakioris, Constantin. "Burden or Allies? Third World Students and Internationalist Duty through Soviet Eyes." *Kritika: Explorations in Russian and Eurasian History* 18, no. 3 (Summer 2017): 539–67.

———. "The Soviet-South Encounter: Tensions in the Friendship with Afro-Asian Partners, 1945–1965." In Babiracki and Zimmer, *Cold War Crossings*, 134–165.

Kenez, Peter. *Cinema and Soviet Society: From the Revolution to the Death of Stalin*. London: I. B. Tauris, 2001.

———. *Hungary from the Nazis to the Soviets: The Establishment of the Communist Regime in Hungary, 1944–1948*. New York: Cambridge University Press, 2006.

Kirschenbaum, Lisa A. *International Communism and the Spanish Civil War: Solidarity and Suspicion*. New York: Cambridge University Press, 2015.

———. *The Legacy of the Siege of Leningrad, 1941–1995: Myths, Memories, and Monuments*. New York: Cambridge University Press, 2006.

Klimešová, Marie. "Czechoslovak Public Sculpture and Its Context from 1945 to the 'Realizations' Exhibition, 1961." In Benton, *Figuration/Abstraction*, 33–50.

Knapík, Jiří. "Czechoslovak Culture and Cinema, 1945–1960." In *Cinema in Service of the State: Perspectives on Film Culture in the GDR and Czechoslovakia, 1945–1960*, edited by Lars Karl and Pavel Skopal, 39–68. New York: Berghahn Books, 2015.

———. *Únor a kultura: sovětizace české kultury 1948–1950*. Prague: Nakladatelství Libri, 2004.

Koenker, Diane P. *Club Red: Vacation Travel and the Soviet Dream*. Ithaca, NY: Cornell University Press, 2013.

Konev, I. S., ed. *Za osvobozhdenie Chekhoslovakii*. Moscow: Voennoe izdatel'stvo Ministerstva oborony SSSR, 1965.

Kotkin, Stephen. *Magnetic Mountain: Stalinism as a Civilization*. Berkeley: University of
California Press, 1995.

——. "Mongol Commonwealth? Exchange and Governance across the Post-Mongol
Space." *Kritika: Explorations in Russian and Eurasian History* 8, no. 3 (Summer 2007):
487–531.

Kozlov, Denis, and Eleonory Gilburd. "The Thaw as an Event in Russian History." In
Kozlov and Gilburd, *The Thaw*, 18–81.

——, eds. *The Thaw: Soviet Society and Culture during the 1950s and 1960s*. Toronto:
University of Toronto Press, 2013.

Kramer, Mark. "The Collapse of East European Communism and the Repercussions
within the Soviet Union (Part I)." *Journal of Cold War Studies* 5, no. 4 (Fall 2003):
178–256.

——. "The Czechoslovak Crisis and the Brezhnev Doctrine." In *1968: The World
Transformed*, edited by Carole Fink, Philipp Gassert, and Detlef Junker, 111–171.
Cambridge: Cambridge University Press, 1998.

Krementsov, Nikolai. *The Cure: A Story of Cancer and Politics from the Annals of the Cold
War*. Chicago: University of Chicago Press, 2002.

Křesťan, Jiří. "KSČ, Společnost pro hospodářské a kulturní styky s SSSR a obraz
Sovětského svazu v prostředí české levicové inteligence (1925–1939)." In *Bolševismus,
komunismus a radikální socialismus v Československu*. Vol. 2, edited by Zdeněk
Kárník and Michal Kopeček, 84–109. Prague: Ústav pro soudobé dějiny AV ČR,
Dokořán, 2004.

Kundera, Milan. "The Tragedy of Central Europe." Translated by Edmund White. *New
York Review of Books* 31, no. 7 (April 16, 1984): 33–38.

Latysh, M. V. *"Prazhskaia vesna" 1968 g. i reaktsiia Kremlia*. Moscow: Tipografiia RAN,
1998.

Lovejoy, Alice. *Army Film and the Avant Garde: Cinema and Experiment in the Czechoslovak Military*. Bloomington: Indiana University Press, 2014.

Lukes, Igor. *Czechoslovakia between Hitler and Stalin: The Diplomacy of Edvard Beneš in
the 1930s*. New York: Oxford University Press, 1996.

——. *On the Edge of the Cold War: American Diplomats and Spies in Postwar Prague*.
New York: Oxford University Press, 2012.

Macura, Vladimír. *The Mystifications of a Nation: "The Potato Bug" and Other Essays on
Czech Culture*. Edited and translated by Hana Pichová and Craig Cravens. Madison:
University of Wisconsin Press, 2010.

Maddox, Steven. *Saving Stalin's Imperial City: Historic Preservation in Leningrad, 1930–
1950*. Bloomington: Indiana University Press, 2014.

Majstorović, Vojin. "The Red Army in Yugoslavia, 1944–1945." *Slavic Review* 75, no. 2
(Summer 2016): 396–421.

Mar'ina, V. V. *Sovetskii Soiuz i chekho-slovatskii vopros vo vremia Vtoroi mirovoi voiny:
1939–1945 gg*. Moscow: Indrik, 2007–2009.

Mark, James. "Remembering Rape: Divided Social Memory and the Red Army in Hungary, 1944–1945." *Past and Present* 188, no. 1 (August 2005): 133–161.

Martin, Terry. *Affirmative Action Empire: Nations and Nationalism in the Soviet Union, 1923–1939*. Ithaca, NY: Cornell University Press, 2001.

Massino, Jill. "From Black Caviar to Blackouts: Gender, Consumption, and Lifestyle in Ceausescu's Romania." In Bren and Neuburger, *Communism Unwrapped*, 226–249.

McDermott, Kevin. *Communist Czechoslovakia: A Political and Social History*. London: Palgrave Macmillan, 2015.

———. "A 'Polyphony of Voices'? Czech Popular Opinion and the Slánský Affair." *Slavic Review* 67, no. 4 (Winter 2008): 840–865.

———. "Stalinist Terror in Czechoslovakia: Origins, Processes, Responses." In *Stalinist Terror in Eastern Europe: Elite Purges and Mass Repression*, edited by McDermott and Matthew Stibbe, 98–118. Manchester: Manchester University Press, 2010.

McGuire, Elizabeth. *Red at Heart: How Chinese Communists Fell in Love with the Russian Revolution*. New York: Oxford University Press, 2017.

———. "Sino-Soviet Every Day: Chinese Revolutionaries in Moscow Military Schools, 1927–1930." In *Every Day Life in Russia Past and Present*, edited by Choi Chatterjee, David L. Ransel, Mary Cavender, and Karen Petrone, 329–349. Bloomington: Indiana University Press, 2015.

McLellan, Josie. *Love in the Time of Communism: Intimacy and Sexuality in the GDR*. Cambridge: Cambridge University Press, 2011.

Mëhilli, Elidor. *From Stalin to Mao: Albania and the Socialist World*. Ithaca, NY: Cornell University Press, 2017.

Michálkovi, Irena, and Ladislav. *Olšany hrdinské*. Prague: n.p., 2008.

Moulis, Vladislav. *Podivné spojenectví: k československo-sovětským politickým a hospodářským vztahům mezi dubnem 1945 a únorem 1948*. Prague: Karolinium, 1996.

Murashko, G. P., T. V. Volokitina, and A. S. Stykalin, eds. *1968 god: "Prazhskaia vesna," istoricheskaia retrospektiva, sbornik statei*. Moscow: ROSSPEN, 2010.

Naimark, Norman M. *The Russians in Germany: A History of the Soviet Zone of Occupation, 1945–1949*. Cambridge, MA: Harvard University Press, 1995.

———. "The Sovietization of Eastern Europe, 1944–1953." In *The Cambridge History of the Cold War*. Vol. 1, ed. Melvyn P. Leffler and Odd Arne Westad, 175–197. Cambridge: Cambridge University Press, 2010.

Nakachi, Mie. "N. S. Khrushchev and the 1944 Soviet Family Law: Politics, Reproduction, and Language." *East European Politics and Societies* 20, no. 1 (February 2006): 40–68.

Ninkovich, Frank A. *The Diplomacy of Ideas: U.S. Foreign Policy and Cultural Relations, 1938–1950*. New York: Cambridge University Press, 1981.

Nolan, Mary. *The Transatlantic Century: Europe and America, 1890–2010*. Cambridge: Cambridge University Press, 2012.

Nothnagle, Alan L. *Building the East German Myth: Historical Mythology and Youth Propaganda in the German Democratic Republic, 1945–1989*. Ann Arbor: University of Michigan Press, 1999.

Nye, Joseph S. Jr. *Soft Power: The Means to Success in World Politics*. New York: Public Affairs, 2004.

Orzoff, Andrea. *Battle for the Castle: The Myth of Czechoslovakia in Europe, 1914–1948*. New York: Oxford University Press, 2009.

Overy, Richard. *Russia's War*. New York: Penguin Books, 1998.

Paces, Cynthia. *Prague Panoramas: National Memory and Sacred Space in the Twentieth Century*. Pittsburgh: University of Pittsburgh Press, 2009.

Palmer, Scott W. "How Memory Was Made: The Construction of the Memorial to the Heroes of the Battle of Stalingrad." *Russian Review* 68, no. 3 (July 2009): 373–407.

Patterson, Patrick Hyder. "Risky Business: What Was Really Being Sold in the Department Stores of Socialist Eastern Europe?" In Bren and Neuburger, *Communism Unwrapped*, 116–139.

Pazderka, Josef. *Invaze 1968: Ruský pohled*. Prague: Ústav pro studium totalitních režimů, Torst, 2011.

Pechatnov, V. "Exercise in Frustration: Soviet Foreign Propaganda in the Early Cold War, 1945–1947." *Cold War History* 1, no. 2 (January 2001): 1–27.

Pelikán, Jiří, ed. *The Czechoslovak Political Trials, 1950–1954: The Suppressed Report of the Dubček Government's Commission of Inquiry, 1968*. Stanford, CA: Stanford University Press, 1971.

Pells, Richard. *Not Like Us: How Europeans Have Loved, Hated, and Transformed American Culture Since World War II*. New York: Basic Books, 1997.

Pernes, Jiří, and Jan Foitzik, eds. *Politické procesy v Československu po roce 1945 a "případ Slánský." Sborník příspěvků ze stejnojmenné konference, pořádané ve dnech 14.–16. dubna 2003 v Praze*. Brno: Kateřina Mikšová-Nakladalství Prius pro Ústav pro soudobé dějiny AV ČR v Praze, 2005.

Péteri, György. "Nylon Curtain: Transnational and Transsystemic Tendencies in the Cultural Life of State-Socialist Russia and East-Central Europe." *Slavonica* 10, no. 2 (2004): 113–123.

Pichova, Hana. "The Lineup for Meat: The Stalin Statue in Prague." *PMLA* 123, no. 3 (May 2008): 614–630.

Povolný, Daniel. "Přijeli jsme splnit úkol: Sovětští vojáci a jejich pohled na invazi." In Pazderka, *Invaze 1968*, 16–23.

Reeves, Julie. *Culture and International Relations: Narratives, Natives and Tourists*. London: Routledge, 2004.

Reid, Susan E. "Cold War in the Kitchen: Gender and the de-Stalinization of Consumer Taste in the Soviet Union under Khrushchev." *Slavic Review* 61, no. 2 (Summer 2002): 211–252.

——. "Khrushchev Modern: Agency and Modernization in the Soviet Home." *Cahiers du Monde russe* 47, no. 1–2 (January–June 2006): 227–268.

——. "This Is Tomorrow! Becoming a Consumer in the Soviet Sixties." In Gorsuch and Koenker, *Socialist Sixties*, 25–65.

——. "Who Will Beat Whom? Soviet Popular Reception of the American National Exhibition in Moscow, 1959." In *Imagining the West in Eastern Europe and the Soviet Union*, edited by György Péteri, 194–236. Pittsburgh: University of Pittsburgh Press, 2010.

Reiman, Michal. *The Birth of Stalinism: The USSR on the Eve of the "Second Revolution."* Translated by George Saunders. Bloomington: Indiana University Press, 1987.

——. *Ruská revoluce, 23. únor-25. říjen 1917*. Prague: Naše vojsko, 1967.

Richmond, Yale. *Cultural Exchange and the Cold War: Raising the Iron Curtain*. University Park: Pennsylvania State University Press, 2003.

Richter, Karel. *Dobývání domova: osvobození Československa bez cenzury a legend*. Part 2. Prague: Ostrov, 2005.

Roberts, Geoffrey. *Stalin's Wars: from World War to Cold War, 1939–1953*. New Haven, CT: Yale University Press, 2006.

Roberts, Mary Louise. *What Soldiers Do: Sex and the American GI in World War II France*. Chicago: University of Chicago Press, 2013.

Rubenstein, Joshua. "Introduction: Night of the Murdered Poets." In *Stalin's Secret Pogrom: The Postwar Inquisition of the Jewish Anti-Fascist Committee*, ed. Joshua Rubenstein and Vladimir P. Naumov, 1–64. New Haven, CT: Yale University Press, 2001.

Rupprecht, Tobias. *Soviet Internationalism after Stalin: Interaction and Exchange between the Soviet Union and Latin America during the Cold War*. Cambridge: Cambridge University Press, 2015.

Sayer, Derek. *The Coasts of Bohemia: A Czech History*. Princeton, NJ: Princeton University Press, 1998.

——. *Prague, Capital of the Twentieth Century: A Surrealist History*. Princeton, NJ: Princeton University Press, 2013.

Schmidt, Oliver. "Small Atlantic World: U.S. Philanthropy and the Expanding Exchange of Scholars after 1945." In *Culture and International History*, edited by Jessica C. E. Gienow-Hecht and Frank Schumacher, 115–134. Oxford: Berghahn Books, 2003.

Schwarzmantel, John. "Nationalism and Socialist Internationalism." In *The Oxford Handbook of the History of Nationalism*, edited by John Breuilly, 635–654. Oxford: Oxford University Press, 2013.

Scott-Smith, Giles. "Mapping the Undefinable: Some Thoughts on the Relevance of Exchange Programs within International Relations Theory." *ANNALS of the American Academy of Political and Social Science* 616 (March 2008): 173–195.

Seton-Watson, Hugh. *The East European Revolution*. London: Methuen, 1950.

Shaw, Tony, and Denise J. Youngblood. *Cinematic Cold War: The American and Soviet Struggle for Hearts and Minds*. Lawrence: University Press of Kansas, 2010.

Shore, Marci. "Engineering in the Age of Innocence: A Genealogy of Discourse Inside the Czechoslovak Writers' Union, 1949–67." *East European Politics and Societies* 12, no. 3 (Fall 1998): 397–441.

Šimečka, Milan. *The Restoration of Order: The Normalization of Czechoslovakia 1969–1976*. Translated by A. G. Brain. London: Verso, 1984.

Skilling, H. Gordon. *Czechoslovakia's Interrupted Revolution*. Princeton, NJ: Princeton University Press, 1976.

Skopal, Pavel. "The Cinematic Shapes of the Socialist Modernity Programme: Ideological and Economic Parameters of Cinema Distribution in the Czech Lands, 1948–70." In Biltereyst, Maltby, and Meers, *Cinema, Audiences and Modernity*, 81–98.

Sluga, Glenda. *Internationalism in the Age of Nationalism*. Philadelphia: University of Pennsylvania Press, 2013.

Stangl, Paul. "The Soviet War Memorial in Treptow, Berlin." *Geographical Review* 93, no. 2 (April 2003): 213–236.

Stowe, Leland. *The Story of Satellite Europe: Conquest By Terror.* New York: Random House, 1952.

Stykalin, A. S. "Propaganda SSSR na zarubezhnuiu auditoriiu i obshchestvennoe mnenie stran zapada v pervye poslevoennye gody (po dokumentam rossiiskikh arkhivov)." *Vestnik Moskovskogo universiteta.* Seriia X: Zhurnalistika (1/1997): 57–70.

Suny, Ronald Grigor. *The Soviet Experiment: Russia, the USSR, and the Successor States.* New York: Oxford University Press, 1998.

Svašek, Maruška. "The Politics of Artistic Identity: The Czech Art World in the 1950s and 1960s." *Contemporary European History* 6, no. 3 (November 1997): 383–403.

Szczepanik, Petr. "Hollywood in Disguise: Practices of Exhibition and Reception of Foreign Films in Czechoslovakia in the 1930s." In Biltereyst, Maltby, and Meers, *Cinema Audiences and Modernity,* 166–185.

Tomoff, Kiril. "Agents of Empire: Soviet Concert Tours and Cultural Empire in Eastern Europe, 1945–1958." Paper presented at the annual convention of the Association for Slavic, East European, and Eurasian Studies in New Orleans, November 15–18, 2012.

——. "A Pivotal Turn: Prague Spring 1948 and the Soviet Construction of a Cultural Sphere." *Slavonica* 10, no. 2 (November 2004): 157–176.

——. *Virtuosi Abroad: Soviet Music and Imperial Competition during the Early Cold War, 1945–1958.* Ithaca, NY: Cornell University Press, 2015.

Troitsky, Artemy. *Back in the USSR: The True Story of Rock in Russia.* Boston: Faber and Faber, 1987.

Tromly, Benjamin. "Brother or Other: East European Students in Soviet Higher Education Establishments, 1948–1956." *European History Quarterly* 44, no. 1 (2014): 80–102.

Tsipursky, Gleb. "Having Fun in the Thaw: Youth Initiative Clubs in the Post-Stalin Years." *The Carl Beck Papers in Russian and East European Studies* no. 2201. Pittsburgh: University of Pittsburgh Press, 2012.

Tumarkin, Nina. *The Living and the Dead: The Rise and Fall of the Cult of World War II in Russia.* New York: Basic Books, 1994.

Turovskaya, Maya. "The 1930s and 1940s: Cinema in Context." In *Stalinism and Soviet Cinema,* edited by Richard Taylor and Derek Spring, 34–53. London: Routledge, 1993.

Vail', Pëtr, and Aleksandr Genis. *60-e: Mir sovetskogo cheloveka.* Moscow: Novoe literaturnoe obozrenie, 1998.

Virgili, Fabrice. *Shorn Women: Gender and Punishment in Liberation France.* Translated by John Flower. Oxford: Berg, 2002.

Vukov, Nikolai. "'Brotherly Help': Representations or 'Imperial' Legacy: Monuments to the Soviet Army in Bulgaria before and after 1989." *Ab Imperio* 1 (2006): 267–292.

Wagnleitner, Reinhold. "'No Commodity Is Quite So Strange as This Thing Called Cultural Exchange': The Foreign Politics of American Pop Culture Hegemony." *Amerikastudien/American Studies* 46, no. 3 (2001): 443–470.

Walton, Whitney. *Internationalism, National Identities, and Study Abroad: France and the United States, 1890–1970.* Stanford, CA: Stanford University Press, 2010.

Weiner, Amir. "Déjà Vu All Over Again: Prague Spring, Romanian Summer and Soviet Autumn on the Soviet Western Frontier." *Contemporary European History* 15, no. 2 (2006): 159–194.

———. *Making Sense of War: The Second World War and the Fate of the Bolshevik Revolution*. Princeton, NJ: Princeton University Press, 2001.

Williams, Kieran. *The Prague Spring and Its Aftermath: Czechoslovak Politics, 1968–1970*. Cambridge: Cambridge University Press, 1997.

Wingfield, Nancy M. *Flag Wars and Stone Saints: How the Bohemian Lands Became Czech*. Cambridge, MA: Harvard University Press, 2007.

Wingfield, Nancy M., and Lisa A. Kirschenbaum. "Gender and the Construction of War-time Heroism in Czechoslovakia and the USSR." *European History Quarterly* 39, no. 3 (2009) 471–473.

Wojnowski, Zbigniew. *The Near Abroad: Socialist Eastern Europe and Soviet Patriotism in Ukraine, 1956–85*. Toronto: University of Toronto Press, 2017.

Wolff, M. M. "Some Aspects of Marriage and Divorce Laws in Soviet Russia." *Modern Law Review* 12, no. 3 (July 1949): 290–296.

Wood, Elizabeth A. "Performing Memory: Vladimir Putin and the Celebration of WWII in Russia." *Soviet and Post-Soviet Review* 38 (2011): 172–200.

Youngblood, Denise J. *Russian War Films: On the Cinema Front, 1914–2005*. Lawrence: University Press of Kansas, 2007.

Yurchak, Alexei. *Everything Was Forever Until It Was No More: The Last Soviet Generation*. Princeton, NJ: Princeton University Press, 2005.

Zubok, Vladislav M. *A Failed Empire: The Soviet Union in the Cold War from Stalin to Gorbachev*. Chapel Hill: University of North Carolina Press, 2007.

———. "Soviet Society in the 1960s." In *The Prague Spring and the Warsaw Pact Invasion of Czechoslovakia in 1968*, edited by Günter Bischof, Stefan Karner, and Peter Ruggenthaler, 75–101. Lanham: Rowman and Littlefield, 2010.

ACKNOWLEDGMENTS

Over the decade I've spent researching and writing this book, I've bene-fited enormously from the support of many people and institutions. At the University of Chicago, Sheila Fitzpatrick inspired me to become a social his-torian. I appreciate her support for a topic that ended up extending beyond the borders of the Soviet Union. Michael Geyer urged me to make this book a transnational study—something I've at times cursed but am ultimately very grateful for. Leora Auslander offered helpful suggestions for thinking about Soviet-Czechoslovak relations in a broader European context. I am especially grateful to Tara Zahra for her intellectual guidance and emotional support from the very beginning of this project—when she took me to the National Archive in Prague for the first time—to the very end, when she read a final draft of the introduction. Over the intervening years I've felt privileged to con-sider her not only an advisor and mentor but also a friend.

One of the pleasures of the University of Chicago was the comradery of so many young scholars working on Russian and European history. In partic-ular I'd like to thank Alan Barenberg, Natalie Belsky, Venus Bivar, Edward

Cohn, Leah Goldman, Ke-Chin Hsia, Kristy Ironside, Andrew Janco, Eleanor Rivera, Flora Roberts, Oscar Sanchez-Sibony, and Andrew Sloin, as well all the participants of the modern Europe and Russian history workshops where I presented drafts of several chapters.

Before coming to Chicago I had the pleasure of studying and interacting with a fantastic group of scholars at the University of Toronto, including Robert Austin, Barbara Falk, Robert Johnson, Thomas Lahusen, and Peter Solomon. I am particularly grateful to Thomas, who encouraged me to return to Russia when I was hesitant to go, and who urged me to get my PhD when I was unsure what path to pursue. A semester as an exchange student at the irreplaceable Central European University proved to be a formative experience for the development of this project. I was inspired by the material traces of Soviet power remaining in Budapest to want to better understand the Soviet encounter with Central/Eastern Europe during the Cold War. I'd like to thank Jennifer Cone, Maria Cvitkovic, Nevenka Grceva, Ziva Kokolj, and Lore Vennix for their friendship there.

At Lafayette College, where I spent a year as a visiting assistant professor of modern European history, Paul Barclay, Emily Musil Church, Rachel Goshgarian, Rebekah Pite, and Joshua Sanborn provided a friendly introduction to professional life and an antidote to the stresses of the job market. I still pinch myself that I had the good fortune to spend a year in Florence as a Max Weber postdoctoral fellow at the European University Institute. At the Department of History and Civilization, Pavel Kolář, Stéphane Van Damme, and Dirk Moses provided valuable feedback on this project and advice on the publishing process. I am grateful to my fellow history postdocs for their intellectual support and friendship—especially Ludivine Broch, Franziska Exeler, Eirini Karamouzi, Hassan Malik, Anne McGinness, and Valerie McGuire. The pleasures of a year in Italy with a young child in tow were significantly enhanced by the company of Emily Michelson, Bill Shackman, and their children; Dina Genis, Gur Zak, and their children; and Anna auf dem Brinke, Robert Lepenies, and their son, Samuel. At the Center for the Humanities at Tufts University, where I spent a year as a Mellon postdoctoral fellow, I am especially grateful to Jonathan Wilson, the former director, for his generous support; as well as to Khalilah Imani Tyre, the program assistant; and to my fellow postdocs, Doreen Densky, Irving Goh, and John Robbins.

I have been privileged since 2015 to be a member of the faculty of the Department of History at Tufts. I am grateful to all of my colleagues in the department for providing me with such a warm welcome and for making the department such a collegial and productive place to work. I owe special thanks to Kendra Field, Elizabeth Foster, Gary Leupp, Beatrice Manz, and Alisha Rankin for providing feedback on chapter 1, and to Jeanne Penvenne for being my departmental mentor.

I spent my final year working on this manuscript as a visiting fellow in the history department at Princeton University. I am grateful to the department (especially Michael Gordin) and the English department at Princeton for welcoming me, and for providing me with the space to work and access to Princeton's rich resources.

The research and writing of this book would not have been possible without the generous financial support provided by several institutions: the University of Chicago, the Fulbright Hays Doctoral Dissertation Research Abroad Program, the Kennan Institute at the Woodrow Wilson Center, the American Council of Learned Societies, and Tufts University. I would also like to thank all of the archival staff and librarians who assisted me in the Czech Republic, Hungary, Russia, and the United States. In Prague, Jiří Hoppe at the Institute for Contemporary History deserves special mention: when the reading room closed for the summer, he let me continue my research, and even provided me my own office, complete with a panoramic view of the Prague Castle. At the trade union archive, Alžběta Kratinová went to great lengths to search for material related to my topic. Pavel Baudisch and Tatiana Rohová at the National Archive helped me to quickly obtain the images I wanted for the book. In Moscow, Galina Mikhailovna Tokareva at the Komsomol archive helped bring the period I was writing about to life, by telling me stories about her experiences leading Komsomol groups to Czechoslovakia in the 1960s. At RGANI, the kindness of the director of the reading room, Liudmila Ivanovna Stepanich, made working there so much more pleasant and productive. At the U.S. National Archives in College Park, Cate Brennan helped with a last-minute search for documents. The late June Farris, the Slavic bibliographer at the Regenstein library at the University of Chicago, tracked down sources from all over the world and always sent quick, detailed replies to my queries.

One of the pleasures of my research abroad was the opportunity to make friends with other historians working in the archives. In Moscow, Emily Baran, Rossen Djagalov, Yelena Kalinsky, Peter Kupfer, Michael Paulauskas,

Erik Scott, Victoria Smolkin, and Gleb Tsipursky provided invaluable companionship, as did Alice Lovejoy in Prague.

I thank the organizers of several conferences, workshops, and lecture series where I received helpful feedback on this book over the years: Bradley Abrams, Theodora Dragostinova, Franziska Exeler, Malgorzata Fidelis, Anne Gorsuch, Claire Knight, Diane Koenker, Kyrill Kunakhovich, Nataliia Laas, Bruce Lincoln, Anne O'Donnell, Giles Scott-Smith, Keely Stauter-Halsted, and Ludovic Tournès. I would also like to thank the organizers, co-organizers, and discussants on several ASEEES panels and roundtables I participated in, including Patryk Babiracki, Lisa Kirschenbaum, Andrea Orzoff, Carolin Roeder, and Nicholas Rutter.

I am grateful for the comments, critiques, and other forms of assistance on this book I have received over the years from many scholars: Elizabeth Banks, Jan Behrends, Robert Bird, Shawn Clybor, John Connelly, David Engerman, Eleonory Gilburd, Austin Jersild, Michal Kopeček, Jessie Labov, Paul Lenormand, Margaret Litvin, Elidor Mëhilli, Ethan Pollock, Marci Shore, Lina Steiner, Zbigniew Wojnowski, and Elena Zubkova. Kyrill Kunakhovich provided extremely helpful suggestions for revising chapter 1. Nicole Eaton, Alexis Peri, and Brandon Schechter read several chapters at our Boston-area writing group and made invaluable suggestions for revisions.

At Cornell University Press, Roger Haydon has been a patient and supportive editor. The two anonymous reviewers provided detailed and insightful feedback on the first draft of the manuscript. As I prepared the manuscript for publication, Sarah Rosenthal helped track down documents at the U.S. National Archives in College Park. Michaela Appeltová and Milyausha Zakirova proofread the Czech and Russian in the manuscript and kept my spirits up through the final push.

Earlier versions of parts of chapters 4 and 5 of this book were published previously in *Slavic Review* and *The Socialist Sixties: Crossing Borders in the Second World*.

Throughout the years, my friends and family have provided much-needed distraction and emotional support while I've worked on this project. I'd like to thank my friends Anya Antonovych, Abigail Dean, Julia Drisdell, Bridget Hanna, Katherine Hill Reischl, Ingrid Kleespies, Jessica May, Tracy McDonald, Lucia Somberg, Nicholas Torrey, Irina Tarsis (who also helped with Russian translations), and Ella Vanderbilt. I am grateful to my parents, Lisbeth and Noha Applebaum, for their unconditional love, and for supporting my interest in Russia and Eastern Europe from the beginning. I'd also like to thank my brother and sister-in-law, Theodore and Alyssa Applebaum; my in-laws, David Kotin, Colleen Darragh, Yvonne Patch and Joe McGlynn; Nick and Carrie Patch; and Joel Kotin and Lyda Hill, at whose dining room table in Laguna Beach I first began working on this project. Sadly, my father passed away unexpectedly as I was working on the final edits to this book. He was always a careful reader and honest critic of my work, and I deeply regret that he did not get to see this project completed.

Finally, it is to my husband and daughter that I owe my deepest gratitude and love. Joshua Kotin has been my partner on every step of the long journey it has taken me to produce this book, from accompanying me on my research to Moscow and Prague, to applying his extraordinary intellectual insight and editorial acumen to the text. Eleonora's infancy coincided with this project's. She is now in third grade, and it amazes me how quickly the time has passed. I am so proud of the kind, smart, generous, and curious person she has become.

INDEX

Page numbers in *italics* indicate illustrations.

CPSIA information can be obtained
at www.ICGtesting.com
Printed in the USA
BVHW030554010319
541507BV00004B/30/P